BODIES OF KNOWLEDGE

BODIES OF KNOWLEDGE

Embodied Rhetorics in Theory and Practice

EDITED BY
**A. ABBY KNOBLAUCH
AND MARIE E. MOELLER**

UTAH STATE UNIVERSITY PRESS
Logan

© 2022 by University Press of Colorado

Published by Utah State University Press
An imprint of University Press of Colorado
245 Century Circle, Suite 202
Louisville, Colorado 80027

 ASSOCIATION of UNIVERSITY PRESSES   The University Press of Colorado is a proud member of
the Association of University Presses.

The University Press of Colorado is a cooperative publishing enterprise supported,
in part, by Adams State University, Colorado State University, Fort Lewis College,
Metropolitan State University of Denver, Regis University, University of Alaska Fairbanks,
University of Colorado, University of Northern Colorado, University of Wyoming, Utah
State University, and Western Colorado University.

∞ This paper meets the requirements of the ANSI/NISO Z39.48-1992 (Permanence of
Paper).

ISBN: 978-1-64642-200-5 (paperback)
ISBN: 978-1-64642-201-2 (ebook)
https://doi.org/10.7330/9781646422012

Library of Congress Cataloging-in-Publication Data

Names: Knoblauch, A. Abby, editor. | Moeller, Marie E., editor.
Title: Bodies of knowledge : embodied rhetorics in theory and practice / edited by
    A. Abby Knoblauch and Marie E. Moeller.
Description: Logan : Utah State University Press, [2022] | Includes bibliographical refer-
    ences and index.
Identifiers: LCCN 2021045127 (print) | LCCN 2021045128 (ebook) | ISBN
    9781646422005 (paperback) | ISBN 9781646422012 (ebook)
Subjects: LCSH: Human body and language. | Language and culture. | Rhetoric—Study
    and teaching—Social aspects. | Academic writing—Social aspects.
Classification: LCC P35 .B555 2022 (print) | LCC P35 (ebook) | DDC 808—dc23/
    eng/20211213
LC record available at https://lccn.loc.gov/2021045127
LC ebook record available at https://lccn.loc.gov/2021045128

Cover illustration, "Trio Troublé," © Justin J. Sehorn (www.embodiment.us).

CONTENTS

Preface: The Body's Turn in Rhetorical Studies
    William P. Banks   vii

Acknowledgments   xiii

1. Introduction: Bodies, Embodiment, and Embodied Rhetorics
    A. Abby Knoblauch and Marie E. Moeller   3

    ### PART I: AFFECT, SENSE/S, PERMEABILITY

2. Violence and Beneficence in the Rhetorics of Touch
    Scot Barnett   23

3. Disrupting Embodied Silence
    Katherine Bridgman   43

4. Towards an Olfactory Rhetoric: Scent, Affect, Material, Embodiment
    Sara DiCaglio   57

5. Embodying History: The Bodies and Affects of Museum Rhetorics
    Julie D. Nelson   74

6. The Role of Intrabody Resonance in Political Organizing
    Nadya Pittendrigh   89

    ### PART II: ADVOCACY, POLICY, CITIZENSHIP

7. Discomfort Training in the Archives: Embodied Rhetoric in Feminist Advocacy
    Meg Brooker, Julie Myatt, and Kate Pantelides   107

8. Fannie Barrier Williams's Citizen-Woman: Embodying Rhetoric at the 1893 World's Columbian Exposition
    Kristie S. Fleckenstein   123

9. Rewriting Maternal Bodies on the Senate Floor: Tammy
    Duckworth's Embodied Rhetorics of Intersectional Motherhood
    Ruth Osorio   143

10. Criminals and Victims: The Embodied Rhetorics of Unaccompanied
    Latinx Children as Represented in Spanish- and English-Language
    Media
    Megan Strom   161

PART III: TEXTUALITY, MULTIMODALITY, DIGITALITY

11. The Successful Text Is Not Always the One That Murders Me to
    Protect You
    Vyshali Manivannan   183

12. Hooking Up Embodied Technologies, Queer Rhetorics, and
    Grindr's Grid
    Caleb Pendygraft   199

13. Avowed Embodiment: Self-Identification, Performative Strategic
    Attire, and TRAP Karaoke
    Temptaous Mckoy   219

14. Matters That (Em)Body
    Kellie Sharp-Hoskins and Anthony Stagliano   236

    Index   253

PREFACE
The Body's Turn in Rhetorical Studies

William P. Banks (East Carolina University)

> *The successful scholarly text does not convey pain, even if/when the author radiates nothing but.*
>
> —Vyshali Manivannan

It's a strange moment to be writing the preface to a book called *Bodies of Knowledge: Embodied Rhetorics in Theory and Practice*. It's June—Pride month—and I should be filled with excitement and energy, with the hope I feel each year at this time as so many LGBTQ+ folks get together, march in parades, attend parties, and enjoy a moment when queer and trans visibilities can become more than merely theoretical or textual. There can be all types of bodies, and they can be everywhere: butch and femme bodies, trans and nonbinary bodies, bodies in all sorts of drag, bodies backed by music, bodies moving and gyrating, bodies in glitter and makeup. But mostly, just so many visible bodies . . .

And the Supreme Court just handed us yet another important decision on LGBTQ+ rights, the recognition in *Bostock v. Clayton County, Georgia* (2020) that firing a gay or transgender person just for being gay or transgender violates Title VII of the Civil Rights Act of 1964. In less than twenty years, LGBTQ+ people have won three major court victories: *Lawrence et al. v. Texas* (2003), which applied the right to privacy to LGBTQ+ consenting adults; *Obergefell et al. v. Hodges* (2015), which extended the right to marry to LGBTQ+ adults; and now with *Bostock*, broad civil rights protections.

We should be partying in every street in the United States. Quite frankly, it's a party we've earned!

But it's not just any June; it's June 2020. And we're living through a pandemic; transmission and infection rates of COVID-19 show little sign of slowing as the White House under President Trump continues to ignore the significance of this disease and the impact it will have on all persons in the United States, though most significantly on minoritized and marginalized bodies, on the very bodies we may recognize as

https://doi.org/10.7330/9781646422012.c000

"essential workers" but whose lives the middle classes have decided are fundamentally replaceable so long as folks can still shop, dine out, and have their overpriced coffee. June may be our yearly month for carnival, but the celebrations have been postponed: queer people do not want to be out here fiddling while Rome burns. We know what a pandemic is; the scars from the daily death tolls of the 1980s and 1990s are still all too present for many of us.

And this June, we are also living through yet another—we can hardly call this unprecedented, can we?—yet another moment in which Black and brown bodies are being slain by unregulated police aggression and white nationalist vigilantism. We have borne witness to Ahmaud Arbery's murder in Brunswick, Georgia, at the hands of two white men it took local law enforcement over two months to arrest or charge with the crime. We have borne witness to Breonna Taylor's murder at the hands of plain-clothes metro police in Louisville, Kentucky, who used a no-knock search warrant as cover to enter her apartment and kill her where she slept. And before the mainstream news media could even be bothered to cover Taylor's murder, we bore witness to the murder of George Floyd in Minneapolis, Minnesota, the nation watching in horror as a white police officer used his knee and the full weight of his body to asphyxiate Floyd while three more police officers stood idly by and did nothing to help save Floyd's life. And in addition to these high-profile cases—stories that only broke and made news because friends and family and bystanders made these stories go viral on social media—we have now borne witness to at least five Black men and women who have been found hanged in public places, while stories are beginning to unfold of another five or six Black men and women who have been murdered by police across the country.

How do I begin to talk about "bodies of knowledge" and not recognize these dead bodies? Not recognize that these bodies have been murdered precisely because of the ways language/rhetoric have been used to invalidate these bodies as *human* bodies in the minds of white nationalists and so many police officers, both groups overweaponized by the military-industrial complex and by the anti-Black and anti-Brown rhetorics of the current White House?

This collection of original and engaging scholarship does work we need desperately in the academy, work we need to see filtering out more thoughtfully and deliberately beyond our campuses. The authors included here look to bodies and embodiment as key spaces where languages and epistemologies interanimate each other, where we come to exist at all as knowable and active subjects. Abby Knoblauch and Marie

Moeller have assembled a collection that explores embodied rhetorical practices across a host of contexts. These authors remind us that there are no disembodied rhetorical projects, only our own failures to recognize and/or acknowledge the impacts of bodies on our epistemologies.

At times, the writers here imagine embodiment in deeply sensory ways—linked to touch (Barnett), or smell (DiCaglio), or sound (Bridgman)—or in less individualized ways by looking at how bodies resonate with other bodies in communal acts of meaning making and advocacy (Pittendrigh). Other times, the authors challenge us to rethink internet-based/media-based spaces and platforms (Pendygraft; Strom) as disembodied spaces. Multiple contributors challenge us to return to our archives through methodologies that require us to pay closer attention to the ways historically disenfranchised people have used their bodies as part of their rhetorical projects (Brooker, Myatt, and Pantelides; Fleckenstein; Nelson), and then they return us to the present to recognize how those same sorts of embodied practices are being deployed daily in sites as seemingly disparate as the halls of Congress (Osorio) and the dance floors at TRAP karaoke events (Mckoy). This collection challenges us to think of embodiment in global, macrolevel terms (Sharp-Hoskins and Stagliano) and also in the hyperlocal, where we remember that everything about our writing practices, tools, genres, and conventions is always already impacting (and impacted by) bodies (Manivannan).

While reading this collection, I continually wished that, as a student, I had learned about writing as an embodied act of meaning making, that I had been taught what Vyshali Manivannan teaches me in their contribution: that academic writing is often overly invested in making the reader comfortable . . . but it doesn't have to be so. Our field needs to be more engaged with the disruptive and discomforting work of writing, not just as a trope of/for poetical texts but as a key component of our own academic/rhetorical writing.

It's funny to make this case again now, as part of this preface, as this is exactly what I hoped to do twenty years ago when I was drafting a weekly response paper for a graduate course (Feminist Composition) I was enrolled in at the end of my doctoral coursework. About one-third of the way through the course, the professor, Julie Jung, asked us to connect what we *wanted* to write with what we *needed* to write. It was an alarmingly simple but powerful question about what writing is, what it does—and why any of us (should) bother doing it. What started out of that imagining I eventually turned into my course project, in large part because of the support and critique of Dr. Jung and my wonderful classmates at the time: Lori Ostergaard, Marie Moeller, Teryn Robinson, Zoë Younker, and Tammie Kennedy. I was also fortunate enough to get to revise that project into an article for a special issue of *College English* on "personal writing" that was guest edited by Jane E. Hindman (Banks). At the time, the field felt very much in a particular cultural turn, one often framed more by cultural studies than by cultural rhetorics, where "personal" seemed primarily to be a code word for bourgeois individualism and the failures of understanding the Other. Having grown up in the academy in spaces heavily influenced by women's and gender studies scholarship, however, where the personal and the political were always interwoven, I had found this dismissal of the personal overly simplistic, and I had begun to wonder if dismissing what is "personal" in a writing class is just another way to dismiss the bodies attached to those personal experiences, particularly bodies of queer and trans writers, of Black and Brown writers, of women and working-class writers. Out of those interests and concerns, I composed "Written through the Body: Disruptions and 'Personal' Writing" as an attempt to reembody a sort of deeply personal writing that could also have cultural and political impact (Banks).

But even then, after countless drafts and the most patient and thoughtful feedback Jane could provide, I still wondered if what I was hoping for—that we could imagine writing as a fundamentally embodied and embodying act of composition—if that were really possible in the academy.

There have, of course, long been inklings of this option: early in my teaching career, even before returning to school for my PhD, I had been inspired by Geneva Smitherman's scholarship; her foundational *Talkin and Testifyin: The Language of Black America*, as well as numerous articles afterward, had demonstrated to me how our words and bodies can exist together on the page, how they are, in fact, inextricable from each other when we write through our lived experiences. I had seen it in texts like Cherríe Moraga and Gloria Anzaldúa's *This Bridge Called My Back*. And in the years since, I've been fortunate to read more and more from scholars in writing and rhetorical studies who have also been making those connections, demonstrating through their own writing and storymaking how important it is for us to remember that language is always about bodies and that bodies are always about language. When Malea Powell (Miami/Shawnee) invited a group of folks to join her in a choral presentation of her CCCC presidential address, for example, we saw those bodies and stories intermingle in a powerful way, one that set her address apart from nearly all those that have come before or since: languaging bodies in communal engagement. An increasingly large group of scholars in our field—Angela Haas, Qwo-Li Driskill (Cherokee), Linda Bruggeman, Jay Dolmage, Robert McRuer, M. Remi Yergeau, Abby Knoblauch, Erin Frost, Caroline Dadas, Chanon Adsanatham, Matthew B. Cox, April Baker-Bell, Asao Inoue, Natasha Jones, Carmen Kynard, Stacey Waite, GPat Patterson, Michael Faris, Iris D. Ruiz, to name only a few—are continuing to teach me about the ways bodies, particularly nonwhite, nonmale, and noncis bodies, are erased from our understanding of writing and rhetoric; they, like the scholars in this collection, make clear the damages those erasures enact.

In fact, if I were a bolder writer, I might claim that after the cultural turn in writing studies, we have seen an embodied turn, a turn that centers bodies in our writing as a materialist techné rather than merely a metaphor. This is a good turn.

The joy of reading this rich collection of scholarship comes in knowing how diverse and exciting our work can be when we take bodies and embodiment more seriously. At this moment, as bodies are being ravaged both globally by a pandemic, which is affecting different bodies in vastly different ways, and nationally by our ongoing investment in a white supremacy rooted in colonialist logics of ownership/property and human capital, I am reminded of a point Sara Ahmed makes in *Willful Subjects* about what happens when our bodies feel "nervous": discussing the history of organized resistance/strikes, Ahmed writes, "The politics of demonstrating are indeed messy: but when things become messy we do not lose the point. If anything, becoming nervous shows how we are getting closer to a nerve, to what matters" (164).

Embodied writing and rhetoric get us closer to those nerves. And this is a moment to be on all sorts of people's nerves. This is a moment to unnerve others through our writing, as so many of the contributions in this collection do. This is a moment to make white supremacy nervous by showing up for people of color and queer/trans people in our work and in our teaching and in our daily, embodied practices. This is a moment to be on the nerves of local, state, and national authorities as we protest the ongoing atrocities we are seeing, many of which are centered on the bodies of nonwhite, noncis people. And this is, as always, a moment to stand up and push back against the never-silent voices of white supremacy, heterosexist patriarchy, and colonialism that continue to shape our own academic discipline and organizations to an alarming degree. By paying careful attention to embodiment as a materialist techné, the chapters in *Bodies of Knowledge* provide us with various methods for how our research and scholarship can practice that important work.

WORKS CITED

Ahmed, Sara. *Willful Subjects*. Duke UP, 2014.

Banks, William P. "Written through the Body: Disruptions and 'Personal' Writing." *The Personal in Academic Writing*. Spec. issue of *College English*, vol. 66, no. 1, Sept. 2003, pp. 21–40. *JSTOR*, doi:10.2307/3594232.

Bostock v. Clayton County, Georgia. 590 US___. *Supreme Court of the US*. 2020. www.supreme court.gov/opinions/19pdf/17–1618_hfci.pdf. Accessed 12 July 2020.

Lawrence v. Texas. 539 US 558. Supreme Court of the US. 2003. *Cornell Law School Institute*, Cornell Law School, www.law.cornell.edu/supct/pdf/02–102P.ZS. Accessed 12 July 2020.

Moraga, Cherríe, and Gloria Anzaldúa. *This Bridge Called My Back: Writings by Radical Women of Color*. 2nd ed. Kitchen Table/ Women of Color, 1983.

Obergefell v. Hodges. 576 US___. Supreme Court of the US. 2015. www.supremecourt.gov /opinions/14pdf/14–556_3204.pdf. Accessed 12 July 2020.

Powell, Malea. "Stories Take Place." Conference on College Composition and Communication, 22 Mar. 2012, Renaissance Hotel, St. Louis, MO. Opening General Session.

Smitherman, Geneva. *Talkin and Testifyin: The Language of Black America*. Wayne State UP, 1986.

ACKNOWLEDGMENTS

We want to first thank everyone at Utah State University Press, and especially Rachael Levay. We couldn't have asked for a better, more patient editor. We'd also like to thank our anonymous reviewers for their generous and formative feedback. We give special thanks to Kellie Sharp-Hoskins, who gave us wonderful feedback on the introduction, and to our formatter, Lindsay Steiner: thank you both for your generosity of time and your careful work. Finally, thank you to our contributors, who stayed with this work through truly extraordinary circumstances.

Abby would like to thank Kansas State University for granting my sabbatical, allowing me to start this project. Thank you, too, to Lisa Tatonetti, Tom Sarmiento, Timothy Oleksiak, Phillip Marzluf, Jess Enoch, Will Banks, Kara Northway, Tim Fitzmaurice, Cheryl Glenn, Stephanie Kerschbaum, and the 2019 RSA Feminisms and Rhetorics seminar group. Thank you to my fabulous family—my mom and stepdad, sisters, brothers-in-law, sister-in-law, and especially my brother, who's been down this road before. Thank you to my aunt and uncle, who gave up the cottage to let me work along the shores of Chequamegon Bay. Finally, and always, thank you to my husband, my love.

Marie would like to thank Teryn Robinson, Julie Jung, Kellie Sharp-Hoskins, Erin Frost, Angela Haas, Michelle Eble, Will Banks, Amy Robillard, Lindsay Steiner, Dessa Wander, GPat Patterson, Cecilia Shelton, Laura Gonzales, Julia Johnson, James McFadden, and Annamaria Formichella—these thinkers have kindly and thoughtfully informed my way of being in the world and thus my way of being in this book. I am thankful to my family, whose support of my work was never predicated on their valuation of it but rather its value to me. Finally, my utmost appreciation goes to JBS, whose emotional and physical labor made my work herein possible.

BODIES OF KNOWLEDGE

1

INTRODUCTION
Bodies, Embodiment, Embodied Rhetorics

A. Abby Knoblauch (Kansas State University)
and Marie E. Moeller (UW-La Crosse)

In the early 2010s, Jacqueline Jones Royster and Gesa E. Kirsch postulated that rhetorical studies was on the precipice of (re)definition, one that was "much more fluid, shifting, and expansive" (139). Royster and Kirsch referred to these changes as "tectonic reverberations" that led to ways of "expanding and recasting our ways of seeing and being" (132). *Bodies of Knowledge* explores one such paradigmatic shift: "how lived experiences—such as, inhabiting specific places and particular bodies—can shape research and teaching" (Royster and Kirsch 93). The contributors in this collection focus on the impacts of the body and embodiment on our various interdisciplinary fields; collectively, our goal is to flesh out and flesh up—to be a shudder in rhetorical studies' tectonic shift, to theorize embodied rhetorics.

That goal, however, proved more difficult than we initially anticipated. When we first started reading through submissions for this collection, we were struck by the difficulty of articulating the boundaries of our key terms: *bodies, embodiment,* and *embodied rhetorics.* These are complicated concepts, and the very act of defining them is problematic: Who gets to decide what "counts" as an embodied experience? Who gets to define the body? We begin our collection, then, by working to parse these three ripe and rife terms in order to reflect their complexities and to illustrate the necessity of an interdisciplinary approach to embodied rhetorics.

BODIES

Debra Hawhee tells us that to understand bodies, "a clustering of terms would be the best place to begin" (5). She continues by saying that "when we talk about bodies . . . we talk about sensation, touch, texture, affect, materiality, performativity, movement, gesture, habits, entrainment,

https://doi.org/10.7330/9781646422012.c001

biology, physiology, rhythm, and performance, for starters" (5). Yet, Eli Clare tells us, "I want to write about the body, not as a metaphor, symbol or representation, but simply as the body" (Clare 89). Despite Hawhee's clusters, in some ways, perhaps, defining the body does seem simple. We know what we mean when we talk about our bodies or, more generally, a body. Or do we? As we become more attuned to the importance of the microbiome, for example, it's harder to think of the body as a singular, bounded entity when the bacteria in our gut have their own relationships and life cycles. Are these bacteria (part of) our bodies, or do they *belong* to us? Are they *in* our bodies but not *of* our bodies? When we look inward, where do "our" bodies begin and end?

Sara Ahmed and Jackie Stacey argue that our skin, what we might think of as the outer boundary of our bodies, is actually a "fleshy interface between bodies and worlds" (1). They caution us not to fetishize the bounded body, but instead to think about "how the borders between bodies are unstable" (2). And Donna Haraway famously asks, "Why should our bodies end at the skin" (178)? Building on Haraway, Billy-Ray Belcourt (Driftpile Cree) notes that microbiology and pathology illustrate the "mythical" containment of the body (9). He reminds us that bodies "are inestimably constituted via leakages and exchanges that seep outside themselves, for better or for worse" (9). Molly Kessler's work on fecal-matter transplant (FMT) illustrates this porousness, highlighting how biological bacteria that move from one body to another create complications for regulatory agencies (such as the FDA) that grapple with notions of bodily boundaries.[1] Such complications are reiterated in work such as Teresa Brennan's *The Transmission of Affect*, which further illustrates the body's mutability. As she states, "The transmission [of affect] is also responsible for bodily changes; some are brief changes, as in a whiff of the room's atmosphere, some longer lasting. In other words, the transmission of affect, if only for an instant, alters the biochemistry and neurology of the subject. The 'atmosphere' or the environment literally gets into the individual" (1). A body can be changed by the shared feeling in a room, physically and chemically impacted by the affects swirling around and through us.

Even within these nuanced discussions, though, we encounter the difficulty of ownership: Who is the "we" who claims the body? Such a question leads us back to the persistent (and largely "Western") Cartesian split, separating the mind and the body. And yet we know things are not so simple. The crux of Elizabeth Wilson's *Gut Feminism*, for example, is that "the gut is an organ of the mind: it ruminates, deliberates, comprehends" (5). Wilson makes clear that she does not mean "the gut *contributes* to minded states" but that the gut IS mind (5). In other words, while the brain is part of the body, the body is part of the *mind*. Similarly, Mark Johnson argues that the mind is the term for our engagement with the world, our desire and ability to make sense of that world and to communicate something about it to others (40, 42).

Margaret Price (via Babette Rothschild) prefers to think in terms of *bodymind*. Price explains that "because mental and physical processes not only affect each other but also give rise to each other—that is, because they tend to act as one, even though they are conventionally understood as two—it makes more sense to refer to them together, in a single term" (269).

Price calls us to recognize *bodymind* as "a sociopolitically constituted and material entity that emerges through both structural (power- and violence-laden) contexts and also individual (specific) experience" (271). Conceptually, *bodymind* hails notions of subjectivity, as Sami Schalk shows in her work *Bodyminds Reimagined: (Dis)Ability, Race, and Gender in Black Women's Speculative Fiction*. Schalk articulates how *bodymind* adeptly explicates the intersecting toll racism takes on people of color: as "experiences and histories of oppression impact us mentally, physically, and even on a cellular level, the term *bodymind* can help highlight the relationship of nonphysical experiences of oppression—psychic stress—and overall well-being" (7).

Schalk's work emphasizes the intersectional nature (Crenshaw) of bodies and beings, reminding us again that there is no entity that can be singularly defined, no lived experience that cuts across subjectivities so as to be totalizing. Gail Weiss puts this pointedly when she states that there "is no such thing as 'the' body" (1). "Instead," she continues, "whenever we are referring to an individual's body, that body is always responded to in a particularized fashion, that is, as a woman's body, a Latina's body, a mother's body," and the list goes on (1). As we know, it is many of these things simultaneously. These bodies are judged, controlled, mediated, medicated, incarcerated, all in unequal ways, as those in power react/respond to the physical characteristics of the specific and culturally coded body itself. Bodies are always judged in concert with contexts.

Ahmed encourages us to think about *institutional* contexts and spaces and to recognize the ways that "some more than others will be at home in institutions that assume certain bodies as their norm" (*On Being Included* 3). This fact is keenly illustrated in much of the work in fat studies (Gay; Ioannoni; Lee; West) and disability studies (Dolmage; Kerschbaum; Mairs; Price; Yergeau), as well as in the germinal *Presumed Incompetent:*

The Intersections of Race and Class for Women in Academia (Gutiérrez y Muhs et al.) and its sequel, *Presumed Incompetent II* (Flores Niemann et al.). Texts such as these implicate institutional spaces, making clear that "the" body is an impossibility, as it erases (or attempts to ignore) how all bodies are differently welcomed or excluded, touched and shaped by power.

Such institutional constructions, Jasbir K. Puar reminds us, are often violent. In *The Right to Maim: Debility, Capacity, Disability*, Puar examines the construction of disability and disabled bodies, arguing that "the production of most of the world's disability happens through colonial violence, developmentalism, war, occupation, and the disparity of resources—indeed, through U.S. settler colonial and imperial occupations" (xix). Movements to redress such bodily trauma—Black Lives Matter, anti-Dakota Pipeline protests, calls for socialized health care, protests against the U.S. imperial presence in the Middle East—are, as Puar says, "leading the way to demand livable lives for all" with bodily concerns at the center (xxiv). Such movements depend on bodies showing up, collectively and publicly; as we have seen recently (in Minneapolis, Portland, Louisville, and elsewhere), when (certain) bodies protest state-sanctioned violence, they are met with violence—the severity and frequency of which is impacted by protestors' embodied identities. Bodies materially change other bodies.

Some theorists, though, encourage us to look beyond the relationships of bodies to bodies. Haraway's blurring of the distinction between bodies and what we have thought of as objects creates opportunities for bodily connection and relationships to occur not between identities (female/female) but between affinities (feminist/feminist). Such a shift provides space for posthuman bodies, what J. Halberstam and Ira Livingston articulate as bodies that "emerge at nodes where bodies, bodies of discourse, and discourses of bodies intersect to foreclose any easy distinction between actor and stage, between sender/receiver, channel, code, message, context" (2). Posthumanism forces us to recognize the speciesism perpetuated by a privileging of the *human* body. Such an anthropocentric focus—white, Western, patriarchal—ignores, too, the connection of bodies to place, to *land*: speaking of the devastating impact of settler colonialism on Indigenous bodies, Belcourt explains that "when a population is corralled in land-bases not entirely their own and legally forced to make do with very little therein, bodies will revolt and sometimes shut down" (8). Such trauma has lasting and devastating effects on Indigenous bodies, even at the cellular level: "[W]hen the cell or the nervous system runs amok in response to histories of colonial trauma, there is little you can do to stop it" (10).

Clearly, notions of "body" are complex. While "body" is not the same as "object," it is also not the same as "person." It is not solely biological material, not simply flesh, is not removed from intersecting matrices of institutional power. But bodies, at least human bodies, *are* also flesh, and this fleshiness can't be sidelined or ignored. Whatever bodies are, they are socially constructed, discursively constructed, sociomedically constructed, technologically mediated and constructed, deconstructed, reconstructed, constrained, damaged.

EMBODIMENT

As we continue to grapple with definitions of body, Eleanor Rosch reminds us that "*body* is not necessarily the same as *embodied*" (xxxvi). Thus, we must also ask, What *is* embodiment? Perhaps the answer is simple: embodiment is the process of being a person in a body. Gail Weiss and Honi Fern Haber explain it as "a *way* of living or inhabiting the world through one's acculturated body" (xiv). Diction is important here, though. Elizabeth Grosz chooses her words carefully when she says, "[I]nsofar as I live the body, it is a phenomenon experienced by me and thus provides the very horizon and perspectival point which places me in the world and makes relations between me, other objects, and other subjects possible. It is the body as I live it, as I experience it" (*Volatile* 86). Note that Grosz writes "I live the body" rather than "I live *in* the body." Here, the body and the living of it are one and the same. To have a body is to live the body; there is no disembodied "one" who lives within the body-object. And yet there's slippage in the wording even here: "I live the body," "the body as I live it, as I experience it." We hear in this a distinction between the "I" and "the body" that the "I" lives and experiences.

For some, the space between body and embodying seems to hinge, at least in part, on motion. Merleau-Ponty points to the ways we move our bodies through the world as a key aspect of what separates bodies from objects (Ahmed, *Queer Phenomenology* 53). And of course bodies move even when they are still: air and blood circulate, bacteria mill about, autonomic reflexes twitch—the body moves without conscious effort, but not without bodily effort. But even here, bodies work differently one from another. As James Wilson and Cynthia Lewiecki-Wilson argue, we might even best define embodiment "as difference" (18).

Of course, to assume that embodiment necessitates motion reflects a troubling ableist framework. Weiss, instead, thinks of embodiment in terms of relationality and connection, pointing out that embodiment

"is never a private affair, but is always already mediated by our con-
tinual interactions with other human and nonhuman bodies" (5). Here,
embodiment emphasizes the reciprocal nature of being, the interconnectedness of lives and objects.[2] This echoes Royster and Kirsch, who say
that embodied experiences are "grounded in the sociohistorical context
and cultural conditions of which they are *lived*" (94). N. Katherine
Hayles agrees, arguing, "[E]mbodiment is contextual, enmeshed within
the specifics of place, time, physiology, and culture" (196). For these
scholars, embodiment is a result of connection and interaction; it is a
literal social construction. Such a configuration assumes embodiment
is more than "simply" the experience of being a being with a body but
is instead the experience of orienting one's body in space and among
others, as Ahmed might say, the result of objects and beings acting with
and upon each other.

EMBODIED RHETORICS

Despite the tangled issues that arise when we try to define these terms,
at the heart of this collection is the idea that, as Judith Butler reminds
us, bodies, whatever they are, matter. And whatever they are, they are
rhetorical. Knowledge and meaning are never disembodied—they are
always made by some*body*—and yet, as a field, we've often ignored the
role of the body in knowledge production. As Karma Chávez explains,
"[T]he abstract body on which rhetorical studies is based is, in reality, an actual body, that of particular white men. The white male body
haunts rhetorical practice and criticism. But only due to its presumed
absence do the actual bodies of different others become significant
to rhetorical invention and study" (244). In other words, "only when
actual bodies are *not* white, cisgender, able-bodied, heterosexual, and
male do they come into view as sites of inquiry" (246). The body is often
only seen *as a body* when it is not the presumed norm. Knowledge, then,
is often only seen as *embodied* when the body producing that knowledge
is imagined as Other. The presumed "normative" body and the knowledge made of and through it has "become 'universal' in modernist
discourses because the bodies producing the discourse have been effectively erased, allowing them to become metonymies of experience and
knowledge" (Banks 33).

This erasure further marginalizes embodied knowledge: *that* knowledge, this academic paradigm says, is specific, particular, and limited
because it comes from the body, while "true" knowledge is general,
expansive, universal, and "pure" because it comes from a disembodied

mind. Knowledge for all, written by no one. "The command paradigm," argues Brian Massumi, "approaches experience as if we were somehow outside it, looking in, like disembodied subjects handling an object. But our experiences aren't objects. They're us, they're what we're made of. We are our situations, we are our moving through them" (14). We argue the corollary is also true: our knowledge moves through us and is impacted by that motion. As Royster says, "[K]nowledge is produced by someone" (280). Those knowledge producers, she continues, "are embodied and in effect have passionate attachments by means of their embodiments" (280). It is through our bodies that we know the world, that we make meaning of our experiences. Knowing this is one thing; representing it in a text is quite another.

Drawing on the work of Banks, Jane E. Hindman, and Royster (among others), Abby has previously defined embodied rhetorics as "a purposeful decision to include embodied knowledge and social positionalities as forms of meaning making within a text itself" (Knoblauch 52). This is an attempt to render re-visible the ways in which all of our bodies play a role in knowledge construction. "All rhetoric," says Jay Dolmage, "is embodied" ("What Is"). But embodied rhetorics cannot be simply "a celebration of bodies (which in themselves do not require academic celebration), but more an enjoyment of the unsettling effects that rethinking bodies implies for those knowledges that have devoted so much conscious and unconscious effort to sweeping away all traces of the specificity, the corporeality, of their own processes of production and self-representation" (Grosz, *Space* 2). Embodied rhetorics call for a recognition of that specificity and corporeality in the production and expression of knowledge. Hindman argues, "I can mark my body's presence when I author(ize) texts by calling to the surface at least some of the associations that my thinking passes through, associations evoked by my gender, race, class, sexual orientation, politics, and so on" (104). This is not simply about perspective or experience; instead, it's a recognition of how the body impacts the way we theorize, the way we make meaning because, as Bernadette Marie Calafell argues, "[W]e theorize not simply through experience, but through histories, and I would argue, the relations, that are written in and through our bodies," (7)—what Cherríe Moraga and Gloria Anzaldúa, drawing on Chrystos, call "theory in the flesh" (23). Thus ignoring the body is a political—and violent—act: Malea Powell (Miami) perhaps puts it most clearly when she says, "This is the biggest colonizing trick of them all—erasing real bodies in real conflict in the real world by separating mind from body, theory from practice to keep us toiling away in the service of a discourse that disadvantages almost every one of us" (401).

Embodied rhetorics are textual, but the body is also text: "*[A]ll bodies* do rhetoric through texture, shape, color, consistency, movement, and function," Maureen Johnson, Daisy Levy, Katie Manthey, and Maria Novotny argue (39). Levy further describes embodied rhetorics in terms of the anatomical body, the flesh and bones: "[E]mbodied rhetoric travels through the bones, into the ground, and through all other organic things, which also harness physical energy" (Powell et al.). Ahmed also theorizes the reciprocal nature of bodies and rhetoric, explaining that "the impressions we have of others, and the impressions left by others, are shaped by histories that stick, at the same time as they generate the surfaces and boundaries that allow bodies to appear in the present. The impressions left by others should impress us, for sure; it is here, on the skin surface, that histories are made" ("Collective" 39). Embodied rhetorics are therefore multilayered, encompassing linguistic and textual markers of the body, the body itself as rhetoric, discussions of visual or textual representations of the body, and bodily communicative practices. The contributors in this collection engage (and critique) embodied rhetorics in multiple forms and in multifaceted ways, but always return to how bodies and meaning intersect and interact, creating and leaving impressions upon each other.

ABOUT THIS COLLECTION

Throughout this introduction, we have tried to draw attention to just a few of the many scholars on whose work we build, providing context for the multiple definitions of bodies, embodiment, and embodied rhetorics. As we hope we've shown, these are slippery concepts, but this slipperiness allows for a "roomier" approach to bodies and rhetorics. We believe embodied rhetorics *must* be expansively imagined, sometimes requiring a different kind of looking, listening, writing, and feeling. We're reminded of Shannon Walters, whose work "reveals the limiting ways in which the tradition has shaped certain bodies for rhetoric but also the more expansive possibilities for valuing the widest range of bodies and minds capable of initiating rhetorical identification and transformation" (13). Our rhetorical perspectives are always limited, but an attention to bodies can help us better recognize the bodies and rhetorics too often pushed outside the margins.[3]

We chose the format of an edited collection with this in mind, believing it allows for a breadth of voices, bodies, and frameworks. As you'll see, the contributors approach key concepts in various ways; we celebrate these differences: if our bodies impact the way we interpret and produce knowledge, then different bodies will construct and engage terms differently. By drawing from multiple disciplines and locations, contributors provide further exploration of the rich complexity of embodied rhetoric, its potential and limitations.

And yet, some voices and perspectives are missing. While we knew that no collection would be comprehensive, we recognize our failure to materially address recent critiques of how whiteness permeates the fields of rhetorical and communication studies (see, for example, Chakravartty et al.; Flores; Vega, and Chávez). We recognize the (mal)function of our embodied whiteness in this process: different editors would have written a CFP that might have called differently to different scholars, would have made different selections, different edits. We're particularly troubled by the lack of Indigenous and trans* voices, for example, and we wished to have a wider representation of the voices of people of color. These are glaring absences in our collection; these are often glaring absences in our fields.

While many voices are missing, we are proud of the work here, which we organized into three thematic categories. The first—"Affect, Permeability, Sense/s"—opens with Scot Barnett's chapter, "Violence and Beneficence in the Rhetorics of Touch," which focuses on "the implications violence holds for our emerging understandings of rhetorical touch" (chapter 2). Nadya Pittendrigh, in chapter 6, "The Role of Intrabody Resonance in Political Organizing," also discusses embodied violence in her analysis of supermax prisons and antiprison activism but concludes by arguing for the potential impact of what she calls *intrabody resonance*. In "Towards an Olfactory Rhetoric: Scent, Affect, Material, Embodiment," Sara DiCaglio theorizes the rhetorical work of scent, asking what it makes "possible for our understanding of what counts as sensation, as persuasion, as connection" (chapter 4). Both Julie Nelson and Katherine Bridgman also address forms of sensory rhetorics by illustrating how feelings of (dis)comfort can support or disrupt whiteness. Nelson's "Embodying History: The Bodies and Affects of Museum Rhetorics," analyzes the bodily impact of the International Civil Rights Center and Museum; Bridgman ("Disrupting Embodied Silence") examines her own response to the now infamous 2018 Watson Conference plenary speech.

As is so often true of the boundaries we draw in such collections, Nelson's and Bridgman's chapters might have been just as comfortable in the second section—"Advocacy, Policy, Citizenship"—in which

contributors address the confines and affordances of embodied positions within advocacy work, especially as it's intertwined with nation-state
policies and understandings of citizenship. Leading off this section, Meg
Brooker, Julie Myatt, and Kate Pantelides explore two seemingly disparate archives (the work of early twentieth-century movement theorist
Florence Fleming Noyes, and the 2017 Tennessee "Women's Day on
the Hill" protest) to illustrate how embodied rhetorics intersect with
bodily discomfort in order to effect change. In a similar vein, Kristie
S. Fleckenstein's chapter, "Fannie Barrier Williams's Citizen-Woman:
Embodying Rhetoric at the 1893 World's Columbian Exposition,"
focuses on Williams's speech at the World's Congress of Representative
Women, convened as part of the 1893 World's Columbian Exposition.
Fleckenstein argues that Williams practices "an embodying rhetoric, one that juxtaposes actual bodies . . . with aspirational bodies,"
(re)weaving identifications in order to argue for social change (chapter
8). Ruth Osorio's "Rewriting Maternal Bodies on the Senate Floor"
brings us back to the twenty-first century by analyzing Senator Tammy
Duckworth's maternal body as rhetorical text—one that illustrates "how
multiply-marginalized people can position their biological bodies in
rhetorical ways to imagine new rhetorical possibilities for embodied
difference, identity, and human worth" (chapter 9). To close this section, Megan Strom's "Criminals and Victims: The Embodied Rhetorics
of Unaccompanied Latinx Children as Represented in Spanish- and
English-Language Media" investigates how media-located language
shapes public policy that affects unaccompanied Latinx children
attempting to cross the southwest U.S. border.

The final section—"Textuality, Multimodality, and Digitality"—opens
with Vyshali Manivannan's chapter, "The Successful Text Is Not Always
the One That Murders Me to Protect You." In it, Manivannan calls attention to how Western expectations of disembodied scholarly textuality
perpetuate ableist frameworks, asking, "What becomes of the rhetoricity of a body chronically in pain?" (chapter 11). Next, in "Hooking Up
Embodied Technologies, Queer Rhetorics, and Grinder's Grid," Caleb
Pendygraft uses new materialist and queer theory lenses to show how
embodied technologies shape users' bodies and expand the scope
of embodied rhetorics (chapter 12). This kind of multimodal shaping is echoed in Temptaous Mckoy's chapter, "Avowed Embodiment:
Psychological Transformation, Performative Strategic Attire, and TRAP
Karaoke," in which Mckoy constructs a theory of *avowed embodiment*: "the
rhetorical act of showcasing one's identity through the physical body"
(chapter 13) and illustrates how the uses of performative strategic attire

within the TRAP Karaoke movement constructs and reflects collective action. And it is with collective action that this collection concludes. Kellie Sharp-Hoskins and Anthony Stagliano's chapter, "Matters that (Em)Body," looks to the past, present, and future to show how all bodies and embodiments are haunted by the weight of (often decaying) materiality in our digital world.

In total, the works in this collection reflect the belief that an attention to embodied rhetorics is vital, as embodied rhetorics attempt to make visible and audible the social identities and positionalities so often made to play ventriloquist to majoritized voices, privileging experiences and knowledges best captured by the languages and structures of the presumed norm: white, cisgender, heterosexual, middle/upper-class, able-bodied males. As language is always a reflection of culture, to attempt to erase communicative practices that reflect minoritized cultural experiences is an attempt to silence those ways of knowing. This collection provides space for an exploration of rhetorical practices not always valued, taught, seen, or heard.

OUR BODIES

As one of the underlying tenets of this text is that the experience of moving through the world in our specific bodies impacts the way we make knowledge, we felt it was important that we, as editors, attempt to make the impact of our own embodiments visible, as limited as those attempts must be.

Abby

In so many ways, I move through the world easily. I'm a white cisgender woman[4] who is presumed hetero and is (mostly) able-bodied. I'm more welcome in many spaces than many others are, and I can approximate the embodied expectations in ways many others can't. But being a fat woman carries its own interconnected issues. As I navigate a world not made with me in mind, I'm very aware of how my body takes up space and how I respond to the expectations of bodies, especially women's bodies, in public. When I enter a space, I can't make myself small even if I want to, and some days I do want to. Other days I really don't. This push and pull of wanting to fit in (both literally and figuratively) and wanting to embrace the excess causes me to gravitate toward work that flows over those boundaries, embracing that which is often expected to be excised.

I also grew up white and working class in a smallish rural northern Wisconsin town. Despite the significant Anishinaabe population in the area, my childhood was shaped by whiteness, and I still struggle with how easy that makes it for me to "miss" issues of race. My whiteness makes it easier to "fit" in academia, too, but my class complicates matters—another instance of push and pull. Despite being white and now middle class, I still feel out of place at those fancy restaurants where we take job candidates; I've never known which fork is which.

In so many ways, then, I move through the world easily, but as a child of the working class, as a fat chick, I am painfully aware (often literally) of how I don't fit into places I sometimes desperately want to occupy: academia, the expensive restaurant, the tiny stool at the fancy coffee shop. I watch myself try to squeeze in; I feel myself sit gently, lightly—figuratively and literally—in places others seem to settle into. I look around me, wondering how many can tell that I'm nervous, barely balanced, out of place. And so I look, imperfectly, for bodies and texts that claim a different sort of space even as they bend, sometimes agonizingly, to be included.

Marie

I twice attended Illinois State University in Normal, Illinois. As my family jokes, that's the closest I'll ever get to normal. I like to think that place spurred my intellectual work in disability studies, affect theory, body studies, gender studies, normalcy-challenging. Such study has helped me process my own embodied experience as it has shifted and morphed over time, moving in and out of constellation with bodies, activities, locations, experiences, spaces, emotions, and, of course, normalcy. As a white, fat, queer woman, I hold many markers of privilege and power; those privileges and powers have afforded me access (with student loans: easy to obtain but difficult to dispense) into the world of academia. I am middle class now—it feels odd and is a move I never forget in mixed company.

Others of my bodily experiences, however, have not been so graceful in normalization. I've been six feet tall since I was fourteen; I have gained and lost and gained hundreds of pounds. Anorexic in high school and a binge eater after that, my metabolism is nonexistent and my thyroid resigned. I was a college athlete—the structure of my body in concert with the activity ripped a knee to shreds. I have bone growths, no cartilage, and receive regular medical intervention. The intervention is a point of contention—it was a botched surgery that maimed me so now I prepare for a knee replacement. I am also keenly aware of the inaccessibility of buildings, sidewalks, cities, and spaces. Accessibility shapes questions I ask at departmental search-committee meetings, how I read texts, how I understand people and the larger world.

My passing disabled body has also proved complex relationally—how do I tell potential partners about my mobility issues? Do I parse my body for them in a way that is easy on their ears, if not their eyes? Passing is a familiar phenomenon—my queerness has also given nuance by way of public perceptions, of passing impressions and reality shaping: I am attentive, for example, to the shifts in experiences that depend upon the varying embodiments of my partners.

My embodied reality has shaped the way I have responded to the texts within this collection—having assimilated into traditional academic rhetoric, as well as having experienced the stares of people on a street, I hold tight to the patterns and bodies that brought me power and access. I resist and struggle with pieces that do the very work I am doing in this essay right now. Those tasks fell to Abby, as I couldn't (much as I wanted to) respond without wanting to normalize. Normal is a pathology—as my embodied experience shapes how I interact with the world, it also propels me to grasp at perceived power in truly troubling ways.

CODA

As we revise this manuscript, we're in the midst of a global pandemic that is highlighting the complex nature of bodies. If we venture outside our homes, most of us are hyperaware of what we touch, and our skin has become a danger, something to be cleansed. We currently believe the COVID-19 virus cannot move through skin, but it can move *from* skin into our eyes, our noses, our mouths—the damp gateways of the body. We stay at least six feet away from others so we can't touch but also because this virus seems to be carried through airborne droplets. Our bodies are fluid; we cannot always contain ourselves.

As we write, horrifying decisions are being made around the globe. Ventilators are in short supply, as is personal protective equipment for medical professionals. When the need outstrips the demand, who is treated and who is turned away? In Italy, where cases skyrocketed, doctors refused care to the elderly and those with preexisting conditions. Similar conversations have happened in New York and also in Alabama, where the emergency operations plan explains that if the need for ventilators outnumbers the supply, those who have or have suffered from "cardiac arrest, severe trauma, dementia, metastasized cancer, severe burns, AIDS and 'severe mental retardation'" would not be provided a ventilator (Impelli). In Austin, Texas, a quadriplegic Black man with traumatic brain injuries died after being denied medical treatment for COVID-19, his doctor citing the quality of his pre-COVID life (Shapiro).

In each case, the viability, utility, and value of bodies are being assessed by government officials and doctors; bodies considered nonnormative are deemed more expendable. In the United States, for example, Black Americans are three times more likely to die of COVID-19 than whites (Pilkington). Horrifically, alarmingly, this virus keeps reminding us that, as they always have, bodies matter in material and mortal ways. This is a reality that has recently come into high relief for the two of us as white cis women; for others, it has been omnipresent.

Such institutional and material violence is impossible to ignore, as we, as a nation, bore witness to the state-sanctioned murders of George Floyd in Minneapolis and of Breonna Taylor in Louisville. Over the last six months, we have seen protests and calls for action similar to those in response to the murder of Trayvon Martin that spurred the creation of the Black Lives Matter movement in 2013. These are calls for justice, as Puar says, for livable lives for all. But this work does not happen without people showing up and putting their bodies at risk—and, as always, some bodies are at greater risk than others. Such movements ask us to acknowledge that intersections of bodies, power, privilege, space, and access have serious, real, and sometimes life-ending consequences. They ask us to acknowledge that, for some bodies, it seems there are no consequences at all. As we mourn George Floyd and Breonna Taylor, we also recognize that they are only two of so many who were violently taken from the world this year because of prejudice, ignorance, hatred, and systemic inequities—including the twenty-one transgender people who have been murdered as of July 2020, already surpassing transgender homicide rates for all of 2019 (Aspegren).

These are just some of this year's profound cultural impressions (Ahmed, "Collective"), impressions that leave deep and lasting marks on BIPOC, LGBTQIA+ peoples, and WOC (and on us all, but to such varying effect). As we continue to move forward, we must attend to the gaps, the histories that cannot be recovered or known, future impressions that will never be made. The lives lost. If rhetoric is a form of world-making, let us never underestimate the differences that bodies make in such creation, and in such destruction and violence.

NOTES

1. This is being illustrated in clear and terrifying ways during the COVID-19 pandemic.
2. It's important to remember that not all interactions or objects are available to all people (or bodies) in the same ways. Access to support systems, health systems, economic systems—all are tempered by embodied conditions such as race, gender identity, able-bodiedness, and socioeconomic class. In the midst of the social distancing, self-isolation, and quarantine that accompanies this pandemic, such distinctions are made, again, visible and undeniable.
3. We're reminded here of M. Remi's Yergeau's brilliant and paradigm-shifting work in *Authoring Autism*.
4. I see this particular privilege so clearly in my troubling use of binary gendered pronouns in my earlier work on embodied rhetorics. I am reminded of this privilege as I watch others cite that work and be forced to reproduce that exclusionary language.

WORKS CITED

Ahmed, Sara. "Collective Feelings: Or, the Impressions Left by Others." *Theory, Culture, & Society*, vol. 21, no. 2, 2004, pp. 25–42. *SAGE Journals*, doi:10.1177/0263276404042133.

Ahmed, Sara. *On Being Included: Racism and Diversity in Institutional Life*. Duke UP, 2012.

Ahmed, Sara. *Queer Phenomenology: Orientations, Objects, Others*. Duke UP, 2006.

Ahmed, Sara, and Jackie Stacey. "Introduction: Dermographies." *Thinking Through the Skin*, edited by Sara Ahmed and Jackie Stacey, Routledge, 2001, pp. 1–17.

Aspegren, Elinor. "Transgender Murders Are 'Rampant' in 2020: Human Rights Campaign Counts 21 So Far, Nearly Matching Total of a Year Ago." *USA Today*, 8 July 2020, www.usatoday.com/story/news/nation/2020/07/08/trangender-murders-2020-human-rights-campaign/5395092002/. Accessed 4 Oct. 2020.

Banks, William P. "Written through the Body: Disruptions and 'Personal' Writing." *College English*, vol. 66, no. 1, 2003, pp. 21–40. *JSTOR*, doi:10.2307/3594232.

Belcourt, Billy-Ray. "Mediations on Reserve Life, Biosociality, and the Taste of Non-Sovereignty." *Settler Colonial Studies*, vol. 8, no. 1, 2018, pp. 1–15. *Taylor & Francis Online*, doi:10.1080/2201473X.2017.1279830.

Butler, Judith. *Bodies that Matter: On the Discursive Limits of "Sex."* Routledge, 1993.

Brennan, Teresa. *The Transmission of Affect*. Cornell UP, 2004.

Calafell, Bernadette Marie. "(I)dentities: Considering Accountability, Reflexivity, and Intersectionality in the I and the We." *On Studying Ourselves and Others*. Spec. issue of *Liminalities: A Journal of Performance Studies*, vol. 9, no. 2, 013, pp. 6–13. liminalities.net/9-2/calafell.pdf. Accessed 4 Oct. 2020.

Chakravartty, Paula, Rachel Kuo, Victoria Grubbs, and Charlton McIlwain. "#CommunicationSoWhite." *Journal of Communication*, vol. 68, no. 2, 2018, pp. 254–66. *Oxford Academic*, doi:10.1093/joc/jqy003.

Chávez, Karma. "The Body: An Abstract and Actual Rhetorical Concept." *Keywords: A Glossary of the Pasts and Futures of the Rhetoric Society of America*. Spec. issue of *Rhetoric Society Quarterly*, vol. 48, no. 3, 2018, pp. 242–50. *Taylor & Francis Online*, doi:10.1080/0277394 5.2018.1454182.

Clare, Eli. "Stolen Bodies, Reclaimed Bodies: Disability and Queerness." *Oppression and the Body: Roots, Resistance, and Resolutions*, edited by Christine Caldwell and Lucia Bennett Leighton, North Atlantic, 2018, pp. 89–95.

Crenshaw, Kimberlé. "Demarginalizing the Intersection of Race and Sex: A Black Feminist Critique of Antidiscrimination Doctrine, Feminist Theory and Antiracist Politics." *University of Chicago Legal Forum*, vol. 1989, no. 8, 1989, pp. 139–67. chicagounbound.uchicago.edu/uclf/vol1989/iss1/8. Accessed 4 Oct. 2020.

Dolmage, Jay. *Disability Rhetoric.* Syracuse UP, 2014.

Dolmage, Jay. "What Is Metis?" *Disability Studies Quarterly*, vol. 40, no. 1, 2020. *Disability Studies Quarterly*, doi:10.18061/dsq.v40i1.7224.

Flores, Lisa A. "Between Abundance and Marginalization: The Imperative of Racial Rhetorical Criticism." *Rhetorical Criticism's Multitudes.* Spec. issue of *Review of Communication*, vol. 6, no. 1, 2015, pp. 4–24. *Taylor & Francis Online*, doi:10.1080/15358593.2016.1183871.

Flores Niemann, Yolanda, Gabriella Gutiérrez y Muhs, Carmen G. González, and Angela P. Harris, editors. *Presumed Incompetent II: Race, Class, Power, and Resistance of Women in Academia.* Utah State UP, 2020.

Gay, Roxane. *Hunger: A Memoir of (My) Body.* Corsair, 2017.

Grosz, Elizabeth. *Space, Time, and Perversion: Essays on the Politics of Bodies.* Routledge, 1995.

Grosz, Elizabeth. *Volatile Bodies: Toward a Corporeal Feminism.* Indiana UP, 1994.

Gutiérrez y Muhs, Gabriella, Yolanda Flores Niemann, Carmen G. González, and Angela P. Harris, editors. *Presumed Incompetent: The Intersections of Race and Class for Women in Academia.* Utah State UP, 2012.

Halberstam, Judith, and Ira Livingston, "Introduction: Posthuman Bodies." *Posthuman Bodies*, edited by Judith Halberstam and Ira Livingston, Indiana UP, 1995.

Haraway, Donna. *Simians, Cyborgs, Women: The Reinvention of Nature.* Routledge, 1991.

Hawhee, Debra. *Moving Bodies: Kenneth Burke at the Edges of Language.* U of South Carolina P, 2009.

Hayles, N. Katherine. *How We Became Posthuman: Virtual Bodies in Cybernetics, Literature, and Informatics.* U of Chicago P, 1999.

Hindman, Jane E. "Writing an Important Body of Scholarship: A Proposal for an Embodied Rhetoric of Professional Practice." *JAC*, vol. 22, no. 1, 2002, pp. 93–118. *JSTOR*, www.jstor.org/stable/20866469.

Impelli, Matthew. "Alabama Plan Could Restrict Ventilator Access for People with Advanced Dementia, Severe Cancer and Other Conditions." *Newsweek*, 25 Mar. 2020, www.newsweek.com/alabama-plan-could-restrict-ventilator-access-people-advanced-dementia-severe-cancer-other-1494319. Accessed 8 Apr. 2020.

Ioannoni, Kelsey. "Where Do I Fit? A 'Check-Up' on the Role of the Fat Researcher in Health Care Spaces." *Elevating the Voices and Research of Fat Scholars and Activists: Standpoint Theory in Fat Studies.* Spec. issue of *Fat Studies*, vol. 9, no. 2, 2020, pp. 126–137. *Taylor & Francis Online*, doi:10.1080/21604851.2019.1629759.

Johnson, Mark. *Embodied Mind, Meaning, and Reason: How Our Bodies Give Rise to Understanding.* U of Chicago P, 2017.

Johnson, Maureen, Daisy Levy, Katie Manthey, and Maria Novotny. "Embodiment: Embodying Feminist Rhetorics." *Peitho: Journal of the Coalition of Feminist Scholars in the History of Rhetoric and Composition*, vol. 18, no. 1, 2015, pp. 39–44.

Kerschbaum, Stephanie. *Toward a New Rhetoric of Difference.* NCTE, 2014.

Kessler, Molly. "Accountability in Divergent Healthcare Practices: DIY Treatment Communities and the Role of Technical Communicators." Association of Teachers of Technical Writing Conference, 12 Mar. 2019, Westin Convention Center, Pittsburgh, PA. Conference Presentation.

Knoblauch, A. Abby. "Bodies of Knowledge: Definitions, Delineations, and Implications of Embodied Writing in the Academy." *Composition Studies*, vol. 40, no. 2, Fall 2012, pp. 50–65.

Lee, Jennifer. "'You Will Face Discrimination': Fatness, Motherhood, and the Medical Profession." *Fat Oppression.* Spec. issue of *Fat Studies*, vol. 9, no. 1, 2020, pp. 1–16. *Taylor & Francis Online*, doi:10.1080/21604851.2019.1595289.

Mairs, Nancy. *Waist-High in the World: A Life Among the Nondisabled.* Beacon Press, 2001.

Massumi, Brian. *Politics of Affect.* Polity, 2015.

Moraga, Cherríe, and Gloria Anzaldúa, editors. *This Bridge Called My Back: Writings by Radical Women of Color.* 2nd ed. Kitchen Table/Women of Color, 1983.

Pilkington, Ed. "Black Americans Dying of Covid-19 at Three Times the Rate of White People." *Guardian,* 20 May 2020, www.theguardian.com/world/2020/may/20/black-americans-death-rate-covid-19-coronavirus. Accessed 4 Oct. 2020.

Powell, Malea D. "2012 CCCC Chair's Address: Stories Take Place: A Performance in One Act." *College Composition and Communication,* vol. 64, no. 2, 2012, pp. 383–406. *JSTOR,* www.jstor.org/stable/43490757.

Powell, Malea, Daisy Levy, Andrea Riley-Mukavetz, Marilee Brooks-Gillies, Maria Novotny, and Jennifer Fisch-Ferguson. "Our Story Begins Here: Constellating Cultural Rhetorics." *Enculturation,* 25 Oct. 2014. www.enculturation.net/our-story-begins-here. Accessed 4 Oct. 2020.

Price, Margaret. "The Bodymind Problem and the Possibilities of Pain." *New Conversations in Feminist Disability Studies.* Spec. issue of *Hypatia,* vol. 30, no. 1, 2015, pp. 270–84. *Wiley Online Library,* doi:10.1111/hypa.12127.

Puar, Jasbir. *The Right to Maim: Debility, Capacity, Disability.* Duke UP, 2017.

Rosch, Eleanor. "Introduction to the Revised Edition." *The Embodied Mind: Cognitive Science and Human Experience,* edited by Francisco J. Varela, Evan Thompson, and Eleanor Rosch. Rev. ed. MIT P, 2017, pp. xxxv–lvi.

Royster, Jacqueline Jones. *Traces of a Stream: Literacy and Social Change Among African American Women.* U of Pittsburgh P, 2000.

Royster, Jacqueline Jones, and Gesa E. Kirsch. *Feminist Rhetorical Practices: New Horizons for Rhetoric, Composition, and Literacy Studies.* Southern Illinois UP, 2012.

Schalk, Sami. *Bodyminds Reimagined: (Dis)Ability, Race, and Gender in Black Women's Speculative Fiction.* Duke UP, 2018.

Shapiro, Joseph. "One Man's COVID-19 Death Raises the Worst Fears of Many People with Disabilities." *Morning Edition.* Natl. Public Radio, 31 July 2020, www.npr.org/2020/07/31/896882268/one-mans-covid-19-death-raises-the-worst-fears-of-many-people-with-disabilities. Accessed 4 Oct. 2020.

Vega, Karrieann Soto, and Karma R. Chávez. "Latinx Rhetoric and Intersectionality in Racial Rhetorical Criticism." *Communication and Critical/Cultural Studies,* vol. 15, no. 4, 2018, pp. 319–25. *Taylor & Francis Online,* doi:10.1080/14791420.2018.1533642.

Walters, Shannon. *Rhetorical Touch: Disability, Identification, Haptics.* U of South Carolina P, 2014.

Weiss, Gail. *Body Images: Embodiment as Intercorporeality.* Routledge, 1999.

Weiss, Gail, and Honi Fern Haber. Introduction. *Perspectives on Embodiment: The Intersections of Nature and Culture,* edited by Gail Weiss and Honi Fern Haber, Routledge, 1999, pp. xiii–vii.

West, Lindy. *Shrill: Notes from A Loud Woman.* Quercus, 2016.

Wilson, Elizabeth A. *Gut Feminism.* Duke UP, 2015.

Wilson, James C., and Cynthia Lewiecki-Wilson. "Disability, Rhetoric, and the Body." *Embodied Rhetorics: Disability in Language and Culture,* edited by James C. Wilson and Cynthia Lewiecki-Wilson, Southern Illinois UP, 2001, pp. 1–24.

Yergeau, Remi M. *Authoring Autism: On Rhetoric and Neurological Queerness.* Duke University P, 2018.

PART I

Affect, Sense/s, Permeability

2

VIOLENCE AND BENEFICENCE IN THE RHETORICS OF TOUCH

Scot Barnett (Indiana University)

In *Rhetorical Touch: Disability, Identification, Haptics,* Shannon Walters develops a rhetorical understanding of touch grounded in its ability to "communicate, form messages, persuade audiences, convey emotion, establish identifications, and craft character" (2). Working through theoretical conceptions of touch from Aristotle and Empedocles to Kenneth Burke and Jean-Luc Nancy, Walters demonstrates that touch is not simply the experience of direct contact with the world, as we sometimes take it to be, but a constitutive encounter mediated through other relations, bodies, and technologies. Given its traditional emphases on speech and reason, rhetorical theory, Walters argues, has tended to privilege neurotypical minds at the expense of people with various disabilities who employ touch for distinctly rhetorical purposes. As a method of inquiry, then, rhetorical touch directs attention toward the potential for bodies of diverse abilities to form identifications with others through "physical, proximal, and/or emotional contact" (3). As Walters explains, "Touch . . . is always relational, bringing bodies in contact and creating a new space. Touch, at its most productive, depends on more than one body or a sense of 'the body' that exceeds singularity. . . . Touch [therefore] is often ambiguous, with no clear line separating the body touched and the body touching" (4).

As an extension of work in embodied rhetorics, touch draws attention to how relationality and communication involve not only the transmission of knowledge but also bodily comportments, connections, and dispositions. Rather than turning our attentions to how embodied actions affect the meaning and production of texts—to date one of the key strands within embodied rhetorics (Banks; Fleckenstein; Fountain; Hindman; Knoblauch)—touch asks us to imagine the body itself as rhetorical, a point Debra Hawhee makes in her examination of athletics and rhetorical education in ancient Greece. Conceiving of touch

https://doi.org/10.7330/9781646422012.c002

rhetorically pushes us to think of embodiment not only in terms of texts or writing practices but also as physical, material bodies in the world, moving and interacting with other bodies in ways that involve language and textuality but are not reducible to them. Touch, in other words, is as much a literal form of contact we have with an other as a way of talking about such connections (e.g., "today, I would like to touch on X"). As a material-embodied form of relationality, one always already oriented toward the other, touch is one of the primary ways we have for initiating, establishing, and sustaining meaningful relationships with others in the world.

Accounts of the pleasures and possibilities inherent in touch appear frequently in many theoretical discussions of touch in rhetoric and philosophy. As discussed at greater length below, in many of these accounts, touch assumes a kind of beneficent status insofar as it emphasizes bodily connection over disconnection and affect over reason or rationality. To touch an other is to establish a link that goes far beyond—or at least exceeds—traditional models of communication rooted in rational deliberative discourse. Some theorists have further suggested that the embodied and extrarational aspects of touch productively trouble the liberal humanist subject by calling into question the sanctity and integrity of that figure, which is often imagined as disembodied and walled off from other bodies in the world. As a jumping-off point for critique, then, touch offers a useful antidote to rationalist and ableist thinkers who have tended to bracket the body from consideration while at the same time reducing communication to various sender-receiver models. As a form of intimate embodied interaction, however, touch cannot only be defined by its beneficence, which is to say, by its goodness or its potentially positive effects. As Walters notes in the conclusion of her book, in addition to its generative potential, there is a "darker side of touch—abuse, violence, pain, and force" that must be understood as well (200).

In this chapter, I accept Walters's invitation to take seriously some of these darker sides of touch. I am particularly interested in the implications violence holds for our emerging understandings of rhetorical touch. While we often think of touch in terms of direct contact or immediate sensation, many of the theorists Walters cites remind us touch is no less mediated than the other senses and like those senses possesses strong creative potential. This potential, however, is not only or purely beneficent. As I argue in what follows, embedded within the structure of touch is a general economy of violence that underwrites the very conditions of possibility for touch and its capacities for bringing bodies-in-relation together. Although it can (and sometimes does) result in more physical or direct forms of violence, the form of violence considered here constitutes more of an ontological grounding enabling touch to achieve its ethical and rhetorical ends in the first place. It does this, I argue, by setting into motion an originary disruption that, prior to any physical act of touching or being touched, is always already working to trouble the stability of identity categories like "you" and "I." To illustrate some of the connections between touch and violence, I turn in this chapter's conclusion to a museum art installation, *Telematic Dreaming*, which used telepresence technologies to connect two bedrooms so visitors and performers could interact with each other at a distance. Writing about her experience performing in the installation, Susan Kozel reflects on how the mediated nature of touch—literally, touch mediated through video projections—enabled unique forms of embodied connection between herself and museum visitors. At the same time, she describes instances when her interactions with strangers turned violent, leaving her both wounded and curious about how mediated projections can so easily arouse feelings similar to those felt during physical acts of violence. One possible answer to this paradox, I conclude, can be found within the nature of touch itself and the kind of vulnerability—being open to the other while never being able to fully know the other—touch demands of us prior to anything else. In contrast to some of the major theoretical treatments of touch, *Telematic Dreaming* reminds us of the risks involved in touch, of allowing the other in as neighbor and as intruder.

THE BENEFICENCE OF TOUCH

In a since-deleted 2018 public Facebook post, philosopher Levi Paul Bryant argued that recent theoretical turns in the humanities have tended to treat embodiment and affectivity as "inherently positive." While these turns were originally meant to challenge efforts in Christian and Platonic philosophies to steer attention away from the body and affect, Bryant wonders if, at times, they have gone too far in valorizing the body unconditionally:

> Life is hard. We age. We suffer from fatigue. We suffer terrible sicknesses and terminal illnesses. We ache. We hunger. Our emotions play havoc with our life. We suffer profound grief at the loss of loved ones, family, and friends. Is it a surprise that we would want to turn away from the body, that we would fantasize about another world where we don't suffer gravity and the folds of the world in these ways, and where we would have tranquil reason not haunted by grief, loss, depression, anxiety, envy, rage, anger, hatred, guilt, longing, and all the rest?

Embodiment is not always all it is cracked up to be, in other words, and the same can be said for touch, a point Walters briefly acknowledges in the closing pages of her book. Although touch is sometimes thought of as generative, it can also be "anxiety-provoking and dangerous"; Walters reminds us that "[a]s much as touch supports connection, enables identification, and circulates emotion, it also has the potential to do harm, to injure, and divide" (200). While the bulk of her study focuses more on the generative aspects of touch, Walters recognizes that "power, domination, and control are as much parts of touch as are trust, identification, and fellow-feeling" (200). An ethics of touch, she concludes, "must be responsive to these tangles of touch and especially mindful of the impulses both to guard touch and to realize its power" (200).

Though not completely absent, substantive examinations of the darker sides of touch are not as prevalent in the major theoretical writings about touch. In many of these discussions, the potentially harmful and injurious sides of touch are mostly muted or occluded altogether in favor of more beneficent conceptions that emphasize touch's capacities to facilitate actions that are good, or at least in the service of productive—that is, nonviolent—ends. In *On the Soul*, for instance, Aristotle characterizes touch as a primary or master sense, one that facilitates our existence as embodied beings in the world (in contrast to the other senses we have for the sake of our well-being). Touch is the condition of all sentient life, according to Aristotle. It is what enables human and nonhuman animals to sense the presence of food and to possess capacities for pleasure and pain: "[I]f they have the faculty for sensation then they also have appetite, for appetite consists of desire, inclination, and aspiration, and all animals have at least one sense: touch" (qtd. in Massie 78). With the ability to touch, life is opened up to experiences beyond or outside of itself. As philosopher Pascal Massie explains in an extensive reading of Aristotle's philosophy of touch, "As soon as an animal is capable of touching, it is exposed to a world and responds to it" (78). Unlike other senses, however, which correspond to specific organs of perception (vision with the eye, hearing with the ear, and so on), touch has no single organ, functioning instead through what Aristotle calls the "medium" of the flesh (Aristotle 672). With touch, there can be no perfect correlation between world and sensing body—no direct or unmediated relation between subject and object. For Aristotle, rather, embodiment is a kind of membrane encasing the body in a manner similar to how a wet suit protects a diver's body. In both cases, the feeling of touch is mediated through various layers and materials; so, while touch can seem to offer direct or immediate contact with the world, it is in fact no less partial (and thus no less world *making*) than any of the other senses. If an object touches me, "I experience not only the object but also at once and together my flesh being touched by the object" (Massie 82). In the feeling of the touch, "I sense both the object *and* (simultaneously) my flesh affected by the object. The experience is simultaneously active and passive: touching I am touched" (82). Among other things, the mediated nature of touch is, according to Aristotle, what creates the conditions for community, for our being-with others in the world. As the most "common" of the senses, touch establishes the basis for "common sense" as both a communal value and a political aspiration (Manning 62). In this sense, touch is inherently, if not primarily, rhetorical.

Questions of immediacy and mediation—and their apparent beneficence—have continued to inform treatments of touch in philosophy and cultural theory. In his unfinished and posthumously published work *The Visible and the Invisible*, Maurice Merleau-Ponty offers a vivid and compelling account of touch that foregrounds its embodied, ethical, and relational dynamics. While touch cannot offer us naked or unmediated contact with the world or others in the world, it is nonetheless one of the primary "means of communication" between bodies, according to Merleau-Ponty (135). Evoking Aristotle's notion of the mutuality of touch—that touching and being touched are necessarily bound up in the same intercorporeal process—Merleau-Ponty describes touch as a reversible relation in which the act of touching not only implies but fundamentally in-corporates that which is being touched. "To touch is to touch oneself," Merleau-Ponty says, meaning touch is never anything singular but is instead fundamentally entangled with other things and beings in the world (255). Properly speaking, then, for Merleau-Ponty there is no such thing as "a touch," only a "touching-touched" or a "touching of the touch" that enacts a relational dynamic in which traditional delineations between subject and object, inside and outside, have increasingly less purchase (134). The experience of touching my own hand, for instance, epitomizes this idea of the touching-touched: "If my left hand can touch my right hand while it palpates the tangibles, can touch it touching, can turn its palpation back upon, why, when touching the hand of another, would I not touch in it the same power to espouse the things that I have touched in my own?" (141). As both a site of indeterminacy and communication between bodies, touch for Merleau-Ponty serves as a reminder of the alterity of the other and the responsibility we have to safeguard the vulnerability of the other amid deeply entangled and reversible relations. In her overview of Merleau-Ponty, Walters notes that the ethical and communicative aspects of the touching-touched "embod[y] Burkean notions of the biological and symbolic processes of identification. . . . Touch for . . . Merleau-Ponty is a common sensation that works rhetorically to invite identification," which for Burke indicates the feeling of being both separate and together at the same time (73–74). The connections between theories of touch and Burkean identification are clearly evident; however, as we see in the next section, imagining touch in terms of identification cannot ultimately circumvent the violence inherent in touch, no matter how attuned we are to the limits of touch or the alterity of the other.

Let me close this section, however, by briefly considering another account of touch discussed by Walters that foregrounds touch's benefi-cence, most notably its capacities to bring bodies together for purposes of communion and collective action. Along with Merleau-Ponty, Jean-Luc Nancy is probably the most cited theorist of touch working over the last twenty to thirty years. With Aristotle and Merleau-Ponty, Nancy questions the idea that touch equals immediacy. Touch, Nancy writes, "does not refer to an immediacy preceding or exceeding sense. On the contrary, it is the very limit of sense—and the limit of sense taken in every sense, each producing a breakthrough into the other" (43).[1] The body, for Nancy, is not the space of direct contact between you and me but the absolute limit case for relationality as such; the body is the place where discourse and matter run up against the limits of their powers to define, explain, and contain. Though the body is still vulner-able to disease and damage for Nancy—as illustrated beautifully in his meditation on his own heart transplant—this vulnerability serves mainly to further his view of the body as a generative site for boundary trans-gression between oneself and others (Walters 74). The body covets the other—covets the other's touch—Nancy suggests: "The body delights in being touched. It delights in being squeezed, weighed, thought by other bodies, and being the one that squeezes, weighs, and thinks other bod-ies. Bodies delight in and are delighted by bodies" (117). If bodies do indeed "delight" in being touched, then touch, Nancy reasons, can have "nothing to do with anguish," which, in his understanding, distracts us from the constitutive and mutually informative roles joy and pain play in our experiences of touch (119).[2]

That touch has nothing to do with anguish depends entirely upon Nancy's definition of touch, of course. In an address given in the late 1990s to a colloquium on the body, Nancy confesses to being "extremely troubled" that his remarks must come in the context of headlines announcing "tortures" and "cruelties" being committed in the Bosnian war: "It's just that, I won't know how to put this, I'd like to give some thought to them before starting, to all those tortured, violated, wounded, humiliated bodies in Bosnia, at this very moment" (122). In the following paragraphs, however, Nancy quickly turns away from the specter of these tortured bodies in order to finesse a distinction between touch and the cruelties committed in Europe that, he claims, denied victims "their being as bodies" (122). To be embodied—to touch another body—is, for Nancy, to open oneself to the "infinite of the finite itself" (122). And to be open in this way "is not to tear, dismember, destroy" (122). Under these terministic constraints, touch indeed can have nothing to do with anguish; at the moment our openness toward the other is violated or destroyed, touch ceases to be touch and becomes something else: not the preoriginary openness to the other but the actual displacement of one body by another. Such parsing allows touch to remain firmly on the side of beneficence while at the same time distinguishing it from other forms of relationality that are more agonistic, divisive, and violent.

In each of these cases, from Aristotle to Merleau-Ponty to Nancy, touch is characterized as ambiguous but still (mostly) generative and beneficent. As a form of mediated embodied perception, touch serves in these accounts as a means of attuning us to the limits of language, consciousness, and relationality. As Walters helpfully summarizes, touch "illustrates, in Burkean terms, ways of life that constitute 'acting together,' in which the substances and sensations of touch intermingle bodies with discourse and push the limits of identification and identity" (78). As a form of embodied interaction, touch incorporates others into relations that exceed the problematics of dualism and rationalism and in so doing provides sites for establishing other models of community not founded upon such logics. Touch in this tradition therefore signifies a rupture or departure from what's come before, a metonym of sorts for a more just, ethical, and progressive future to come.

TOUCH AND VIOLENCE

The fact that touch pushes against the limits of discourse, knowledge, and reason is part of what makes it such a compelling subject for embodied rhetorics. In his introduction to *Rhetorical Bodies*, Jack Selzer highlights some of the ways attending to materiality productively challenges rhetoric's traditional privileging of language and discourse. In the wake of the rhetorical turn in the sciences and humanities, "things in themselves" have been "reduced to a function of language," Selzer observes. As a result, "[w]ords have been mattering more than matter" (4). Turning attention (back) to embodiment, and to touch specifically, has thus served as a corrective of sorts, reminding us, as Anne Wysocki notes, that "[w]ithout our bodies—our sensing abilities—we do not have a world; we have the world we do because we have our particular senses and experiences" (3). And as work on embodied rhetorics has continued to develop over the past decade or so, the question of the body itself—What is the body and whose body do we have in mind when we write embodied rhetorics?—has also productively come under scrutiny, especially in terms of disability (Dolmage; McCorkle; Walters) and sexuality (Alexander and Rhodes). Acknowledging bodies as generative sites for analysis and activism, in other words, has been critical for expanding the reach of rhetoric beyond just language and discourse.

And yet, as we have begun to see, implicit in the rhetorics of touch is the presupposition that making the turn from discourse toward materiality constitutes a corrective to prior dismissals and diminutions of the body in Western philosophy. This tendency, despite its usefulness in framing embodiment as important to rhetorical studies, inspires the kinds of qualifications we see above in which theorists acknowledge the risks and realities of embodied relations while continuing to emphasize the productive potential of such relations nonetheless. Of course, embodied relations *are* productive *and* essential aspects of our rhetorical lives and must be understood as such. However, when we emphasize these potentialities at the expense of other capacities and effects, we lose sight of other important aspects of the rhetorics of touch and embodiment, most notably the violent potentials equally constitutive of our experiences and understandings of touch as well. In this section, then, I build on the above discussion of the beneficence of touch by turning to other conceptions that more explicitly consider the violent natures of touch and their implications for embodied rhetorics going forward.

Within rhetoric and writing studies in recent years, violence has become a key concern for scholars working in the areas of visual rhetoric, rhetorical ethics, and composition pedagogy. In "an age of perpetual conflict," to borrow a phrase from the subtitle of Cynthia Haynes's award-winning book, the question of how rhetoricians should respond to the proliferation of violent discourse and the circulation of violent images and media has become increasingly urgent. Building on Emmanuel Levinas's ethical philosophy, for example, Michael Bernard-Donals argues that rhetoric is, by its very nature, violent: "In the rhetorical act, we leave the shelter of silence, the putative safety of the already known, and are wounded by the exposure [to the other]. . . . Speaking comes with a risk to the body, as it exposes us to the response of the other" (404). This kind of rhetorical violence, while inherent in rhetoric's nature as a form of address to the other, is constitutive rather than volitional; according to Bernard-Donals, "It is a violence that we can't avoid, a violence that inheres in the structure of rhetoric itself, stripping the speaker of the assumptions she makes when speaking a name for herself" (404). Acknowledging the violence inherent in rhetorical address, Bernard-Donals concludes, challenges "rhetoric's idea of writing as a refuge, a space, a means by which subjects gain a sense of who they are" by reminding us that any utterance is "radically unstable" and as such "makes us vulnerable . . . to one another and uncomfortable in our own skin" (417).

The form of violence Bernad-Donals sees as inherent in rhetoric is not the only way violence manifests in embodied rhetorics, of course. In their essay "A Pedagogy of Rhetorical Looking: Atrocity Images at the Intersection of Vision and Violence," Kristie S. Fleckenstein, Scott Gage, and Katherine Bridgman carefully lay out several conceptions of violence relevant to their project of developing a pedagogical strategy for addressing atrocity images in the writing classroom. Following Johan Galtung, the authors define violence as "'that which increases the distance between the potential and the actual' in human flourishing" (18). This fairly broad definition, they argue, allows for various manifestations of violence to be considered under the same rubric. With this definition in mind, they identify three major categories of violence: direct, structural, and cultural. Direct violence refers to acts that can be witnessed by other people and often includes physical, emotional, and sexual violence. As a form of institutionalized or institutionally sanctioned violence, structural violence, on the other hand, is less visible than direct violence but can be implicated as a motive for direct violence. Finally, cultural violence occurs at the symbolic level where domains such as language, religion, ideology, and empirical science serve to legitimate both structural and direct forms of violence. These three forms of violence synchronize with one another to create conditions that perpetuate violence. As Fleckenstein, Gage, and Bridgman illustrate, "If a man beating his wife reflects direct violence, and a million men denying women education reflects structural violence, then sexist language or privileged dialects reflect cultural violence" (18). Fleckenstein, Gage, and Bridgman adopt this tripartite conception of violence to help flesh out a pedagogy attuned to the production, analysis, and circulation of violent images. I suggest it may help us better understand the roles violence plays in rhetorics of touch as well.

As we see above, touch is necessarily relational (even if we touch our own hands). When we touch, we reach out toward another body and in this reaching out cross a chasm separating "you" from "me." This in-between space is fraught with risk and complexity, both for the potential consequences that can follow from touch but also for how that initial gesture—that reaching out toward another body—ruptures the self at the same time it tries to invite an other outside of themself as well. Touch wrenches selves out of themselves and toward relations that disrupt easy distinctions between "you" and "me." The rupturing of identity categories we experience during such interactions suggests something violent is underwriting our motives and experiences when it comes to touch and touching. Much like rhetoric, violence likely, if not inevitably, inheres within touch, even in gestures intended in the most mundane or tender senses. Touch and violence cannot be easily separated from each other, in other words. As most of us know intuitively, if not unfortunately from experience, touch can sometimes turn violent in the direct and cultural ways described by Johan Galtung (as in, for example, the cultural logics of misogyny that trivialize consent, or ignore it altogether, and thus perpetuate instances of rape and abuse). At the same time, the violence of touch can also be structural, which is to say inherent within the general economy of touch itself. And as in the example cited above, cases in which touch becomes harmful are likely informed by all three forms of violence operating in tandem with the others.

Diverting slightly from Fleckenstein, Gage, and Bridgman, I see the structural violence of touch as not only one of three forms violence can take but as the condition of possibility that makes possible—and legible—direct and cultural forms of violence as well. For Fleckenstein, Gage, and Bridgman, structural violence occurs primarily "through the uneven distribution of power systematized on the institutional level" (17). In addition, structure can also be understood in a broader sense as *infra*structure or as a set of internal logics that make possible other forms of violence and, perhaps, even touch itself. Thought of in this way, structural violence precedes other forms of violence, not in the temporal sense of "before" and "after" but in the ontological sense of a primordial grounding giving rise to more complex iterations that further clarify and extend the violent potentialities already present within touch. As A. Abby Knoblauch reminds us, few if any of us imagine ourselves as Cartesian minds-in-a-vat or, for that matter, postmodern "amalgamations of discourse" (60). Someone must walk the dog in the morning, after all, she says. We experience our bodies not abstractly but in the feelings, actions, and relations we have in the world and with others in the world. This holds true for touch and violence as well. As Knoblauch eloquently writes, "This body, my body, has been cut into, has had violence inflicted upon it, has inflicted violence upon others, has been ignored and silenced, has been touched and celebrated" (60). Knoblauch's experiences, while no doubt familiar to some readers, cannot be substituted for the experiences of bodies in general. The irreducibility of individual embodied experience is very much at the heart of what it means to study embodied rhetorics, Knoblauch argues. And yet, even as we continue to emphasize specific bodies and lived experiences, we can still inquire into the ontological conditions that give rise to such experiences—the same conditions that help make these experiences, while distinct, common enough for us to share so we are able to commiserate with others who have had similar experiences. Attending to the structural violence inherent in touch, I'm suggesting, offers one such move in this direction.

From an ontological and structural perspective, the main problem we face is figuring out what enables violence through touch and what this means for understandings of touch, especially those mentioned above. In her book *Politics of Touch: Sense, Movement, Sovereignty*, philosopher Erin Manning explores this problem by posing a seemingly odd question: "Can I touch without violence?" (11). The answer, for Manning, is *no*, though the consequences of violence change considerably as touch moves from intercorporeal relations to state-sanctioned gestures that seek to constitute stable and submissive bodies for the body politic.[3] With respect to the "you" and "me," Manning describes touch in ways familiar to some of the accounts detailed above: touch, she says, makes evident the limits of knowledge while at the same time challenging assumptions about where one body begins and the other ends. In touching, Manning writes, "our bodies gesture toward each other and themselves, each time challenging and perhaps deforming the body-politic, questioning the boundaries of what it means to touch and be touched, to live together, to live apart, to belong, to communicate, to exclude" (9). Touch belongs to the other: "[I]t comes to me from an other, already addressing itself to an other" (11). Echoing Merleau-Ponty and Nancy, Manning conceives of touch as a form of interruption, one that calls us into a relation in which I am moved by you and in which I move (with) you, and yet neither of us is ultimately touchable or knowable to the other. When we touch, what we touch is untouchability itself: when I reach out to touch you, "I negotiate that untouchability, that surface that cannot be penetrated, the unknown and (in)finite distance which separates me and you" (11).

The infinite distance separating you from me poses challenges for touch as a rhetorical means of establishing identification between bodies-in-relation or, in Walters's terms, "bringing bodies together in dynamic potentials" (35). When we use touch to "respond to specific situations and craft specific meaning contingent to a particular time, place, and culture," we are having to contend with the underlying structure of touch that makes it difficult, if not impossible, to fully bridge the divide separating you from me (35). It is perhaps more accurate to say, then, that touch doesn't facilitate identification but rather functions as the "communication of communicability" itself, the bodily opening of oneself to an other that sets into motion the potentialities of future rhetorical identifications to come (61). Touch in this sense, and within a general economy of violence, remains firmly within the realm of rhetoric, even if it asks us to conceive of simultaneity not in terms of Burkean identification but as the in-between of bodies that paradoxically touch and yet remain untouchable to each other (13). In a departure from what we see with Merleau-Ponty or Nancy, this conception of rhetorical touch does not end with the beneficence touch unquestionably enacts in some instances but reaches further to understand how touch—the touching of the touch—is itself predicated upon an intrinsically violent structure in which stable notions of "you" and "me" are necessarily sacrificed in the service of intercorporeal relations to come:

> In reaching out to you, I entice you to become a medium of expression. I ask you to participate. I invite you to experience. As my sensation translates itself into you, you immediately convey to me a response to this touch. This multidimensional movement of desire is violent, for it presupposes a certain demand, a decision, an instance of response-ability. This response charges your body with the potential seduction of wanting to re-embody itself with and alongside mine. . . . Touching—this articulation toward an other—therefore occurs in a general economy of violence. (Manning 51)

Structural violence both enables and underwrites touch insofar as touching demands a different relationship between self and other. The violence one encounters in the desire to touch, however, "is not necessarily a violence toward you or toward the space time we create through our touch. This violence is symbolized through the entry into the realm of unknowability" (56). For Manning, to enter willingly into an economy of violence "is to engage the relation between touch and untouchability, between touch as reaching and touch as an erring that never quite succeeds in finalizing its approach to the other" (70). In this way, the violence that underwrites and constitutes the touching-touched holds the potential to redirect violence toward other ends and possibilities.

Touch itself, then, always already comes marked by the specter of violence that cannot be transcended through any gesture or reaching out to the other, however tender that action may have been intended or received. This fact is not something we should lament, but it does need to be understood and thought about in the context of other conceptions of violence and the uses they make of touch as well. What Walters calls the darker side of touch no doubt refers to the direct and cultural forms of violence that use touch to injure, divide, and control others. But it may—and probably should, I argue—also call to mind the structural violence of touch itself, the ontological grounding that, while potentially enabling identification, unmoors self and other by opening both up to a relation that can only result in unknowability and untouchability.

TOUCHING (ON) VIOLENCE: MEDIATIONS OF TOUCH

Touch is risky, in other words. To touch is to agree to enter into a relation in which both you and the other are opened up to bodily modification, change, and displacement. Such effects are structurally violent insofar as their emergence takes place within a general economy of violence that makes it impossible to transcend or fully escape the disruptive power touch introduces into corporeity. Much like the violence that underwrites rhetoric as a mode of address, this economy of violence can still be generative, especially when it disrupts fixed and stable identity categories in favor of creating new bodies and new worlds. And yet, it is not enough to say touch is ontologically violent and leave it at that (or that it's inherently beneficent, for that matter). As with any form of embodied relation, there is always a risk structural violence will slide into—and/or be subsumed under—direct or cultural violence. This potential must be kept in the front of our minds when considering rhetorics of touch. In this concluding section, then, I consider how the forms of violence discussed above intersect with each other and in particular how touch as a mediated and disruptive force can harm even as it attempts to establish identifications between bodies-in-relation. I do so by turning to a provocative performative art installation, one intended to explore the nuances and complexities of touch but that actually ended up revealing a great deal more about the general economy of violence undergirding touch.

Designed by artist Paul Sermon in 1992 and performed multiple times by phenomenologist and performance artist Susan Kozel, *Telematic Dreaming* sought to create spaces for digitally mediated interactions between the public and performers. Using telepresence technologies such as video projectors and monitors, visitors in a gallery were invited to interact with Kozel's digital projection, which was being recorded live in a separate room elsewhere in the museum. Adding further layers to these interactions, in both of the rooms in the museum, Sermon placed a bed, which allowed visitors to lie with Kozel, whose image was projected onto the visitor's bed in the museum gallery. By encouraging participants to share such an intimate space, *Telematic Dreaming* created opportunities for them to explore embodied mediations as relational techniques, or what Nancy might call the "*technē* of the neighbor"—"the sharing of bodies" and their exposedness together (91). As both an installation and a provocation for thought, *Telematic Dreaming* plays with boundaries between physical and mediated interactions. At the same time, the piece raises important questions about touch as a mediated form of relation and a gesture fraught with ambiguity and potential risk and harm. With respect to embodied rhetorics specifically, *Telematic Dreaming* foregrounds (and problematizes) the body's role as a conveyor of meaning, affect, and intensity, one that helps mediate and facilitate communication between bodies-in-relation.

Kozel performed in *Telematic Dreaming* for four consecutive weeks in 1994. Her days were long—between eight and ten hours a day—and the performance quickly took a toll on her body. After two days, the pain in her back became intense and she was made constantly aware of the invisible and unconscious aspects of her body: digestion, intestines, breathing. Writing about her experience performing in the installation, Kozel notes that, in her technologically mediated interactions with museum visitors, "interaction was reduced to its simplest essence: touch, trust, vulnerability" (93). Though not able to experience direct physical contact, touch became a central takeaway for visitors and performers alike. Kozel vividly describes being able to feel the sensation of touch when visitors reached out a virtual hand or finger. As in many of the theoretical accounts examined above, the experience of touch for Kozel became highly mediated and reversible. In her reflections on the performance, Kozel turns to Merleau-Ponty and his conception of touching-touched as part of the inspiration for her performance. For Kozel, touch is simultaneously active and passive: touch, she says, "always bends back on itself and that which seems to passively receive touch subtly, latently, covertly can be felt to exert its own touch, touching that which it touches" (37–38). This playful dynamic between active and passive touching—between the touching and the touched—significantly informed Kozel's experience performing in *Telematic Dreaming*. In her reflections, she recalls an interaction with a visitor in which she momentarily confused his projected leg with her own. In this brief instant, Kozel's body became foreign to herself—something altogether other or

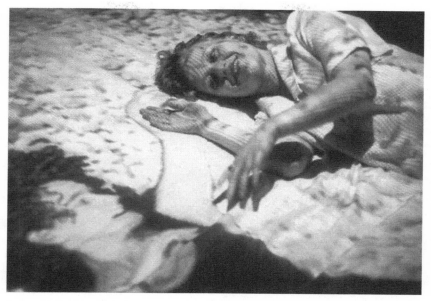

Figure 2.1. Susan Kozel performing in Paul Sermon's Telematic Dreaming, 1994.

separate from her own sense of herself as a singular and stable embodied being. This disorientation, she writes, "made me reassess what I took to be the frontier of my own body. Could it still be called a frontier if it was no longer fixed, but highly flexible and constantly changing" (101)? Although Kozel reserves the term *violence* for more direct actions, the out-of-body experience she describes nonetheless recalls the structural violence inherent in touch in which "there is a losing of oneself in the chiasmic composition of touch, vision, and movement, a destabilization of identity that is fundamentally creative" (39). The reversibility of touch disrupts identity categories ("you" and "me") even as it works to redirect the energy of such disruptions toward creative potentialities.

For much of her time performing in *Telematic Dreaming*, interactions were mostly playful for Kozel, resulting in what she describes as a "hypnotic feeling of not knowing what is coming next but letting the strong flow of movement carry you onward" (94). The installation's uncanny computerization of human experience left many, Kozel included, overwhelmed but still energized by their experiences on the bed. "Some felt protective toward me, or stayed on the bed because they didn't want me to be alone in my virtual world. Others claimed to have been 'changed' by the experience," Kozel recalls (95). Through all of these encounters, mediation played a significant role. The mediation of the video equipment mirrored (or perhaps literalized) the ways touch itself mediates our interactions in the world and others in the world. And it was these layers of mediations—embodied and technological—that made possible interactions between bodies-in-relation that, in spite of their intimacy, actualized the fact that touch (no matter its mode of mediation) never fully enables us to know the other as such.

The experience was not all positive for Kozel, however. At one point, someone took out a knife. Not in a threatening way, Kozel explains, but enough for her to feel the "predictable shiver" and to experience a "set of alarm bells" going off in her head (96). "The most he could do was slash the duvet," Kozel reminds herself, "but I still felt uncomfortable" (96). Five minutes later, Kozel experienced the worst cybersexual violence of her time performing in *Telematic Dreaming*. Here is how she describes the attack:

> Two men in leather jackets jumped my image on the bed. One attacked my head and the other my pelvic area. After three or four body twisting blows they fled. It was a back-alley scenario. What did I feel? Very little. This amazed me, after my body had felt so much in the subtly erotic context and through earlier acts of aggression. I believe that the extreme violence of the attack caused me to separate my physical self from my virtual self. A split-second after they began to hit me I found myself watching my image in the video monitor, paralysed with horror at what they were doing to the woman's body—no longer *my* body. This was the only moment in the entire four weeks when I divorced my two selves, and it was the result of an involuntary act of self-preservation—a primordial reaction in a sophisticated technological context. (98)

Being physically separated from her attackers could not fully shield Kozel from the dangers touch poses for any given moment. Far from establishing identifications between bodies, instances like this demonstrate just how risky being open to the other can be.[4] Touch—the reversibility of touch that bends back on itself—became here an instrument for committing violence. In the terms we have been using, the structural violence inherent in touch (and its potential for productive disruption) was subsumed under the regimes of cultural violence (misogyny and rape culture) and its methods of enforcement through more direct forms of physical and sexual violence. Such amplifications of violence not only endangered Kozel's well-being but also violated the ethical imperative woven into the ontological structure of touch itself, which is predicated upon radical openness to the other and a willingness to let the other in rather than sublimate the other into another (more recognizable) version of the self. As Manning warns, "If I attempt to subsume you through touch, I will not reach you. Instead, I will inflict the worst kind of violence upon your body: your body will act only as the recipient of my directionality. Your body will become prey. If, instead, I acknowledge the ephemerality of the gesture, I risk an opening toward 'the sphere of *ethos* of the most proper sphere of that which is human' " (60). As Kozel's experience in *Telematic Dreaming* attests, it is easy to turn touch's structure against itself—to amplify the force of its disruptive violence for purposes other than openness, intimacy, and connection.

That Kozel's experiences with touch and violence were not physical (i.e., involving actual contact between bodies) reminds us there can never be a perfect correlation between touch and world (Aristotle 672–673; Walters 174). Touch is always mediated in one way or another, whether ontologically, physiologically, or electronically, even if we don't always think of touch in this way. The disorientation Kozel experienced while performing in *Telematic Dreaming* may therefore have stemmed from the assumptions she (and we) has about touch and its physicality and immediacy. While she clearly experienced physical pain and pleasure, these sensations did not come about through direct contact but through a hypermediated context designed to mimic and intensify the mediated nature of touch (Kozel). For Kozel, this context provided space for exploring what Merleau-Ponty calls the touching-touched, the chiasm between actively touching an other and letting oneself be touched by other people, things, or the world. Though the touching and the touched ("you" and "me") intertwine, "they do not coincide in the body," according to Merleau-Ponty: "[T]he touching is never exactly the touched. This does not mean that they coincide 'in the mind' or at the level of 'consciousness.' Something else than the body is needed for the junction to be made: it takes place in the *untouchable*. That of the other which I will never touch" (254). Whereas haptic technologies tend to imagine touch as natural and immediate and thus as a way of dissolving the medium of the interface altogether (consider the hype surrounding the initial launch of Apple's iPad), *Telematic Dreaming* allowed technology to interrupt the feeling of immediacy we typically associate with touch. In so doing, it invited participants to play not only with touch and interaction but also with the untouchability of touch itself—to experience the mediated essence of touch dramatically and in the company of others.

Looking back on her experience performing in this installation, Kozel is left with a more ambivalent understanding of touch than what we find in many of the theoretical accounts discussed above. At minimum, what Kozel's reflections on her performance suggest is the importance of developing an ethics of touch attuned to its generative *and* violent potentialities. Such an ethics would consider touch's generative possibilities as described by Merleau-Ponty, Nancy, Manning, and others. At the same time, it would stop short of assuming a priori that something generative is by definition positive and beneficent. As Bryant and others remind us, embodiment and embodied rhetorics are ambivalent at best; we relate to others through our bodies, we communicate and form attachments with them, and yet we also experience pain, anxiety, depression, loss, and disease in our bodies. And sometimes we experience nothing at all with our bodies. Violence is thus a fundamental part of our experiences as embodied beings, a point William P. Banks made over a decade ago in terms of embodied rhetorics when he observed that "violence is always already embodied. The violence, once inscribed on the body, is difficult to erase and, as such, may control the readings we do of ourselves, our experiences, and others" (25). Violence in its many forms must be at the fore of our thinking in embodied rhetorics, Banks believes, not only because violent acts leave (sometimes literal) marks on us but also because the structure of embodied relationality—an idea implicitly at the heart of many theories of embodied rhetorics—is itself enabled by a form of violence similarly difficult to erase but no less constitutive than the direct forms of bodily violence more visible and immediate for us. This form of violence is ambiguous in the sense that it enables the openness necessary for actions such as touch to have any meaning or effect at all. At the same time, however, through such entanglements—the reversible relation that throws into question where you begin and I end—we become increasingly vulnerable to harm and injury. Violence is indeed always already embodied. Our bodies can be—and frequently are—intruded upon, and an ethics of touch must account for the intruder as well as the invited guest, the one, as Nancy says in the context of his heart transplant, who "introduces himself forcefully, by surprise or by ruse, not, in any case, by right or by being admitted beforehand" (161).

NOTES

1.   Writing for and about Nancy, Jacques Derrida similarly stresses the impossibility of direct contact when it comes to touch. The very structure of touch, according to Derrida, "assumes the solitude that conditions touch and which touches upon its limit, the untouchable" (Ben-Naftali 663).

2.   Nancy sees joy and pain as related aspects of touch: "A body is *also* enjoyed in pain (and this remains absolutely alien to what gets called masochism). It remains extended, exposed there—yes, to the point of unbearable rejection. This unshareable division of delight twists thought and drives it insane" (119).

3. Manning contrasts the structural violence inherent in touch with its amplifications and distortions through state sovereignty, which attempt to discipline bodies by insisting upon fixed and stable notions of identity, embodiment, and agency. What makes the structural nature of touch productive, for Manning, is how it serves to contest the disciplinary logics of sovereignty while at the same time opening bodies-in-relation up to new political potentialities irreducible to the politics of late modernity.

4. Levinas understood that openness to the other makes one uniquely vulnerable to violence or erasure, thus his move to install a third party into the ethical relation—justice, law, politics—which attempts to establish order and intelligibility for the relation. Perhaps we could argue that the cameras or the other visitors stand in for the third party in *Telematic Dreaming*, but in this instance of simulated rape, the trust and responsibility Kozel demonstrated in the face of the other is what was directly targeted and exploited by these two men.

WORKS CITED

Alexander, Jonathan, and Jacqueline Rhodes. "Queerness, Multimodality, and the Possibilities of Re/Orientation." *Composing (Media)=Composing (Embodiment): Bodies, Technologies, Writing, the Teaching of Writing*, edited by Kristin L. Arola and Anne Francis Wysocki, Utah State UP, 2012, pp. 188–212.

Aristotle. "On the Soul." Translated by J. A. Smith. *The Complete Works of Aristotle*, edited by Jonathan Barnes, Princeton UP, 1991, pp. 641–92.

Banks, William P. "Written through the Body: Disruptions and 'Personal' Writing." *College English*, vol. 66, no. 1, 2003, pp. 21–40. *JSTOR*, doi:10.2307/3594232.

Ben-Naftali, Michal. "Deconstruction: Derrida." *Edinburgh Encyclopedia of Continental Philosophy*, edited by Simon Glendinning, Edinburgh UP, 1999, pp. 653–664.

Bernard-Donals, Michael. "Divine Cruelty and Rhetorical Violence." *Extrahuman Rhetorical Relations*. Spec. issue of *Philosophy and Rhetoric*, vol. 47, no. 4, 2014, pp. 400–18. *JSTOR*, doi:10.5325/philrhet.47.4.0400.

Derrida, Jacques. "Violence and Metaphysics." *Writing and Difference*. Translated by Alan Bass, U of Chicago P, 1978, pp. 79–153.

Dolmage, Jay Timothy. *Disability Rhetoric*. Syracuse UP, 2014.

Fleckenstein, Kristie. *Embodied Literacies: Imageword and a Poetics of Teaching*. Southern Illinois UP, 2003.

Fleckenstein, Kristie, Scott Gage, and Katherine Bridgman. "A Pedagogy of Rhetorical Looking: Atrocity Images at the Intersection of Vision and Violence." *College English*, vol. 80, no. 1, 2017, pp. 11–34.

Fountain, T. Kenny. *Rhetorics in the Flesh: Trained Vision, Technical Expertise, and the Gross Anatomy Lab*. Routledge, 2014.

Galtung, Johan. "Cultural Violence." *Journal of Peace Research*, vol. 27, no. 3, 1990, pp. 291–305.

Hawhee, Debra. *Bodily Arts: Rhetoric and Athletics in Ancient Greece*. U of Texas P, 2004.

Haynes, Cynthia. *The Homesick Phonebook: Addressing Rhetoric in the Age of Perpetual Conflict*. Southern Illinois UP, 2016.

Hindman, Jane E. "Writing an Important Body of Scholarship: A Proposal for an Embodied Rhetoric of Professional Practice." *JAC*, vol. 22, no. 1, 2002, pp. 93–118. *JSTOR*, www.jstor.org/stable/20866469.

Knoblauch, A. Abby. "Bodies of Knowledge: Definitions, Delineations, and Implications of Embodied Writing in the Academy." *Composition Studies*, vol. 40, no. 2, 2012, pp. 50–65. *JSTOR*, www.jstor.org/stable/10.2307/compstud.40.2.0050.

Kozel, Susan. *Closer: Performance, Technologies, Phenomenology*. MIT P, 2007.

McCorkle, Ben. "Who's Body? Looking Critically at New Interface Designs." *Composing (Media)=Composing (Embodiment): Bodies, Technologies, Writing, the Teaching of Writing,* edited by Kristin L. Arola and Anne Francis Wysocki, Utah State UP, 2012, pp. 174–87.

Manning, Erin. *Politics of Touch: Sense, Movement, Sovereignty.* Minnesota UP 2007.

Massie, Pascal. "Touching, Thinking, Being: The Sense of Touch in Aristotle's *De anima* and Its Implications." *Minerva,* vol. 17, 2013, pp. 74–101. www.minerva.mic.ul.ie/ Vol17/Touching%20.pdf. Accessed 27 June 2020.

Merleau-Ponty, Maurice. *The Visible and the Invisible.* Translated by Alphonso Lingis, Northwestern UP, 1968.

Nancy, Jean-Luc. *Corpus.* Translated by Richard A. Rand, Fordham UP, 2008.

Selzer, Jack. "Habeas Corpus: An Introduction." *Rhetorical Bodies,* edited by Jack Selzer and Sharon Crowley, U of Wisconsin P, 1999, pp. 3–15.

Walters, Shannon. *Rhetorical Touch: Disability, Identification, Haptics.* U of South Carolina P, 2014.

Wysocki, Anne Francis. "Introduction: Into Between—On Composition in Mediation." *Composing (Media)=Composing (Embodiment): Bodies, Technologies, Writing, the Teaching of Writing,* edited by Kristin L. Arola and Anne Francis Wysocki, Utah State UP, 2012, pp. 1–22.

3

DISRUPTING EMBODIED SILENCE

Katherine Bridgman (Texas A&M–San Antonio)

In October of 2018, I attended a keynote address at the Thomas R. Watson conference during which the speaker told a story about an experience she had in elementary school. In retelling this story, she repeated a racial slur used by an adult in reference to Black children. I sat silently as the keynote progressed. I continued to sit silently during the Q&A, and my silence continued during the conversations that ensued across platforms such as e-mail and Twitter.

What was this silence I embodied? Was it deference? Respect for a more senior scholar? Was it reflection? Was it a perpetuation of white supremacy?

More than simply an absence, silence can be "an emptiness that deafens" (Torrey 160). Silence, as Cheryl Glenn points out, is rhetorical; it always has a broader function that must be accounted for. Silence has been recognized across contexts as a powerful form of rhetoric, as more than the submissive silence that "has long been considered a lamentable essence of femininity, a trope for oppression, passivity, emptiness, stupidity, or obedience" (Glenn, *Unspoken* 2). Instead, Glenn and Krista Ratcliffe write that the rhetorical arts of silence "have been conceptualized and employed in different times and places by many different people—some with power, some without—for purposes as diverse as showing reverence, gathering knowledge, planning action, buying time, and attempting to survive" (2). Silence is also "unavoidably an embodied phenomenon," as it is "unavoidably referential, expressive, and rhetorical" and "can never be removed from [its] historical context nor separated from the (inter)subjectivity of speakers and actors" (Acheson 542). As such, "silence can deploy power; it can defer to power" (Glenn, *Unspoken* 4). In its relationship to power, "the meaning of silence depends on a power differential that exists in every rhetorical situation: who can speak, who must remain silent, who listens, and what those listeners can do" (9).

In this chapter, I turn to examine the relationship between power and silence as this relationship manifested itself across my silent white

https://doi.org/10.7330/9781646422012.c003

body. To do so, I examine my own embodied silence at the 2018 Thomas R. Watson Conference, and I seek to enact part of my larger response to a call from the Black, Latinx, American Indian, Queer, and Asian/Asian American caucuses of NCTE and CCCC to conference organizers and attendees "to speak out and speak up about this event to address how they plan to respond more adequately in the future and more importantly to add and affirm that *Black Lives Matter*" (1). I open this chapter with an examination of my embodied silence, a silence I initially justified to myself as that of reflection. Next, I examine the white body as a location needing transformative change, and I think through two embodied rhetorical strategies that can initiate this change: disorientation and indirection. I close by looking back at my silence during the 2018 Watson conference and forward at the other locations where my silences thrive, and I describe some of the ways disorientation and indirection could have been embodied at the Watson conference and can be embodied moving forward.

SILENT BODIES

The Thomas R. Watson conference reimagines the logistics of the traditional keynote by inviting speakers to offer brief opening remarks followed by a discussion with audience members that ties into the broader conference theme. These remarks draw from longer published pieces all attendees have access to beforehand. For example, the 2018 Watson keynote remarks were drawn from a text published shortly before the conference by the Computers and Composition Digital Press titled *Making Future Matters*, edited by Rick Wysocki and conference director Mary Sheridan and sharing the title of that year's conference. It was at one of these keynotes that Laurie Gries spoke about her current project, *The Swastika Counter Initiative*. Extending the methodology she developed in *Still Life with Rhetoric*, Gries uses iconographic tracking in this project "to account for the ways that images are constantly circulating, transforming (in form, media, and/or genre), and acquiring diverse meaning as they become embroiled in various rhetorical activities" ("Swastika Monitoring"). In her opening comments to a discussion of this work at Watson, Gries "chose to use [her] keynote to explain how [she] experienced racist indoctrination as a child" (Black, Latinx, American Indian, Queer, and Asian/Asian American caucuses). Gries used a number of examples to illustrate this indoctrination, including a time in elementary school when an adult used a racial slur to describe Black children. In retelling this story, Gries repeated the racial slur.

Although this decision went unaddressed during the discussion that followed, and at any other point publicly during the conference, it quickly became apparent online that many had concerns about Gries's use of a racial slur. For example, Gavin P. Johnson, a first-generation PhD student presenting at Watson, commented on Twitter: "ok #watscon18—i truly appreciate laurie gries' work and her points about white scholars confronting their privilege and ties to racism—but are [*sic*] just gonna ignore that she dropped the N word in her talk? i understand it was in a specific context—but still . . ." (@gavyJ). Others replied, signaling the breadth of concerns about what had happened. However, these conversations did not seem to gain much visibility at the conference beyond brief appearances on social media and private exchanges among some attendees. It was not until an e-mail sent to conference attendees about a month after the conference that Gries's inclusion of a racial slur in her remarks was formally addressed by conference organizers, who shared a letter from Gries in which she offered a formal apology (Letter). A few days later, the Black, Latinx, American Indian, Queer, and Asian/Asian American caucuses of NCTE and CCCC responded with an open letter expressing concern over Gries's use of the slur "and the anti-Blackness that it signifies." Additionally, the caucuses expressed their disappointment that no "formal institutional action was taken to address this matter in a conscious and timely manner." All the while, I looked on silently.

This exchange of open letters by conference organizers, Gries, and the Black, Latinx, American Indian, Queer, and Asian/Asian American caucuses broadly provides two approaches to the silence I participated in at the conference. While the caucuses are clear that my "[s]ilence is complicity," Sheridan and Gries both describe their silence in terms that suggest reflection. While Sheridan (Letter) acknowledges silence can be complicity and offers "a heart-felt apology for what has been described as my silence-as-complicity," she also challenges this categorization of her silence, explaining that she had no "playbook of responses" to work from and "we had no way of anticipating" what unfolded during Gries's keynote. Sheridan describes her silence as her "wrestling, listening, and trying to do better in working to redress deeply entrenched racism in our field." Sheridan asks, "How do we honor folks who need time to think about the ethical and responsible ways to respond before we call them out in public for silence and complicity?" A similar approach to silence as emerging from reflection comes through in Gries's description of her own "thinking deeply for the last month about my keynote address." I, too, would have described my silence as reflection, as taking time to step back and understand what had transpired and my role in it.

SILENT EMBODIMENTS OF REFLECTION

In *Reflection in the Writing Classroom,* Kathleen Blake Yancey describes reflection as prompting a "growth of consciousness" (5). She describes herself as a teacher looking for students to use reflection to go "beyond the text to include a sense of ongoing conversations that texts enter into" (5). Silence has frequently been accepted as a given part of this reflective practice. For example, Pat Belanoff describes the role of silence in reflection writing: "What is it that comes before the utterance of or inscribing of a word that can be tagged as, in a sense, its parent? The obvious (and only logical) answer, of course, is 'silence' and 'emptiness'" (400). She immediately follows up, asking, "What happens in silence?" Eva Alerby and Jo´runn Eli´do´ttir Alerby describe what happens during this silence as a "sense-making process" (42) in which "[r]eflection needs to be given space to breathe and emerge and for that needs space for silence" (45). As we reflect in professional contexts, reflection frequently becomes part of the "sense-making process" (42) through which we—especially white bodies—come to understand the "ongoing conversations that" (45) we enter into as embodied participants.

This embodied silence, however, is never neutral and instead participates in deferring and deploying power through the racialized discourse of reflection silence perpetuates (Glenn). In their discussion of reflections by Hmong writers, Asao Inoue and Tyler Richmond highlight three facets of white discursive practices that also shape reflective practices: whiteness treated as an unspoken, unnamed, and unmarked category (136); whiteness "associated with an individual who is detached, objective, and demonstrates abstract reasoning" (137); and whiteness assumed to be "universal, neutral, and the norm" (137–138). Thus, rather than simply giving reflection a space to "breathe" and "emerge," silence embodied by the reflecting white body allows the white body to enact "[a] style of embodiment that is invisible to the person or voice, a way of inhabiting spaces that is comfortable (allows the person to 'sink into the space' around the body); the space becomes an extension of the white body and its discourse in such a way that it is hard to distinguish where the white body ends and the world begins" (Inoue, "Classroom" 399).

As I embodied the racialized discourse of reflection through my silence at Watson, my body functioned rhetorically to afford me this comfortable presence in the auditorium where my whiteness went unnamed, allowing my ostensibly neutral body to recede from its accountability for the violence that unfolded in that space through the recirculation of a racial slur.

Through the silences of reflecting white bodies such as mine, the white body is awarded an autonomy Virginia Held describes as a "splendid independence, self-sufficiency and easy isolation of the traditional liberal ideal of the autonomous rational agent" (49). Iris Marion Young describes "the knowing subject" embodied through my reflection as a "gazer, an observer who stands above, outside of, the object of knowledge. In the visual metaphor the subject stands in the immediate presence of reality without any involvement with it" (156). Thus, at the same time the autonomous body is awarded the power to move from reflection to action, so too is this body awarded the privilege of inaction when inaction preserves its privilege. The white body cloaked in silence thus becomes "autonomous, neutral, abstract, and purified of particularity" (155), enacting what Donna Haraway describes as "a conquering gaze from nowhere" (677). This "conquering gaze" is replicated through the white body's rhetorical presence as it claims "the power to see and not be seen, to represent while escaping representation," all of which ostensibly relieves the silent white body from its complicity in broader systems of white supremacy (677). Such rhetorical embodiments allow white bodies to "not overtly acknowledge their white privilege because they think of themselves as average, morally neutral non-racists. They do not see racism as an ideology that protects the interests of all white people; rather, they envision racism in the form of white hooded Klansmen engaged in acts of racial hatred" (Crenshaw 255). This purported moral neutrality was enacted at Watson as bodies such as mine reflected in silence, ostensibly removing ourselves from the violence that unfolded.

POWER AND THE WHITE BODY

The rhetoricity of the body demonstrates the ways the body is a "field on which the play of powers, knowledges, and resistances is worked out" (Grosz, *Volatile* 146). In moments such as my silence at Watson, this occurs through approximations of the normate body, an ideal that "is used to control bodies—normalcy, as a social construct, *acts* upon people" (Dolmage, *Disability* 9). What Nirmal Puwar describes as the ostensible "universal human" (8), the "normate body" is a cisgender, able-bodied, middle-class, white male we are taught to approximate often from the earliest days of our schooling, if not before (Dolmage, "Writing"; Garland-Thomson; Puwar; Villenas et al.). While this ideal can only ever be partially achieved, some bodies, such as mine, are able to be more successful than others in this approximation. Such bodies are able to achieve a "constructed identity of those who, by way of the bodily configurations and cultural capital they assume, can step into a position of authority and wield the power it grants them" (Garland-Thomson 8). I was able to do this at Watson as I sat silently, justifying my silence as reflection and reasserting my ostensible distance from the violence. The violence enacted by and through my successful approximations of the normate body becomes difficult to name and disrupt because, as Jeremy Engels reminds us, "It is hard to see the violence inherent in what we take to be normal" (142).

Disorienting the White Body

Disrupting the "centrality, naturality, neutrality, and unquestionability of the normate position" (Dolmage, "Writing" 111) allows us to see the body as "an event, an active merging, emerging, and re-emerging that opens up options for transformative change" (Grosz, *The Incorporeal* 2). This transformative change is resisted by white bodies entrenched in successful approximations of the normate body, as such change would lead to a loss of power and privilege and an acknowledgment of complicity. However, the Black, Latinx, American Indian, and Queer caucuses assert that transformative change by white bodies is necessary if white scholars are to be "answerable in the positions they take in their work." The caucuses go on to explain that being answerable means creating disciplinary spaces that locate white scholars within a "paradigm of moral accountability as opposed to anonymity." This anonymity is a barrier to moral accountability and emerges from the ability of whiteness to remain unmarked and neutral, allowing white bodies to assert power yet at the same time withdraw, as I did, unanswerable for this power. Embodied disorientations of the white body resist this anonymity of the white body and initiate transformative change through the body.

Embodied disorientation is a strategy through which white bodies, which can never exist outside their whiteness, go beyond working in the abstract to describe or critique their privilege and move to disrupt this privilege through embodied action. Through embodied disorientation, white bodies move to recognize themselves in relation to others instead of only recognizing others in relation to their whiteness. bell hooks describes how she learned to belong in space, writing, "In rooms full of objects, crowded with things, I am learning to recognize myself. She hands me a mirror, showing me how to look" (121). While this learning to belong in space was not disorienting to hooks, a Black woman, learning to recognize oneself through a process of belonging in spaces shared with others is disorienting for the white body, a body that has ostensibly always already belonged in spaces through its embodiment of a habitus that allows it to simply "sink into space" (Inoue, "Classroom" 399). Such a shift disorients the white body by disrupting its embodied autonomy and its status as "universal human" (Puwar 8). This disorientation exposes the docile orientations of bodies such as mine that are perpetuating systems of power and violence. At Gries's 2018 keynote, embodying disorientation would have disrupted my sense of always already belonging in a space that is oriented around my whiteness, a space in which my embodied silence sustained the white privilege accrued through my successful approximations of the normate body.

For Sara Ahmed, disorientation allows "the oblique to open another angle on the world," reorienting the body and disrupting the white body's approximations of the normate body ("Orientation" 566). This opening creates an opportunity for the transformative change described by Grosz and positions the white body for potential accountable action. Ahmed explains the potential for such disorientations to shift embodiments, writing, "The phenomenological attitude in reflecting on the previous attitudes is thus a new style; a theoretical attitude that is new in relation to what already exists because *in* reflecting on what exists, it withdraws from an immersion, such that an existence is transformed" (*On Being* 174). Here, in addition to identifying how change happens *through* the body rather than *to* the body, Ahmed also provides us with a model of reflection that does not reenact the autonomous normate body by ostensibly pulling this body from contexts it is complicit in through strategies such as silence, but instead accountably reanimates and reconnects this body to its surroundings. Through this reconnection, the disoriented body is forced to learn to recognize itself through a process of coming to belong.

For white bodies such as mine, this disorientation takes place at a somatic level wherein my "white racial equilibrium" that facilitates a false sense of belonging is disrupted (DiAngelo 54). As a set of "processes and practices," the white habitus maintained by the normate body often escapes the cognitive awareness of those enjoying its privileges and can instead reside in the bones and flesh of learned habits and ways of being (56). DiAngelo goes on to write that "[t]hese processes and practices include basic rights, values, beliefs, perspectives and experiences purported to be commonly shared by all but which are actually only consistently afforded to white people" (56). She reminds us that in this way, "[w]hiteness is dynamic, relational, and operating at all times on a myriad of levels" (56). Disorientation of this whiteness thus requires an embodied rhetorical response that resists the trained impulse to preserve the comfort of the white body and acknowledges the body as a manifestation of larger systems of violence and power. For example, such disorientation invites the white body to root its action in rhetorical embodiments that resist comforting responses (such as silence) to what DiAngelo terms "racial stress" (54). Without disrupting these embodiments, the white body continues to approximate the normate body, sustaining the "white racial equilibrium" through the "outward display of emotions such as anger, fear, and guilt, and behaviors such as argumentation, silence, and leaving the stress-inducing situation" (54). The silence DiAngelo includes in this list is the silence I embodied at Watson as I sought to preserve my white racial equilibrium in a moment that laid bare the "systemic conditions that foster hurtful events," like the recirculation of a racial slur (Black, Latinx, American Indian, Queer, and Asian/Asian American caucuses). Embodying disorientation resists such strategies for recovering a white racial equilibrium and creates the opportunity for embodiments that disrupt and even dismantle the ostensible neutrality and naturality afforded to centered white bodies.

Embodying New Relations through Indirection

In the Black, Latinx, American Indian, and Queer caucuses' letter to conference organizers and attendees, they point out the ways the relationships forged by even the most well-meaning white scholars doing antiracist work often fall short. They write, "As the Watson incident illustrates, too often white scholars who attempt to engage in anti-racist work help to maintain white supremacy by disregarding the perspectives and voices of those on whose behalf they claim to speak, leading to a recentering of whiteness and the preservation of hostile spaces" (2). While disorientation contributes to the decentering of white bodies, it is not enough and must be accompanied by embodied strategies that attend to the relationships white scholars embody with others. A key embodied strategy for the white body seeking to build these relationships is embodied indirection.

Trinh T. Minh-ha writes that, forging relationships through indirection, "one not only goes toward the subject of one's focus without killing it, but one also allows oneself to get acquainted with the envelop, that is, all the elements which surround, situate or simply relate to it" (4). Embodied indirection thus builds on the process of coming to recognize oneself in space initiated for white bodies through disorientation. Indirection carries this work into the relationships white bodies build by disrupting the ways the "detached, objective," and "abstract reasoning" of white discourse is embodied through the relationships white bodies forge with others—especially in professional contexts (Inoue and Richmond 137). The white body, for example, is likely to remain focused on a task or goal, giving little thought to the relationships that must be forged to reach that goal. Indirection prompts an embodied awareness that "activities are no longer compartmentalized as if they could be sufficient in themselves, and what is thought to be personal can no longer be limited to the individual and the singular" (Minh-ha 13).

Embodying indirection, white bodies are prompted to "let things resonate and approach them indirectly . . . opening up a space in which absence and presence never work as mere oppositions" (Minh-ha 8). For white bodies, this requires first decentering our embodiments through disorientation, relinquishing the somatic autonomy of the white body that makes it "the preserve of rational, adult (male) actors unfettered by affectionate ties with concrete others" (Keller 154). Strategies of indirection not only open the white body to these affectionate ties but also move the body to rhetorically embody these ties, continuing the somatic disruption of its own comfort and privilege.

Indirection also resists the ways white bodies so often claim to speak for others as autonomous moral agents. White bodies embodying indirection resist what Minh-ha describes as "diverse forms of centralization—the indulgence in a unified self, in a locus of authority, or in words and concepts whose formulation comes to govern the textual (and extratextual) space" in moments in which white bodies claim the space of speaking for nonwhite bodies (Minh-ha 6). Through indirection, white bodies prepare to no longer speak for nonwhite bodies and instead learn to speak beside these bodies. This indirection ensures that the actions of white bodies "are no longer compartmentalized as if they could be sufficient in themselves, and what is thought to be personal can no longer be limited to the individual and the singular" (Minh-ha 13). Such an approach creates a space for embodying relationships that are not the result of linear processes. Instead, white bodies approach relationships through embodied indirection that highlights interconnection and deemphasizes the comfort of white bodies.

LOOKING BACK AND LOOKING FORWARD

Looking back to October of 2018, a rhetorical reorienting of my white body would have decentered it, jostled it from the comfort of my silence—a silence that sought to deny my complicity in the violence of Gries's slur. Occupying this space of embodied disorientation would have opened my body to embodiments of indirection that could have allowed me to speak beside rather than for the nonwhite bodies in the room, especially those who have been labeled with the racial slur that was recirculated at the conference. In moments such as the Watson keynote, embodying indirection would have rhetorically resituated my body to see myself as one among many in that moment and to recognize the relationships I was already entering into just by sitting in that auditorium, relationships too frequently obscured by my embodied silences that deny the accountability of my own white body. Embodied strategies of indirection, however, go beyond simple moments of reflection in relation to others and also work to reshape my presence in that space. Such a reshaping would make Gries's recirculation of a racial slur not about my whiteness but instead about the violence enacted on so many of the other bodies in that space.

In that moment, I could have used my body rhetorically to disrupt my whiteness by standing up, perhaps during Gries's address, and turning my back to the stage. I could have also addressed this issue during the Q&A. Embracing embodied indirection, I could have used that opportunity to embody relations rather than speaking just for myself and distancing myself from Gries's slur. Speaking beside others in the room, embodying disorientation and indirection would have led me to resist simply recentering either through a comment I might have made during the Q&A or the silence that emerged from my reflection on what transpired. Speaking beside the scholars represented by the Black, Latinx, American Indian, Queer, and Asian/Asian American caucuses, I would have acknowledged my complicity alongside Gries in any comment I chose to make, using my body to rhetorically dislodge my privilege and inviting a space for others to speak from their experience. Other responses in that moment could have taken place through the forging of relationships outside the keynote through discussions and the building of relationships. Indirection disrupts the problem-solution orientation of the white body and would have pushed my white body to engage in processes of building relationships with those most directly impacted by this recirculation of a racial slur.

Looking forward, white bodies must hear the caucuses' assertion that "[b]eing answerable also means understanding that apologies must go beyond surface-level acknowledgments of wrongdoing to focus attention on the systemic conditions that foster hurtful events like the one we denounce here" (2). This chapter, for example, is a surface-level acknowledgment of my own wrongdoing. Such acknowledgments are put to the test every time I walk into a classroom at the minority-serving institution where I work, every time I participate in a hiring committee, every time I sit down to participate in or chair a committee meeting. How often do I claim to speak *for* the needs of nonwhite students rather than speaking *beside* these students and creating spaces where their voices can be heard? How often have I recentered my whiteness by walking into a committee meeting with a problem to be solved, ignoring the relationships and the communities both in and outside the room? How often have I chaired a committee and let my whiteness go unnamed, rampantly preserving the "white racial equilibrium" of not only myself but of the institution I work for (DiAngelo 54)?

CONCLUSION

The Black, Latinx, American Indian, Queer, and Asian/Asian American caucuses remind us that the violence of Gries's racial slur does not simply exist within the bounds of our field and the pages of our scholarship. Instead, they remind us that "[b]eing answerable means being conscientious and sensitive to our present context in which hate crimes are currently on the rise" (1). William Banks echoes this reminder, challenging us to resist abstracting our discussions and eliding the role of bodies in any antiracist project. We cannot think our way to disrupting systems of racism and ending the violence that thrives within these systems. Instead, we must always return to the bodies that enact change. Banks writes, "[R]egardless of how distant we can get ourselves from the embodied experiences of our lives, if we do not find ways back to those bodies, those experiences, we run the risk of impoverishing our theories and pedagogies. More specifically, when we ignore the 'embodied' in discourse, we miss the ways in which liberation is always both social and individual, a truly symbiotic relationship" (22). Too frequently, when white bodies seek to enact change in systems of racism, they turn to what Asao Inoue describes as a white racial habitus we see enacted through my embodied silence at the Watson keynote. My embodiment of silence in this moment protected the privilege accrued through my approximations of a white normate body. As I find my way back to and confront this white body, I am prompted not only to *do* better but to *be* better. Such *being* better requires that I recognize the rhetorical embodiments my approximation of the normate body elide—and the habits of whiteness that enable these approximations—that I have learned and internalized. Beyond simply acknowledging these embodiments, I must also do the work of shifting them, of using my white body to disrupt the privileges of my whiteness. Rhetorical, our embodiments in the world are malleable, as our flesh is never neutral but instead always involved in negotiations of power. As I affirm that Black Lives Matter, so too must I interrogate my white embodiment, an embodiment that is both a location perpetuating white supremacy and a location for potential disruptions of white supremacy.

White bodies taking action from embodiments that preserve their privilege maintain and perpetuate the systems of white supremacy that cohere to these bodies, that make them "the problem" (Inoue, "How Do We Language"). Inoue confronted white bodies about this during his CCCC keynote saying:

> How does it feel to be the problem? How does it make you feel to be the one in the way of progress, no matter what you have said or what your agendas are, how hard you worked, or how sincere you are? It's unfair, isn't it? You are good people. And yet you are the problem, but you don't want to be. Think about that for a minute. You can be a problem even when you try not to be. Sit and lament in your discomfort and its sources. Search. If our goal is a more socially just world, we don't need more good people. We need good changes, good structures, good work that makes good changes, structures, and people.

The discomfort Inoue created for many white bodies listening to and reading his keynote is a transformational discomfort that, if allowed, can powerfully reorient white bodies and the relationships they enter into. As the silence that became deafening at Watson illustrates, "[M]ore good people" fail at "good changes, good structures, [and] good work that makes good changes" when their embodiments of whiteness remain intact and allow them to sit silently, to "sit on their hands, with love in their hearts, but stillness in their bodies" ("How Do We"). As white bodies take up this challenge, the discomfort of these bodies, as Meg Brooker, Julie Myatt, and Kate Pantelides (chapter 7) point out, can lead to powerful embodiments that are answerable, reaching beyond reinscribing the autonomy of the white body and instead dismantling this autonomy and the privileges it preserves.

WORKS CITED

@gavyJ. "ok #watscon18—i truly appreciate laurie gries' work and her points about white scholars confronting their privilege and ties to racism—but are just gonna ignore that she dropped the N word in her talk? i understand it was in a specific context—but still . . ." *Twitter*, 26 Aug. 2018, 4:54 p.m., twitter.com/gavyj/status/105 5940838461718534?lang=en. Accessed 27 June 2020.
Acheson, Kris. "Silence as Gesture: Rethinking the Nature of Communicative Silences." *Communication Theory*, vol. 18, no. 4, 2008, pp. 535–55. *Wiley Online Library*, doi:10.11 11/j.1468–2885.2008.00333.x.

Ahmed, Sara. *On Being Included.* Duke UP, 2012.

Ahmed, Sara. "Orientation: Toward a Queer Phenomenology." *GLQ: A Journal of Lesbian and Gay Studies*, vol. 12, no. 4, 2006, pp. 543–74. *Duke UP*, doi:10.1215/10642684-2006-002.

Alerby, Eva, and Jo´runn Eli´do´ttir Alerby. "The Sounds of Silence: Some Remarks on the Value of Silence in the Process of Reflection in Relation to Teaching and Learning." *Reflective Practice*, vol. 4, no. 1, 2003, pp. 41–51. *Taylor & Francis Online*, doi:10.1080/1462394032000053503.

Banks, William P. "Written through the Body: Disruptions and 'Personal' Writing." *College English*, vol. 66, no. 1, 2003, pp. 21–40. *JSTOR*, doi:10.2307/3594232.

Belanoff, Pat. "Silence: Reflection, Literacy, Learning, and Teaching." *College Composition and Communication* vol. 52, no. 3, 2001, pp. 399–428. *JSTOR*, doi:10.2307/358625.

Black, Latinx, American Indian, Asian/Asian American, and Queer caucuses. Letter to Watson Conference. 4 Dec. 2018. https://docs.google.com/document/d/1fsD-D5Y-KyQ007lLiMDmuIv7QV2TJ07qMUxJqQZIzHk/edit.

Crenshaw, Carrie. "Resisting Whiteness' Rhetorical Silence." *Western Journal of Communications*, vol. 61, no. 3, 1997, pp. 253–78. *Taylor & Francis Online*, doi:10.1080/10570319709374577.

DiAngelo, Robin. "White Fragility." *International Journal of Critical Pedagogy*, vol. 3, no. 3, 2011, pp. 54–70.

Dolmage, Jay. *Disability Rhetoric.* Syracuse UP, 2014.

Dolmage, Jay. "Writing against Normal: Navigating the Corporeal Turn." *Composing (Media)=Composing (Embodiment): Bodies, Technologies, Writing, the Teaching of Writing*, edited by Kristin Arola and Anne Wysocki, UP of Colorado, 2012, pp. 110–26.

Engels, Jeremy. *The Politics of Resentment: A Genealogy.* Pennsylvania State UP, 2015.

Garland-Thomson, Rosemarie. *Extraordinary Bodies: Figuring Physical Disability in American Culture and Literature.* Columbia UP, 1997.

Glenn, Cheryl. *Unspoken: A Rhetoric of Silence.* Southern Illinois UP, 2004.

Glenn, Cheryl, and Krista Ratcliffe. *Silence and Listening as Rhetorical Arts.* Southern Illinois UP, 2011.

Gries, Laurie. Letter to Watson Conference Organizers, Participants, and Audience Members of my Keynote Address. Distributed to conference participants via e-mail. 28 Nov. 2018.

Gries, Laurie. "Swastika Monitoring: Developing Digital Research Tools to Track Visual Rhetorics of Hate." Making Future Matters. Thomas R. Watson Conference, 26 Oct. 2018, Stickler Auditorium, Louisville. Keynote Address.

Gries, Laurie. "Swastika Monitoring: Developing Digital Research Tools to Track Visual Rhetorics of Hate." *Making Future Matters*, edited by Rick Wysocki and Mary Sheridan, Computers and Composition Digital, 2018. ccdigitalpress.org/book/makingfuturematters/gries-intro.html. Accessed 27 June 2020.

Grosz, Elizabeth. *The Incorporeal: Ontology, Ethics, and the Limits of Materialism.* Columbia UP, 2017.

Grosz, Elizabeth. *Volatile Bodies.* Allen and Unwin, 1994.

Haraway, Donna. "The Persistence of Vision." *The Visual Culture Reader*, edited by Nicholas Mirzzoff, Routledge, 2002, pp. 677–84.

Held, Virginia. *The Ethics of Care: Personal, Political, and Global.* Oxford UP, 2006.

hooks, bell. *Belonging: A Culture of Place.* Routledge, 2009.

Inoue, Asao. "Classroom Writing Assessment as an Antiracist Practice: Confronting White Supremacy in the Judgements of Language." *Pedagogy*, vol. 19, no. 3, 2019, pp. 373–404. *Duke UP*, doi:10.1215/15314200–7615366.

Inoue, Asao. "How Do We Language So People Stop Killing Each Other, or What Do We Do about White Language Supremacy?" Performance-Rhetoric, Performance-

Composition. Conference on College Composition and Communication, 14 Mar. 2019, David L. Lawrence Convention Center, Pittsburgh. Keynote Address.

Inoue, Asao, and Tyler Richmond. "Theorizing the Reflection Practices of Female Hmong College Students: Is Reflection a Racialized Discourse?" *A Rhetoric of Reflection*, edited by Kathleen Blake Yancey, Utah State UP, 2016, pp. 125–45.

Johnson, Gavin. "Re: Request to quote a tweet." Received by Katherine Bridgman, 18 June 2000.

Keller, Jean. "Autonomy, Relationality, and Feminist Ethics." *Hypatia*, vol. 12, no. 2, 1997, pp. 152–64. *JSTOR*, www.jstor.org/stable/3810475.

Minh-ha, Trinh T. "The Undone Interval in Conversation with Annamaria Morelli." *The Post-Colonial Question*, edited by Iain Chambers and Lidia Curti, Routledge, 1996, pp. 3–16.

Puwar, Nirmal. *Space Invaders*. Berg, 2004.

Sheridan, Mary. Letter to Watson attendees. Distributed to conference participants via e-mail. 10 Dec. 2018.

Torrey, KT. "Silence." *Keywords in Writing Studies*, edited by Paul Heilker and Peter Vandenberg, Utah State UP, 2015, pp. 160–64.

Villenas, Sofia, Francisca E. Godinez, Dolores Delgado Bernal, and C. Alejandra Elenes. "Chicanas/Latinas Building Bridges." *Chicana/Latina Education in Everyday Life*, edited by Dolores Delgado Bernal, C. Alejandra Elenes, Francisca E. Godinez, and Sofia Villenas, State U of New York P, 2006, pp. 1–10.

Wysocki, Rick, and Mary P. Sheridan, editors. *Making Future Matters*. Computers and Composition Digital, 2018, ccdigitalpress.org/makingfuturematters. Accessed 27 June 2020.

Yancey, Kathleen Blake. *Reflection in the Writing Classroom*. Utah State UP, 1998.

Young, Iris Marion. *Justice and the Politics of Difference*. Princeton UP, 1990.

4

TOWARDS AN OLFACTORY RHETORIC
Scent, Affect, Material, Embodiment

Sara DiCaglio (Texas A&M University, College Station)

Rhetorical scholarship is increasingly concerned with the molecular, the material, the sensorial, the embodied. Through the no-longer-so-recent material turn, rhetoricians have argued that the kinds of persuasions we are interested in examining do not happen only on the level of language; rather, language is just a part of a larger network of persuading forces, of experiences and embodiments that allow us to perceive and be persuaded, of human and nonhuman forces that control the possibilities of what can be argued and of what can be thought or said. Rhetorical scholarship engaged in object-oriented and new materialist rhetorics (Pfulgedger; Rickert; Rivers) and examinations of what Debra Hawhee calls "rhetoric's sensorium" (Ball and Hawk; Hawhee; Walters) have illustrated that the ways we perceive are broader, and less in our control, than we have previously imagined. In this article, I am particularly interested in the role of the senses in relation to these persuasive forces, human and nonhuman, linguistic, and material.

Or, rather, I am concerned with scent. Because, as our scholarship has expanded to examine visual rhetorics (Finnegan; Gries; Kaszynski), haptic rhetorics (Hanson; Loe; Walters), sonic rhetorics (Ball and Hawk; Comstock and Hocks; Gunn et al.; Hawk; Rickert), and even rhetorics of taste (Branch; Wells), rhetoricians have still largely overlooked scent. This elision not new; Plato and Aristotle, in their own studies of the senses, seem thoroughly befuddled, speaking of scents largely in terms of the challenges of discerning them from other senses and their mediums. More recently, scent merits mention in a number of pieces related to Hawhee's "rhetoric's sensorium," but its mention is often brief, lumped into a larger discussion of the critical hole around senses or the rhetorical potentials of those senses. Hawhee, for example, writes of her own work in *Rhetoric in Tooth and Claw* that her findings "often highlight and perhaps replicate, which is to say follow, a historical preference for

https://doi.org/10.7330/9781646422012.c004

the visual, but not without acknowledging the omnipresence and simultaneity of other senses, especially the sonic and the haptic, though there is surely work to be done on notions of taste and smell" (171). As this example illustrates, even in overviews of the relationship between senses and rhetoric, scent is generally left to the end, functioning as an afterthought. Hawhee is far from anomalous here, as this move is repeated across the century by rhetoricians such as Edward Corbett, who writes "of a complete immersion in an experience that involves the senses of sight, hearing, touch, and *even smell* simultaneously" (292; emphasis added), and Jenell Johnson, who writes, "Most humans perceive the feelings of others through gestures, bodily postures, and facial expressions *(and, perhaps, smell)*" (3; emphasis added). Smell is cast either as an almost unbelievable other or as something we don't quite know what to do with—an ongoing challenge for future scholarship.

I am interested in thinking about scent because the turn to the senses has important implications for rhetoric, particularly embodied rhetorics. As Hawhee notes, "The idea of a sensing package, a bundle of constitutive, participatory tendrils, may help press past commonplace conditional observations—e.g., *that* rhetorical activity is embodied—and could offer a way to think about the connective, participatory dimensions of sensing" (5). Later, she writes, "Sensation needn't become encased in language to be known—the epistemic approach to rhetoric has run its course; rhetoric is not, or not only, a means of knowing and needn't be so attached to meaning" (13). In other words, the unknown within the sensorium, the aspects of our senses that may be outside of control and even easy perception, still may be vital for rhetoric itself.

Scent is arguably the sense hardest to translate into language, the most unknowable and uncontrollable—but also constantly and consistently with us. In order to better understand what encountering this very embodied sensation means for our considerations of rhetoric, in this article I construct a theory of *olfactory rhetorics*, or rhetorics of scent. As Lisa Phillips conceives of it, olfactory rhetorics are "concerned with how we write, think, talk about, and experience smell and scent in different environments, cultural contexts, and disciplinary domains" (36). As Phillips notes, a richer rhetorical sense of olfaction is vital to a quest for ethical relations and social justice; to attend to those ethical relations, I would add, we must think carefully about scent as an embodied process, an ongoing series of material changes and responses within our embodied selves and entangled worlds.

Taking up Phillips's challenge to consider our material and rhetorical entanglements through olfactory rhetorics in order to consider our material and rhetorical entanglement, I argue that attention to the rhetorical powers of scent can allow for a heightened understanding of the interaction among embodiment, environment, and rhetoric—between our physical beings and related perceptions, between and among what we might consider ourselves and the physical, molecular, and chemical world just outside our (porous) boundaries. Of course, these boundaries and terms are in many ways limited—what does it mean to speak of boundaries and surfaces as somehow external when our interiors too are filled with surface and boundary and porousness, for instance (Colls and Fannin)? But as rough categories, these terms point to the question of how our material bodies—both our perception of that materiality and what we do not perceive about or with it and the other material within and without our bodies we engage with, take in, and are taken in by—affect, define, and create one another. By turning our attention to this interaction, we are forced to confront rhetoric's less controllable, visible, individual distinctly human aspects. As Teresa Brennan has written, scent is a particularly powerful tool for the understanding of affect, community, and discernment, as it is rapid, relational, and incapable of deceit, though it, like senses and embodiment more generally, is often read as less intelligent and organized than more logic-based forms of knowing (136). And since, as Jay Dolmage argues, "rhetoric has ignored the body" and "this ignorance is reinforced by a fear of imperfection, a fear about the boundaries around our bodies, and a fear of the strange bodies of Others," it seems natural that scent—the most intermingling, potentially off-putting, and strange of senses—has been most ignored (5).

In order to theorize olfactory rhetorics, then, I first examine what we might think of as rhetorics *about* scent—understandings and discussions of how we conceive of scent itself. Following this discussion, I consider olfaction's possibilities as an organizing feature of a process-based understanding of the body. Through this examination, I ask how attention to olfactory rhetorics might build upon our understandings of rhetoric as embodied, affective, and new materialist, pushing us towards a rhetorical theory that embraces vulnerability, interconnectedness, and materiality as central to our understanding of what it means to be embodied rhetorical creatures.

UNPACKING OLFACTION, OR SMELLY RHETORICS

Scent is political. It is cultural. It is individual. It affects access and air, public spaces, public health. As a migraine sufferer, I must occasionally take refuge inside my office when certain air fresheners make the air in the hallway feel as if it is pressing directly on my brain. I duck away from candle shops and other places where scents mean my sensitive body is not welcome. When I was a high schooler in the late 90s, a primary mode of bonding among many groups of girls was the passing of Bath and Body Works moisturizer and the frequent question, "Do you have any lotion?" As a middle-school teacher, I had discussions with home-rooms overfilled with thirty-seven seventh-grade boys about hygiene and puberty coded through scent; I also had even gentler conversations with and about students who could not afford enough school uniforms and access to laundry to make it through the week—something I could discern primarily through scent. And despite my scent sensitivities, my relation to scent is rather privileged. I do not live near a pig-feces lagoon or a meat-packing plant or a processing plant that releases not just waste but *scent* into the air, spaces largely occupied by poor people of color in this nation and elsewhere (Jackson; Mele; Phillips; Purifoye). The history of miasma and the connection of scent to disease further highlights the political nature of scent; as Emily Winderman, Robert Mejia, and Brandon Rogers write, "Olfactory rhetorics are central to disease rhetoric because disgust evoked by 'diseased' smells can encourage visceral publics to avoid or demonize bodies visually represented as occupying disgusting spaces" (121).

Beyond or as a part of its politics, scent is affective. Think of your own favorite scent—the mustiness of library books, the sharpness of fresh-cut grass, the warmth of rain. For me, it is the smell of snow, though I struggle to discern in my scent memory which part is scent and which is simply chill. The smell of the mercaptan and other odorants added to gas so we will know if there's a leak—odorants added as a safety measure shortly after a 1937 Texas schoolhouse explosion—is to our contemporary noses the very essence of the gas itself. This sensory and affective confusion between scent and object is, as I argue in later parts of this piece, vital to our understanding of olfactory rhetorics, as it illustrates the deep connections that occur throughout and in conjunction with scent itself. Scent connects us through space and memory. It separates us, marks neighborhood communities, communicates back to us.

In other words, though scent has been largely undertheorized, particularly within rhetorical studies, it is far from neutral. Indeed, scents are regularly used to influence human conduct, particularly in terms of consumption. For example, ambient scents are used to encourage certain behaviors, be they performance, purchasing, or otherwise. As Kevin D. Bradford and Debra M. Desrochers write in the *Journal of Business Ethics*, "[S]mell is a sense that we cannot suspend, it is engaged whether or not we are aware of it, and it is directly tied to our memory and emotions" (151). Scent's connections function at an affective or otherwise nonlinguistic level, prefiguring our awareness but still persuading, affecting. Though we are aware of and respond logically to some scents, reacting to them through, among other things, choices about proximity, our impossible-to-suspend sense of smell also operates on fully embodied levels we are unaware of. And, as Phillips notes, scent highlights "our vulnerability to desensitization," bringing attention to our ability to grow used to and therefore ignore or no longer notice an odor—as well as the dangers of this ability (38).

All of this is to say that scent, while shifting and complex, is ever present, vital to our own embodiment, but also invisible, forgotten. Scent directs our behaviors and affects, tells us what we are and are not even while becoming a part of our physical being. Despite this, as I have previously mentioned, extended attention to olfaction has been largely absent from rhetorical scholarship.[1] There are many reasons for this absence. For one, scent has an uncomfortable relation to the private-public boundary. Even as we move to digitize the chemical senses to enhance virtual reality and entertainment (Spence et al. 64), and even as that digitization reaches into more serious realms like military training and telesurgery, chemical senses remain difficult to operationalize, difficult to share. As a child of the 80s and 90s, I grew up in the age of the scratch-and-sniff everything, and perhaps this colors my own inability to take scent seriously—but it is hard for me not to think of projects related to the development of experiential, virtual scents as gimmicky, a scratch and sniff 2.0. Beyond this form of resistance, smell is hard to make virtual in part because it is difficult to make as private as a pair of headphones or a smartphone or even an *amuse bouche* might make another sense.

Moreover, scent is, for lack of a more precise term, *funny*. Think, for instance, of that darling of the preteen coming to understand bodies as hilarious and shameful—the common fart joke. In some ways, these jokes are about the sonic quality of flatulence separated from the smell, but in many others, they're about discernment. Thus—not to get too sidetracked into a rhetorical analysis of jokes about flatulence—the common refrains of *whoever smelt it, dealt it* and its response, *whoever made the rhyme, did the crime*, are about the creation of a(n unwanted) scent as a part of the act of discernment itself. In other words, the act of noticing ties one to the creation of the scent, which, in the fairly circular logic of this humor, would not exist had it not been noticed. To note a smell is therefore to be guilty—to discern is to create. This complicated sense of guilt and silence is compounded by the fact that when we talk about smell, we imagine we are speaking only of the nose—another often giggle-worthy body part. And yet olfactory receptors appear throughout our body, including in the "gastrointestinal (GI) tract, muscle, heart, pancreas, liver, lung, and skin," as well as sperm and kidneys (Shepard and Pluznick 715). As I discuss in my next section, it is precisely an attention to the specific mechanisms of scent—as well as what we do not know about those mechanisms—that can help us take the rhetorical power of scent more seriously.

WHAT'S THAT SMELL, OR ONTOLOGIES OF OLFACTION

The consideration of olfactory rhetorics is not simply about the ways we think about or consider smell, either linguistically or in an embodied matter. It is also about the ways we contend with the biological, with biological processes and our knowledge about them. That is not to say the biological or scientific has any sort of ontological claim to a higher level of knowledge based on its very existence. However, it does mean attention to the senses can and very well should contend with how those actual processes occur. As Elizabeth Wilson writes of feminist theory, we have too long "talked about the body as if anatomy did not exist," thought about the body as theoretical but not material (69).

Sensation seems a vital space through which to consider our material selves as they meet one another, particularly when we speak specifically of the mechanisms through which bodily sensations occur. Those mechanisms are easy to overlook for fear of biological essentialism, but they provide a rich way to rethink our assumptions about what embodiment is and what it brings to us. As Samantha Frost writes, "With some notable exceptions, I think theorists are more comfortable with general or theoretically abstracted notions of embodiment. . . . To describe someone as a living body, as alive, seems at once to be absurdly obvious and also theoretically suspect—as if the statement of something so clearly incontrovertible must carry another agenda, that is, the aim to reduce someone to a biological substrate" (23). Scent as a rhetorical process does indeed seem both "absurdly obvious and also theoretically suspect." That is, we are deeply aware we all have scents, that scent is a thing used to communicate that we, to different degrees and at different levels of awareness, perceive—and also that theorizations built in scent threaten to knock us away from the pedestal of logic. An overly intimate understanding of scent has been culturally cast as otherworldly, the stuff of horror (see, for example, *Perfume* or *The Silence of the Lambs*). Scent, in this understanding, threatens to control our instincts, and any discussion of pheromonal attraction to intimate partners turns quickly to a fearful erasure of human agency. And we are deeply uneasy with recognizing that our bodies may therefore work in ways we are not fully aware of. As Jennifer Saltmarsh writes in her consideration of bacterial rhetorics, "If we recognize relationships (or the lack thereof) through nonconscious odor cues, we may be inclined to communicate and interact differently toward different people, which could possibly interfere with our desires for and conscious efforts at inclusion and tolerance" (74). We are rightly cautioned here that a lack of attention to odor doesn't make our relationship to it any simpler or less visible; however, within Saltmarsh's statement also lies an intriguing divide between embodiment and desire. As Saltmarsh notes, our embodied selves may react to cues and therefore act in ways our logical minds might not agree with. But, we might then ask, are our embodied actions therefore not encompassed by or a part of our desires? The relationship between embodiment, desire, persuasion, and the particularities of bodily processes is a challenging problem for rhetorical scholarship more broadly, which may examine sensation but not its specific processes and expansions throughout the body. So here, I consider what we know about how smell—"one of the most important means of communication with the environment"—works, what that tells us about what smell is, and what that means for our understandings of olfactory rhetorics (Strous and Shoenfield 55).

Upon beginning the research for this project, I assumed—perhaps naïvely—that, scientifically speaking, the mechanisms of scent would be settled, if not straightforward. However, the more I researched the mechanisms of scent, the more I realized how little we know about it. At its most basic definition, "Olfaction registers chemical information in organisms ranging from insects to humans, including marine organisms. For terrestrial animals, its stimuli comprise airborne molecules. The typical stimulus is an organic chemical with molecular weight below 300 Daltons; about a half million such substances exist" (Cain). It is posited that smell is intimately related to autoimmunity; as Carlo Perricone, Netta Schoenfeld, Nancy Agmon-Levin, Catarina de Carolis, Roberto Perricone, and Yehuda Shoenfeld write, "The sense of smell is an ancient sensory modality vital for sampling and perceiving the chemical composition of the surrounding environments" (87). But as biophysicist Jennifer C. Brookes writes, "Human sensory processes are well understood: hearing, seeing, perhaps even tasting and touch. But we do not understand smell—the elusive sense" (3491). Recent conversations about olfaction center around what is known as the "vibration theory of olfaction," which posits that odor operates through a kind of electron tunneling rather than a more physical exchange (Turin). The other most central theory is referred to as "shape," "docking," or "lock-and-key" theory (Horsfield, Haase, and Turin; Hoehn et al.).[2] The debate over the vibrational theory implies that scent, long recognized as a "chemical sense," might instead be a "spectral sense" (Hettinger E349). In other words, what we see in this debate is an ontological question about what scent itself is. And thus, when we talk about smell, or any sense, what are we talking about?

Olfaction operates outside the realm of our easy understanding; our language about, and even our scientific understanding of, scent extends beyond what we think scent embodies. This is doubly complicated by the fact that odor sensitivity is not a fixed attribute, either across the population or even within a single subject (Simsek et al.; Trimmer et al.). What I perceive changes over time. What I perceive also is different from what those around me perceive, with less of an agreed-upon center point than say in vision or hearing. However, regardless of this lack of fixedness and the exact mechanism of olfaction, scent is unarguably intimate and public facing, affective. As Brookes writes, "It is imperative to realize that, in the first stages of any sensory process, we are physically interacting with the outside world. Smell is arguably the most intimate of all the senses" (3492). But smell, while having rhetorical effects, is only partially controllable, only partially purposeful—and this is hard for us to come to terms with.

SMELLING THE SENSES

The expansion of sensory rhetorics allows for a broader understanding of flows and materialities in our embodied communication. In his theorization of sonic rhetoric, Byron Hawk writes, "A sonic approach to rhetoric, then, would mean that the rhetorical is at stake in every circulation of energy, every resonant encounter, and every unfolding future" (322). The resonance of sound, its multiplicity and reverberations, links sound to and through the relation of our bodies to the material world. But this definition is also, for lack of a better word, loud. Even in its verbs, sonic rhetoric "mak[es]" and "attun[es]"; "bodies are entangled through circulatory waves of *energy* and *force*" (317; emphasis added). Olfactory rhetorics, which deemphasize energy in exchange for a vulnerable intermingling, feel quieter than all that. There is a vulnerability in this understanding of scent, one that contrasts an olfactory rhetoric with other sensory rhetorics. Immanuel Kant notes, "[T]aking something in through smell (in the lungs) is even more intimate than taking something in through the absorptive vessels of mouth or throat" (50). Scent is one of the hardest senses to shut off, though it is also perhaps one of the most often altered due to things like allergens, air pollution, and congestion from illness. And when scents get, well, loud, becoming too strong, they make us long to move outside the language of scent itself, landing on phrases like *a smell you can taste*—or to otherwise neutralize the scent through myriads of air fresheners and other products designed for such purposes.

That desire to move outside scent's language reflects our discomfort with scent itself; however, it's also reflective of the interconnectedness of the sensorium. As we have turned to more precisely examine senses and the body, we've come to understand senses are not quite singular, not located in limited body parts. As Steph Ceraso writes, thinking about what she calls "multimodal listening," "It is also possible to feel sound in one's stomach, throat, legs, and other areas of the body—a common occurrence at clubs where music is amplified. As these examples suggest, identifying the ear as the body part that enables listening does not capture all that is involved in experiencing a sonic event. Listening is a multisensory act" (102). Scent, too, is not just about the perception of odors in and around the nose—rather, as mentioned above, scent receptors exist throughout the body, such that what we think of as scent is not its end or limit. But, if bringing sonic resonances into the rhetorical frame is complicated, considering smell's complexities is perhaps even more complicated. It is perhaps easier to talk about the act of listening than about the baser act of smelling, which ties us quickly not to the symphonic but to the bodily, not the orchestral but the rank, which gets us quickly to trash, to sewage, to sweat, to refuse. Though the things we smell are certainly as positive as they are negative, as much neutral as either, when we think of smell we often jump to excess, to illness, to what should be cast off. And why wouldn't we, when some of the smells we most frequently interact with in our own bodies are scents we try to hide, to send away, to ignore? Smell ties to bodily attempts to flush away what does not belong, what cannot be assimilated, what must be removed.[3]

But of course, that's far from all scent encompasses or describes. Smell is also about the boundaries of others in relation to us. To understand these ideas of boundaries, it is useful to first turn to thinking about another space of intermingled boundaries: touch. As Shannon Walters has argued about haptic rhetoric, touch requires a turning beyond boundaries: "The body is less a singular entity and more accurately described as inhabiting various points of contact among itself, other bodies, entities, and the world" (18). This is true even when, or especially when, bodies come into contact with themselves. Understanding this breakdown—or rather this absence—of boundaries and boundedness within our sense of what an organism is, as well as our definition of the senses, is central to making sense of embodiment as sensorial. Kelin Loe, in arguing for a haptic rhetoricity in resistance to anthropocentrism, states, "I find that haptics can be a vocabulary for vulnerability, the existence of the exposedness that constitutes rhetoricity" (42).

Scent, I argue, is similar in its possibilities for identification and connection. Walters argues that haptic rhetorics allows us to rethink "what kinds of bodies and minds have access to rhetorical production and its elements, purposes, and possibilities" (2). So, too, does scent broaden what kinds of bodies and minds we might think of as rhetorical, as participating in and through rhetoric. For one thing, scent is bacterial; as Saltmarsh has noted, bacteria, not the animal body itself, are responsible for many of the odor cues most central to our communication. Bacteria metabolize a full variety of human hormones and materials, creating different odors and looping the organic production of these hormones and materials back through those scent cues and other input. In other words, even our smells are affected by the causes of our smells. Moreover, scent is responsible for many communicative loops—for example, the smell of a newborn, posited to be related to leftover amniotic fluid or vernix, has been found to activate reward sectors in women's brains regardless of their maternal status (Lundström et al.), and studies abound on the effect of pheromones on mate selection in animals and humans alike.

The nonindividuality of scent provides us with the perception that this sense is, by its nature, nonbounded, communal, connected. But the rhetoric of scent moves us quickly to ecologies, to air quality and pollution—to who is affected by what kind of olfactory elements and who can make olfactory choices. As environmental pollutants have been found to affect olfactory receptors and olfaction more generally (Cheng et al.), and as other states, including depression (Croy and Hummel), also have been found to negatively affect olfaction, we return to a politics of whose sense of smell is allowed to matter. Olfactory connections open us without our awareness, leaving us vulnerable to pollutants, to pheromones, to processes—but they also may open each of us differently, and differently at different times. To consider an olfactory rhetoric is to consider how we might communicate about and through all these layers of scent reception—and how we already are doing so.

SMELLING THE FUTURE, A CONCLUSION

Throughout this chapter, I ask what it would mean for scholars to take seriously as rhetorical the work of olfaction. What does olfactory rhetoric make possible for our understanding of what counts as sensation, as persuasion, as connection? What relations, interactions, perceptions do olfaction make us aware of, and how might we take those perceptions and relations back into other senses, other rhetorics? The question of scent is ultimately one of boundaries; odors link us, are difficult to contain or to control, may be perceived differently than we believe (experience the smell of Axe body spray in the halls of your local middle school for reference)—they do not respect our attempts at control or boundary. And thus olfactory rhetorics enter into questions of what Johnson calls "visceral publics," about which she writes, "Controversies over fluoridation, vaccination, and 'genetically modified organisms' are charged by fears that motivate passionate defense of the porous boundaries between our bodies, our selves, and the world" (14). The space of the boundary is a space of intense—to use her word, drawn from Hawhee drawing on Ann Czetovich—*feeling*. We are afraid of being crossed, contaminated, opened, undone; we fear the unknown in the vaccine, the choice to have our bodies punctured, though we forget the constant entrance of microbes, the constant threat of illness. We have, as Johnson argues, collective intense feelings about different spaces and processes through which we become aware of our bodies' boundedness, their openness. As I note throughout this chapter, olfactory processes are also about the destruction of boundaries, the threat of the Kristevan abjection, "what disturbs identity, system, order. What does not respect borders, positions, rules. The in-between, the ambiguous, the composite" (Kristeva 4). Molecules that waft, enter our noses, our cells; detritus of cellular processes we inhale. Our bodies are never without scent, nor is the air ever without the "impurities" our scent receptors receive.

We describe the most abject of scents outside the realm of language about odor, highlighting the way they have broken sensorial boundaries, become the "smell you can taste." But this language, our disgust at this move outside the imagined boundaries of our senses, fails to imagine the presence of olfaction as a fully embodied practice taking place throughout the body. As Wilson argues about the presence of serotonin receptors in the gut, our imagining of states like depression, or processes such as, in this case, smell, is often based on a model of embodiment that emphasizes parts rather than wholes. But just as it makes sense to think of the depressed gut, it also makes sense to think of olfaction as occurring in our kidneys, in our digestive processes. A new understanding of ontologies of olfaction, therefore, understands scent as a rhetorical agent that occurs at many levels, that is sensed beyond our understanding of sensing. What scent am I experiencing within my gut right now? I might ask. Whose molecules are in me?

But what do these intimate relations of scent—physical, material, affective—mean for rhetoricians as we continue to think through what it means to be embodied, relational, and entangled? Brennan, incidentally making a case for olfaction as rhetorical, argues we are disposed "to see activity as mindless when it is not directed from the point of self-interest" (136). In other words, is what cannot be purposefully controlled at all times still potentially rhetorical? What does it mean for rhetorical effects if, though I do not know you, throughout olfaction your bits circulate around and throughout me—though I do not know how, through vibrations or lock and key or some other mechanism? The inherent vulnerability, intimacy, and—dare I say it—sensuality of a rhetoric of olfaction pushes us to consider what it is we might do as we grow together, what effects we have on one another, on what surrounds us, and on ourselves, and through which processes.

As we expand our rhetorical thinking to consider more and more our entangled molecular selves, scent provides a trace we might together view, one that pushes us to think also about the ways the cuts we make effect our larger sense of boundedness, relationality, and even decision making. An olfactory rhetoric, then, allows us to think more robustly about the unknown forces of embodiment, the ways we are consistently implicated in relation with the outside world. New materialists have clearly illustrated that thinking of our bodies—and our rhetorics—as in any way set apart from materials and worlds overlooks a great deal of what it means to communicate, to exist, to be persuaded and to persuade in that world. But the turn to olfactory rhetorics—to the complicated ways not just the nose but the entire the body communicates with, learns from, and responds to both its environment and its embodied states—represents the possibility of an environmental, sensorial, affective, and medical rhetoric that pays careful attention to the processes of the body-environment assemblage as a part of a shifting, turning rhetorical situation that cannot be easily figured, easily mapped.

An olfactory rhetoric asks us to focus on interrelation through the very air we breathe, the entangled web we participate in. And thus an olfactory rhetoric would ask for attention to the silent affect of a room, to the act of standing near, of breathing with and among, of crafting the air. A turn to the olfactory lets us consider rhetoric beyond the verbal, beyond the object, beyond the visual, and in turn turns our attention to invisible porousness and interconnectedness, to the innumerable things that happen at the speed of scent. It asks what rhetorical effects might come from understanding the ways our molecules mix, discern, and entangle as we breathe together, inhaling one another.

NOTES

1. Outside of Philips's work, I could find only one full-length discussion of scent and rhetoric at the time of writing this chapter, Janet Miller's 2010 *Making Rhetorical Scents*. Miller's discussion focuses mainly on language, scent, and metaphor rather than phenomenological and ontological questions about scent as a material rhetoric. Jane Sutton's discussion of "rhetoric's nose" theorizes scent briefly but is more concerned with the idea of accidents and metaphors within rhetoric. However, her argument ends by asking us to "look for rhetoric where it has not been found," which calls us again to olfactory rhetorics (138).

2. The debate between these theories, and particularly the effort to disprove the vibrational theory, by some, is described by Andrew P. Horsfield, Albrecht. Haase, and Luca Turin as "intense" (937). Publications with titles like "Laying a Controversial Smell Theory to Rest," and "Implausibility of the Vibrational Theory of Olfaction," which spawned multiple series of replies between the two camps, attempt to settle the disagreement by characterizing the vibrational theory as old-fashioned and "fringe" (Burr). Further reading about these two theories can be found in "Molecular Vibration-Sensing" (Franco et al.) and "Reply to Hettinger" (Franco et al.); "Implausability" (Block, Jang, Matsunami, Sekharan et al.); "Reply to Turin et al." (Block, Jang, Matsunami, Batista et al.); and "Plausibility" (Turin, Gane, et al.).

3. Though I lack the space to talk about the implications of this idea of disgust and removal in this article, one way of understanding it might be through Scot Barnett's thinking in this collection (chapter 2) about the violent aspects of senses. As he writes, "Of course, embodied relations *are* productive *and* essential aspects of our rhetorical lives and must be understood as such. However, when we emphasize these potentialities at the expense of other capacities and effects, we can lose sight of another important aspect of the rhetorics of touch and embodiment: the violent potentials equally constitutive of our experiences and understandings of touch as well." Scent's extremities, and our tendency to think only about the extremely good and extremely bad scents, as well as its relations to what is taken in and removed from the body, might also help us consider how violence and disgust are a part of a rhetorical understanding of sensation.

WORKS CITED

Ajmani, Gaurav S., Helen H. Suh, and Jayant M. Pinto. "Effects of Ambient Air Pollution Exposure on Olfaction: A Review." *Environmental Health Perspectives*, vol. 124, no. 11, 2016, pp. 1683–93. *EHP*, doi:10.1289/EHP136.

Aristotle. *De Anima*. Translated by Christopher Shields, Oxford UP, 2016.

Ball, Cheryl E., and Byron Hawk. "Letter from the Guest Editors." *Sound in/as Composition Space*. Spec. issue of *Computers and Composition*, vol. 23, no. 3, 2006, pp. 263–65. *ScienceDirect*, doi:10.1016/j.compcom.2006.06.002.

Block, Eric, Seogjoo Jang, Hiroaki Matsunami, Sivakumar Sekharan, Bérénice Dethier, Mehmed Z. Ertem, Sivaji Gundala, Yi Pan, Shengju Li, Zhen Li, Stephene N. Lodge,

Mehmet Ozbil, Huihong Jiang, Sonia F. Penalba, Victor S. Batista, and Hanyi Zhuang. "Implausibility of the Vibrational Theory of Olfaction." *Proceedings of the National Academy of Sciences*, vol. 112, no. 21, 2015, pp. E2766–74. *PNAS*, doi:10.1073/pnas .1503054112.

Block, Eric, Seogjoo Jang, Hiroaki Matsunami, Victor S. Batista, and Hanyi Zhuang. "Reply to Turin et al.: Vibrational Theory of Olfaction Is Implausible." *Proceedings of the National Academy of Sciences*, vol. 112, no. 25, 2015, pp. E3155. *PNAS*, doi:10.1073 /pnas.1508443112.

Bradford, Kevin D., and Debra M. Desrochers. "The Use of Scents to Influence Consumers: The Sense of Using Scents to Make Cents." *Sixth Annual Ethical Dimensions in Business*, supplement of *Journal of Business Ethics*, vol. 90, Nov. 2009, pp. 141–53. *SpringerLink*, doi:10.1007/s10551-010-0377-5.

Branch, Erin L. "'Taste Analytically': Julia Child's Rhetoric of Cultivation." *Rhetoric Society Quarterly*, vol. 45, no. 2, 2015, pp. 164–84. *Taylor & Francis Online*, doi:10.1080/0277394 5.2015.1007518.

Brennan, Teresa. *The Transmission of Affect*. Cornell UP, 2003.

Brookes, Jennifer C. "Science Is Perception: What Can Our Sense of Smell Tell Us about Ourselves and the World Around Us?" *Visions of the Future for the Royal Society's 350th Anniversary Year*. Spec. issue of *Philosophical Transactions of the Royal Society A: Mathematical, Physical and Engineering Sciences*, vol. 368, no. 1924, 2010, pp. 3491–3502. *The Royal Society Publishing*, doi:10.1098/rsta.2010.0117.

Burr, Chandler. *The Emperor of Scent*. Random House, 2002.

Cain, William S. "Olfaction." *McGraw Hill AccessScience*, 2014, doi.org/10.1036/1097 -8542.467900.

Ceraso, Steph. "(Re)Educating the Senses: Multimodal Listening, Bodily Learning, and the Composition of Sonic Experiences." *College English*, vol. 77, no. 2, 2014, pp. 102–23. *JSTOR*, www.jstor.org/stable/24238169.

Cheng, Hank, Arian Saffari, Constantinos Sioutas, Henry J. Forman, Todd E. Morgan, and Caleb E. Finch. "Nanoscale Particulate Matter from Urban Traffic Rapidly Induces Oxidative Stress and Inflammation in Olfactory Epithelium with Concomitant Effects on Brain." *Environmental Health Perspectives*, vol. 124, no. 10, 2016, pp. 1537–46. *EHP*, doi:10.1289/EHP134.

Colls, Rachel, and Maria Fannin. "Placental Surfaces and the Geographies of Bodily Interiors." *Environment and Planning*, vol. 4, no. 10, 2013, pp. 1087–1104. *SAGE Journals*, doi:10.1068/a44698.

Comstock, Michelle, and Mary E. Hocks. "The Sounds of Climate Change: Sonic Rhetoric in the Anthropocene, the Age of Human Impact." *Rhetoric Review*, vol. 35, no. 2, 2016, pp. 165–75. *Taylor & Francis Online*, doi:10.1080/07350198.2016.1142854.

Corbett, Edward P. J. "The Rhetoric of the Open Hand and the Rhetoric of the Closed Fist." *College Composition and Communication*, vol. 20, no. 5, 1969, pp. 288–96. *JSTOR*, doi:10.2307/355032.

Croy, Ilona, and Thomas Hummel. "Olfaction as a Marker for Depression." *Journal of Neurology*, vol. 264, no. 4, 2017, pp. 631–38. *SpringerLink*, doi:10.1007/s00415-016-8227-8.

Dolmage, Jay. *Disability Rhetoric*. Syracuse UP, 2014.

Finnegan, Cara A. "Review Essay: Visual Studies and Visual Rhetoric." *Quarterly Journal of Speech*, vol. 90, no. 2, 2004, pp. 234–47. *Taylor & Francis Online*, doi:10.1080 /0033563042000227454.

Frost, Samantha. *Biocultural Creatures: Toward a New Theory of the Human*. Duke UP, 2016.

Franco, Maria Isabel, Luca Turin, Andreas Mershin, and Efthimios M. C. Skoulakis. "Molecular Vibration-Sensing Component in *Drosophila Melanogaster* Olfaction." *Proceedings of the National Academy of Sciences*, vol. 108, no. 9, 2011, pp. 3797–3802. *PNAS*, doi:10.1073/pnas.1012293108.

Franco, Maria Isabel, Luca Turin, Andreas Mershin, and Efthimios M. C. Skoulakis. "Reply to Hettinger: Olfaction Is a Physical and a Chemical Sense in Drosophila." *Proceedings of the National Academy of Sciences*, vol. 108, no. 31, 2011, pp. E350. *PNAS*, doi:10.1073 /pnas.1107618108.

Gries, Laurie. *Still Life with Rhetoric: A New Materialist Approach for Visual Rhetorics*. Utah State UP, 2015.

Gunn, Joshua, Greg Goodale, Mirko M. Hall, and Rosa A. Eberly. "Auscultating Again: Rhetoric and Sound Studies." *Rhetoric Society Quarterly*, vol. 43, no. 5, 2013, pp. 475–89. *Taylor & Francis Online*, doi:10.1080/02773945.2013.851581.

Hanson, Valerie. *Haptic Visions: Rhetorics of the Digital Image, Information, and Nanotechnology*. Parlor, 2015.

Hawhee, Debra. *Rhetoric in Tooth and Claw: Animals, Language, Sensation*. University of Chicago Press, 2017.

Hawhee, Debra. "Rhetoric's Sensorium." *Quarterly Journal of Speech*, vol. 101, no. 1, 2015, pp. 2–17. *Taylor & Francis Online*, doi:10.1080/00335630.2015.995925.

Hawk, Byron. "Sound: Resonance as Rhetorical." *Keywords: A Glossary of the Pasts and Futures of the Rhetoric Society of America*. Spec. issue of *Rhetoric Society Quarterly*, vol. 48, no. 3, 2018, pp. 315–23. *Taylor & Francis Online*, doi:10.1080/02773945.2018.1454219.

Hettinger, T. P. "Olfaction Is a Chemical Sense, Not a Spectral Sense." *Proceedings of the National Academy of Sciences*, vol. 108, no. 31, 2011, pp. E349. *PNAS*, doi:10.1073/pn as.1103992108.

Hoehn, Ross D., David E. Nichols, Hartmut Neven, and Sabre Kais. "Status of the Vibrational Theory of Olfaction." *Frontiers in Physics*, vol. 6, no. 25, 2018. *Frontiers*, doi:10.3 389/fphy.2018.00025.

Horsfield, Andrew P., Abrecht Haase, and Luca Turin. "Molecular Recognition in Olfaction." *Advances in Physics: X*, vol. 2, no. 3, 2017, pp. 937–77. *Taylor & Francis Online*, doi :10.1080/23746149.2017.1378594.

Jackson, Deborah Davis. "Scents of Place: The Dysplacement of a First Nations Community in Canada." *American Anthropologist*, vol. 113, no. 4, 2011, pp. 606–18. *AnthroSource*, doi:10.1111/j.1548–1433.2011.01373.x.

Johnson, Jenell. " 'A Man's Mouth Is His Castle': The Midcentury Fluoridation Controversy and the Visceral Public." *Quarterly Journal of Speech*, vol. 102, no. 1, 2016, pp. 1–20. *Taylor & Francis Online*, doi:10.1080/00335630.2015.1135506.

Kant, Immanuel. *Anthropology from a Pragmatic Point of View*. Edited by Robert Louden, Cambridge University Press, 2006.

Kaszynski, Elizabeth. " 'Look, a [Picture]!': Visuality, Race, and What We Do Not See." *Quarterly Journal of Speech*, vol. 102, no. 1, 2016, pp. 62–78. *Taylor & Francis Online*, doi: 10.1080/00335630.2015.1136074.

Kristeva, Julia. *Powers of Horror: An Essay on Abjection*. Translated by Leon Roudiez, Columbia UP, 1982.

Loe, Kelin. "Let's Listen with Our Feet: Animals, Neurodivergence, Vulnerability, and Haptic Rhetoricity." *Rhetorical Animals: Boundaries of the Human in the Study of Persuasion*, edited by Alex C. Parrish and Kristian Bjørkdahl, Lexington, 2017, pp. 41–60.

Lundström, Johan N., Annegret Mathe, Benoist Schaal, Johannes Frasnelli, Katharina Nitzsche, Johannes Gerber, and Thomas Hummel. "Maternal Status Regulates Cortical Responses to the Body Odor of Newborns." *Frontiers in Philosophy*, vol. 4, no. 597, 2013. *Frontiers*, doi:10.3389/fpsyg.2013.00597.

Mele, Christopher. "Casinos, Prisons, Incinerators, and Other Fragments of Neoliberal Urban Development." *Social Science History*, vol. 35, no. 3, 2011, pp. 423–52. *JSTOR*, doi:10.1215/01455532–1273357.

Miller, Janet. "*Making Rhetorical Scents: An Olfactory Grammar of Motives Based on Kenneth Burke's Pentad*." MS thesis. Clemson University, 2010. *TigerPrints*, tigerprints.clemson .edu/all_theses/798. Accessed 26 June 2020.

Perricone, Carlo, Netta Schoenfeld, Nancy Agmon-Levin, Catarina de Carolis, Roberto Perricone, and Yehuda Shoenfeld. "Smell and Autoimmunity: A Comprehensive Review." *Clinical Reviews in Allergy & Immunology*, vol. 45, no. 1, 2013, pp. 87–96. *SpringerLink*, doi:10.1007/s12016-012-8343-x.

Pflugfelder, Ehren Helmut. "Rhetoric's New Materialism: From Micro-Rhetoric to Microbrew." *Rhetoric Society Quarterly*, vol. 45, no. 5, 2015, pp. 441–61. *Taylor & Francis Online*, doi:10.1080/02773945.2015.1082616.

Phillips, Lisa L. "Smellscapes, Social Justice, and Olfactory Perception." *Rhetoric Across Borders*, edited by Anne Teresa Demo, Parlor, 2015.

Plato. "The Timaeus." *Dialogues of Plato*. Translated by Benjamin Jowett, vol. 3, Macmillan, 1892, pp. 339–517.

Purifoye, Gwendolyn. "Transporting Urban Inequality through Public Transit Designs and Systems." *City and Community*, vol. 16, no. 4, 2017, pp. 364–68. *Wiley Online Library*, doi:10.1111/cico.12266.

Rickert, Thomas. *Ambient Rhetorics: The Attunements of Rhetorical Being*. U of Pittsburgh P, 2013.

Rivers, Nathaniel. "Deep Ambivalence and Wild Objects: Toward a Strange Environmental Rhetoric." *Rhetoric Society Quarterly*, vol. 45, no. 5, 2015, pp. 420–40. *Taylor & Francis Online*, doi:10.1080/02773945.2015.1086491.

Saltmarsh, Jennifer. "Human Boundary Seepage, Bacterial Rhetorics." *Rhetorical Animals: Boundaries of the Human in the Study of Persuasion*, edited by Alex C. Parrish and Kristian Bjørkdahl, Lexington, 2017, pp. 61–80.

Shepard, Blythe D., and Jennifer L. Pluznick. "How Does Your Kidney Smell? Emerging Roles for Olfactory Receptors in Renal Function." *Pediatric Nephrology*, vol. 31, no. 5, 2016, pp. 715–23. *SpringerLink*, doi:10.1007/s00467-015-3181-8.

Simsek, Gokce, Nuray Bayar Muluk, Osman Kursat Arikan, Zeynep Ozcan Dag, Yavuz Simsek, and Ersel Dag. "Marked Changes in Olfactory Perception during Early Pregnancy: A Prospective Case-Control Study." *European Archives of Oto-Rhino-Laryngology*, vol. 272, no. 3, 2015, pp. 627–30. *SpringerLink*, doi:10.1007/s00405-014-3147-7.

Spence, Charles, Marianna Obrist, Carlos Velasco, and Nimesha Ranasinghe. "Digitizing the Chemical Senses: Possibilities and Pitfalls." *Multisensory Human-Computer Interaction*. Spec. issue of *International Journal of Human-Computer Studies*, vol. 107, 2017, pp. 62–74. *ScienceDirect*, doi:10.1016/j.ijhcs.2017.06.003.

Strous, Rael D., and Yehuda Shoefeld. "To Smell the Immune System: Olfaction, Autoimmunity and Brain Involvement." *The Bled Autoimmunity Meeting*. Spec. issue of *Autoimmunity Reviews*, vol. 6, no. 1, 2006, pp. 54–60. *ScienceDirect*, doi:10.1016/j.autrev.2006.07.002.

Sutton, Jane. "Rhetoric's Nose: What Can Rhetorical Historiography Make of It?" *Theorizing Histories of Rhetoric*, edited by Michelle Ballif, Southern Illinois UP, 2013, pp. 128–138.

Trimmer, Casey, Andreas Keller, Niall R. Murphy, Lindsey L. Snyder, Jason R. Willer, Maira H. Nagai, Nicholas Katsanis, Leslie B. Vosshall, Hiroaki Matsunami, and Joel D. Mainland. "Genetic Variation across the Human Olfactory Receptor Repertoire Alters Odor Perception." *Proceedings of the National Academy of Sciences*, vol. 116, no. 19, 2019, pp. 9475–80. *PNAS*, doi:10.1073/pnas.1804106115.

Turin, Luca. "A Spectroscopic Mechanism for Primary Olfactory Reception." *Chemical Senses*, vol. 21, no. 6, 1996, pp. 773–791. *Oxford UP*, doi:10.1093/chemse/21.6.773.

Turin, Luca, Simon Gane, Dimitris Georganakis, Klio Maniati, and Efthimios M. C. Skoulakis. "Plausibility of the Vibrational Theory of Olfaction." *Proceedings of the National Academy of Sciences*, vol. 112, no. 25, 2015, pp. E3154. *PNAS*, doi:10.1073/pnas.1508035112.

Walters, Shannon. *Rhetorical Touch: Disability, Identification, Haptics*. U of South Carolina P, 2014.

Wells, Justine B. *A Taste for Things: Sensory Rhetoric Beyond the Human.* 2015. Diss. University of South Carolina, 2015. *ScholarCommons,* scholarcommons.sc.edu/etd/3694. Accessed 26 June 2020.

Wilson, Elizabeth A. *Gut Feminism.* Duke UP, 2015.

Winderman, Emily, Robert Mejia, and Brandon Rogers. "'All Smell Is Disease': Miasma, Sensory Rhetoric, and the Sanitary-Bacteriologic of Visceral Public Health." *Rhetoric of Public Health.* Spec. issue of *Rhetoric of Health and Medicine,* vol. 2, no. 2, 2019, pp. 115–46. *U of Florida P,* doi:10.5744/rhm.2019.1006.

5

EMBODYING HISTORY
The Bodies and Affects of Museum Rhetorics

Julie D. Nelson (University of Tampa)

The International Civil Rights Center and Museum (ICRCM) in Greensboro, North Carolina, commemorates the site of a remarkable example of embodied rhetoric and protest: the segregated Woolworth lunch counter where four African American college students staged a sit-in that inspired desegregation of public spaces across the South. Sit-ins were successful rhetorical tactics during the civil rights movement because, as Carole Blair and Neil Michel claim, they "disrupted (peacefully) the ordinary activities of towns, businesses, and citizens"; "announced the resilience and determination of those pledged to civil rights"; and "situated the individual observer as the agent of change, by placing their cause—and the often cruel counter-reaction—visually and materially in the space of the everyday" (34). Unwitting Woolworth shoppers and diners faced the fight for civil rights amid their errands and lunch-counter meals, and as the Greensboro sit-in gained national attention, the public saw violent, unjustified responses to the peaceful protest. The silent presence of Black bodies in a public space designated for white bodies disrupted the status quo and embodied a powerful argument for equality.

It is fitting, then, that the ICRCM uses embodied rhetorics to create a museum experience that expresses the magnitudes of social, psychological, and bodily oppression during Jim Crow. The museum, which opened in 2010 on the fiftieth anniversary of the Greensboro sit-ins, aims to "inspire the vigilance and fortify the spirit of all oppressed people to step forward in the on-going struggle for human freedom" (International). More than focusing solely on the past, the ICRCM urges visitors to consider how historical injustices continue in the present and, without intervention, will continue into the future. In addition to telling the story of the Greensboro Four (Ezell Blair Jr., now known as Jibreel Khazan; Franklin McCain; Joseph McNeil; and David Richmond) as it

https://doi.org/10.7330/9781646422012.c005

fits into civil rights history, the goal of those working at the ICRCM is "to bring down barriers of all kinds that divide and weaken us as human beings. It is that drive that calls us to strengthen ourselves, our community, and our world" (International). Tour guides communicate this message as they lead groups of visitors through an expansive foray into segregation in the United States. Unlike museums that foreground the logocentric—chronological presentation of facts, events, and people in an illusion of coherence—the ICRCM privileges embodied rhetorics that expose the everyday, material impact of racism during Jim Crow. Using affect theories to supplement an embodied rhetorical methodology, this chapter considers how museums portray embodied knowledges and move visitors on a bodily level.

Through embodied and affective rhetorics, the ICRCM educates visitors, inspires reflection, and (re)presents a critical era in US history. Public memory is animated by affect, assert Carole Blair, Greg Dickinson, and Brian Ott: "Perhaps the most underdeveloped of public memory's assumptions, it may also be one of the most central" (6–7). While embodied rhetoric scholarship accepts affect (i.e., bodily feeling and precognitive emotion) as central to bodily experience, few scholars have used affect theories to further elucidate embodied rhetorics. Reflecting the "affective turn" in the humanities, this chapter considers how affects are transmitted through museum texts and spaces—manifesting in and through bodies to shape experiences (Clough and Halley; Massumi). I begin with a brief survey of scholarship, which identifies three main features of affect theory: (1) affects are culturally determined capacities; (2) affects attach to bodies and mediate relationships among bodies; and (3) affects can be rearticulated to support bodies that have been historically marginalized. Building on recent rhetoric scholarship, I assert that representing bodies as moving and generative is necessary for ethical representations of race in museums. Following an analysis of several exhibits at the ICRCM, I argue that affective and embodied rhetorics are invaluable for conserving marginalized and contested histories.

AFFECTING BODIES

Embodied-rhetorics scholarship seeks to dissolve dichotomies between the mind (associated with reason) and body (associated with emotion). Historically, of course, rhetoricians privileged *logos*, suggesting the body and its passions undermine or interfere with rational discourse. Despite excellent scholarship mending the mind-body split and asserting the rationality and ethical nature of emotions (Ballif; Damasio;

Hawhee, *Bodily*; Kopelson; Nussbaum; Solomon), we are still immersed in Cartesian paradigms. However, affect theory and scholarship, because of its distinct vocabulary and theories of bodily feeling, avoids some of the historical baggage attached to studies of *pathos* or emotions, encouraging a more nuanced understanding of rhetorical experience and embodied rhetorics. Affects—and how they mediate, work on, and define bodies—underlie museums' embodied, sensory rhetorics.

Since the "affective turn" (coined by Patricia Clough and Jean Halley's 2007 collection), scholars across disciplines have used affect theories to consider the extralinguistic aspects of experience. In rhetorical studies, that means focusing on how bodily feeling, other bodies, space, and materiality interact to influence communication and persuasion. Scholars have defined affect in many ways; some use it interchangeably with emotion, mood, or feeling, while others assert fixed definitions that differentiate affect from other related concepts. Many affect scholars draw on one of two traditions: Spinoza→Deleuze→Massumi or Tomkins→Sedgwick→Ahmed. While the former tradition has a philosophical foundation often used to study mediated or political affects, the latter invokes psychology and is often used in studies of cultural or queer affects. For studying public-memory places, I suggest we draw from both traditions because each captures valuable conceptualizations of affect as it relates to rhetorical experience.[1] The theories I review here depict affect in action, which is imperative for scrutinizing how marginalized bodies are represented and move through the world. Thus, this section draws on Spinoza to define affects as capacities, Eve Kosofsky Sedgwick and Sara Ahmed to illustrate affect's attachment, and Jenny Edbauer Rice to consider how affective attachments can be rearticulated.

Defining bodies by their affects instead of inherent qualities foregrounds the cultural contexts in which they live. Many current affect theories emerged from the seventeenth-century work of Baruch Spinoza, who suggests bodies are not defined by shape or as subjects but by their affects (actual effects) or capacities (potential or real). Bodies move and are allowed to move through the world according to the societal constructs that support or inhibit them—a first important feature of affect. As Spinoza writes in his *Ethics*, "By affect I understand the affections of the body, by which the power of acting of the body itself is increased, diminished, helped, or hindered, together with the ideas of these affections" (106). In his work on Spinoza, Gilles Deleuze asserts, "[I]t is the relations of motion and rest, speeds and slowness between particles" and "the capacity for affecting and being affected" that define an individual body (123). Deleuze explains that a plow horse is more similar to an ox than to a racehorse because their affects are similar. Through this lens, we see bodies within their cultural and material contexts, which name and ensnare them based on their perceived identities. While white bodies could sit, eat, and move freely at the 1960 Woolworth lunch counter, seated Black bodies defied the capacities (affects) available to African Americans during Jim Crow. By exercising affects deemed unavailable to them, the Greensboro Four protested how African Americans were perceived, controlled, and segregated. These cultural contexts can be recreated in museum exhibits through material and sensory engagement using artifacts, images, sounds, interactive media, interviews, reenactments, and so forth. Though recreations always fall short in composing the past, they can be dynamic ways to communicate a cultural milieu to modern audiences.

This contextual perspective of bodies extends to any gathering of human and nonhuman things, including objects, media, environments, groups of people, and so forth. As bodies interact, Spinoza theorizes, they transition from one state to another, increasing or decreasing the power to act rhetorically. The relations to other people, ideas, environments, and media propel or inhibit bodies and their rhetorical opportunities. A successful protest movement, for example, must involve many human and nonhuman bodies to make a significant social intervention. The Greensboro Four's affects were bold but socially acceptable enough that the protest was allowed to go on, showing a careful consideration of the actions (affects) and embodied rhetorics available to them. Shirking popular portrayals of protesters as aggressive or rude, their silent, nonviolent bodily presence pushed, but didn't break, the boundaries of social acceptability. The affects (physical actions and emotional expressions) of the Greensboro Four attracted the attention of other bodies (news media, counter protesters, satellite protesters, etc.) in a way that sustained protests and national discussions about segregation. When museums and memorials involve other bodies, like employees, investors, and visitors, they expand their potentials for social intervention.

Through their attachment or "stickiness," affects uphold cultural stereotypes and biases. Exposure to repeated affective associations, Sedgwick and Ahmed maintain, creates cultural patterns of belief and interaction, which can be detrimental for marginalized people who often have negative associations. Ahmed ("Affective"), for example, analyzes how discourses on an Aryan Nations Web site generate solidarity and attach hate, anger, and fear to "others." Because they define affect more broadly to include bodily feelings and recognized emotions, Sedgwick's and Ahmed's theories often include discussion of emotions.[2] Affects are versatile, Sedgwick asserts: "[A]ffects can be, and are, attached to things, people, ideas, sensations, relations, activities, institutions, and any number of other things, including other affects" (19). Through affective attachments, affects are associated with public bodies (e.g., with Black, female, or queer bodies) in ways that shape perception. Ahmed describes this as "stickiness": "This is what I would call the rippling effect of emotions; they move sideways (through 'sticky' associations between signs, figures, and objects) as well as backward (repression always leaves its trace in the present—hence 'what sticks' is also bound up with the 'absent presence' of historicity)" ("Affective" 120). The absent presences of enslavement and segregation support racist notions of African American inferiority and depravity; racial profiling, police brutality, and news media portrayals continue to proliferate the negative affects "stuck" to Black people. The challenge for museums of marginalized histories is undermining sticky associations. Embodied rhetorics offer strategies to do this, "[drawing] attention to embodied knowledge—specific material conditions, lived experiences, positionalities, and/or standpoints" (Knoblauch 62). Featuring reenactments, historical footage, mediated exhibits, and narratives, museums draw on embodied knowledges in ways that can undermine negative affects.

Ahmed and Edbauer Rice use metaphors of economy and ecology to illustrate the multiple dimensions of emotion/affect—as it is simultaneously represented, transmitted, and personally felt. Ahmed's concept "affective economy" suggests emotions do not lie within people or objects; rather, they "mediate the relationship between the psychic and the social, and between the individual and the collective" ("Affective" 119). Because they mediate relationships among bodies, emotions are the lenses through which we express and perceive embodied rhetorics. In the affective economy of a museum, emotions are deeply personal and material but also attached to the desires and affective investments of others. Thus, emotions emerge within affective economies amid other moving bodies and depending on individuals' motivations and backgrounds. Visitor interaction with embodied rhetorics, then, is always variable. Like Ahmed, Edbauer Rice points out how emerging and circulating affects impact marginalized bodies in disproportionate ways. She suggests a contextual, adaptive framework: "Rather than primarily speaking of rhetoric through the terministic lens of conglomerated elements, I look towards a framework of *affective ecologies* that recontextualizes rhetorics in their temporal, historical, and lived fluxes" ("Unframing" 9). Affective economies and ecologies reorient conceptualizations of museums away from a unilateral imparting of information to a living, emerging experience.

The "unsticking" or rearticulating of emotions is a promising strategy for museums of marginalized histories. While it may seem we have little control over whether and how affects are attached to our and others' bodies, Ahmed asserts that affects and emotions can be "unstuck" through awareness and conscious effort (*Cultural*). This "unsticking" is a third feature of affect theory that attempts to reverse harmful historical and cultural affective attachments. Edbauer Rice describes the potential for reforming public memory: "Theories of affect suggest a process of disarticulation, or an unsticking of those figures that seem to be glued together, followed by a rearticulation, or a new way of linking together images and representations that is less oppressive" ("New" 210). Edbauer Rice maintains that affect can be rearticulated in public discourse through integration of positive associations to bodies and ideas that have been ignored or devalued. She describes how public discourses about HIV/AIDS were rearticulated from disgust and fear to health and hope through public campaigns ("New"). The challenge for public-memory places is to connect marginalized people to representations that are empowering, socially just, and multifaceted. Because people of color are often represented by the dominant culture in simplistic ways, the work of rearticulating should undermine affects that diminish marginalized people and reassert empowering, ethical, and positive affects instead. Museums can do this by making "purposeful decision[s] to include embodied knowledge and social positionalities as forms of meaning making within a text itself" (Knoblauch 52). In addition to featuring embodied knowledges, museums create meaning for visitors and rearticulate affects by captivating their senses.

Affects are the vehicles of embodied knowledges, the "gut feelings" Knoblauch describes. Museums include embodied and affective rhetorics through sensory and material engagement. As Lauren Obermark asserts in her study of the Oklahoma City National Memorial Museum, material rhetorics "circulate messages and educate visitors in ways that resonate and remain, and powerfully so, in a way that a discrete, 'finished' text struggles to achieve" ("Assurance" 104). Material rhetorics—everyday objects and official artifacts—encourage visitors to "dwell, reflect, imagine, and engage" in ways that support museums' civic and pedagogical goals (102). Sensory engagement with artifacts and media, and the corresponding feelings it incites, binds visitors to people represented, to other visitors, and to imagined events. Because of the attachment and stickiness of affects, museums inherently portray bodies that support or oppose historical and contemporary affective attachments. Museums like the ICRCM attach a wide range of affects to

African Americans, portraying a nuance and complexity often missing in historical representations. Unsticking and rearticulating affects is a powerful strategy museums can use to bolster specific associations and viewpoints, similar to Kristie S. Fleckenstein's concept of "reanimation," which is articulated as a means to reconfigure oppressive and oppressed practices of living (chapter 8). Material and sensory rhetorics have often been neglected in public-memory places, yet, as Obermark's work illustrates, they are compelling avenues for educating visitors and fulfilling museums' civic missions.

RHETORICAL BODIES

Affect theories reinforce the study of bodies as moving and generative. To undermine negative associations and stereotypes, marginalized people must be represented with nuance and complexity. Debra Hawhee asserts, "The bind for body theorists is that bodies become a problem when they come to 'stand in' for subject positions. . . . Contemporary theory thus has a tendency to freeze bodies, to analyze them for their symbolic properties, thereby evacuating and ignoring their capacity to sense and to move through time" (*Moving* 7). Ethical commemoration requires bodies and history to be captured as *living*—not just in static photographs but also in exhibits that ask visitors to watch, listen, and feel. Visual, audio, and digital media can contribute a more complicated representation of fraught periods of US history. Despite the tendency to "freeze bodies," rhetoric scholars have also pursued more complicated studies, such as the role of the body in invention (Holding) and public memory (Marback). However, disability studies offers a fruitful supplement to theorizing marginalized bodies as fluid and changing.

In addition to dismantling the West's default conception of *the* body (i.e., male, white, able), disability studies illustrates how bodies are generative and rhetorical (Wilson and Lewiecki-Wilson). As Jay Dolmage suggests in his study of the mythical Greek god Hephaestus, bodies considered to be "different" or "abnormal" were valued and even celebrated for their abilities in classical times ("Breathe"). He employs an embodied rhetoric that interrogates discourses of normalcy/ableness and cultural perceptions of bodies and their rhetorical abilities. Consideration of *mêtis* ("wise and wily intelligence"), Dolmage suggests, encourages focus on the rhetorical skills of all bodies since Greek mythology often gave characters with bodily differences distinct intellectual abilities ("Metis" 5). Because bodily difference can be rhetorically advantageous, he argues for an approach to embodied rhetorics that "[affirms] the possibilities and the limitations of the body" and "[refuses] rhetorical and philosophical economies that silence, that deny the body or normalize it" (21). Dolmage asserts, "[I]nstead of stigmatizing embodied difference, we might advocate for a range of body images, an awareness of body values and a critique of the powerful discourses of silencing and delimitation that surround embodied rhetoric" (21). This awareness expands theorization of the rhetorical possibilities for bodies that have been historically marginalized and aligns with scholars who have studied the innovative, adaptive rhetorical approaches of African Americans (Gilyard and Banks; Jackson and Richardson; Logan; Richardson and Jackson; Royster). Though "disabled" bodies and racially marginalized bodies are distinct and shouldn't be simply compared, Dolmage's work portrays bodily difference as generative and urges us to critique social processes that stigmatize bodies. For museums, this means highlighting how bodies are racialized, marked as inferior, and segregated; however, it also means showcasing the distinct rhetorical abilities and approaches of people historically marked as "different."

As rhetorical spaces, museums literally represent historical bodies (and their embodied knowledges) and create embodied rhetorical experiences for visitors. Because, as Elizabeth Grosz suggests, the body is culture's "preeminent object," embodied rhetorics may be the most powerful avenue to re-present history. Representing bodies through photos, videos, and reenactments, the ICRCM privileges African American embodied knowledges, recognizing that, as Jacqueline Jones Royster explains, "knowledge is produced by someone . . . its producers are not formless and invisible. They are embodied and in effect have passionate attachments by means of their embodiments. They are vested with vision, values, and habits; with ways of being and ways of doing" (280). These passionate attachments are revealed in exhibits, and they play out in visitors' embodied experiences.[3] Seeing historical bodies in various states of demoralization and protest inspires affective responses; the intensity of these responses, however, depends on our social/political contexts and our own willingness to acknowledge and reflect on embodied experience. As Derrick Brooms asserts,

> When people enter museums they do not leave their cultures and identities at home; nor do they respond passively to museum displays. They interpret museum exhibitions through their prior experiences and through the culturally learned beliefs, values, and perceptual skills that they gain through membership in multiple communities. As such, museums are symbols and sites for the playing out of social relations of identity and difference, knowledge and power, and theory and representation. (511)

To consider how bodies and rhetorics converge in public-memory places, we must, as Brooms suggests, be aware of how our own perspectives
and motives might influence our experience. Visitors are not passive observers but active participants in creating meaning in museums, as their
histories and values intersect with museum content and affects. However,
as Brooms asserts, museums are also cultural microcosms that reveal political investments and leanings.[4] As with embodied rhetorics, "it is, quite
simply, impossible (and irresponsible) to separate the producer of the
text from the text itself," as William Banks claims (33). For civil rights
museums, this means highlighting the activist heroes of the movement
and exposing the white supremacists (from lawmakers to everyday folks)
who produced racist and segregationist texts.

However, simply entering a museum like the ICRCM doesn't guar-
antee transformative experiences. We must be open to being affected,
to listening rhetorically: taking a "stance of openness that a person may
choose to assume in relation to any person, text, or culture" (Ratcliffe
17). Rhetorical listening is a conscious practice that requires cultivation; it is a bodily, material process. Casie Cobos, Gabriela Raquel Ríos,
Donnie Johnson Sackey, Jennifer Sano-Franchini, and Angela Haas
claim, "[L]istening is a mode of interpretative production that is based
in the body. Listening becomes a method for enacting and illustrating how bodies hold meaning, make meaning, and are meaningful"
(150). Listening is an embodiment, a willingness to contemplate what
in public-memory places are often complicated or traumatic events.
Despite the tendency to avoid discomfort in memorials and museums,
"[a] pedagogy of memory," Obermark claims, "should open space to
dwell in difficult topics, ones that might seem too hard, depressing or
easier to avoid" ("Assurance" 98). Material and sensory rhetorics open
such spaces, urging audiences to feel and reflect. Undoubtedly, some
visitors are not moved by their visit to museums like the ICRCM, and
others intentionally disengage with its embodied rhetorics. However, for
those willing to listen to the affects and bodies around them, the ICRCM
portrays the lives and stories of African American people in ways often
historically absent.

HISTORICAL BODIES

The ICRCM commemorates the many people who devoted their lives to
the pursuit of human rights and equality. Featuring texts that viscerally
move visitors—graphic images of racist violence, public signs that were
used to enforce segregation (e.g., "Whites Only," "Colored Entrance"),

and separate but not equal public facilities (e.g., drinking fountains, polling-tax forms, bus seats)—the museum overwhelms visitors with artifacts that reflect/recreate the racism and segregation preceding and following the Greensboro sit-in. From atrocities to inconveniences, visitors see firsthand the realities of Jim Crow. Because, as Brooms suggests, visitors bring their own histories and proclivities into museums, it's impossible to generalize about visitors' embodied experiences at the ICRCM. Thus, I look specifically for "purposeful decision[s] to include embodied knowledge and social positionalities, as forms of meaning making" within the museum's exhibits (Knoblauch 52). By applying the three features of affect theory identified earlier—(1) affects are culturally determined capacities, (2) affects attach to bodies and mediate relationships among bodies, and (3) affects can be rearticulated to support bodies that have been historically marginalized—I consider how affects elucidate embodied rhetorics and reveal strategies for creating texts that leverage bodily feelings.

Throughout the museum's images, videos, and reenactments, visitors come to see how African American bodies were publicly defined by the affects they were denied. The sheer number of artifacts across the sixteen galleries in the permanent exhibit called *The Battlegrounds* expose the many sites of African American restriction during Jim Crow: schools, beaches, churches, voting booths, public transportation, movie theaters, and so forth. Though many museums focused on a specific era rely on chronologies, the ICRCM is organized around places of segregation, giving visitors a broad view of how daily life was obstructed. Images of segregated classrooms portray Black students physically packed into a dilapidated schoolhouse with small rugged desks. Magnified *Green Book* pages map how few hotels people of color could stay in while traveling across the United States. An image of a beach shows a fence down the middle segregating Black people to the smaller and less attractive side. A two-sided Coke machine sells warm soda for twice the cost on the side facing the train lobby for Black travelers. In these examples, the affects (physical actions and emotional expressions) available to African Americans are predetermined by white-supremacist societies. The overwhelming evidence of how everyday actions like eating, traveling, praying, and learning were regulated sparks affective responses, as visitors process a museum experience that might bolster, undermine, or disturb preconceived notions of life during Jim Crow.

Negative affective attachments to African Americans are implicit in the many artifacts documenting racist rules and laws. Affects like inferiority, disgust, or depravity provided the rationale for segregation, and showcasing them makes visible their attachment and stickiness, as Sedgwick and Ahmed describe. A dimly lit gallery titled *The Hall of Shame* features only graphic photos of racist violence: the aftermath of the Birmingham Church bombing, the Freedom Rider bus attack, lynchings, a KKK rally, and so forth. Each photo is blown up on a large piece of glass broken into a handful of fragments; as visitors walk through the hall, glass fragments light up from behind and soft audio accompanies the images (e.g., sounds of protesters being hosed, a tree branch breaking from the weight of a lynched man, people yelling). These disturbing images confront the danger and volatility of being Black during Jim Crow. Explicitly drawing on visitors' senses may have profound effects on how people relate to museum exhibits (see Scot Barnett's work on touch in chapter 2). In this case, seeing dead, impaired, or tortured bodies created an affective, embodied response that was visible in other visitors (i.e., silence, gaping mouths, tears, shrinking posture) during each of my three tours of the museum.

The infamous photo of Emmitt Till's bloated and beaten face is a focal point for the hall and an image all guides spend significant time discussing. Affectively, visitors may encounter the image in a number of ways, invoking historical and contemporary affective attachments. Historically, the image of Till could incite acknowledgment of the racist affects originally stuck to him: disgust, hatred, anger, and so forth. Currently, as Till has become a symbol for the worst of Jim Crow, different affects may be stuck to him, such as pity, shame, and sadness. Visitors might even simultaneously feel historical affects, symbolic affects, and individual affects that reflect their racialized identities and values. The embodied affective negotiation visitors are encouraged to experience in *The Hall of Shame* calls attention to the multiple meanings of symbolic racist imagery and exposes the feelings of rage and fear that fueled violence against African Americans. A growing amount of research suggests powerful emotional experiences become more ingrained in our memories as time goes on; thus, appealing to visitors' emotions is a significant strategy for inciting long-lasting memories (Phelps and Sharot; Tambini et al.). Visitors' affective responses in this gallery mediate their understanding of Jim Crow, civil rights, and legacies of African American oppression. Of course, visitors who are racially marginalized come with a visceral understanding of these legacies; for white visitors, this gallery encourages dwelling in discomfort and reflecting on white racial identity and oppression.

The affects that emerge for individuals within the ICRCM must be negotiated within the collective of the tour group, similar to Ahmed's affective economy. Sharing an extreme emotional experience with a group—a randomly assigned collection of fellow citizens of varying races and backgrounds—could incite feelings of community, resentment, guilt, or confusion toward others and their perceived racial identities. Given that all tours are guided, visitors must stay together, often participating with each other, as guides continually direct visitors' attention and ensure they engage with the focal points of the museum. Collective feelings culminate in the final gallery that focuses on more recent international examples of human rights violations and urges visitors to become involved in current civil rights struggles. With artifacts ranging from South African apartheid to the Berlin Wall and Tiananmen Square, this gallery works to transpose visitors' affective, embodied reactions to Jim Crow to ongoing social injustices. If visitors were horrified by the atrocities of 1960 America, they should be horrified by the atrocities of 2019 Syria. Guides stress that all the featured movements began with average citizens deciding to take action, and they directly ask visitors what they will do to support civil rights. Throughout the tour, the ICRCM employs a rhetorical education, as Obermark describes it, specifically encouraging listening, dwelling, and conversing through interaction with guides (*Rhetorical*).

Rather than treating visitors as passive receptacles, the ICRCM places visitors' bodies in strategic places, potentially rearticulating their affective relationship to the sit-in movement. This is especially true in the portion of the tour that focuses on the planning and execution of the sit-in protest. Prior to seeing the original lunch counter, visitors watch a film reenactment of the young men's planning session the night before amid a re-creation of the dorm room featuring furniture from North Carolina A&T State University. Seeing Blair's, McCain's, McNeil's, and Richmond's embodied communication—even in a re-creation—helps visitors feel they're a part of the secret meeting where the men debated whether and how to accomplish the sit-in. Following this gallery, guides lead visitors down the same hallway the men walked before launching their protest and ask visitors to consider how the Greensboro Four must have felt at that time. Bolstering images of the Greensboro Four as relatable young college students who were at once determined, fearful, and hopeful, guides explicitly ask visitors to empathize with them.

The ICRCM creates a similar bodily experience in the lunch-counter gallery, which includes the original counter, place settings, stools, advertisements, and signs that indicated where people of color were to pick up their food orders.[5] Guides lead visitors to stand exactly behind the four stools where the men sat, and a mirror behind the counter allows visitors to see themselves in their places. Next, a reenactment is superimposed on the mirror so visitors see the men's bodies sit down, attempt to order food, begin their protest, and suffer harassment. Many visitors have likely seen an image of the Greensboro Four before entering the museum, yet being in front of the original stools and counter, seeing the men's bodies in front of them, and hearing the attempted food order, refusal, and harassment *feels* different. While it's impossible and unethical to recreate the protest for visitors, providing a sensorial context encourages visitors to interact with the sit-in on an embodied level, connecting to the era, movement, and protest as their own racialized identities are highlighted. Many of the galleries showcase the negative affects historically attached to African American people; however, the lunch-counter gallery puts visitors in a position to rearticulate or unstick those affects. Through depictions of nervous excitement, moral obligation, and silent perseverance, the Greensboro Four reenactments showcase embodied knowledges and the rhetorical potentials of African American bodies.

Employing embodied rhetorics and creating embodied rhetorical experiences, museums can harness visitors' attention to form new attachments and memories. Just as embodied rhetoric "connects the personal to the larger social realm, and makes more visible the sources of *all* of our knowledge," so does affect, as it defines, attaches, and restricts people (Knoblauch 62). Affect theories contribute to the study of embodied knowledges and rhetorics, especially when interrogating beliefs and biases viscerally felt but not yet articulated in language. Given new media and technologies that proliferate dehumanizing affective attachments, we need more methodologies for responding to rhetorics that we may not fully or always consciously recognize—yet that are working on our bodies. Affective, embodied rhetorics make clear that logocentric methodologies have reached their limit in adequately theorizing rhetorical discourse and experience. The feelings and sensations we have been taught to understand as ephemeral underlie our beliefs about race and our social commitments. Museums, like the ICRCM, can leverage affective and embodied rhetorics to challenge hegemonic histories and reinvigorate the stories of overlooked and forgotten people.

NOTES

1.   I draw on Brian Massumi's definition of affect as precognitive bodily intensity, Spinoza's use of "affect" to describe capacity or action, and Ahmed's ("Affective," *Cultural*) theories of affect that include emotions and feelings.

2.   In this section, I use *emotion* as Sedgwick and Ahmed do, as an expression of affect.

3.   Similarly, scholarship in trauma studies has suggested museums and memorials can communicate embodied trauma, incite lasting affective response, and encourage empathy (Choi).
4.   Scholars in cultural geography have begun studying race in museums using affect theories. For example, Divya Tolia-Kelly asserts, "The presence of bodies of the 'other' effectively destabilise the technologies of racialisation, including tropes of 'victimage' or 'savage'" (899).
5.   People of color could take out food orders but could not dine at the counter.

WORKS CITED

Ahmed, Sara. "Affective Economies." *Turning Pro: Professional Qualifications and the Global University.* Spec. issue of *Social Text*, vol. 22. no. 2, 2004, pp. 117–39. *Project MUSE*, muse.jhu.edu/article/55780.

Ahmed, Sara. *The Cultural Politics of Emotion.* Routledge, 2012.

Ballif, Michelle. *Seduction, Sophistry and the Woman with the Rhetorical Figure.* Southern Illinois UP, 2001.

Banks, William. "Written through the Body: Disruptions and 'Personal' Writing." *The Personal in Academic Writing.* Spec. issue of *College English*, vol. 66, no. 1, 2003, pp. 21–40. *JSTOR*, doi:10.2307/3594232.

Blair, Carole, and Neil Michel. "Reproducing Civil Rights Tactics: The Rhetorical Performances of the Civil Rights Memorial." *Rhetoric Society Quarterly*, vol. 30, no. 2, 2000, pp. 31–55. *JSTOR*, www.jstor.org/stable/3886159.

Blair, Carole, Greg Dickinson, and Brian Ott. "Rhetoric/Memory/Place." Introduction. *Places of Public Memory: The Rhetoric of Museums and Memorials*, edited by Greg Dickinson, Carole Blair, and Brian Ott, U of Alabama P, 2010, pp. 1–54.

Brooms, Derrick. "Lest We Forget: Exhibiting (and Remembering) Slavery in African-American Museums." *Journal of African American Studies*, vol. 15, no. 4, Dec. 2011, pp. 508–23. *SpringerLink*, doi:10.1007/s12111-011-9165-2.

Choi, Suhi. "Can a Memorial Communicate Embodied Trauma?: Reenacting Civilian Bodies in the No Gun Ri Peace Park." *Rhetoric & Public Affairs*, vol. 19, no. 3, 2016, pp. 465–489. *JSTOR*, doi:10.14321/rhetpublaffa.19.3.0465.

Clough, Patricia Ticineto, and Jean Halley, editors. *The Affective Turn: Theorizing the Social.* Duke UP, 2007.

Cobos, Casie, Gabriela Raquel Ríos, Donnie Johnson Sackey, Jennifer Sano-Franchini, and Angela Haas. "Interfacing Cultural Rhetorics: A History and a Call." *Rhetoric Review*, vol. 37 no. 2, 2018, pp. 139–54. *Taylor & Francis Online*, doi:10.1080/07350198.2018.1424470.

Damasio, Antonio. *Descartes' Error.* Harper, 1995.

Deleuze, Gilles. *Spinoza: Practical Philosophy.* Translated by Robert Hurley, City Lights, 1988.

Dolmage, Jay. "'Breathe Upon Us an Even Flame': Hephaestus, History, and the Body of Rhetoric." *Rhetoric Review*, vol. 25, no. 2, 2006, pp. 119–40. *JSTOR*, www.jstor.org/stable/20176710.

Dolmage, Jay. "Metis, Mêtis, Mestiza, Medusa: Rhetorical Bodies across Rhetorical Traditions." *Rhetoric Review*, vol. 28, no. 1, 2009, pp. 1–28. *JSTOR*, www.jstor.org/stable/25655927.

Edbauer Rice, Jenny. "The New 'New': Making a Case for Critical Affect Studies." *Quarterly Journal of Speech*, vol. 94, no. 2, 2008, pp. 200–12. *Taylor & Francis Online*, doi:10.1080/00335630801975434.

Edbauer Rice, Jenny. "Unframing Models of Public Distribution: From Rhetorical Situation to Rhetorical Ecologies." *Rhetoric Society Quarterly*, vol. 35, no. 4, 2005, pp. 5–24. *JSTOR*, www.jstor.org/stable/40232607.

Gilyard, Keith, and Adam Banks. *On African-American Rhetoric.* Routledge, 2018.

Grosz, Elizabeth. *Space, Time, and Perversion.* Routledge, 1995.

Hawhee, Debra. *Bodily Arts.* U of Texas P, 2005.

Hawhee, Debra. *Moving Bodies: Kenneth Burke at the Edges of Language.* U of South Carolina P, 2009.

Holding, Cory. "The Rhetoric of the Open Fist." *Rhetoric Society Quarterly,* vol. 45, no. 5, 2015, pp. 399–419. *Taylor & Francis Online,* doi:10.1080/02773945.2015.1058973.

International Civil Rights Center and Museum. "About." *International Civil Rights Center and Museum,* 2018, sitinmovement.org/about/. Accessed 21 Sept. 2018.

Jackson, Ronald, and Elaine Richardson, editors. *Understanding African American Rhetoric: Classical Origins to Contemporary Innovations.* Routledge, 2003.

Knoblauch, A. Abby. "Bodies of Knowledge: Definitions, Delineations, and Implications of Embodied Writing in the Academy." *Composition Studies,* vol. 40, no. 2, 2012, pp. 50–65. *JSTOR,* www.jstor.org/stable/compstud.40.2.0050.

Kopelson, Karen. "Rhetoric on the Edge of Cunning; Or, The Performance of Neutrality (Re)Considered as a Composition Pedagogy for Student Resistance." *College Composition and Communication,* vol. 55, no. 1, 2003, pp. 115–46. *JSTOR,* doi:10.2307/3594203.

Logan, Shirley Wilson. *We Are Coming: The Persuasive Discourse of Nineteenth-Century Black Women.* Southern Illinois UP, 1999.

Marback, Richard. "Detroit and the Closed Fist: Toward a Theory of Material Rhetoric." *Rhetoric Review,* vol. 17, no. 1, 1998, pp. 74–92. *JSTOR,* www.jstor.org/stable/465744.

Massumi, Brian. *Parables for the Virtual: Movement, Affect, Sensation.* Duke UP, 2002.

Nussbaum, Martha. *Upheavals of Thought: The Intelligence of Emotions.* Cambridge UP, 2001.

Obermark, Lauren. "'Assurance That the World Holds Far More Good Than Bad': The Pedagogy of Memory at the Oklahoma City National Memorial Museum." *Rhetoric Review,* vol. 38, no. 1, 2019, pp. 93–107. *Taylor & Francis Online,* doi:10.1080/07350198.2019.1549410.

Obermark, Lauren. *Rhetorical Education at Historical Museums: Public Pedagogies of Civic Engagement.* Southern Illinois UP, forthcoming.

Phelps, Elizabeth, and Tali Sharot. "How (and Why) Emotion Enhances the Subjective Sense of Recollection." *The Interface between Neuroscience and Psychological Science.* Spec. issue of *Current Directions in Psychological Science,* vol. 17, no. 2, 2008, pp. 147–52. *JSTOR,* www.jstor.org/stable/20183269.

Ratcliffe, Krista. *Rhetorical Listening: Identification, Gender, Whiteness.* Southern Illinois UP, 2005.

Richardson, Elaine, and Ronald Jackson, editors. *African American Rhetoric(s): Interdisciplinary Perspectives.* Southern Illinois UP, 2004.

Royster, Jacqueline Jones. *Traces of a Stream: Literacy and Social Change Among African American Women.* U of Pittsburgh P, 2000.

Sedgwick, Eve Kosofsky. *Touching Feeling: Affect, Pedagogy, Performativity.* Duke UP, 2003.

Solomon, Robert. *The Passions: Emotions and the Meaning of Life.* Hackett, 1993.

Spinoza, Baruch. *Ethics.* Translated by Stuart Hampshire, Penguin, 1996.

Tambini, Arielle, Ulrike Rimmele, Elizabeth Phelps, and Lila Davachi. "Emotional Brain States Carry Over and Enhance Future Memory Formation." *Nature Neuroscience,* vol. 20, no. 2, 2017, pp. 271–78. *NYU Scholars,* doi:10.1038/nn.4468.

Tolia-Kelly, Divya. "*Feeling* and *Being* at the (Postcolonial) Museum: Presencing the Affective Politics of 'Race' and Culture." *Bringing it "Home"? Sociological Practice and the Practice of Sociology.* Spec. issue of *Sociology,* vol. 50, no. 5, 2016, pp. 896–912. *SAGE Journals,* doi:10.1177/0038038516649554.

Wilson, James, and Cynthia Lewiecki-Wilson, editors. *Embodied Rhetorics: Disability in Language and Culture.* Southern Illinois UP, 2001.

6

THE ROLE OF INTRABODY RESONANCE IN POLITICAL ORGANIZING

Nadya Pittendrigh (University of Houston-Victoria)

Here is a story told by a friend, who recalls an experience of sympathetic bodily shock: years ago in New York City, he saw a young man in a subway car. Standing upright, involved in his headphones, the young man suddenly lost consciousness and collapsed, making no attempt to break his fall. The sound of his 170 pounds hitting the hollow floor was incredibly alarming. My friend recalls people rushing to help him as the young man composed himself and insisted he was fine, but once he was up he promptly fell again, and with that second fall real fright set in for my friend. Though my friend's body did not directly mirror what the young man experienced, his body vibrated with an urgent sense of visceral emergency related to the survival of this stranger. Yet his feeling of extreme anguish on behalf of the young man did not formulate itself in words. Rather, the sensation was so prerational it was as if he had witnessed himself collapse. This anguish on behalf of the man took my friend by surprise in the same way witnessing many citizens rally to help a stranger in a supposedly hard-hearted city might also surprise. Words and thought came later, my friend recalls, along with his own habitual selfishness and relief that others were helping (so he did not have to).

My friend recounted this experience because he believed it spoke to the phenomenon at the center of this chapter, namely the tendency of our bodies to resonate in sympathy with one another. He had the hypothesis that in some sense, we are all one body; there is not always actually a chasm between us in the way we might assume. As my friend described it, he felt the anguish he might have felt for himself had he been on an operating room table and heard the doctors say, "Okay, that's it, the heartbeat is fading, administer emergency measures." This visceral sense of alarm on behalf of a stranger seems worth considering, insofar as it represents an underrecognized subcategory of rhetoric. In

https://doi.org/10.7330/9781646422012.c006

the analysis that follows, I refer to this category as *intrabody resonance*, which I distinguish from empathy, sympathy, pathos, and identification for its nonratiocinative characteristics. Though it is not all-powerful and not decisive, it is a common but underrecognized element of grass-roots persuasion.

Based on my participation in a campaign in Illinois to close the state supermax prison, my observations of the contributions of former prisoners to that activism, and my own experience of their effects, I argue that even though intrabody resonance does not always supersede other obstacles to solidarity, it had a role to play in the prison-reform campaign that provides the impetus for this discussion. Using the situation of the supermax, which is widely characterized in the United States by indefinite solitary confinement, prolonged isolation, sensory deprivation, and a lack of human touch, this chapter articulates intrabody resonance as a subcategory of persuasion that operates routinely between bodies.

Following the publication of Teresa Brennan's *The Transmission of Affect* in 2004, many scholars have theorized affect as at least in some sense communal, providing a prompt for this investigation of intrabody resonance and its implications for community activism. As Brennan asserts, if I walk into an "atmospheric room . . . and it is rank with the smell of anxiety, I breathe this in" (68). Her claim that "we are not self-contained in terms of our energies" challenges individualist conceptions of our presumed separateness (6). Similarly, in her contribution to *Thinking Through the Skin*, Jennifer Biddle defines corporeality as explicitly not a "private individual experience or expression" and "not determined by the muscular skeletal conceptions that physiology and biology afford us" (190). Biddle suggests instead that our "bodily potentiality" or permeability "derives from a literal sharing in the bodies of others" (190). This volatile sharing points to an overlooked communal dimension of embodiment, which Sara DiCaglio also discusses in this collection, arguing, "The question of scent is ultimately one of boundaries; odors link us, are difficult to contain or to control" (chapter 4). Sara Ahmed and Jackie Stacey also address the volatile borders of bodies in their very title, *Thinking Through the Skin*, and their conception of "inter-embodiment" articulates "a politics attuned to the fleshy interface between bodies" (1). Likewise, the term *intrabody resonance* also gestures towards Karen Barad's conception of "intra-action;" her focus on "the entanglements and responsibilities of which one is a part" hints at ethical entanglement as part of our proximity to one another (ix). If these authors all emphasize interconnectedness through various forms of affective permeability, then the conditions of isolation that characterize supermax confinement represent a particularly acute case for investigating connection across our purported separateness because supermax prisoners are stigmatized and because prisoners' bodies undergo extreme experiences in prolonged isolation.

TAMMS SUPERMAX

In the 1990s, Illinois officials supported the creation of an all-solitary-confinement supermax prison in the context of prison crowding and gang violence, bolstered by the argument that it would function as added punishment for those prisoners already incarcerated who commit further crimes while in prison. The original warden estimated prisoners would be held in isolation at the supermax as temporary shock treatment for approximately a year and then would be sent back to the regular prison population. In practice, during its decade and a half of operation, Illinois's Tamms C-MAX prison (or Tamms) mostly held suspected gang leaders and prisoners with mental illnesses, and because no system existed for prisoners to earn their way out, many stayed there for years. In 2008, staff estimated that approximately 30% of prisoners had been there for ten years (John Howard Association Visit). In 2013, following both the economic downturn and an intense protest campaign, the governor of Illinois shut the prison down.

As opponents continue to argue nationwide, the conditions that characterize supermax confinement—such as those at Tamms—can trigger and exacerbate mental illness. A well-established body of research documents a predictable set of psychiatric disturbances associated with the social and sensory deprivation typical of supermax prisons, sometimes referred to as " 'SHU' (security housing unit) syndrome" (Haney 137). A Wisconsin judge cites that research, describing increased "paranoid delusional disorder, dissociative disorder, [and] schizophrenia and panic disorder" along with higher rates of self-mutilation, smearing feces, and suicide (qtd. in Golden 282). Another judge suggests supermax prisons "are virtual incubators of psychoses-seeding illness in otherwise healthy inmates and [are] exacerbating illness in those already suffering from mental infirmities" (qtd. in Golden 282). These problems were born out in Tamms. In their final report on the prison, a local prison-monitoring group, the John Howard Association (JHA), documented varying degrees of mental disintegration among the prisoners they encountered while touring Tamms. In a report issued in 2012 just before the prison closed, the JHA documented "a significant number of inmates with scars and wounds from acts of self-mutilation and self-harm" (John Howard Association 18). The report also describes one prisoner with a paranoid narrative about being poisoned becoming disconsolate during the interview and simply repeating "I'm so lonely." Such encounters with suffering, related by witnesses or journalists, proved pivotal in mobilizing opposition to the prison. Yet this analysis seeks to articulate a different element of the activist rhetoric against Tamms, which this chapter refers to as *intrabody resonance*. As I elaborate later, this intrabody resonance, which entangled activists in the affects of former prisoners and their families, depended upon directly witnessing the prisoners' suffering at organizing meetings and public forums and ultimately motivated continued engagement.

INTERRUPTED TOUCH AS A FORM OF PUNISHMENT

According to G. Patrick Murphy, US District Court Judge in the case *Westefer v. Snyder*, conditions in the Illinois supermax were characterized by an exceptional degree of isolation, amounting to "virtual sensory deprivation" (24). Murphy conducted an extensive investigation and in 2010 issued a report highlighting testimony of prisoners who had spent time at Tamms. All of the prisoners quoted insist, as this prisoner does, that the isolation took a real toll their bodies.

> A. Well, I'm stressed out most of the time. A lot of anxiety. If I even think that I'm getting a call pass[1] my stomach starts to hurting, I have murmurs—palpations [*sic*], I mean. The mornings of yard, stressed out. I'm not good around people anymore. I don't want to be around people.
>
> Q. And were you that way before you went to Tamms?
>
> A. No. (qtd. in Murphy 22)

Many others insist that the difference between being in Tamms and being in segregation at other prisons is access to at least some social interaction. Those imprisoned at Tamms repeatedly assert that interacting with others constitutes a fundamental lifeline that depends on "communicating with other people": "[J]ust to go on the yard with other people, you know. To have that connection with someone, you know. [At Tamms, y]ou can talk to someone behind a door and you are isolated 23 hours a day. But it is a totally different situation if you are allowed to be with other inmates around and communicate, you know. . . . You got to have—you got to be in that situation to understand that. And it takes a toll. And it takes a big toll. I don't feel the same" (qtd. in Murphy 17). Insisting that the sociality and varied sensation described by this prisoner play a vital role in mental health, many former Tamms prisoners also testify that touching others and being touched plays an essential part in their ability to not only feel socially connected but also to connect one day meaningfully to the next. In a conversation about how Tamms is different, one prisoner contrasts Tamms with segregation in another Illinois prison, where the cells have bars: "You know, you could reach out, you know, you could touch a person's hand which was a significant difference. If you have never—if you have been—if you have been isolated for so long, just putting your hands on another human being was like . . . wow. You know the feeling if you ever been thirsty and you just drink a cold glass of water. It's like that. It's strange at first but it's—well, it's free" (qtd. in Murphy 46). The fact that these prisoners treasure an almost meaningless touch and the fact that touch is the essential thing Tamms withheld highlight one of the principles of the prison's design.

By design, Tamms operates through logics of permeability and touch. Officials who lobbied for its construction wanted to minimize not only the influence of gang leaders in the general prison population but also physical contact, which speaks to Scot Barnett's reminder in this collection not to treat touch as a strictly prosocial force (chapter 2). The officials who wanted the supermax wanted it precisely because of the desire to control the violent potential of touch. At the same time, the prisoners housed there argued that spending ten years in isolation without ever being touched by another human (except by the gloved hand of a guard) represents its own kind of violence.[2] In this sense, the supermax's attempt to institute a hyperimpermeable form of incarceration can be understood as its own violent permutation of "thinking through the skin," with the result that prisoners themselves routinely described conditions in the supermax as "no-touch torture." Here, the rhetoric of the supermax and of prisoners themselves can be understood to function, in Shannon Walters's terms, "in the visceral locations that touch creates between more and less verbal, often working to facilitate identifications spontaneously, intuitively, and unconsciously" (42). Thus, without denying Barnett's point that touch is partly violent, I stay closer to Walters's focus on its nonratiocinative dimensions, including intrabody resonance and its potential to connect people in spite of immense obstacles. At the same time, I argue in the following section that intrabody resonance, or the tendency of bodies to resonate in sympathy with one another, is not confined to physical touch. Touch, while important, is not my focus. The central concern guiding the rest of this chapter is intrabody resonance as a force in activism, and though it may occur along with touch as a part if activism, physical touch is not required: most lawmakers never physically touch a prisoner but they can be exposed to the resonant body of a prisoner or the mother of a prisoner on a stage, at a meeting, or even through filmed images, all of which represent their own form of affective—but not physical—touch, which I call *intrabody resonance*.

INTRABODY RESONANCE

For people involved in anti-Tamms activism, Brian Nelson and his mother were important catalysts from the moment he was sent to the prison in 1998. His mother served as head of the Tamms Committee, a group that organized mail for the prisoners and bus trips for visitation. The parents of Tamms prisoners had been told their children were monsters, and they felt ashamed and responsible, so connecting with others who had someone in the prison relieved some of the isolation the families themselves experienced. Years later, the prison-reform activism of the Tamms Year Ten campaign was organized by Laurie Jo Reynolds. Reynolds built on her involvement with the Tamms Committee; being connected to mothers and family members of prisoners in that group helped galvanize the work of the campaign to reform and eventually close the prison.

When I first met her, Reynolds repeatedly tried to persuade me and others in our social group to attend Tamms Committee meetings. She reassured us we didn't need to become deeply involved, but she insisted we just come and hear what the family members of prisoners had to say. Attending Tamms Committee meetings attached me to the cause of reforming Tamms through contact with the people most directly affected by it. That same strategy of affective attachment through exposure to people directly affected by the prison was repeated in building a large coalition to address inhumane conditions at the prison. All our organizing meetings, public events, and lobbying of state officials centrally featured family members and former prisoners describing the effects of long-term isolation, the mental deterioration of prisoners at the prison, and the lasting psychological effects after release. Based on my own initial resistance to becoming involved, followed by my eventual intense participation, I experienced campaign meetings as working to entangle me with suffering bodies of former prisoners and family members. These meetings bodied forth the otherwise hidden reality that the prison was a shared responsibility, not to be borne just by the families of the prisoners. As the lives of people who had not been directly touched by incarceration at Tamms became entangled with those who had, their proximity, or simply being near one another, illustrated the "responsibilities" Karen Barad associates with proximity (ix). Certainly, participants were not all equally receptive, but many were; the movement grew from a few core organizers to thousands who signed on to attend rallies, call their legislators, and help make a public case for reform.

As a result of the group's monthly mailings to prisoners in Tamms, many of the prisoners wrote back describing their experiences of being incarcerated there. One prisoner wrote he had forgotten what body language looked like. He also said, having lived without a mirror for years, he could no longer conjure the image of his own face. Others complained of being unable to sleep or experience sustained quiet because of the disturbances caused by mentally ill prisoners on the cell-block, while others wrote of being fearful for their own mental states. These written testimonies from prisoners from inside the supermax performed an incalculable role. Yet, as I argue below, the affective power of the many written descriptions of what it was like to be incarcerated in Tamms operates by other means, distinct from the resonance between bodies that took place during organizing meetings and other events where former prisoners were present.

In 2010, shortly after Brian Nelson got out of Tamms, he attended a meeting organized by the Tamms Year Ten campaign at New Saints of Humboldt Park in Chicago. As was customary at meetings, family members of prisoners and former prisoners spoke. Brian sat next to another recently released prisoner who mostly declined to speak except to say crowds made him extremely uncomfortable. They both kept their coats on and their backs against the wall, which Brian explained as part of the paranoia both of them felt in the space. To elaborate on the ongoing discomfort after being released, Brian talked about what it was like for him immediately after he got out: "So, it's 10 min. out of Tamms, I had the first psychotic episode where I'm ready to hurt somebody, and the rest of the way home I wouldn't get out the car. And it's just, it sucks. My family started getting all jittery because I'm so bad. I mean it's. . . . How do you go from being in a box by yourself for 12 years, and some-body wants to walk up behind you. Even people you know, your family, they love you, it's don't get close." Here, I want to direct attention away from the transcript of what Nelson said and towards the verbal gaps in his speech—moments when he says, "And it's just, it sucks" and "I mean it's . . ." Here, and when he testified about Tamms elsewhere, he choked up and said he couldn't explain the experience. Similar versions of this scene reoccurred with many other former Tamms prisoners. At one meeting, a new attendee was asked to describe what it was like to be iso-lated for so long. After a few attempted sentences, he simply wept and said, "I don't know how to explain what happened to me." Everyone in

the room was acutely aware that several mothers of currently incarcerated Tamms prisoners were present, and we all hung on his words, wanting to know if it really was as bad as they feared. There was a sensation of
suspense or slow motion, and as one mother audibly caught her breath
in response to the man's emotion, we all caught our breath and waited
to see if the shared affect in the room would tip over into weeping.

In attempting to understand the rhetoric operating in such an experience, I reach for Brennan's description of walking into an "atmospheric
room." Yet I distinguish bodies sharing affects in a shared physical space
from the kind of affective contagion that takes place online, or, in the
case of the Tamms prisoners, letters through the mail.[3] Borrowing a
term from neurology, Brennan refers to the process of transmission as
"entrainment," which involves "one person's or one group's nervous and
hormonal systems" being "brought into alignment with another's" (9).
Brennan's description of aligned nervous systems matches the direct,
visceral impact I experienced and saw in others most clearly in moments
when people visibly choked up. Though narratives written by Tamms
prisoners stirred our imaginations, delivered information, and elicited
pathos, they did not elicit body resonance. In the same sense my friend
on the subway would not have felt emotional emergency if someone had
merely told him the story of the man collapsing on the subway because
there would have been no body to resonate with, letters from prisoners
inside Tamms likewise did not elicit body resonance.

There is a scene in *Anna Karenina* (Tolstoy) that illustrates the tendency of intrabody resonance to circumvent ratiocination and other
signals that can prevent what Brennan calls "alignment," or what some
might call siding with the prisoners. The scene focuses primarily on the
male protagonist's anxiety in contemplating his newborn baby and its
mother. As the infant breastfeeds and then falls asleep, the protagonist
is aware that "[t]his beautiful baby only inspire[s] him with a sense of
repulsion and pity" as he considers the enormity of what he has done
in fathering the child (782). But then suddenly the baby sneezes, which
in an instant replaces doubt with fatherly pride; he is brought back into
alignment with the baby through the sneeze. It is in this same sense that
the suffering of supermax prisoners, a deeply a stigmatized population,
has the potential to circumvent skepticism. Certainly, the existence of
intrabody resonance doesn't mean it will persuade everyone, and even
if there is intrabody resonance, it is a relatively weak force—not decisive. Yet there are moments when intrabody resonance is the rhetor's
best hope. The skeptic in the audience asks, "Why should I care about
gang members and murderers when there are so many other people

more deserving of my time, attention and resources?" If something, like intrabody resonance, circumvents that response, it could be effective when nothing else works.

Imagine a former supermax prisoner attempting to persuade judges, journalists, or legislators through the force of reason to take seriously the idea that long-term solitary confinement causes invisible psychological damage. For many audiences, those reasons will be insufficient, in part because supermax prisoners are considered by many to be among the least sympathetic people in society.[4] In fact, a multitude of forces in the popular imagination function to block public audiences from being able to see prisoners as worthy of rights, due process, or resources. Not least among these are widely used stigmatizing labels in the popular discourse, including references to the prisoners as "the worst of the worst" or as monsters. Such language was routinely used at public forums on Tamms issues, including these public comments from a 2012 Commission on Government Forecasting and Accountability (COGFA) hearing about whether to keep the prison open:

> This facility is serving the purpose for which it was built to house the worst of the worse. (*Tamms Correctional* 32)
>
> The knowledge that Tamms is the destination of the "worst of the worst" has always been evident. (*Tamms Correctional* 33)
>
> I want those people to know that as long as the monsters that caused you such great lose are housed at tamms they can never harm another innocent person. (*Tamms Correctional* 44)

These habitually applied labels, "worst of the worst" and "monsters," effectively naturalize the apparent need for the prison in the imaginations of those using the terms, as though the existence of the moniker "worst of the worst" demonstrates the existence of such so-called monsters.

Meanwhile, the very gesture of their banishment functions to persuade many audiences the prisoners involved must have deserved it. For example, Brian Nelson spent twelve years in solitary confinement in Tamms. The extremity of that fact gives society pause, suggesting this prisoner is unfit for contact. The degree of banishment involved is almost worse than if the prisoner had been sent to a deserted island, insofar as at least on an island the person would be able to walk around. In a supermax cell, the island is the size of a bathroom and every wall, every surface, says this is a toilet. There is no exercise equipment in the yard. When the prisoner receives a rare visit, he is chained to a concrete stump, arms behind his back. Visits are conducted through the intercom, with no touch involved. At Tamms, there were no accommodations for children during visitation. There were no educational programs. Yet when these conditions are described as deprivation, public audiences very commonly respond with disdain: "Seems to be a lot of 'mamas' that think their kids have to sleep on concrete beds. That is by far not true seeing how they all have a very thick brand new mattress, television, radio, air conditioning, and a recreation yard" (*Tamms Correctional* 41). Besides the obvious cognitive obstacles to aligning with the prisoners, there was also the indisputable structural fact that the prison represented the main source of jobs in the area. As Ahmed comments, "Some feelings are blocked (or there is an attempt to block their transmission) if the expression of those feelings would challenge the rights of others" (*Cultural Politics* 225). Indeed, there were powerful obstacles in place that potentially blocked the possibility of siding with the prisoners.

As is evident in the public comments above, such blockages are often expressed in the rational language of triage. For instance, as a prison-reform activist, one is inevitably asked, Why are you helping these people? Why them, when so many people are in need? In fact, many activists ask themselves these questions. In this sense, the extrarational bonds between bodies who show up again and again to share the burden of activist work actually seem quite necessary. Activists themselves stand in need of a visceral boost, an experience of alignment with one another or the cause, precisely insofar as the grinding work of activism contradicts their own self-interest in important ways. Here again, intrabody resonance demonstrates its power to circumvent rational will and self-interest.

My claim is that in the context of all this already-operative skepticism, reasons are inherently weak without the physical presence and the undeniable bodily evidence of former prisoners. Certainly, for some people, for those already primed to be receptive to what former Tamms prisoners had to say, the prisoners' direct testimony might have been sufficient to persuade them that conditions in the supermax were unacceptable. Yet the intuitive response for other audiences was, "Oh, you were tortured? Did you want it to be a vacation?" In such a context, verbal bridge making between the prisoner and the highly skeptical audience member seems impossible.

Yet in some contexts, public audiences did resonate with the suffering of the mothers of Tamms prisoners and the former prisoners themselves, and I contend that this unwilled sympathetic intrabody resonance represents an underrecognized political opening. When one sees a person reduced to a broken state for reasons they're not giving—one can simply sense their brokenness—the unwilled, intrabody resonance is made perceptible. When Nelson says through tears that he still can't hug his family members and feel comfortable, intrabody resonance is a part of the rhetorical situation, even potentially for the most skeptical audience members. It will likely exist simultaneously with other contradictory signals, yet the existence of such internal contradictions itself represents an opening.

In emphasizing the unwilled, instantaneous, or nonratiocinative nature of what I am calling *intrabody resonance*, I do not intend to imply such resonance takes place universally. I take Ahmed's caution that "there is nothing more mediated than immediacy" ("Making Strangers"), and in important ways, this argument affirms the position that the conditions that make intrabody resonance effective between some bodies and not others is mediated by social structures. Yet Ahmed's claim can actually be taken too far. Despite such obstacles to alignment, immediacy does commonly take place; it is not true that there is no such thing as immediacy,[5] and depending on the receptiveness of the people involved, it can have persuasive power.

THE WORK ETHIC REQUIRED FOR IDENTIFICATION

Intrabody resonance differs from pathos, as well as from empathy or sympathy, insofar as it operates independently of the conscious strategic work of the mind. On this account, I understand pathos as the primary operative element involved in the narratives Tamms prisoners wrote in their letters to the Tamms Year Ten campaign; in this case, pathos involves someone telling a story and the audience understanding someone's plight in the story. Intrabody resonance, on the other hand, does not require such understanding. Similarly, if empathy means imaginatively putting oneself in the place of others, intrabody resonance also differs from empathy. This notion of empathy is commonly distinguished from sympathy, which is often understood as more shallow: as one scholar suggests, sympathy risks condescension, or projecting ethnocentric pity onto the other (Valovirta, *Sexual* 34). Thus empathy means using one's imagination to feel someone else's pain, while sympathy means using the imagination to acknowledge another's pain. In this sense, empathy is commonly understood as superior to sympathy, yet both are distinct from intrabody resonance for their reliance on imagination, or hauling one's understanding over a presumed radical separation. Important, empathy and sympathy are subject to the will—after all, they can both be intentionally withheld. Intrabody resonance, by contrast, refers to a visceral state of alarm, fear, or tenderness on behalf of the other, which happens in a visceral flash, without imagination, ratiocination, or will.

Much of the rhetoric of anti-Tamms activists was intended to cause in receptive members of the public a *pang*. In everyday speech, we might say such bodily rhetorics of suffering caused audiences to identify with the prisoners, but recall Kenneth Burke's discussion of the term, which pivots on a sense of shared interests and assumes separateness as a starting point. As he puts it, "Identification is affirmed with earnestness precisely because there is division. If men were not apart from one another, there would be no need for the rhetorician to proclaim their unity" (22). He goes on to affirm the view that the unavoidable biological fact of our separateness, or the "individual centrality of the nervous system, in the divisiveness of the individual human organism, from birth to death," is precisely what motivates identification (130). Thus, for Burke, identification involves agency, action and work, figured as the building of a bridge between people who operate from neurologically separate experiences. Identification is goaded by our separateness, and from that default position, we launch communication over an abyss, whereas the bodily rhetoric I'm pointing to suggests there is also something more like nonvolitional flow between bodies. If we needn't be by default radically out of sympathy with one another, if instead the social and political reality founds our separateness, then perhaps, as Burke suggests, we can in important ways build bridges through identification or shared interests. But in the meantime I argue there's a more direct route already operating by way of intrabody resonance that doesn't require overlapping self-interests among the parties.

Diane Davis's fundamental point in *Inessential Solidarity* is that there are various illusions related to communication, community, and our ability to align ourselves in solidarity with one another created by the physical gap between people. Obviously, this physical separation between us really does exist: if I hit my hand with a hammer, the person sitting next to me will not feel it insofar as our nerves end at the borders of our bodies. Yet Davis, despite this actual physical gap between bodies, challenges Burke's view that rhetoric is brought into being by our fundamental isolation from one another. Instead, she argues that our being already receptive to each other reveals the origin of our rhetoricity. Her investigation resists the notion that community formation is always exclusionary—togetherness is too important. In setting out to investigate whether communication is inherently founded on social division, Davis discovers an underappreciated, already-operative receptiveness to each other that is "oblivious to borders" and operates outside of "symbolic identification and therefore any prerequisite for belonging" (2). Against Burke, she highlights a version of togetherness that already exists, right at the "intersection of rhetoric and solidarity that neither references a preexisting essence" nor "installs, as a product of human work, an essence of the community" (1). This notion of communication not being a matter of hard work (or rhetorical work ethic) is the note I end on.

If we take Davis's view, which assumes that on some level we are already receptive to one another, then why doesn't communication work more smoothly more often? To be clear, Davis is not arguing that we already understand each other. Instead, she asks which is the default/ starting point: everyone fundamentally separate and isolated (so it is a challenge to communicate) or everyone already equipped with ready receptivity for each other (and stepping away from *that* is what makes communication difficult)? Intrabody resonance, the unwilled body rhetoric investigated in this analysis, is more easily pictured in Davis's terms because body rhetoric proceeds as a matter of flow. According to such a view, it is not a miracle that we can communicate over an abyss; the miracle is that we don't. In truth, it turns out it doesn't take much to remind us we are, in a sense, all one organism. My neighbor revving his motorcycle loudly and at length, which raises my blood pressure, blocks my identification with him—but from another perspective, he and I are just different cells in the big organism. From a similar perspective, we can see it takes surprisingly little to bring people to a sense of unity. An audience's ready sympathy when a former Tamms prisoner chokes up, or must leave the room in the middle of an organizing meeting because he can no longer be comfortable around people, seems potentially sig-nificant and promising.

Davis's analysis resists conventional intuitions about rhetorical agency, namely that through sheer force of rhetorical effort, we throw a rope bridge across the Grand Canyon. That view of communication is even more exaggerated if what we are talking about is communicating across a chasm with the so-called worst of the worst. Yet the unwilled, mutual resonance between bodies I have pointed to, and Davis's sense that we communicate not strictly from the default of personal separateness, sug-gests there are lines of communication and receptiveness available to us that tend to be overlooked. Instead of a rope bridge over an abyss, per-haps the effect of body resonance can more closely resemble being in a pool with other bodies, being buoyed by the waves their bodies cause. The question for political rhetors is whether or not we can actually use that sort of resonance. The case I have made here is that we can. There may be a variety of things we do as activists that are effective, that we are only dimly aware of, and that we don't do on purpose. Such tactics have nothing to do with building an impossible bridge, a model of communication that makes it seem like the situation might be hopeless.

CONCLUSION

I found in my research, through interviews with legislators and Department of Corrections employees, that many self-announced law-and-order hardliners happily express their belief that they are intractable when it comes to people who commit crimes. Yet, in fact, many who pronounce themselves as having no sympathy for criminals go on later in the same conversation to affirm their belief in second chances or rehabilitation. Thus, if the reform-minded activist is tempted to regard the tough-on-crime senator or hard-line warden as absolutely closed to persuasion, in fact their very philosophical incoherence suggests an opening, which is where the Burkean move to appeal to shared interests might come in; the standard rhetorical move would be to play to that aspect of their values that seems to overlap with that of the prison reformer. Yet this analysis points to a deeper incoherence, suggesting that the resistance of the law-and-order hard-liner comes partly from the fact that they are potentially resonant with other suffering bodies; they don't want to be exposed to Brian Nelson's tears because they don't want to cry on his behalf. If we were to ask hard-liners why they are closed to the suffering of prisoners, they might adopt an affect of exaggerated impermeability and say that they don't need to listen, that they have heard it hundreds of times. They would not likely say (because it would take exceptional self-knowledge to do so) they do not want to listen to the testimony of a former prisoner because if they did listen, they might experience bodily alignment with that prisoner or momentarily occupy their suffering: *I don't want to listen to their testimony because I might share in their bodily misery and it might weaken my resolve to punish them.*

I am suggesting that when exposed directly to the experiences, testimony, suffering, and tears of people who have been touched by supermax incarceration, the ideologically opposed senator participates, possibly against their own will, in visceral community with the criminal. I am not suggesting such people are lying when they vehemently assert they have no sympathy for criminals, though their very vehemence against what they deny, namely the capacity to feel anything for a prisoner, can be understood in Freudian terms: one swears up and down that one does not feel, the better to deny the body's reactions. Certainly, whoever structures their life to keep a safe distance from prisoners can safely despise them, and maybe that person really does have no sympathy for them. Maybe they have no empathy. Yet the intrabody resonance at issue here goes beyond both empathy and sympathy.

It is not necessarily to the advantage of the activist to make their political opponents aware of this intrabody resonance and argue the value of it. Just the same, to channel the power of intrabody resonance is to make use of an underutilized potential. Naturally, there is no way to measure exactly how much of the success of our campaign depended on intrabody resonance, but that the role was not insubstantial stands to reason. The potency of the effect I have discussed here is as reliable as it is overlooked.

NOTES

1. An official summons to leave one's cell for healthcare, visitation, yard time, etc.
2. See also Chris S. Earle, who links the type of punishment in the supermax to liberal logics of responsibility in "Just Violence? California's Short Corridor Hunger Strikes and Arguments Over Prison Legitimacy."
3. In their article "Contagious Bodies. An Investigation of Affective and Discursive Strategies in Contemporary Online Activism," Britta Timm Knudson and Carsten Stage, for instance, consider the persuasive power of hunger strikes, as word spreads online and exerts moral pressure on remote audiences who imagine the "starving bodies" involved. Here affect spreads through verbal relay, which I distinguish from the transmission at issue in Brennan's analysis "whereby people become alike" in each other's presence (9).
4. See "Never Innocent" by Erica R. Meiners, which draws connections between "public panic" regarding "the worst of the worst," supermax prisons, and sex offenders (43–44).
5. Here I cite the emerging body of literature on the biology of emotion, which resists social constructionist absolutism. See for instance, *The Emotional Mind: The Affective Roots of Culture and Cognition*, by Stephen Asma and Rami Gabriel.

WORKS CITED

Ahmed, Sara. *The Cultural Politics of Emotion.* Routledge, 2004.
Ahmed, Sara. "Making Strangers." *feministkilljoys,* 4 Aug 2014, feministkilljoys.com/2014/08/04/making-strangers/. Accessed 12 June 2020.
Ahmed, Sara, and Jackie Stacey. *Thinking Through the Skin.* Routledge, 2001.
Asma, Stephen T., and Rami Gabriel. *The Emotional Mind: The Affective Roots of Culture and Cognition.* Harvard UP, 2019.
Barad, Karen. *Meeting the Universe Halfway.* Duke UP, 2007.
Biddle, Jennifer. "Inscribing Identity: Skin as Country in the Central Desert." *Thinking Through the Skin,* edited by Sara Ahmed and Jackie Stacey, Routledge, 2001, pp. 177–93.
Brennan, Teresa. *The Transmission of Affect.* Cornell UP, 2004.
Burke, Kenneth. *A Rhetoric of Motives.* U of California P, 1969.
Davis, Diane. *Inessential Solidarity: Rhetoric and Foreigner Relations.* U of Pittsburgh P, 2010.
Earle, Chris S. "Just Violence?: California's Short Corridor Hunger Strikes and Arguments Over Prison Legitimacy." *Argumentation and Prison Activism.* Spec. issue of *Argumenta-*

tion and Advocacy, vol. 51, no. 3, 2015, pp. 185–199. *Taylor & Francis Online*, doi:10.108 0/00028533.2015.11821849.

Golden, Deborah. "The Federal Bureau of Prisons: Willfully Ignorant or Maliciously Unlawful?" *Michigan Journal of Race & Law*, vol. 18, no. 2, 2013, pp. 275–294.

Haney, Craig. "Mental Health Issues in Long-Term Solitary and 'Supermax' Confinement." *Crime and Delinquency*, vol. 49, no. 1, 2003, pp. 124–156. *SAGE Journals*: doi:10 .1177/0011128702239239.

John Howard Association. "A Price Illinois Cannot Afford: Tamms and the Costs of Long-Term Isolation." 2012, static1.squarespace.com/static/5beab48285ede1f7e8102102/t /5d1b8101b79cae000124ade9/1562083586930/TammsReport.pdf. Accessed 27 June 2020.

John Howard Association and Tamms Year Ten Visit. Tamms C-MAX prison. 2008. Tamms, IL.

Knudson, Britta Timm, and Carsten Stage. "Contagious Bodies. An Investigation of Affective and Discursive Strategies in Contemporary Online Activism." *Practising Emotional Geographies*. Spec. issue of *Emotion, Space and Society*, vol. 5, no. 3, 2012, pp. 148–155. *ScienceDirect*, doi:10.1016/j.emospa.2011.08.004.

Meiners, Erica R. "Never Innocent." *Meridians*, vol. 9, no. 2, 2009, pp. 31–62. *JSTOR*, www .jstor.com/stable/40338782.

Nelson, Brian. Public Comments at Tamms Year Ten Meeting. Saints of Humboldt Park, 2010. Chicago, IL.

Westefer v. Snyder. Civil no. 00-162-GPM. US District Court for the Southern District of Illinois. 2010. https://casetext.com/case/westefer-v-snyder-17.

Tamms Correctional Center Public Comments as of 05/21/2012. cgfa.ilga.gov/upload/Tamms CCpublicComments.pdf. Accessed 3 Sept. 2019.

Tolstoy, Leo. *Anna Karenina*. OM Books International, 2018.

Valovirta, Elina. *Sexual Feelings: Reading Anglophone Caribbean Women's Writing Through Affect*. Rodopi, 2014.

Walters, Shannon. *Rhetorical Touch: Disability, Identification, Haptics*. U of South Carolina P, 2014.

PART II

Advocacy, Policy, Citizenship

7

DISCOMFORT TRAINING IN THE ARCHIVES
Embodied Rhetoric in Feminist Advocacy

Meg Brooker, Julie Myatt, and Kate Pantelides
(Middle Tennessee State University)

FRAGMENTED MEMORIES

JULIE: November 2016, disillusionment descends. Following the election, I'm sad and frustrated. I desperately need to be reminded not everyone subscribes to the policies of the president elect. I did jack shit before Trump was elected and feel culpable. Sure, I voted, and I donated some money, but I wasn't involved in politics in a meaningful way. Post-election, I realize that needs to change. I want to get involved. I hear of a local organization offering lobbying training, and I ask my friend Kate to come with me. We go, and we are both inspired by this powerful collective of women and taken aback by their open acknowledgment that lobbying work means subjecting one's body to the unwelcomed scrutiny of the male legislators. We're told to expect them to stare at our breasts and that we need to be cautious about how we respond, as calling out the legislators' inappropriate behavior could jeopardize a potential alliance. As soon as we get in the car, we shake our heads and share our astonishment at the apparent contradictions.

MEG: January 2017, International Women's March, Nashville, Tennessee. We marched together, Julie, Kate, and I. We made signs, we shared emergency contacts, we prepared for activism, for protest, for crowds, for potential separation, for the unknown. We marched from Cumberland Park, across the bridge in downtown Nashville, to Public Square and the Tennessee state capitol building. We showed up, in solidarity with marchers in Washington, DC, and around the world. I wore my white tunic, in homage to the suffragists, to dancer Florence Fleming Noyes, and to Hillary Clinton's white pantsuit. We celebrated the record turnout, the global demonstration, women's bodies moving freely through public spaces. Our path was unobstructed, and the mood was joyous, celebratory, allied. We marched freely, but we did not forget that unimpeded flow of women's bodies in public spaces is not the historical or the global norm.

https://doi.org/10.7330/9781646422012.c007

KATE: March 2017, Women's Day on the Hill, Nashville, Tennessee. I was excited to lobby for the first time. After listening to different organizations describe the exigence for their bills, we queued in front of the metal detectors, waiting to enter the capitol building. Julie and I were paired with a young lobbyist new to Nashville and a former House member who, though recently unseated, was very comfortable in the legislature. She knew everyone, and she was incredibly generous with us. Folks ranged from polite, to indifferent, to gracious: one former politician even engaged in extended discussions of education reform with us and later sent signed copies of his book. The ickiest moment was when we were leaving a legislator's office and he grabbed the hand of our lobbyist companion, inviting her to stay and linger. While we had been in his office, he openly stared at her, and, we learned in talking to her later, told her she looked like Kerry Washington. He offered her his number, ostensibly to give her organization financial support, but she wasn't sure in retrospect if that was all he intended.

We foreground our activist experiences, and especially our discomfort in these experiences, to frame our examination of how sites of discomfort produce embodied rhetorics. As Kristie Fleckenstein notes, as researchers, our bodies "hover over this account" (chapter 8). Following A. Abby Knoblauch's assertion that "[e]mbodied rhetoric is a purposeful decision to include embodied knowledge and social positionalities as forms of meaning making," we define sites of discomfort as physical spaces in which bodily affect is influenced by architecture, history, and unspoken codes of conduct and norms of dress; we also define sites of discomfort within bodies themselves, the aspects of bodies that manifest tension, that become immobile or mobilize subversively (52). We call the experience of learning to navigate these spaces *discomfort training*[1]—the process of learning to ignore or suppress embodied knowledge for strategic means or to purposefully put one's body in an uncomfortable space in order to persuade; such training is instructive in attunement to embodied knowledge and, subsequently, constructing embodied rhetorics.

In examining how discomfort training is deployed across time and space, we offer fragments from our experiences of two feminist rhetorical archives, situated one hundred years apart: first, women marching in the nation's capital for the right to vote, and now, women protesting outside and then marching right on in to capitol buildings to make their arguments. The historic archive includes choreography and performances by the understudied rhetor and movement theorist Florence Fleming Noyes, and we specifically focus on her role as an artist in the women's suffrage movement in the 1910s. A contemporary of the suffragists in the early twentieth century, Noyes trained movers to develop sentiency, an increased awareness of the body as receptive, responsive, alive, and expressive. Her system, Noyes Rhythm, asks dancers to notice and become aware of movement impulses before they manifest in action. The contemporary archive includes training practices and recommendations for lobbying by a Tennessee advocacy group focused on supporting legislation to protect women and children. Their discourse draws lobbyists' attention to how their bodies signify in political spaces and the potential of embodied rhetorics.

We posit sites of discomfort as spaces occupied by Sara Ahmed's notion of "willful subjects." Ahmed writes, "Feminist, queer, and anti-racist histories can be thought of as histories of those who are willing to be willful, who are willing to turn a diagnosis into an act of description" (134). Ahmed recognizes that claiming willfulness, choosing to assume the "charge" of willfulness, is a subversive act (134). To be called willful is a reprimand, a reminder to adjust behavior, to submit. The refusal to submit is a purposeful choice. To choose to move into a space of discomfort, and to act from that position, reflects Knoblauch's assertion that "an embodied rhetoric that draws attention to embodied knowledge—specific material conditions, lived experiences, positionalities, and/or standpoints—can highlight difference instead of erasing it in favor of an assumed, privileged discourse" (62).

Sites of discomfort must be inhabited by bodies, and the purposeful navigation of these bodies and these sites is one path to generate embodied rhetoric. Judith Butler identifies the body as a "cultural sign" and gender as a mode of signification, with high stakes for acceptable, or correct, performance. Framing the context for gender performance as a "situation of duress," Butler asserts, "The historical possibilities materialized through various corporeal styles are nothing other than those punitively regulated cultural fictions that are alternately embodied and disguised under duress" (522). It is similarly uncomfortable to act against one's bodily impulses and desires, to mask or stifle them out of fear of triggering verbal or physical attacks. Discomfort training develops a heightened threshold for discomfort in one's body, a kind of discomfort endurance. This choosing of discomfort is also an iteration of Ahmed's willful bodies. Ahmed writes, "A history of willfulness is a history of those who are willing to put their bodies in the way, or to bend their bodies in the way of the will" (161). Willingness to sustain discomfort is a learned behavior, one we develop through the repetition of performative acts.

In order to cultivate this discomfort endurance, one must be able to notice, to locate the discomfort. The act of noticing, of identifying, of locating discomfort provides the opportunity to make a choice, to either enter into and sustain the sensation of discomfort or to transform it, to release the tension. This is a somatic act, a heightening of awareness of sensation in order to cultivate and increase conscious control of physiological processes. Somatic training teaches us to notice sensation in the body. In her historiography of somatic studies, Martha Eddy recognizes that "the body is perceived as *the* source of human intelligence . . . the body awareness senses of proprioception and kinesthesia form the underpinning of communication networks within the living body, the soma" (7). Susan Foster, in examining the embodied relationships between dancers and audiences in the context of performance, demonstrates "how dance practices have been aligned with rather than isolated from other forms of cultural knowledge production" and focuses attention on the interrelationship between "choreography, kinesthesia, and empathy," demonstrating "how they function together to construct corporeality in a given historical and cultural moment" (12–13). In line with Knoblauch's point that "embodied rhetoric, like all rhetoric, is purposeful," we argue that somatic training and awareness increase the rhetor's ability to engage in embodied rhetorical practices precisely because there is increased conscious, bodily choice making (57). This awareness of our bodies and how we can choose to use them has potential to make us more aware of how others' bodies move—or how their movements are inhibited in ways that differ from the ways we ourselves have felt constrained.

Discomfort training broadens the signifying potential of the body as both a cultural sign and as a cultural actor. Ahmed cites Eve Kosofsky Sedgwick's work on voluntary stigma, noting, "To be involved in a protest can mean not only to assume the sign of willfulness but to be willing to carry the sign for others" (162). Ahmed is referring to a specific incident narrated by Sedgwick in which she carries a sign handed to her by a friend. Ahmed extends the metaphor of the protest sign to include "different sides of the placard," inviting the possibility of complicating the signifying power of the sign by recognizing the potential for conflicting messages on either side of the sign (166). The potential for conflicting messages inherent in a multidimensional signifier is another reminder of the dynamic nature of embodied rhetoric. Discomforted bodies signify from the sidelines, from the margins, and they both draw attention to their discomfort and reveal, through their decentralized stance, the tension of their position. In recognizing difference and offering solidarity by carrying the sign for others, we become aware of our own privilege: others may not physically carry a sign—either because their bodies aren't allowed in that space or because it is dangerous for their bodies to inhabit that space.

We choose the historic archive, the Florence Fleming Noyes archive, and the contemporary one, a Tennessee lobbying group, not just because they offer perspectives of women's advocacy one hundred years apart but also because they were our own sites of discomfort training. These archives allow us to analyze how discomfort training can serve as preparation for inhabiting sites of discomfort towards effecting political change through embodied rhetoric. We trace the role discomfort plays—in architectural spaces, in how bodies relate to other bodies, and within bodies themselves—as examples of how discomfort training can be used to foreground embodied rhetorics. Further, we draw on Ahmed's portrayal of the protest sign, particularly its ability to broadcast potentially conflicting messages in pursuit of a liberatory ideal, in reading these two archives and their import for our understanding of the long arc of women in protest. We find the parallels between these archives unsettling, and it is our recognition of our collective unease that illuminates these historically distinct moments as instances of discomfort training in action.

> JULIE, KATE, AND MEG: 2019. Bodies communicate. Bodies stride forth, visible with strength and courage, and they disappear, unnoticed, slinking through shadows. Bodies band together to form crowds, creating publics, and bodies separate, individuate, living out personal narratives, fleshed with hope, longing, loss, and joy. We are all born into bodies, and yet our bodies are all different, and bodies experience differently, experience difference. Some bodies move freely, and some bodies don't. Some bodies stand tall with weight grounded, and some bodies bend and twist. Bodies burst forth into motion, flooded with endorphins, and bodies fold in, immobile with pain. Bodies claim space, take power, and establish and enforce legislation, regulating bodily freedom and access. Some bodies lead, some bodies (are expected to?) follow.

THE CAPITAL AS A SITE OF DISCOMFORT

For the women rhetors we examine, the political spaces they inhabit/ed are fraught sites of discomfort. In what follows, we trace women's "strategies" (Butler) of embodiment in sites of discomfort—in and around capitol buildings, across two archives, and through our personal experiences with these archives. We read the suffragists' embodied experiences during their 1913 demonstration in our nation's capital, Washington, DC, and we reflect on our collective experiences in the recent women's marches in our state capital, Nashville, Tennessee. Despite the time and space that separate these archives, each reveals the ways women learn to suppress embodied knowledge to perform appropriately or act upon embodied knowledge only in carefully chosen moments. We identify somatic awareness of discomfort in advocacy work and frame it as a choice, as a means to claim agency for marginalized bodies and their allies. In acknowledging the body's layered function as a historiographically specific cultural signifier and a potential catalyst for change, we aim to make discomfort visible as embodied rhetoric. Dance theorist Ann Cooper Albright identifies the "slippage between the lived body and its cultural representation, between a somatic identity . . . and a cultural one" as a productive space where the performing body can challenge cultural assumptions about identity based solely on what a body looks like or how it appears to the viewer (4).

In her performance work as a women's-suffrage artist, Florence Fleming Noyes physically illustrates this tension between somatic experience and cultural representation. During her work with the suffrage movement, Noyes danced in multiple civic pageants, symbolically enacting an idealized version of women's significance in society. The roles she danced included Liberty, Washington, DC, 1913 ("Dances"); Hope, Metropolitan Opera, New York, 1913 ("Roosevelt Centre"); The Spirit of Triumph, Armory, New York, 1914 ("Women of Many"); and Columbia, leading the Manhattan delegation in the New York City suffrage parade, 1915 ("Real Beauty"). In all these performances, Noyes functioned as an embodied metonym in which her physical presence stood in for these US ideals, yet, as dancers, she and her students were still real women, engaged in the real labor of physical performance. Noyes and her dancers performed in silk tunics and bare feet. Their move away from corsets and restrictive nineteenth-century dress was considered radical and was a subject of debate in the press leading up to the 1913 performance of Hazel MacKaye's *Suffrage Allegory* on the steps of the Treasury building as part of the National American Woman Suffrage Association (NAWSA) march. A caption underneath a photo of Noyes in a white, lightweight tunic cautions in advance of the event, "It is to be hoped that Miss Noyes will not appear on the treasury steps in this costume, for the first part of March in Washington is likely to be cold and damp, and she would be more than likely to get pneumonia" ("Will Take Part"). Due to the winter weather, the suffrage pageant performers opted for wool tunics, but Noyes famously refused to cover her feet ("Suffragists to Wear Wool"). Her choice to leave her feet (and legs) bare reflects Noyes's commitment to endure the physical discomfort of cold weather and to use her body in positioning her advocacy work (see figure 7.1).

Figure 7.1. *Florence Fleming Noyes as Liberty in the* Suffrage Allegory, *Washington, DC, March 3, 1913 (L & M Ottenheimer).*

Noyes not only endured physical discomfort to illustrate her right to make choices about how she dressed but also used discomfort as a performance tool to illustrate women's oppression. Her solo choreography *Dance of Freedom*, performed at the Biltmore Hotel for Anna Howard Shaw's birthday party, is a metaphor for women's struggle for freedom of movement and control over our own bodies.[2] Noyes begins her dance wrapped in ten yards of chiffon fabric, symbolically struggling to break free. She first frees her arms, then her head and torso, and finally her legs. There is gesture in celebration of each stage of freeing the body, only to realize that another part of the body remains restricted. When she is finally fully unbound, she dances around the space, gesturing with the fabric as if it is a flag, "symbolic of the 'unshackling' of women" and "the slow process of winning freedom" ("Dance of Freedom"). The *Dance of Freedom* also illustrates the disconnect that can occur when one becomes unconsciously accustomed to discomfort—for instance, the torso celebrates its freedom, but the legs are still bound—further highlighting the importance of freeing all the parts. This piece is particularly poignant as a lens to view Noyes's sartorial choices at the march. She and her dancers free themselves from corsets and the binding clothes of the time only to find they're still not free, and thus their purposeful choice of discomfort—to be barefoot in the cold, to wear tunics to perform willfulness with their bodies, makes a particularly strong argument for suffrage. By bringing visibility to physical discomfort and struggle, Noyes's dance illustrates the power of discomfort as embodied rhetoric.

In practice, the suffragists for whom Noyes danced failed to protect and advocate for the needs of all women in their march for enfranchisement; in the 1913 march in Washington, the NAWSA segregated the marchers, visibly and visually relegating women of color to the end of the parade line. In the 1913 suffrage events, not only was the allegorical pageant carefully choreographed and scripted, but so was the parade. The timing, the day before Woodrow Wilson's inauguration, and the location of the pageant and parade in the nation's capital, Washington, DC, were careful choices. According to historian Lucy G. Barber, "Wilson's inaugural committee refused to allow women to march in the actual inaugural parade. [Alice] Paul wanted to highlight this exclusion of women from public life. She explained her choice of date by saying it would show that 'one-half of the people have not participated in choosing the ruler who is to be installed'" (51). While Noyes and her associates occupied a focal point, Paul decided to segregate the parade, instructing Black women to march at the back. Yet, Ida B. Wells-Barnett, an African American journalist and woman suffrage leader, chose to break rank and join her white colleagues during the parade. She embraced potential discomfort—and took a physical risk—to place her Black body in line, alongside white women's bodies, in a space resistant to intersectional embodied representation and in a time when that language did not yet exist. Her physical choice recalls Ahmed's two-sided placard and reminds us of the multidimensional nature of embodied rhetorics. Wells-Barnett's choice to embrace discomfort as a strategy of embodied rhetoric illustrates how discomfort functions differently, and at different levels of risk, for racialized bodies. Rosalyn Terborg-Penn asserts that Wells-Barnett understood what was at stake for Black women in a racially segregated march and made a significant, purposeful, and visually symbolic choice to integrate the march while it was in procession (59).

The pageant and parade were timed so the parade would approach the Treasury building, the site of the pageant, just as the pageant concluded, with the allegorical figures of Columbia (representing the nation) and her court, including Justice, Charity, Liberty (portrayed by Noyes), Peace, and Hope, witnessing the women's procession. The pageant was performed as rehearsed, but, according to Annelise K. Madsen, "Columbia and her attendants waited and waited, with no parade line in sight" (300). What was planned as a peaceful march ended up as a bottleneck, with the 5,000 marchers struggling to advance through an antagonistic crowd of over 200,000 who "physically impeded [the women's] progress" (Madsen 301–302; "5,000 Women"). Despite having proper permits and a police presence, the women's right to march was not protected. United States cavalry troops were called in to push the crowds back, and Congressional hearings later investigated the failure of the police to provide protection for the marchers and to preserve peace during the protest. When placed side by side, images of the women's parade on March 3 (see figure 7.2) and Woodrow Wilson's inaugural parade on March 4 (see figure 7.3) dramatically illustrate differences between the two events. The photograph of the women's march is a chaotic blur, and the *Tennessean* characterized it as a "near-riot," ("Suffrage Pageant"), while the inaugural procession appears orderly, and individual marchers are clearly visible (Madsen 309). This visually demonstrates a clear difference in the way men's and women's bodies were able to occupy political and public spaces in 1913.

Though the presence of women's bodies in capitol buildings may no longer be transgressive, many still perceive it as a threat to what has historically been, and remains, a male-dominated space. Megan Boler explains how confronting an individual's "cherished assumptions may be felt as a threat to their very identity" (191), and thus nonmale presence in the legislature invites discomfort for bodies considered 'other' because of gender or race. As Ahmed notes, "Just being is willful work for those whose being is not only not supported by the general body, but deemed a threat to that body" (160). Thus, we turn to the other side of Ahmed's protest sign, from the rear guard to the avant-garde, exploring the capitol as site of discomfort but from a different vantage point.

The clever protest sign was a stalwart of the Women's March in January 2017. Outside the capitol building in Nashville, Tennessee, we marched and were buoyed by the presence of allies. Everywhere we looked, signs were held aloft, proclaiming women's bodily autonomy, expressing a refusal to allow male legislators to make choices for us and our bodies. Many of these signs were bold and in your face. They foregrounded women's bodies to make arguments: "Keep your filthy laws off my silky drawers," "Resisting bitch face," and "We need to talk about the elephant in the womb." These signs called to mind the uninhibited expression Noyes championed. For us, the march, with its attendant multiplicity of perspectives, experiences, and voices, offered a space in

Figure 7.2. Crowd converging on marchers in the Woman Suffrage Procession, Washington, DC, March 3, 1913 (Leet Brothers).

Figure 7.3. Inaugural procession for President Woodrow Wilson, Washington, DC, March 4, 1913 (Bain News Service).

which to articulate our vision of the world as we want it to be, not as we have experienced it. Ahmed proclaims this generative potential of protest, noting, "[T]he act of assembling does more than disagree: the bodies that gather also reclaim time and space" by making room for the bodies and voices that have been relegated to the margins, silenced, and subjected to violence (163). "To reclaim the streets," she says, "is to enact what we will: a world in which those who travel under the sign of women can travel safely, in numbers: feminist feet as angry feet" (163). In this moment, our collective anger was motivating, reassuring, sustaining. Seeing the sheer number of bodies gathered in that public space reminded us that we were not alone, that together we can be heard, together (despite our differences) we are a force to be reckoned with.

This experience was powerful because "in asserting ourselves, we [were] asserting more than ourselves" (Ahmed 160). And yet, as soon as we (Kate and Julie) entered the capitol building for Women's Day on the Hill in March 2017, the feeling changed: the power we felt standing in front of the capitol building surrounded by other smart, strong allies left us. At the march, breasts and female genitalia were openly celebrated on signs, and being subject to the male gaze was the butt of jokes, not reality. But we soon stopped laughing. Walking through the doors, we felt the weight of scrutiny; we knew our bodies were highly visible as we and other women lobbyists descended upon the male-dominated home of the Tennessee General Assembly, and as a defense mechanism, we covered them. We weren't powerless exactly, but we were less certain of ourselves in this context than we had been at the march. As we took our possessions out of our pockets and allowed our persons to be scanned by metal detectors, we were reminded we were moving within a space where women's bodies are sexualized. We had to remind ourselves to restrain our impulses to share a truth, to be careful about what we said. We had been given a script to follow, and thankful for it though we were as first-time lobbyists, that script and the context and audience for which it was written changed the very nature of the conversation. How we brought our bodies into our arguments changed—we were once again polite and deferential, informed yet restrained.

Our bodily discomfort while lobbying was prompted in part by the lobbying training we attended before the march. Concerns about how women's bodies occupy traditionally gendered political spaces animate many of the lobbying group's recommendations. Since they consider policy change the central mechanism for advancing a progressive legislative agenda, recommendations they give potential volunteers candidly address the fact that the Tennessee political arena is often not friendly or safe for bodies that aren't clearly white, traditionally conforming men. A handout distributed at our training, "Lobbying 101: Tips for Successful Advocacy," covers innocuous logistics (how to contact legislators to make an appointment, how long these meetings generally last, the value of following up with a thank-you letter containing the bill number, etc.) and the importance of researching one's representative (know where they stand on issues such as "women's healthcare, gun ownership, civil rights, religion, and school vouchers," whether they have children, whether they serve on the board of any organizations with similar missions, etc.). In discussing these recommendations with volunteers during their Lobbying 101 sessions, a form of discomfort training, organization leaders note that women can expect their bodies to be scrutinized in ways that may make them uncomfortable. For example, one volunteer reported how a legislator stared at her chest during her entire lobbying pitch; other seasoned lobbyists reported the same experience with different legislators. They recommend being prepared for such behavior and to ignore it when it inevitably happens.

Even as the organization's website invites participation by including empowering messages ("Lobbying is fun and anyone can do it") and references how this work enacts change ("Even if you meet with only one legislator, you can make a difference"), this recruitment tool reassures prospective volunteers that they will not be alone: "You'll always be with a more experienced buddy." Given the climate in the male-dominated Tennessee General Assembly in the 2010s, it is no wonder the group suggested lobbying in pairs. A legislator was expelled in 2016 after multiple allegations of sexual misconduct. Just the newspaper headlines from the time tell a troubling story about the political climate: "Jeremy Durham Expelled from Tennessee House in 70–2 vote" (Ebert and Boucher), "Married Politician Nicknamed 'Pants Candy' Harassed at Least 22 Women on Job" (Associated Press), "Tennessee Lawmaker Questions Motives of Female Accusers" (Mattise), and "Jeremy Durham Banished after AG probe Finds 'Inappropriate Physical Contact'" (Boucher and Ebert). Further, "A lobbyist told investigators he once closed the door to his office, made sexual comments and gave her a 'full frontal hug, squeezing her breasts into him and making a sound like 'mmmmmm'" (Associated Press).[3]

Clearly, within the capitol building, predatory practices are too often at play, and it is difficult not to read the lobbying advice as evidence of the lobbying group's acceptance of discomfort as part of advancing its progressive work. What discomfort should we accept to meet liberatory goals? We're left to wonder: How is it possible to advance social justice projects that benefit women when women's bodies continue to be objectified and/or excluded in the political arena? When must we stop and object to the ways our bodies are treated or read? To return to Noyes's *Dance of Freedom*: Should we celebrate when we realize our arms are unbound? Or is it folly when our legs continue to be constrained? The example of the lobbying organization (and the success of their predecessors such as the temperance women and the suffragists) leads us to a troubled realization: as women today, we would expect to have more freedom than Noyes and many of her contemporaries, and we do. But how much more? Our discomfort training requires us to move in spaces in which uninhibited expression may not be welcomed, in which we must increase somatic attention of self and consciously tuck embodied knowledge away so the performance for legislators can be seamless. This tension is the source of much of our own discomfort training.

CONCLUSION: DERIVING AN EVOLVING THEORY OF EMBODIMENT FROM THE ADVOCACY ARCHIVES

Both these archives, sites of discomfort for women across generations, produce embodied rhetorics. Perhaps this operationalization of discomfort training is most clear in the selection by these groups of embodied exemplars, women who are chosen to use their bodies to make an argument for the movement, to use their discomfort to forward an argument, to demonstrate embodied rhetoric. We argue that Noyes and her contemporary protesters, as well as modern-day women's marchers (including us), all use embodied rhetoric to make arguments—to use their (our) bodies as arguments—sometimes silencing discomfort to persuade. Yet the chosen exemplar is the curated selection of a body to stand in metonymically for a broader movement, to serve as the embodied rhetor for a cause. The *Suffrage Allegory* pageant cast is evidence of this tactic, as is the well-publicized choice of Inez Milholland, a New York attorney noted for her physical beauty, to lead the parade on horseback. Suffragists sought "to dispel the popular misconception that women who sought the vote were mannish in attire, strident, lacking in domestic accomplishments, and distinguished by particularly unattractive personalities" (Moore 92). The leaders of the NAWSA instead presented an image of the future woman voter as white, upper class, and educated but always beautiful and feminine; this effectively erased women's very real class and race differences.

Similarly, the lobbying group is purposeful in their selection of the exemplar who becomes the face and body of each new piece of legislation. The exemplar is a body that calls to mind Ahmed's notion of at once being both yes and no, subversive and sympathetic, beautiful and pathetic. Essentially, she is "willing to appear *with* so [she can] work *against*" (Ahmed 152).

For example, they selected a woman to use her body as an argument to help pass their recent legislation, a bill that decriminalized crimes associated with prostitution. The white woman who was asked and who agreed to participate was essentially asked to place her body in the public eye to represent impacts of sex work, to ignore embodied knowledge that might suggest that she turn away, to use her face to allow legislators to see sex workers as people. By agreeing to this representational role, this woman also had to take on the burden of increased speculation about her behavior, critiques of how effectively/not effectively she performs both "white woman" and "former sex worker."

We suggest there is value in inhabiting sites of discomfort, developing somatic attention to our discomfort, and choosing how to respond to this embodied knowledge. As Boler notes, our discomfort can serve as a form of "inquiry and invitation" (200). Though occupying such a position can be difficult, there is worth, too, in being the embodied exemplar, in making an argument with our presence, as we do in a dance performance, at a protest, or in a lobbying context; after all, "discomfort calls not only for inquiry but also, at critical junctures, for action—action hopefully catalyzed as a result of learning to bear witness" (179). Fleckenstein (chapter 8) describes this phenomenon as *bodying*, "encompassing the dynamic play of relationships by which any single body serves as a contingent expression of a tangle of corporeal relationships with other bodies." This important, sustaining work is an example of what Ahmed calls a "memory project": as we seek to reclaim and advocate for the aspects of our bodies and identities others wish we would forget, our collective efforts allow us and our bodies to "recover a will that has not been fully eliminated," to "remember what has not been fully erased" (140). This act of self-recovery offers hope, for "[w]illfulness can be a trace left behind, a reopening of what might have been closed down, a modification of what seems reachable, and a revitalization of the question of what it is to be for" (140). Even so, we understand that change is a process not unlike Noyes's freedom dance and that with each successive victory, we may well come to realize how constricted we (and others) remain. Thus collectives that remind us our discomfort is worth attending to and that we need not act alone in addressing it are crucial in helping us remember who we are and, together, who we can become.

JULIE, MEG, KATE: January 2019, Nashville, Tennessee. This year, there was no permit for a march because of the governor's inauguration. Many stayed home (and perhaps questioned the wisdom of marching). We talked about the controversies surrounding the national march and its organizers—concerns about intersectional representation, race, ideology, politics. But we still gathered to rally, directly in front of the capitol, showing up, temporarily emboldened by each other. We assembled, shivering in the rain, in the mud, a weathered group toting umbrellas we hesitated to raise, sensitive to obstructing others' views. We were well trained. We marveled once again at the boldness and creativity in others' signs. We listened, chanted, sang, and were changed. Someone from a progressive political organization handed us empty placards. We lifted our pens to finish the sentence: "I march because . . ."

NOTES

1. Education scholar Megan Boler introduces the concept of a pedagogy of discomfort, characterizing it as a process of learning to "see differently" (176) so we can understand the "complexity of ethical interrelations" (197). Boler asserts that "[t]he aim of discomfort is for each person . . . to explore beliefs and values; to examine when visual 'habits' and emotional selectivity have become rigid and immune to flexibility; and to identify when and how our habits harm ourselves and others" (186). Though our advocacy efforts further called our attention to restrictive beliefs and practices, our application of the term *discomfort* departs from Boler's in that our discomfort arose not from seeing but rather from the strategic choice to suppress our emotions in service of the causes we supported. At times, our advocacy work demanded we "inhabit a morally ambiguous self" in order to achieve our desired outcome of inclusion and equality (187).

2. This feels very contemporary in 2019 as state legislators are radically limiting women's choices regarding reproductive healthcare, including abortion.

3. With each consecutive revision of this article, we have had to add new details about the debauchery characterizing the Tennessee General Assembly. Most recently, in 2019, we learned that the legislator involved in the "Kerry Washington incident" Kate describes earlier was accused of sexual harassment. Also troubling is the revelation that the speaker of the house and his chief of staff sent each other "sexually explicit text messages about women" (Ebert and Allison).

WORKS CITED

"5,000 Women March Beset by Crowds." *New York Times,* 4 Mar. 1913, p. 5.

Ahmed, Sara. *Willful Subjects.* Duke UP, 2014.

Albright, Ann Cooper. "Mining the Dancefield: Feminist Theory and Contemporary Dance." *Choreographing Difference: The Body and Identity in Contemporary Dance.* Wesleyan UP, 1997.

Associated Press. "Married Politician Nicknamed 'Pants Candy Sexually Harassed at Least 22 Women on Job." *Daily News,* 14 July 2016, www.nydailynews.com/news/politics/pol -nicknamed-pants-candy-sexually-harassed-22-women-article-1.2711986. Accessed 23 June 2020.

Bain News Service. *Inauguration.* 4 Mar. 1913. Library of Congress Prints and Photographs Division, Washington, D.C. *Library of Congress,* www.loc.gov/item/2014691429/. Accessed 27 April 2020.

Barber, Lucy G. *Marching on Washington: The Forging of an American Political Tradition*. U of California P, 2002.

Boler, Megan. *Feeling Power: Emotions and Education*. New York: Routledge, 1999.

Boucher, Dave, and Joel Ebert. "Jeremy Durham Banished after AG Probe Finds 'Inappropriate Physical Contact.'" *The Tennessean*, 21 Sept. 2016.

Eddy, Martha. *Mindful Movement: The Evolution of the Somatic Arts and Conscious Action*. Intellect, 2017.

Butler, Judith. "Performative Acts and Gender Constitution: An Essay in Phenomenology and Feminist Theory." *Theatre Journal*, vol. 40, no. 4, 1988, pp. 519–531. *JSTOR*, doi: 10.2307/3207893.

"'Dance of Freedom' Symbolizes Suffrage Cause." 1914. Noyes School of Rhythm Foundation Archive, Portland, CT.

"Dances for Suffrage Pageant Are Being Rehearsed in New York." *New York Sun*, 24 Feb. 1913. Noyes School of Rhythm Foundation Archive, Portland, CT.

Ebert, Joel, and Natalie Allison. "Rep. Glen Casada, Cade Cothren Sent Sexually Explicit Text Messages about Women." *Tennessean*, 6 May 2019, www.tennessean.com/story /news/politics/2019/05/06/house-speaker-glen-casada-cade-cothren-sent-sexual-texts -women/1122490001/. Accessed 13 May 2019.

Ebert, Joel, and Dave Boucher. "Jeremy Durham Expelled from Tennessee House in 70–2 Vote." *Tennessean*, 13 Sept. 2016, www.tennessean.com/story/news/politics/2016/09 /13/house-prepares-jeremy-durham-expulsion-vote/90127546/. Accessed 7 Oct. 2017.

Foster, Susan. *Choreographing Empathy: Kinesthesia in Performance*. Routledge, 2011.

Knoblauch, A. Abby. "Bodies of Knowledge: Definitions, Delineations, and Implications of Embodied Writing in the Academy." *Composition Studies*, vol. 40, no. 2, 2012, pp. 50–65. *JSTOR*, www.jstor.org/stable/compstud.40.2.0050.

L & M Ottenheimer, Baltimore, Md. *Liberty and Her Attendants—(Suffragette's Tableau) in Front of Treasury Bldg. March 3, 1913—Washington, D.C.* 3 Mar. 1913, Records of the National Woman's Party, Washington, D.C. *Library of Congress*, www.loc.gov/item/mn wp000279/. Accessed 27 Apr. 2020.

Leet Brothers, Washington, DC. Crowd Converging on Marchers and Blocking Parade Route During March 3, Inaugural Suffrage Procession, Washington, D.C. 3 Mar. 1913, Records of the National Woman's Party, Washington, DC. *Library of Congress*, www.loc .gov/item/mnwp000443/. Accessed 27 Apr. 2020.

Madsen, Annelise K. "Columbia and Her Footsoldiers: Civic Art and the Demand for Change at the 1913 Suffrage Pageant-Procession." *Winterthur Portfolio*, vol. 48, no. 4, 2014, pp. 283–310. *JSTOR*, doi: 10.1086/679369.

Mattise, Jonathan. "Tennessee Lawmaker Questions Motives of Female Accusers." *Daily News*. 30 Mar. 2018.

Moore, Sarah J. "Making a Spectacle of Suffrage: The National Woman Suffrage Pageant, 1913." *Journal of American Culture*, vol. 20, no. 1, 1997, pp. 89–103.

"Real Beauty Show in League Pageant: Handsomest of Their Sex Chosen for Suffrage Allegorical Scene." *New York Times*, 18 Apr. 1914, p. 11.

"Roosevelt Centre of Suffrage Host." *New York Times*, 3 May 1913, p. 1.

"Suffrage Pageant a Near Riot." *Nashville Tennessean and the Nashville American (1910–1920)*, 4 Mar. 1913, p. 1. *ProQuest*, ezproxy.mtsu.edu/login?url=https://search.proquest.com /docview/905806068?accountid=4886.

"Suffragists to Wear Wool." *New York Times*, 7 Feb. 1913.

Terborg-Penn, Rosalyn. *African American Women in the Struggle for the Vote: 1850–1920*. Indiana UP, 1998.

"Will Take Part in Washington Pageant." *Daily State Gazette* [Trenton, NJ], Feb. 1913.

"Women of Many Organizations March." *New York Times*, 31 Oct. 1915, p. RP8.

8

FANNIE BARRIER WILLIAMS'S CITIZEN-WOMAN

Embodying Rhetoric at the 1893 World's Columbian Exposition

Kristie S. Fleckenstein (Florida State University)

Speaking at the World's Congress of Representative Women,[1] a week-long conference convened in 1893 as part of the World's Columbian Exposition,[2] Fannie Barrier Williams presented "some lines of progress" achieved by African American women in the three decades since emancipation (698). Concerned that "less is known of our women than of any other class of Americans," Williams sets out to share how African American women have struggled "to emancipate themselves from the demoralization of slavery" (697). As this Northern daughter of free-born parents describes the ways liberation has widened the purview of previously enslaved women to encompass moral growth, religious fervor, educational ambitions, and career hopes, she subtly delineates a vision of what she calls "the citizen-woman," one who, regardless of color, embraces, in a spirit of unity with fellow women, accountability to country, community, and companions (710). However, while her topic focuses on Black women—past, present, and future—her rhetorical goals focus on white women in that Williams implicitly argues for female coagency across color lines to secure collective progress for the female gender. In brief, she envisions not only a new Black citizen-woman but a new White citizen-woman, both of whom, as collaborative instruments of change, work together toward progressive ends. This was a daunting goal, one requiring Williams to transform minds and bodies, ranging from an array of Black women reckoning with the violence of the post-Reconstruction Jim Crow era to an equal array of white women facilitating or impeding the drive for a more equitable and racially just twentieth century. Thus, achieving her rhetorical ends required Williams to grapple with a constellation of bodies as a means to reconfigure all female bodies in service of the future. To forward her aims, she enacts an *embodying rhetoric,* one that juxtaposes actual bodies, marked

https://doi.org/10.7330/9781646422012.c008

by a range of "practices of living"—including habits, affective ecologies, corporeal stylistics, physiological traits, and action protocols—with aspirational bodies, such as the Black citizen-woman and, by implication, the white citizen-woman (Grosz 21).[3]

Defined as a mode of discourse enmeshed within and dependent on a complex tangle of bodies, embodying rhetoric honors the sinuous movement of bodies twisting in and out of any performance of rhetoric. In doing so, it fosters individual and mutual transformation by undermining the temptation to reduce "actual bodies to abstract conceptualizations of 'the body'" (Chávez 248). As Karma R. Chávez contends, replacing real bodies with the categorical body—coded white, and, generally, able-bodied male—"enforces and animates systemic oppressions" rather than resisting them (248). Williams's speech, considered "the most important" of more than three hundred papers delivered throughout the eighty-one sessions of the congress, seeks to actualize abstract bodies as a means to transform bodies, and she does this through an embodying rhetoric (Deegan xxix; Weimann 531). Complementing rather than displacing embodied rhetoric—one that often focuses on a discrete and bounded body, object, performance, or proposition—embodying rhetoric elicits transformation through *bodying*: a phenomenon encompassing the dynamic play of relationships by which any single body serves as a contingent expression of a tangle of corporeal relationships with other bodies. Moira Gatens emphasizes the processural nature of bodying, noting that a fleshy form "does not have a 'truth' or a 'true nature' since it is a process and its meaning and capacities will vary according to its context" (57). In addition, as Elizabeth Grosz points out, the bodying process consists of an ongoing transaction fusing materiality, or practices of living, and the idea(l), or the dynamic of relating. Finally, bodying extends that transactional process to incorporate not *the* or *a* body but multiple bodies. Bodying highlights that a titular body exists as an array of contingent connections among myriad bodies similarly constituted from conditional, vibrant connections. Gloria Anzaldúa acknowledges just such an array, contending that "'us' and 'them' is interchangeable," especially within a colonized subjectivity; as a result, she has "a White man . . . and a White woman in here [body-mind]" (qtd. in Lunsford 8). However, she continues, both the "White woman" and "White man" also have her "in their heads, even if it is just a guilty little nudge sometimes" (qtd. in Lunsford 8). Embodying rhetoric thus directs attention to the activity of body unities emerging as they cohere through different patterns, opening the door to changing those unities.

I begin my exploration of Williams's embodying rhetoric with the concept itself, attending particularly to the paradoxical monism of what Grosz calls the "material-idea(l)" as it incorporates multiple bodies. I then illustrate the confluence of different white and Black female bodies entangled in Williams's embodying rhetoric by examining the trope of the sexual savage, the material-idea(l) she evokes and then transforms into the citizen-woman. I identify and trace two strategies—animation and reanimation—guiding Williams's deconstruction and reconstruction of this material-idea(l). First, animation summons forth the sexual savage's materiality as a means to disinter and dismantle the idea(l), or the organizing principle by which the various qualities of the material—the practices of living—coalesce into a coherent pattern. Second, reanimation embodies a new material-idea(l)—the citizen-woman—reshaping the organizing principle construing the sexual-savage trope as a means to reshape oppressive and oppressed practices of living. Together, these strategies characterize Williams's embodying rhetoric and her efforts to reweave a web of bodies that can jointly work for the social good.

EMBODYING RHETORIC: A MATERIAL-IDEA(L) MONAD

Dominated by a present participle—simultaneously verb/process, noun/state of being, and adjective/modifier and limiter—embodying rhetoric attends to the dynamic of negotiating multiple porous bodies situated within overlapping temporal lines and physical spaces. By capitalizing on the fraught activity of becoming, being, and transforming, embodying rhetoric underscores the messy recursive corporeality characterizing Williams's advocacy of Black and white female collaboration at the Chicago Exposition, a world's fair sited within what was admiringly called the *White City*, a term constituting a racist description, a metaphor, and an agenda.[4] Thus, Williams existed as a Black female body invited to speak formally at an international event; at the same time, she existed as a member of the African American community systematically excluded from contributing either to planning the fair or to creating a display of African American progress (Ballard; Carby; Rydell; Weimann; Wells et al.). Furthermore, even as Williams stood as a self-identified Black woman, seemingly empowered to speak by the Board of Lady Managers, the committee of women with international control over women's representation at the fair, she also stood disempowered by that very group, which refused to seat an African American woman on their board (Weimann).[5] Included and excluded, empowered and disempowered by the exposition's white power brokers, Williams finally took her place on the dais as a professional freeborn Northern Black female body paradoxically speaking for herself and for Southern Black women who were born into slavery. So even as she is her own body, comprised of a set of practices of living unique to her, she is simultaneously a muddle of bodies, a composite of bits and pieces of different habits, corporeal stylistics, affective triggers, and action plans that connects Williams with other bodies in asymmetrical configurations. As a result, Williams's rhetorical presence, performance, and goals highlight the necessity and the value of embodying rhetoric, revealing the degree to which the struggle to give birth to the new citizen-woman relied on the fluid processes of bodying to change all female bodies—white and Black, past and present—entangled within that vision.

Embodying rhetoric as conceived in this chapter grounds itself in Grosz's ontoethics, "a way of thinking about not just how the world is but how it could be, how it is open to change, and, above all, the becomings it may undergo" (1). That ontoethics emerges from a deliberate effort to return the idea(l), or the incorporeal, to materiality, or the corporeal, without erecting a false dichotomy between the two phenomena separated only through the auspices of language. Drawing on the Stoics, Grosz defines materiality as active causes, a capacious category including "anything capable of action and influence" (24), of acting and being acted on, biological and nonbiological (25, 27). However, materiality is inextricable from ideality, the means by which materiality actualizes itself in one particular form rather than another. Referred to variously as "the incorporeal, sense, the immaterial, or the idea(l)," ideality consists of relationships—of pattern making—operating as both the connection between active causes and the organizational logic by which some patterns form rather than others (18). Ideality is, as Grosz describes, a predicate. She offers the example of *Cato walking* to illustrate ideality. Cato is an active cause, as is walking, for each is capable of action and influence. However, *Cato walking* consists of neither one nor the other or even a sum of the two. Rather, it consists of a relationship that cannot be reduced to either (38). That relationship is incorporeal, while the materialities—Cato and walking—are corporeal, only encompassing incorporeality when joined in a pattern. Furthermore, the idea(l) contributes more than linkages: it provides the logic, the organizing principle, guiding the union of active causes; thus, Cato walks, but Cato does not fly except, perhaps, in his dreams.

The transaction of materiality and ideality integral to bodies underscores the challenge facing Williams: changing the practices of living—a loosely bound category including habitus, bodily disciplines, affective constellations, physiology, and action protocols that secure particular social orders and distributions of power—requires changing the organizing principle by which practices of living cohere and gain salience. However, because ideality does not exist outside materiality, subsisting instead within qualities and practices as potential relatings, changing ideality requires changing practices of living. Both practices and patterns must be transformed simultaneously, pointing to the need for embodying rhetoric. Grosz makes clear the mutual dependence of the material-idea(l)'s "nonreductive monism" (249).

Grosz describes the dance of materiality and ideality as "the subsistence of the ideal in the material" or the "immanence of the ideal in the material and the material in ideality" (5). While "today just about everyone is a materialist," Grosz avers, and while not everyone embraces the same approach to materialism, most conceive of a materialism that negates the "idea(l)" or subsumes the idea(l) into its account of materialism, becoming a product of material forces (Marx), of biological forces in conjunction with environmental contingency (Darwin), or of corporeal forces clashing inter- and intrapersonally (Nietzsche) (15). However, Grosz pursues a different agenda. Her approach concerns itself with neither materialism nor ideality as separate fields but with materialisms that transform "to accommodate a fringe or force of the ideal inevitably surrounding and infiltrating even composing matter" (18). Such an agenda eschews any "binarization" between matter and ideal, emphasizing instead the necessary affinity of material and idea(l) (18). Thus, Grosz places material and idea(l) in a "paradoxical dualist monism" of cocreation, emphasizing the dynamism as well as the contingency of the material-idea(l) (249). Such dynamism is the key to transformation in Williams's speech.

Embodying rhetoric's transformative potential arises out of ontoethics' ongoing transaction within any material-idea(l) body, a dynamic traceable in Williams's presentation to her international audience. From the perspective of Grosz's ontoethics, a body is neither material nor idea(l); it is an event, an active merging, emerging, and reemerging that opens up options for transformative change (2). By extension, then, an embodying rhetoric is also an event, enacting and revealing the constant dance of materiality and ideality. Within this pas de deux, the singular *body*—the Fannie Barrier Williams body, the body formerly enslaved now freed, and the white female body sitting on the Board of Lady Managers—is a contingent placeholder for the myriad bodies at play in each singularity, a placeholder with significant sociopolitical implications.

Embodying rhetoric emphasizes not only what is actualized—the enmeshed bodies with their varying positionalities—but also the actualizing itself, highlighting the continuous negotiations of multiple, many times competing, practices of living, organizing principles, and constraints. More specifically, for Williams, the exigencies of her effort to midwife the new Black citizen-woman—the African American woman as social activist—require her to engage at the same time in an embodying rhetoric that midwifes the new white citizen-woman: a civically engaged white woman who, unlike the Lady Board of Managers, clubwomen, temperance activists, suffragists, and other progressives, works integrated with rather than segregated from her African American sisters. The new white citizen-woman systematically includes rather than excludes the Black citizen-woman, a radical transformation of the late nineteenth-century status quo (see Bordin; Gere; Terborg-Penn). In aid of this goal, Williams's performance at the World Congress of Representative Women harnesses two key strategies—animation and reanimation—to transform one material-idea(l) body—that of the sexual savage—into a different material-idea(l) body—that of the new citizen-woman—as a means of recalibrating one set of the relationships between white and Black female bodies and the patterned practices of living they enact.

ANIMATING THE SEXUAL SAVAGE'S MATERIAL-IDEA(L)

The nonlinear corporeality of embodying rhetoric is readily evident in the different material-idea(l) bodies connecting, contesting, and reconnecting in Williams's speech. As this clubwoman, social reformer, and ardent Christian stood before the audience crowding the Hall of Columbus at the Memorial Art Palace on the evening of May 18, she recognized the complex confluence of bodies in that moment: the past bodies of Southern Black women, who, trapped in the "mean vocabulary of slavery" had "no definition of any of the virtues of life" (Williams 697); the past and present bodies of the African American women of the North, who, like herself, "were free from the vicious influence of slavery" (702); the bodies of white women, past and present, including the "saintly women of the white race" who dedicated themselves to teaching those newly freed from bondage (697), and the less saintly white women "responsible for the wrongs we suffer" (710). All existed within her mind as well as her speech. Attending to Black women's progress as a means to birth the new Black citizen-woman, as well as her companion the new white citizen-woman, thus required Williams to perform an embodying rhetoric that would establish relationships among the multiple material-idea(1)s forming and re-forming that evening. More particularly, Williams takes the first step toward the new citizen-woman by animating the trope of the "sexual savage," a product of slavery's "long-enforced degradation," a particularly trenchant material-idea(1) body obstructing opportunities for joint activism across color lines (697).

A crucial move in Williams's embodying rhetoric consisted of the need to recognize and defuse the white manufactured threat of the sexual savage, a material-idea(1) within which both Black and white bodies converged in a complicated relationship of negation: the body of the Black female sexual savage, mythologized by the white patriarchal culture, was everything the body of the white cultured female, equally mythologized by white patriarchy, was not. The affiliations, practices of living, and power of each material-idea(1) are diametrically opposed in the dynamic of antithesis, presenting a substantial obstacle to Williams's goal of cross-racial collaboration. Williams acknowledges the danger posed by the sexual savage material-idea(1) to the progress of African American women and the unity of all woman, noting that "the morality of our home life has been commented upon so disparagingly and meanly that we are placed in the unfortunate position of being defenders of our name" (702). Her allusion to white critics, female and male, who excoriate all Black women on the basis of a material-idea(1) that serves white interests at the same time it circumscribes racial uplift, attests to the mix of white male and female bodies hindering the rise of the new citizen-woman, Black and white. Thus, to bring to fruition her vision of shared progressive agency, Williams had to redeem the maligned body along with the promiscuous and immoral lifestyle ascribed to it, a process that sets the stage for transmuting all bodies—white and Black, past and present—entangled within that of the sexual savage. By actualizing—bringing to life—a particular material-idea(1) body, animation, first, illuminates the multiple bodies—white and Black—implicated in the practices of living that punctuate the existence of the sexual savage; and second, animation exposes the flawed ideality, or the relationships—the organizational logic—that compose materiality in particular ways that serve some agendas and not others. Within the scope of embodying rhetoric, then, animation forwards transformation by disentangling the bodies latent in this demeaning material-idea(1).

To call into question the entrenched white myth of the sexual savage, Williams brings to life the materiality ascribed to this debased figure in the white cultural imaginary. She begins by addressing the quality of savagery white critics, especially white female critics, assign to the Black female body. That barbarism, she implies, results from a body perceived as bereft of a rational mind, one capable of learning and thus of acquiring culture. Without the capacity to learn, such a body can only be uncivilized, its actions driven by unrestrained desires. Williams gestures to this demeaning trait assigned to enslaved African American women for whom, seemingly, "the blue-black speller, the arithmetic, and the copy-book contain[ed] no magical cures for inherited inaptitudes" (697). She provides metonymic evidence of the impact of such supposedly "inherited inaptitudes" through the practices of living enacted by the sixty-nine African men, women, and children inhabiting the Dahomey Village, a tourist site and sight on the Midway Plaisance, the exposition's almost mile-long amusement park (697). Resonating with what Meg Brooker, Julie Myatt, and Kate Pantelides call *sites of discomfort*, or "physical spaces in which bodily affect is influenced by architecture, history, and unspoken codes of conduct and norms of dress" (chapter 7), the Dahomey Village made manifest in material terms the tropic savagery of the Black female body that inhabited the white mind and haunted the Black mind.

Sponsored by the fair's Department of Ethnology, the Dahomey Village and its inhabitants functioned as a "living display," ostensibly replicating the traditional huts, tools, dress, and tribal rituals of the peoples of West Africa, the ancestral land of many African Americans (Ballard 31). Even though never directly referenced in Williams's speech, the Dahomey Village insinuates itself into that discourse—nested within the white and Black bodies filing into the Hall of Columbus—supplying details of life lived in a supposedly mindless body, the source of the enslaved Black women's inherent and irredeemable savagery. Hazel Carby argues as much, contending that the physical distance between the Dahomey encampment and Williams's presentation was specious at best; instead, Williams's part in the Congress of Representative Women served merely as an extension of the Dahomeans, of the "discourse of exoticism that pervaded the fair" (5). She, too, was a living display, the savage body entangled within her own, constituting what Julie D. Nelson identifies as a museum exhibit that expresses the "immediate, everyday impact of racism" (chapter 5). Frederick Douglass concurs. Condemning the immensely popular Midway, Douglass points out that the "Dahomians [*sic*] are also here to exhibit the Negro as a repulsive savage" and thereby "shame the Negro," suggesting the ways those bodies are always present, troubling Williams's embodying rhetoric (13).

Implicitly evoking the Dahomeans in her speech, Williams entangles her body with that of the vilified West Africans by exposing tenacious white illusions of the untutored—and untutorable—Black body. For instance, she notes that, supposedly cursed by a "heredity that bound them [enslaved Black women] to the lowest social level" (703), these "non-progressive peasants of the 'black-belt' of the South" (705)—these bodies of the past—were forced into a life construed by white stakeholders as unclean and chaotic, filled with "dross coarseness," subjected only to sullied "affections" and lost to a "proper sense of all the sanctities of human intercourse" (704). But those bodies of the past did not remain in the past. In the guise of the Dahomey Village, they tethered themselves to Williams even as she sought to unknot the bindings. The West African villagers, brought to the Exposition specifically to embody Black savagery, thus provided performances of practices of living meant to make manifest a life governed by coarseness and impropriety, an interpretation promulgated by the dominant white culture. Such practices included the Dahomean dress, food preparation, music, and dancing, described by the white fairgoers in shivering delight as uncivilized, unhygienic, discordant, and frenzied. Thus, the villagers—"barbarians and cannibals, the most savage of all the conquered peoples at the exposition"—reified by analogy white beliefs about enslaved Black females of the past and the current Black-belt African Americans suffering under late nineteenth-century peonage (Ballard 31). They too, and Williams as their spokesperson, are similarly savage. As one white female journalist sensationalized, the Dahomey Village—analogous to Williams in the Hall of Columbus—formed the boundary "Where Savage and Barbarian Mingle with Their More Enlightened Fellows," a boundary separating uncivilized from civilized on the basis of the capacity (or incapacity) to learn (Shaw 56). By subtly spotlighting the tenacity and currency of the white version of the savage body, Williams's embodying rhetoric highlights the presence of that body not only in Williams but also, and more important, within the white female bodies populating her audience, an alleged savagery that expressed itself in the practice of sexual profligacy.

Adding to the savage essence of the dominant white version of the Black female body, Williams uses embodying rhetoric to materialize the quality of unrestrained sexuality. In radical juxtaposition to the mythologized refined white female body, the white cultural narrative depicts the Black savage as irredeemably promiscuous. Thus, African American women, like Williams, are perceived as inherently licentious because they are perceived as inherently savage. Williams directly grapples with this skewed logic. Based on a white historical record, she says, enslaved Black women were understood to be incapable of learning "such precious terms as marriage, wife, family, and home" (697); thus, cultural stereotypes represented them as defaulting to arcane practices, "witch-craft, sensual fetishes, and the coarse superstitions of savagery" (698), in the service of sexual gratification. The obduracy of those stereotypes haunted post-Emancipation Black women. Supposedly betrayed by their roots in (West) Africa—in the Dahomey Village—African American women were configured by white culture as possessing an inbred sexual depravity so wanton it appeared to be a manifestation of "evil and magic" (Carby 26). As Williams points out, the white-constructed "slave code" only recognized "animal distinctions between the sexes," resulting in an almost "complete extinction of all the moral instincts" in Black women, thereby reducing them, in the white imaginary, to pawns of their own irresistible carnality (703). Such is the convenient logic used by white men to justify their sexual abuse of Black women and by white women to excuse their men for such abuse (Carby 26).

By pointing to the "vile imputations of a diseased public opinion," Williams animates the practices of living ascribed to the sexual savage by white female critics and animates the white female critics' need for the sexual savage. The bodies are locked together, a degraded Black material-idea(l) necessary for an ennobled white body. For example, Marian Shaw, a white journalist, recounts the mindless pleasures of the Midway in the chapter "On the Midway" of her book *World's Fair Notes* and in so doing instates her own superiority. While remaining only "a short time" with the Dahomey Village, she still concludes that the music produced by the Dahomeans is quite "nerve-wracking" and "the fetish Amazonia [*sic*] war dance leaves us little choice between this and the other barbarous so-called dances" (59). The activities of the Dahomey Villagers as depicted in guidebooks also manifest a similar intertwining of bodies: to reify their own virtuous bodies, white culture required the sexual savagery and availability of the Black woman's body, whether that body be on the Midway or on a dais in the Memorial Art Palace. Exposition guidebooks promulgated this idea and reinforced white female chastity. The guidebooks warned (and titillated) young white ladies and men with their descriptions of the dangers of the Dahomean women dancing, a sight so salacious, they were told, it will "deprive you of a peaceful night's rest for months to come" (qtd. in Sund 457). As a result, pure white wives and sweethearts were urged to keep their signifi-cant others away from the displays or risk their loved ones succumbing to improper behavior inspired by the sexual wantonness of the West African women (457). Pertinent to Williams's embodying rhetoric, then, and the entanglement of bodies is the degree to which the intensity of the white commitment to the Black female body as savage and sexual signals the intensity with which the two bodies were intertwined in a knot of subjectivity: the sexual savage in the white mind, the vituperative white critic in the Black mind. Bodies collide in a pattern of negation, signaling the need to transform white and Black bodies as a means to secure joint social action.

Through animation, Williams actualized the materiality of the sexual savage *and* of the stakeholders in that construct, implicitly weaving a pattern out of past African American female bodies, absent-present Dahomean bodies, and white female bodies. However, materiality is only part of the strategy of animation; dismantling the sexual savage as a prelude to transformation also includes addressing the ideality by which materiality becomes pattern. As Grosz argues, materiality is shaped through relationships that are themselves incorporeal. So, while the first step in animation involves evoking the corporeality of the sexual savage, an evocation that reveals the tangle of bodies, Black and white, tightly joined within it, the necessary second step involves exposing the ideality, the logic, structuring corporeality. Williams uses embodying rhetoric to take this next step. Via animation, she unearths the logic invigorating the sexual savage—the imputation that such savagery is a product of inheritance—to illuminate the flaws in this logic, arguing that environment rather than nature shaped the enslaved Black female body. And, because environments can be changed, so too can the material-idea(l) constituting both Black and white bodies.

While Williams readily admits that past associations promulgated by white patriarchal culture between promiscuity and Black female identity have plagued African American women, such associations ensue not from heredity, as imputed by whites, but from the environmental exigencies imposed by slavery itself (697). The proof of such an assertion, and thus a refutation of the logic of inheritance organizing the materiality of the sexual savage, is found in the life of Black women postemancipation. When released from "the mean cabin life of their bondage," African American women promptly laid claim "to all that there is in human excellence," Williams insists (697). In the face of this pursuit of excellence, witchcraft and sensuality yielded to the "blessedness of intelligent womanhood," demonstrating that any isolated evidence of sexual savagery stemmed not from blood but from environment (697). Furthermore, Williams points out, these "children of darkness" made strides in "their new life of freedom" without the direction or support of "a guide, a teacher, or a friend" (697). In essence, they disinterred themselves from the system of slavery responsible for "every moral imperfection that mars the character of the colored American" (703). A mindless savage could not have effected such a significant change in practices of living; therefore, the Black body is neither savage nor sexual.

Dismantling the logic of inheritance by which the white dominant culture organizes the materiality of the sexual savage enables Williams to undermine not only the ideality shaping the Black female body but also the ideality shaping the white female body. Without the crutch of inheritance, white women can no longer cling to the sexual savage as a negative expression of their own positive white feminine identity. Breaking the pattern of one means breaking the pattern of both, for, as embodying rhetoric emphasizes, the two material-idea(l)s—sexual savage and cultured white female—exist coupled together, inhabiting the same mind. Thus, through animation, Williams sets the stage for reanimation, the second strategy of her embodying rhetoric, by which she transforms the material-idea(l)s of the Black female body and the white female body into a different material-idea(l): the new citizen-woman.

REANIMATING THE NEW CITIZEN-WOMAN MATERIAL-IDEA(L)

As Williams narrates the intellectual progress of African American women in the thirty years since emancipation, she does so not only to celebrate such progress but also to advocate for thirty years of additional progress. Or, perhaps more accurately, she advocates for continued gender uplift through the joint efforts of white and Black women working together and apart as equals. To secure a seat at this particular activist table, however, Williams needed to do more than just expose the flawed logic structuring the sexual savage, more than laud the evolution of those formerly enslaved in the Southern Black belt into a force for human excellence. Instead, to gain the sanction of resistant white women, she needed embodying rhetoric to reanimate—transform—the material-idea(l) of the Black female body and the white female body woven with it. Williams does this by evoking a vision of the new citizen-woman who, both Black and white, arises out of a shared organizational principle—that of good character—that inspirits collaborative activist reform. In brief, the new citizen-woman, whether Black or white, lives according to the dictates of good character and acts on those dictates to seek the well-being of democracy on local and national levels for everyone, regardless of race or class. The white woman in the Black body—Anzaldúa's "White woman in here"—would then act not through a pattern of "vile imputations" but through one of affirmation. Analogously, the Black body in the white female mind would operate not through a pattern of alienation but through one of camaraderie.

Embodying rhetoric works to change both bodies, and reanimation initiates that transformation with the ideality of the new citizen-woman's good character.

Reanimation in Williams's embodying rhetoric unfolds by attending to the principle by which the new citizen-woman material-idea(l) coheres: the ideality of character, or a set of habits, ethical attitudes, and virtues that structures both African American and white women's bodies. As Grosz notes, bodies encompass not just flesh but also qualities such as truthfulness, empathy, courage, patriotism, spirituality, and sexual reticence, all elements of character that direct an individual's actions, or "what they cause in themselves" (28). In her May 18 speech, Williams emphasizes repeatedly the formative power of good character in the lives of African American women, noting that "force of character" provided the impetus "enabl[ing] them to escape the slavery taints of immorality" (702–703). It was strength of character, rather than direct guidance or the pressure of societal expectation, that motivated these "trustful and zealous students of freedom" to strive through their own efforts to become that new citizen-woman, joining with her sisters in "the constant striving for equality" (697). In addition, these Black women could undertake such self-improvement on their own because they already possessed the necessary character—the "native gentleness, good cheer, and hopefulness"—crucial for nurturing righteousness (704). In sum, Williams shares, it is the "longing to be something better than they were when freedom found them" that has been "the most notable characteristic in the development of these women" (697). Two particular virtues acquired by African American women—purity and piety, qualities prized by the late Victorian white community and promulgated by the Board of Lady Managers (Sund 444)—reflect the power of good character to transform rather than disavow white or Black bodies, for, as Anzaldúa reveals, "they are all in me" (qtd. in Lunsford 8).

To begin, reanimation in Williams's embodying rhetoric brings into view the force of purity as an organizing principle, signaling the entanglement of white bodies and Black bodies in a virtue prized by Eurocentric, white, middle-class, patriarchal culture. As Williams claims, with the cessation of slavery and escape from the moral vacuum of forced sexual contact, African American women immediately enacted a life marked by its moral purity: "[T]he recuperative power of these women to regain their moral instincts and to establish a respectable relationship to American womanhood is among the earlier evidences of their moral ability to rise above their conditions" (703). Thus, Black women, excoriated by white culture as bereft of clean hearts and bodies, in fact developed chasteness by sheer dint of character, Williams points out: "[E]verywhere there is witnessed a feverish anxiety to be free from the mean suspicions that have so long underestimated the character strength of our women" (704). They consciously and conscientiously obtained knowledge of chastity on their own and enacted that virtue in their lives, suggesting such integrity resided in their bones. Furthermore, these standards of moral rectitude and personal worth not only shaped the pattern constituting the idea(l) of African American women but also effected changes in the idea(l) of African American men. Inspired by the pure bodies of African American women, African American men gained a "chivalric sentiment and regard" that provided the virtuous African American women with "a new sense of protection" (703). By implication, such purity of heart transforms white female bodies even as it transforms Black male bodies, moving white women, like Black men, from threat to helpmeet. Williams then forwards her embodying rhetoric by reanimating the character trait of piety, further aligning the ideality of the Black and white new citizen-woman.

Williams's strategy of reanimation in her embodying rhetoric complements the purity of Black female bodies with piety, a quality important to the good character of respectable, middle-class white women. In the process, it reconfigures the white female body in the Black mind as a mentor rather than a critic, just as the Black body in the white female mind changes from danger to collaborator. To illustrate, Williams details the African American woman's adherence to Christian teachings. Not only is the African American woman's body wholesome and untainted, but it is also pious, an avatar of Christian precepts and values. "In their religious life . . . our women show a progressiveness parallel in every important particular to that of white women in all Christian churches," Williams attests (698). Disputing white perceptions of the African American woman as a devotee of carnality, Williams recrafts her as a soul longing for Christianity, guided by a heart "singularly tender, sympathetic, and fit for the reception of its doctrines" (704). In addition, piety among African Americans evinces behaviors warranted by the new citizen-woman, especially those that safeguard the well-being of her community. Thus, as a result of their Christian devotion, these pious Black women perform their beliefs by "clean[ing]" their religious houses, as well as their own family homes, reestablishing godliness in parishioners and ministers (698–699). Working individually and collectively, devout African American women have done much "to elevate the tone of worship and to magnify all that there is blessed in religion," rendering safe not only the bodies of women but also the body of the church (699). Finally, the most vivid sign of the piety of African American women, and the most vivid sign of their ability to unify across color lines to achieve shared progress, stems from their renunciation of race hatred. Williams emphasizes this aspect of Black benevolence in the new citizen-woman. "The hearts of Afro-American women are too warm and too large for race hatred" (701), she says, for the righteous women of color have no thought of revenge despite two hundred years of mistreatment (698). Instead, possessing in abundance "those gracious qualities of heart that characterize women of the best type," African American women live guided by the principles of virtue and devoutness treasured by the women of the dominant white community, embodying themselves through the very organizing principle espoused and supposedly embodied by their white sisters (702).

Through reanimation—the strategy in embodying rhetoric that forwards transformation of a material-idea(l)—Williams's speech configures character as the organizational logic by which Black and white female bodies can find hospitable spaces within mind and world to dwell peaceably. But, in the spirit of Burkean identification, Williams's embodying rhetoric also extends that ideality into materiality, or the practices of living that actualize ideality in the corporeal form of the new citizen-woman, a figure neither solely white nor Black but encompassing both as she dedicates herself to the service of country, community, and gender. The first such practice constituting the life of the new citizen-woman consists of patriotic acts. Williams repeatedly celebrates the action protocols and affective investments reflected in African American dedication to the United States as a nation, a way of living that embraces all Americans and mirrors the exposition's theme. African American women, she says, are as "thoroughly American in all the circumstances of citizenship as the best citizens of our country" (706), partaking of the same patriotic fervor as their white counterparts. Indeed, the race of African American women has "never faltered in its support of the country's flag" (708). Even more, Williams singles out African American women as "daughters of men who have always been true as steel against treason," reminding her audience of the blood spilled by African Americans to protect the nation throughout its—and their—history. "We are so essentially American in speech, in instincts, in sentiments and destiny that the things that interest you equally interest us," Williams affirms, thereby attesting to the ingrained practices of living the white and Black citizen-women jointly enact (708). As a result, white and Black women share country, interests, and "a destiny that will certainly bring us closer to each other" (710). But the materiality of the citizen-woman extends beyond patriotism to encompass specific reform agendas that benefit individual communities, entangling white and Black bodies—those in the mind and those in the world—through a spirit of affirmation.

"The contentions of colored women are in kind like those of other American women for greater freedom of development," Williams points out, a goal that directly connects new citizen-women across color lines in the unified pursuit of progressive goals (708). Such compatible causes involved the pursuit of education, the road to economic uplift for African American women, one already well traveled by white female activists. Thus, it is a road on which the two races as new citizen-women can walk together. "For thirty years education has been the magic word among the colored people of this country," Williams emphasizes, under-scoring the "greedy" desire since emancipation for "mental uplifting of a whole race of people" (699). Like the dominant white race, African American men and women demand the best education possible so they can take their place as "eager students of intelligent citizenship" (700). The desire for education as a democratic duty is matched by the acquisition of that education, evident in the intellectual development of African Americans, which, given their starting point in the forced illit-eracy of slavery, "has been a little less than phenomenal" (699). Thus, the need to secure education for African American men and women aligns with like needs addressed by white citizen-women for members of their own cohort, a need that would enable African American women to enact the new citizen-woman material-idea(l) with their white sisters within the local contexts unique to each. However, Williams concedes, education will take the new citizen-woman, whether white or Black, only so far. What is also necessary for the flourishing of women regardless of race, class, or geography is professionalization, a further practice of linking the bodies of new citizen-women and highlighting their ability to work toward reform regardless of race.

Ultimately, the goal of reanimating the material-idea(l) of the new citizen-woman through an embodying rhetoric highlights the limits, as well as the power, of identification. For that goal consists of the desire to work together as equals, similar to but also different from each other. By altering the tangle of bodies through embodying rhetoric, new citizen-women are partners, fortified in rather than divided by their dif-ferences. Williams illustrates the vision of a civil and civic collaboration that honors rather than despises or erases difference by pointing to the specific reform goal of professionalization. The new citizen-women share a commitment to education as central to gender uplift, Williams argues, because it opens up opportunities for employment suitable to a woman's talents, training, and aspirations. African American and white women all seek to increase women's employment prospects, mentorship, and pay to a level equal to that of their (White) male counterparts. But it is also a goal that emphasizes the disparities in the realities of Black and white women. Williams articulates this crucial variance, claiming that "this question of employment for the trained talents of our women is a most serious one" because "employment of colored women bears a distressing burden of mean and unreasonable discrimination" (705). Whereas white women only contend with gender discrimination, African American women bear the intersectional burden of gender and race discrimination. Thus, while the aim for professionalization remains a bridge between the new white and Black citizen-women, it illuminates rather than elides the diverse obstacles facing women on opposite sides of the bridge; the realization of these significant dissimilarities thus requires the new citizen-women to seek solutions together without erasing differences. It is only through a partnership forged in equality, not identification alone, that the new citizen-women will be able to reinstate the rule of fair play so central to the ethos of the nation, Williams claims (707).

The ideality of good character infuses practices of living to con-figure the material-idea(l) of the new citizen-woman as one who can work with her sisters for the betterment of all. It is through the "spirit of organization," of creating change together, that change can best be accomplished for womanhood, not just white or Black women, Williams contends (701). "The highest ascendancy of woman's development has been reached when they have become mentally strong enough to find bonds of association interwoven with sympathy, loyalty, and mutual trustfulness. To-day union is the watchword of woman's onward march," she continues (701). The fledgling new Black citizen-woman—who three decades earlier emerged from slavery with "no sentiments of association"—now finds within herself a provident rather than adver-sarial white female body; thus, she has "begun to recognize the blessed significance" of uniting "in work for a common destiny" (701). Similarly, Williams implies—and hopes—the emergence of the new white citizen-woman, who finds within herself a Black female body blessed with grace and an educated mind, will likewise embrace unity as a means of bring-ing their common destiny to fruition.

CONCLUSION

"Liberty to be all that we can be, without artificial hindrances, is a thing no less precious to us than to women generally," Williams asserts (709).

Securing that liberty requires remaking Black and white bodies into new citizen-women who can work together to achieve common goals while honoring the differences of each. Williams lays out the means of doing exactly that through her embodying rhetoric, with its twin strategies of animation and reanimation. Thus, this examination of Williams's speech on the intellectual progress of postemancipation Black women highlights the importance of embodying rhetoric, especially for marginalized peoples held hostage by a phenotype used to legitimate social and economic injustice.

First, by underscoring bodies as webs of contingent connections immersed within webs of similarly constituted bodies, embodying rhetoric dispels the polite myth of a single or singular body. From the perspective of embodying rhetoric, bodies are palimpsestic, changing as past, present, and future bodies bleed in, out, and through, turning attention to all the myriad biological and nonbiological active causes invested in bodying. Williams's speech illustrates exactly this, for the material-idea(l)s of the sexual savage and the new citizen-woman both consist of fragmented, cobbled together, and frequently fraught combinations of bodies and organizing principles that reinforce each other. Second, embodying rhetoric with its palimpsestic material-idea(l) highlights the importance of the ethic of accountability, of responsibility for all the myriad bodies entangled within any body. Because of multiple connections, bodies are answerable to bodies—rejected, repressed, or embraced—for such bodies constitute the realities surrounding and saturating us. That ethic of accountability circulates throughout Williams's speech, both in the rescue of the tropic sexual savage and in the practices of living characterizing the unified activism of the new citizen-woman. The progressive reforms she pursues reflect her sense of accountability within her racial cohort and, just as important, across color lines. Finally, because embodying rhetoric emphasizes the material-idea(l) as a conditional pattern—privileging neither the actual nor the abstract incorporeal relationships from which the actual is formed—it opens up spaces for change. Williams's vision of the new citizen-woman capitalizes on exactly this transformative quality of embodying rhetoric. Born out of the dark days of slavery, a darkness created by white ideality and materiality, the new citizen-woman embraces new duties to and new opportunities for gender and racial uplift. But such a transmutation involves not merely the Black female body but also the white female body so tightly intertwined with it. A volatile composite of materialism and ideality, the new citizen-woman taking shape at the Chicago Exposition in the Memorial Art Palace exists as and through a muddle of Black and white female bodies that must all take on new patterns to effect change. Anzaldúa warns that "nothing happens in the 'real' world unless it first happens in the images in our heads" (87). Williams might add that nothing happens in the "real" world until we change the *bodies* in our heads and worlds. Embodying rhetoric provides a means to do both.

NOTES

1. Envisioned, organized, and sponsored by the Woman's Branch of the World's Congress Auxiliary, an arm of the Board of Lady Managers responsible for celebrating "all lines of thought connected with the progress of women" (Palmer qtd. in Weimann 529), the World Congress of Representative Women constituted a major contribution to the congresses featured throughout the Columbian Exposition, all of which served to "add intellectual flavor to the circus atmosphere of the fair" (546).

2. After more than eight years of planning, politicking, and production (Appelbaum 1), the World's Columbian Exposition drew to Chicago, its host city, an estimated 27 million paying participants, including approximately one-tenth of the US population (Hales x).

3. Other bodies are at play in Williams's embodying rhetoric, including white and Black male bodies, both of which she alludes to in her speech. In addition, hovering over this account is the researcher's own body, an integral component of any account of embodying rhetoric (see Chávez). However, explicit discussion of those bodies remains outside the parameters of this chapter.

4. As a description, *White City* referred to the white stucco façade that graced the surfaces of the fair's main buildings, a deliberate decision designed to communicate a sense of "serene whiteness" (Appelbaum 5). As a metaphor, *White City* fixed attention on white presence, erasing bodies of color from public perception. Beyond a few clerical positions, most African Americans were employed as laborers, porters, or janitors, and those positions were scarce (Weimann 123). As an agenda, *White City* celebrated not human progress but white progress, refusing any acknowledgment of African American contributions (see Wells et al.).

5. After considerable rhetorical work on her part, Williams briefly served in an unpaid clerical role on the Board of Lady Managers before even that position was eliminated (Weimann).

WORKS CITED

Anzaldúa, Gloria. *Borderlands/La Frontera: The New Mestiza.* Aunt Lute, 1987.

Appelbaum, Stanley. *The Chicago World's Fair of 1893: A Photographic Record.* Dover, 1980.

Ballard, Barbara J. "A People without a Nation." *Chicago History,* vol. 28, no. 1, 1999, pp. 27–43. *Living History of Illinois,* livinghistoryofillinois.com/pdf_files/African%20Americans%20at%20the%201893%20Worlds%20Columbian%20Exposition,%20A%20People%20Without%20a%20Nation.pdf. Accessed 27 June 2020.

Bordin, Ruth. *Woman and Temperance: The Quest for Power and Liberty, 1879–1900.* Rutgers UP, 1990.

Carby, Hazel. *Reconstructing Womanhood: The Emergence of the Afro-American Woman Novelist.* Oxford UP, 1987.

Chávez, Karma R. "The Body: An Abstract and Actual Rhetorical Concept." *Keywords: A Glossary of the Pasts and Futures of the Rhetoric Society of America.* Spec. issue of *Rhetoric Society Quarterly*, vol. 48, no. 3, 2018, pp. 242–50. *Taylor & Francis*, doi:10.1080/0277394 5.2018.1454182.

Deegan, Mary Jo. "Fannie Williams and Her Life as a New Woman of Color in Chicago, 1893–1918." *The New Woman of Color: The Collected Writings of Fannie Williams, 1893–1918*, edited by Mary Jo Deegan, Northern Illinois UP, 2002, pp. xiii–lx.

Douglass, Frederick. Introduction. *The Reason Why the Colored American Is Not in the World's Columbian Exposition: The Afro-American's Contribution to Columbian Literature* by Ida B. Wells, Frederick Douglass, Irvine Garland Penn, and Ferdinand L. Barnett. Edited by Robert W. Rydell, U of Illinois P, 1999, pp. 7–16.

Gatens, Moira. *Imaginary Bodies: Ethics, Power and Corporeality.* Routledge, 1996.

Gere, Anne Ruggles. *Intimate Practices: Literacy and Cultural Work in U. S. Women's Clubs, 1880–1920.* U of Illinois P, 1997.

Grosz, Elizabeth. *The Incorporeal: Ontology, Ethics, and the Limits of Materialism.* Columbia UP, 2017. *JSTOR*, www.jstor.org/stable/10.7312/gros18162.6.

Hales, Peter Bacon. "Photography, Architecture, Civilization and the Spectacle of the White City." Introduction. *Spectacle in the White City: The Chicago 1893 World's Fair*, by Stanley Appelbaum, Calla Editions, 2009, pp. ix-xx.

Lunsford, Andrea A. "Toward a Mestiza Rhetoric: Gloria Anzaldúa on Composition and Postcoloniality." *Exploring Borderlands: Postcolonial and Composition Studies.* Spec. issue of *JAC*, vol. 18, no. 1, 1998, pp. 1–27. *JSTOR*, www.jstor.org/stable/20866168.

Rydell, Robert W. Editor's Introduction. *The Reason Why the Colored American Is Not in the World's Columbian Exposition: The Afro-American's Contribution to Columbian Literature by* Ida B. Wells, Frederick Douglass, Irvine Garland Penn, and Ferdinand L. Barnett. Edited by Robert W. Rydell, U of Illinois P, 1999, pp. xi–xlvii.

Shaw, Marian. *World's Fair Notes: A Woman Journalist Views Chicago's 1893 Columbian Exposition.* Pogo, 1992.

Sund, Judy. "Columbus and Columbia in Chicago, 1893: Man of Genius Meets Generic Woman." *Art Bulletin*, vol. 75, no. 3, 1993, pp. 443–66. *JSTOR*, doi:10.2307/3045968.

Terborg-Penn, Roslyn. *African American Women in the Struggle for the Vote, 1850–1920.* Indiana UP, 1998.

Weimann, Jeanne Madeline. *The Fair Women.* Academy Chicago, 1981.

Wells, Ida B., Frederick Douglass, Irvine Garland Penn, and Ferdinand L. Barnett. *The Reason Why the Colored American Is Not in the World's Columbian Exposition: The Afro-American's Contribution to Columbian Literature*, edited by Robert W. Rydell, U of Illinois P, 1999.

Williams, Fannie Barrier. "The Intellectual Progress of the Colored Women of the United Stated since the Emancipation Proclamation: An Address by Fannie Williams of Illinois." *The World's Congress of Representative Women*, edited by May Wright Sewall, Rand, McNally, 1894, pp. 696–712. *Internet Archive*, ia802604.us.archive.org/31/items/worldscongressof00worluoft/worldscongressof00worluoft.pdf.

9

REWRITING MATERNAL BODIES ON THE SENATE FLOOR
Tammy Duckworth's Embodied Rhetorics of Intersectional Motherhood

Ruth Osorio (Old Dominion University)

On April 19, 2018, Maile Pearl Bowlsbey made history: at ten days old, she was the first infant permitted on the United States Senate floor (Viebeck). Her mother, Senator Tammy Duckworth, held the newborn on her lap as she rolled into the Capitol Building, initiating national conversations about postpartum bodies, work, and governance. Days before the vote, the Senate passed a resolution—drafted by Duckworth—to change standing rules and allow infants under the age of one onto the Senate floor. After the historic vote, images and videos from Duckworth and Bowlsbey's entrance into the Capitol circulated widely, sparking celebration from working mothers, disabled parents, and women of color. In articles and interviews about Bowlsbey's Senate debut, Duckworth articulated the importance of supporting new parents. For instance, Duckworth wrote in an *LA Times* editorial, "I'll always be proud that my daughter Maile helped bring the Senate into the twenty-first century. But the reality is, this country can't afford to wait 229 more years to pass laws that look out for families beyond the Senate chamber." Her words continue to bring attention to the lack of support working parents receive in the United States, but her words do not work alone. Rather, I argue it was Duckworth's and Bowlsbey's bodies together on the Senate floor that sparked collective knowledge making about maternal bodies, work, governance, and disability.

Duckworth's vote with Maile Pearl Bowlsbey on her lap illustrates the power of bodily acts of rhetoric—particularly how multiply marginalized people can position their biological bodies in rhetorical ways to imagine new rhetorical possibilities for embodied difference, identity, and human worth. Such bodily action and attention to the body are hallmarks of Duckworth's career, as evidenced by the series of firsts she can

https://doi.org/10.7330/9781646422012.c009

claim: the first Asian American woman elected to Senate from Illinois, first woman with double amputations in the Senate, and first Senator to give birth while in office ("Sen. Tammy Duckworth's Pregnancy").[1] Discourse surrounding Duckworth's career, then, is intertwined with her body, and especially her race, gender, and disability. Indeed, discussions about Duckworth's political achievements are filtered through her identity as a disabled veteran, a mother, and mother of color—a fact Duckworth herself leverages persuasively when speaking about healthcare or foreign policy.[2]

In this chapter, I argue that Senator Tammy Duckworth and Maile Pearl Bowlsbey's embodied presence on the Senate floor catalyzed collective knowledge making about raced motherhood, governance, work, and disability. With her multiply marginalized mothering body, Duckworth authored an argument about the importance of supporting and including mothers in the workplace while confronting deeply entrenched narratives about the role of postpartum bodies in United States society. My reading of this moment involves embodied rhetorics in two significant ways: first, I approach Duckworth's maternal body as a rhetorical text, and second, I examine how her embodied knowledge as a disabled woman, a nursing mother, and a *woman of color* shaped her argumentative strategies. To that end, I explore how Duckworth's embodied needs as a disabled and nursing mother of color shaped the invention and delivery of her argument. I begin by fleshing out my intersectional framework for an embodied-rhetorics methodology. Then, I identify three binaries Duckworth's embodied argument deconstructed: (1) motherhood and work, (2) motherhood and governance, and (3) motherhood and disability. In these sections, I analyze how Duckworth's vote on the Senate floor rewrote dominant narratives about motherhood, catalyzing collective knowledge making about the political power and resilience of postpartum bodies. By refusing to follow centuries-old rules dictating who can have babies and where babies can be brought, Duckworth offered new scripts for nonwhite disabled parents and mothers who work outside the home.

INTERSECTIONAL APPROACHES TO EMBODIED RHETORICS

Studying a body as a text is not an easy task. Bodies are ephemeral—I cannot go back to April 19, 2018, and examine Duckworth's and Bowlsbey's bodies in the Capitol. Therefore, to study physical bodies as embodied rhetorics, we must depend on other texts. In this essay, I look to photographs, videos, and written descriptions of Duckworth's entrance into the US Capitol, triangulating those images with larger discourse about motherhood and work, governance, and disability. Though I look to images for my analysis, I situate this project firmly in embodied rhetorics rather than visual rhetorics because of its central research question: How did Duckworth's embodied needs, and the embodied knowledges that emerge from those needs, shape her bodily argument? Karma R. Chávez insists that rhetorical studies of the lived, actual body "demand intersectional analysis to understand bodies in rhetorical practice" (245). Thus, to attend to Duckworth's body-as-text, I follow Chávez's call to perform an intersectional analysis, one that attempts to account for the embodied knowledges, needs, and arguments emerging from her gendered, raced, and disabled body.

Like all practitioners of embodied rhetorics, Senator Duckworth's embodied text and her embodied knowledges cannot be reduced to one aspect of her identity. Duckworth's rhetoric necessitates an intersectional approach: one that accounts for the complex, messy ways her multiple marginalized identities intersect. Kimberlé Crenshaw coined the term *intersectionality* in 1989, giving a name to the concept that Black feminists in the United States have been describing since the nineteenth century. Crenshaw explained that because "the intersectional experience is greater than the sum of racism and sexism, any analysis that does not take intersectionality into account cannot sufficiently address the particular manner in which Black women are subordinated" (140). Since Crenshaw's 1989 article, intersectionality has transcended disciplinary boundaries and transformed the field of women's studies (McCall; Nash). Intersectionality adds a critical analytical framework to the study of embodied rhetoric: bodies are never just one thing, and the material realities—and thus embodied knowledges—of any individual body cannot be divorced from intersections of power, privilege, and oppression. Sumi Cho, Kimberlé Crenshaw, and Leslie McCall write,

> [W]hat makes an analysis intersectional—whatever terms it deploys, whatever its iteration, whatever its field or discipline—is its adoption of an intersectional way of thinking about the problem of sameness and difference and its relation to power. This framing—conceiving of categories not as distinct but as always permeated by other categories, fluid and changing, always in the process of creating and being created by dynamics of power—emphasizes what intersectionality does rather than what intersectionality is. (795)

Cho, Crenshaw, and McCall emphasize that an intersectional analysis acknowledges the fluidity and complexity of identity and its connection to power. For embodied rhetorics, an intersectional analysis prompts us to acknowledge that rhetors embody a multitude of identities, and that complex matrixes of identities and power shape the available means of persuasion. In other words, Duckworth's rhetorical choices, as well as the rhetorical situation itself, were influenced by her embodied identities—and the needs, wisdom, and experiences her body has generated moving though this world.

Crenshaw's original writings on intersectionality did not focus on disability, a critical aspect to Duckworth's political identity, body, and arguments. Thus, I turn also to the disability justice (DJ) movement, started and sustained by queer and trans disabled people of color, for an articulation of intersectionality that foregrounds disability. As Patricia Berne explains in Sins Invalid's *Skin, Tooth, and Bone. The Basis of Movement Is Our People: A Disability Justice Primer:* "The mechanical workings of oppression and how it outputs shift depending upon the characteristics of any given institutional or interpersonal interaction; the very understanding of disability experience itself is being shaped by race, gender, class, gender expression, historical moment, relationship to colonization and more" (16). Within a DJ framework, disability cannot be separated from other identities because ableism and racism, among other systems of oppression, coconstruct each other. What DJ offers to the conversation about intersectionality is not merely the inclusion of disability but also the focus on embodied needs. Berne succinctly writes, "A Disability Justice framework understands that all bodies are unique and essential, that all bodies have strengths and needs that must be met" (Sins Invalid 14). Embodied needs, such as the need for a ramp or a private space to nurse, are often framed as burdens, but DJ argues that our diverse needs are what make us human. Every body has different needs because of the complex intersections of identity, location, and time, and those needs can change. And those diverse needs have wide-ranging impacts on the shape of rhetorical invention, production, and delivery.

Because Duckworth's body so visibly defies singular categorization, so does my methodological framework. This study braids cultural, disability, and maternal rhetorics in its embodied approach, as all three fields focus on the materiality and rhetorics of the body. More specifically, cultural rhetorics offers an emphasis on relationality in embodiment. In the collaboratively written "Our Story Begins Here: Constellating Cultural Rhetorics," Daisy Levy describes embodied rhetoric in terms of the anatomical body, the flesh and bones: "[E]mbodied rhetoric travels through the bones, into the ground, and through all other organic things, which also harness physical energy" (Powell et al.). Cultural rhetorics asks for more than merely acknowledging the body's presence or importance in rhetorical production; it stresses the body's relational-ity to other bodies, space, and meaning. As Levy says, rather than treat bodies as "objects used to gather and excavate meaning from," a cultural rhetorics framework calls for "relationality, as a rhetorical framework, [which] gives us a way to do something besides objectify" (Powell et al.). I interpret cultural rhetorics' call by approaching Duckworth's body not as my object of study but as a body in constellation with other maternal bodies. Relationality is a focal point for my embodied-rhetorics meth-odology: to see Duckworth's flesh-and-bone body as connected to the legions of working mothers of color, disabled mothers, and postpartum parents of all genders—including my own white nondisabled body, nurs-ing my five-month-old child as I watched Duckworth and Bowlsbey enter the Capitol Building.

Maternal rhetorics share an important relationship to disability rhetorics, and to think intersectionally about Duckworth's argument, I bring together the field's theorization of embodied difference and care. In his book *Disability Rhetoric*, Jay Dolmage argues, "Disability shapes our available means of persuasion. Embodied difference can actually be read as the very possibility of meaning" (289). For Dolmage, embodied difference creates the possibility for meaning to be created, understood, and shared. Thus, disability rhetorics puts into focus how disabled rhetors tap into their lived experiences of embodied difference as a source of rhetorical invention. Maternal bodies also offer insight into how flesh-and-blood-and-milk bodies carry both flesh and mean-ing. Cynthia Lewiecki-Wilson and Jen Cellio write in the introduction to their collection *Disability and Mothering*, "Mothering is a relation to another and an experience in flux, and like disability, an experience that is both personal and social, bodily and socially shaped by local as well as broader cultures" (3). The maternal body, then, cannot be studied as purely a biological reality or a socially constructed phenomenon: it is discursive and material, with discourse about maternal bodies shaping their physical realities and vice versa. Dorothy Roberts's pivotal research on Black maternal mortality and criminalization, for instance, illustrates the embodied consequences of cultural myths for Black women.[3] There is no singular maternal body, for the rhetorics of motherhood impact different maternal bodies in different, intersectional ways. As a disabled mother of color, Duckworth's embodied argument demands an inter-sectional framework to understand the ways race, disability, and gender shape interpretations of her maternal body.

Before proceeding, I want to be clear that in writing about the post-partum body, it is important to recognize not all people who give birth are mothers and not all mothers give birth. The embodied knowledges that emerges from birth and nursing are not limited to cisgender women. Nonbinary and trans men also partake in responsibilities traditionally coded as *female* and *maternal*, including giving birth and nursing infants. My use of the words *mother* and *maternal* is not meant to erase the diverse manifestations of family making and caretaking; rather, as my analysis illustrates, I observe how Duckworth's embodied argument catalyzed collective knowledge making about traditional, and thus gendered, understandings of the postpartum body.

READING THE DISABLED MATERNAL BODY OF COLOR

Motherhood, disability, and race cannot be neatly divided from the body, from other bodies, or from discourse. Duckworth seems to acknowledge this in her rhetorical performance within the Capitol Building: her embodied knowledge as a disabled woman of color shapes each canon of rhetoric—the invention of the argument itself and how she arranges, styles, and delivers that argument. Discourse surrounding Duckworth's vote highlighted her arguments about motherhood in particular. Indeed, Duckworth leverages her maternal body to upend the myths of the "bad mother," a myth Molly Ladd-Taylor and Lauri Umansky argue is ubiquitous, ever shifting, and most often applied to nonwhite, career-focused, and disabled moms. As a disabled working mother of color, Duckworth's embodied argument deconstructs these pernicious tropes and offers a new rhetoric of motherhood: one that derives rhetorical power, rather than shame or weakness, from disabled maternal bodies. Duckworth's new maternal rhetoric defies dominant narratives about motherhood and work, motherhood and governance, and motherhood and disability. I organize the remainder of this chapter around these three embodied arguments, explicating how Duckworth reimagines the intersectional and politically powerful maternal body.

Conversations about Work and Motherhood

By entering her workplace with a newborn baby snuggled close to her body, Duckworth authored an embodied argument about mothers who work outside the home. Importantly, Duckworth did not actually start working full time just ten days after giving birth, nor was she advocating for postpartum people to return to work so quickly. She took three months of unpaid leave, only coming into the Capitol with Bowlsbey for important votes. By bringing Bowlsbey to her office during her parental leave, Duckworth argued for workplace policies and cultures that allow postpartum parents to more comfortably blend their identities as parents and workers. On the day of the vote, Amy Joyce published an editorial in the *Washington Post* with the headline "Few Mothers Could Do What Tammy Duckworth Did, but She May Still Pave a Way for Working Parents." *The New York Times* (Lett), *NBC News* (Mandel), *InStyle* (Pulia), *Fox News* (DeBellis), and the online publication *Working Mother* (Foye) all featured editorials drawing connections between Duckworth's vote on the Senate floor and the policies and cultural norms that dictate the presence, comfort, and well-being of postpartum bodies in the workplace. Duckworth's embodied argument was widely interpreted as a statement on the importance of supporting new parents in the workplace.

Indeed, work culture in the United States is not kind to parents immediately after birth. A quarter of postpartum people return to work within two weeks of the birth, and those who return to work sooner report greater likelihood of depression (Lerner). At the same time, workplace cultures often demand new parents contain signs of their postpartum status. As Caroline Gatrell argues, the maternal body and its "exhaustion, anxiety and the potential . . . to change shape and produce fluids" produce profound discomfort in the workplace (622). For this reason, new parents are pressured to return to work at the same time they are pressured to hide the embodied realities of giving birth and nurturing an infant—thus, they are pushed to create stark demarcations between their mothering identity and worker identity (Buzzanell et al.; Gatrell; Turner and Norwood). Duckworth, then, worked to upend the deep-seated trope that being a good worker precludes good mothering and vice versa (Turner and Norwood). At the same time, Duckworth's embodied argument destabilizes the dominance of whiteness in discussions about working moms. Studies on the obstacles for working mothers often overlook race, leaving little engagement with how structural racism might impact how mothers of color move through careers and family life (Cuddy and Wolf). Furthermore, resources that do exist for mothers working in professional fields are often race neutral and thus assume whiteness.[4]

Duckworth resists the binary between worker and mother and the whitewashing of working-mom discourse by bringing her nonwhite maternal body and newborn child into her office. Duckworth does not look like the typical postpartum person who just gave birth ten days ago: dressed professionally, wearing either a long-sleeved blouse or blazer, Duckworth looks the part of the Senator. The only departure from the standard dress code: a young baby in a tiny pink beanie curled up and strapped to her chest, wrapped in a baby carrier. In pictures of Duckworth's entrance into the Capitol, she looks radiant—smiling widely as the wind sweeps her hair. Inside the building, her smile continues. Lindal Buchanan writes that maternal rhetorics "produce rich rhetorical resources capable of advancing women and their civic agendas while simultaneously reinforcing limiting stereotypes and inequitable gender relations" (14). Duckworth, I contend, avoids this trap by rewriting maternal rhetorics, expanding the motherhood *topos* to represent nurturing as well as working. Within the Capitol, Duckworth's body reconciles the tension between the good mother and good worker, a tension complicated already by her nonwhite and disabled body. Her body refuses binaries, projecting professionalism, mothering, and joy all at once.

Duckworth's decision to bring Bowlsbey onto the Senate floor for the vote was spurred by her breastfeeding body's needs, needs often at odds with workplace cultures. Gatrell describes postpartum bodies as "leaky," explaining that "maternal 'leakage'—such as bleeding, breast milk, amniotic fluids/breaking waters, vomiting and tears (caused by supposedly unpredictable hormones)—is regarded as inappropriate within workplaces and most mothers feel under pressure to hide this" (624). Duckworth's body was indeed leaky, and that reality did prompt discomfort, particularly from male senators (Kellman). Duckworth, like so many nursing parents, was subjected to what Amy Koerber describes as conflicting disciplinary rhetorics of breastfeeding: "[T]he disciplinary power of breastfeeding discourse lies not in any single message about what women should do, but in mixed messages that circumscribe what their bodies can do" (88). She wanted to nurse, a decision supported by major pediatric health organizations, at the same time her workplace attempted to prevent bodily leakage by not allowing her on the Senate floor with her newborn. Duckworth refused to submit to the disciplinary rhetorics of her colleagues and the space of the Senate floor. Postponing breastfeeding or pumping breastmilk can lead to visible milk leakage, pain, potential infection from plugged breast ducts, and a lower milk supply. Rather than hide her body's leakiness, Duckworth highlighted it in her deployment of embodied rhetoric; indeed, Duckworth's leaky body, and its physical needs to express milk regularly, shaped her argument and its delivery.

By refusing to succumb to the disciplinary rhetorics of breastfeeding, Duckworth offered a powerful embodied depiction of an Asian American breastfeeding mom and worker. In this way, Duckworth performed what

Paaige K. Turner and Kristen Norwood call "unbounded motherhood," which they describe as nursing parents "insert[ing] breastfeeding into work in ways that [do] not abide by the rules of masculinity that underlie organizations" (416). Duckworth, then, challenged dominant rules about workplace culture by incorporating her embodied needs as a breastfeeding parent into her embodied argument. What Turner and Norwood's analysis overlooks, however, is that breastfeeding discourse is often raced, with resources and representations of nursing often focusing on white mothers. Asian American mothers often face additional hurdles when attempting to breastfeed, including language and cultural barriers in the postpartum wing of the hospital (Lai; Tseng). As an Asian American nursing senator, Duckworth, then, collapsed the boundaries between good worker and good mother and in doing so served as an embodied reminder that such divisions are often poignantly raced. Bowlsbey slept the entire time in the Capitol, so Duckworth did not need to nurse her. Still, Duckworth never hid the fact she was breastfeeding, never sought to obscure her maternal leaky body by hiding in private. Duckworth unsettled assumptions about breastfeeding, the maternal body, whiteness, and work, demonstrating she did not need to separate these critical aspects of her embodied reality in order to succeed as both a mother and a senator.

Conversations about Motherhood and Governance

Duckworth's workplace is not any old workplace, of course. When Duckworth and Bowlsbey entered the Capitol Building, they authored an embodied argument about governance and motherhood. Bodies do not construct arguments in a vacuum: bodies comingle with the space they occupy to make meaning, often to activist ends (Endres and Senda-Cook). Duckworth's vote was historic precisely because of the space she and Bowlsbey entered—the Senate floor of the Capitol Building, a space that represents governance, decorum, and prestige.

The Senate floor, and the United States government generally, has historically not been a welcoming place for maternal bodies. Senator Duckworth is the first—and as of this writing, the only—United States Senator to give birth while in office. Furthermore, prior to April 2018, Senate rules prohibited infants under the age of one to enter the Senate floor—sending a clear message that babies, and, importantly, their caregivers, do not belong in the decision-making spaces of the United States. Such rules, both written and unwritten, have worked to keep women out of government. In the United States, women—and especially disabled women of color—are drastically underrepresented in elected political positions (Fox and Lawless; Gerrity, Osborn, and Mendez; Paxton and Hughes). The *Washington Post* reports that, as of February 2018, "for every woman in political office in the United States, there are three men" (Cameron and Soffen). Of course, not all women will or can become mothers. Still, research has consistently shown that family-friendly workplace policies, such as paid parental leave, lead to increased and sustained women's participation in the workplace, as well as increased wages for women (Rossin-Slater, Ruhm, and Waldfogel).

Policies, therefore, carry immense power in allowing or banning the presence of maternal bodies and women in government. In order for Duckworth to vote ten days after giving birth, she had to first contend with centuries of patriarchal norms inscribed in the rules of the Senate: particularly, she had to roll back the Senate rule that forbade infants from the Senate floor. The Senate voted unanimously to do so.[5] The straightforward resolution reads, "[A] Senator who has a son or daughter . . . under 1 year of age may bring the son or daughter onto the floor of the Senate during votes." Senate regulations may seem mundane, but as Nathaniel Rivers and Ryan Weber assert, mundane documents, while "not always as exciting or visible as the rhetorical fireworks of more obvious public displays . . . are no less necessary for the creation and re-creation of publics" (188). Duckworth's Senate rule change illustrates the connection between policies and embodied arguments: policies dictate the movement and presence of bodies. By moving to change the rules of the Senate to allow the presence of babies on the floor, Duckworth was able to participate in governing, leaky maternal body and all, and opened the door for more potential maternal bodies to run for elected office.

Duckworth's embodied argument offered new narratives for non-white maternal bodies in particular. Few elected officials across the globe have brought their babies into work. Those who do garner international attention for doing so—Licia Ronzulli of the European Parliament and Australian Member of Parliament Larissa Waters have brought their children when they vote and address their parliaments—tend to be white ("Senator Becomes First"). Asian American mothers are rarely, if ever, presented as governing figures or nurturing mothers. As Yoonsun Choi argues, stereotypes abound of the "devoid of warmth, controlling, unfeeling, and undemocratic" Asian-American mother (qtd. in Whitaker). Such stereotypes work to minimize the political power of the Asian American mother by assigning her the responsibility of grooming her children to become leaders rather than being a leader herself. Thus,

Duckworth's revised Senate policy, which enabled her embodied argument on the Senate floor, offers a new narrative: that Asian American maternal bodies can nurture, govern, and set the stage for more maternal bodies of color to join in leadership ranks.

Conversations about Motherhood and Disability

Just as Duckworth offers new possibilities for imagining the Asian American maternal body, she generates new pathways for disabled motherhood. Kristin Lindgren observes, "[W]hen disability and maternity register visibly in the same body, they sometimes create a visual and cognitive dissonance, as if one can be either a mother or a disabled person—not both at once" (90). Duckworth's embodied argument refuses this dichotomy by presenting her body as both disabled and maternal, never attempting to hide either part of her identity. Indeed, disability was present throughout Duckworth's advocacy to allow infants on the Senate floor. When older male senators suggested Duckworth vote from the Senate cloakroom rather than bring her child onto the Senate floor, for example, they overlooked the fact that the cloakroom room is not accessible for people who use wheelchairs. Though disabled maternal bodies are often rendered invisible, as Lindgren argues, Duckworth's disability actually prevented her from being hidden away in the Senate cloakroom, and it supported her argument to allow infants on the Senate floor. Yet again, Duckworth's embodied needs—the need for a wheelchair-accessible space wherein she could vote and hold her newborn—shaped the delivery of her argument.

Duckworth's refusal to choose between her disabled identity and mothering identity strikes against the common misconception that disabled people are unfit or even dangerous mothers. On their own, disabled bodies conjure anxiety in nondisabled people, a physical and visual reminder of the human body's frailty (Garland-Thomson; Siebers). The disabled maternal body in particular provokes unrest and fear. Disabled people are assumed to be unable to care for a child, or presumably worse, at risk for passing their disability onto their child (Farber; Leweicki-Wilson and Cellio; R. Powell). As disability studies scholars have documented, these ableist and racist anxieties have historically manifested in eugenic rhetoric and practices, including forced sterilization, removal of children from disabled parents and families of color, and proposals to ban disabled people from marrying each other (Carey; Dolmage, *Disabled Upon Arrival*; Leweicki-Wilson and Cellio 19–20). While forced sterilizations have decreased in the twenty-first century, more subtle forms of eugenic rhetoric and practice continue. The National Council of Disability (NCD) reports, "The power of the eugenics ideology persists. Women with disabilities still contend with coercive tactics designed to encourage sterilization or abortion because they are not deemed fit for motherhood. Equally alarming, a growing trend is emerging toward sterilizing people with intellectual or psychiatric disabilities" (13–14). The NCD report underscores how policies, ideologies, and medical practices can dictate the treatment and very existence of disabled bodies, an urgent reminder that eugenic rhetoric carries embodied, material risks for disabled people—and particularly for nonwhite disabled people (National Council). Far too often, disabled mothers are labeled as selfish and unfit, accused of the crime of supposedly putting their desire to have children over the well-being of their children (R. Powell).

Duckworth's embodied argument strikes at the core of eugenic rhetoric. On the day of the vote, Duckworth is visibly disabled, visibly nonwhite, and visibly mothering. Duckworth makes no effort to hide her prosthetic leg or wheelchair. A staff member pushes Duckworth in her wheelchair, presumably so Duckworth can use her arms to hold Bowlsbey on her chest. Duckworth, then, embodies what Eva Feder Kittay calls *doulia*, the "relations of 'nested dependencies' through which caregivers also receive care," as Duckworth's body is at once receiving care from the staff member pushing her wheelchair and providing care to her infant child sleeping on her chest (qtd. in Lindgren 95). In the photographs from the vote, Duckworth's body resists narratives of shame that surround motherhood, disability, and interdependence: that her maternal body needs care is not a weakness but rather a human reality.

In a world where the disabled mother figure, and especially the nonwhite disabled mother figure, is often presented as unfit or dangerous, Duckworth presents her disabled maternal body as a site of caregiving and political power. Duckworth's spoken rhetoric focused on supporting working mothers but neglected to mention disability or race. But Duckworth did not need words to spark celebration from disabled activists of color—her body conveyed enough on its own. Asian American woman disability activist and wheelchair user Alice Wong describes Duckworth's embodied rhetoric as a source of validation for disabled women of color: "The joy on her face, the sight of her newborn nestled to her chest, her prosthetic leg and wheelchair in full view, and her use of an accessible entrance that wouldn't exist without the Americans with Disabilities Act all coalesced into an immense feeling of disability pride." Wong applauds the way Duckworth "unapologetically brings her full self into every space she navigates as a parent, veteran, politician, and disabled woman of color." Wong's response to Duckworth underscores the generative power of Duckworth's disabled maternal body. By entering the Senate as a fully visible disabled mother of color, Duckworth's body articulates a radical refutation of eugenic rhetoric. As Duckworth and Bowlsbey illustrate, disability and mothering are not mutually exclusive but rather can come together and generate collective wisdom, affirmation, and political power.

REIMAGINING MATERNAL BODIES IN POWER

In this chapter, I approach Duckworth's historic vote on the Senate floor as an act of embodied rhetoric, offering an opening to a conversation that has predominantly focused on written texts. Here, I see embodied rhetorics as working together with other frameworks invested in bodily acts of rhetoric; for example, Duckworth's act was absolutely a form of visual rhetoric. It could also be read as performance rhetoric, especially in how Bernadette M. Calafell describes performance: a "theory of the flesh with a critical rhetorical perspective immersed in the politics of performance" (106). Indeed, Duckworth's entrance into the Capitol was photographed and circulated by the media, and in the vote itself, Duckworth's performance merged her flesh with her rhetorical and political goals. I do not see embodied rhetorics, visual rhetorics, and performance rhetorics as neatly divided, distinct realms of inquiry. Rather, I chose to write about Duckworth's vote as embodied rhetoric because I was fascinated with how her embodied knowledges—as a nursing parent and a disabled woman of color—catalyzed her argument, and in turn, sparked collective knowledge making about maternal bodies, identity, and power. Applying an embodied-rhetorics framework to bodily acts of rhetoric can highlight how the embodied needs of maternal, disabled, and other marginalized rhetors can shape and even enrich the production of their argument. Duckworth embraced her embodied differences, needs, and experiences as sources of invention and delivery and thus highlighted for her audience the rhetorical power of maternal disabled bodies of color.

Duckworth's body was the text, the invention, and the delivery of her argument. By bringing her maternal body and newborn child into her office, Duckworth boldly broke down the racialized boundaries between mother and worker, mother and legislator, mothering and disability. Duckworth has written editorials and spoken publicly about the importance of supporting mothers in United States society, but her embodied presence authored a more visible argument than her words alone could, illustrating the rhetorical power of the disabled nonwhite maternal body in governing spaces. As this edited collection demonstrates, I am not alone in insisting bodies are rhetorical. My goal is to echo and expand the claims of embodied rhetorics by highlighting how multiply marginalized rhetors leverage their material bodies to catalyze collective knowledge making. Embodied rhetorics encompasses so much more than alphabetic writing, with rhetorical bodies outlining new possibilities for community, transformation, and liberation. Furthermore, by centering the body, embodied rhetorics provides frameworks for understanding how the needs of the human body can dictate the manifestation of rhetoric. Duckworth's embodied argument illustrates how the biological body is integral to the invention and delivery of rhetoric, with her needs as a nursing parent and disabled person shaping her argument.

Duckworth rewrote cultural scripts—as well as literal Senate policy—to make space for new ways of working, governing, and mothering. Her body exists in relation to bodies across space and time, with her movement onto the Capitol floor affirming the wisdom and resilience of pregnant, postpartum, nonwhite, and disabled bodies. I was one such maternal body, watching videos of Duckworth while home with my second child, just five months old, sleeping soundly on my chest as I prepared for my dissertation defense. After nursing my first child at a standing group meeting at CCCC in 2015 and pumping for my second child during campus interviews three years after, I cannot separate my academic identity from my mothering identity. Scholars of embodied rhetoric remind me I never need to divorce my physical body from my scholarship. And Duckworth's embodied rhetoric specifically reminds me our leaky maternal bodies and their needs are not sources of shame but rather sources of wisdom, connection, and rhetorical and political power.

NOTES

1. Duckworth has spoken directly about the pressure, and at times dismay, of consistently being "the first" (qtd. in Kahn). After describing the issues she faced as a woman of color in the military and then a disabled veteran, she explains, "I have won historic elections, but it feels like these 'firsts' are so overdue. I never set out to be the first in anything, and with a lot of these 'firsts' it really makes me wonder how it's taken so long. It also underscores how much farther we have to go to have representation in our government" (qtd. in Kahn).

2. For instance, in a May 1, 2018, press release announcing Duckworth's support for expanding access to Medicare, Duckworth's staff overtly identifies how she weaves her embodied knowledges into her policy stances and rhetoric. The statement

reads, "She has drawn on her own experiences to highlight how certain communities, such as Veterans and people with disabilities, would be especially devastated by these bills" ("Duckworth Announces Support").

3. Discourse about the "negligent Black mother" trope is etched upon Black bodies through family separations, forced sterilization, and an astronomically high maternal mortality rate for Black mothers. Indeed, as of 2017, Black mothers were 243% more likely to die due to pregnancy or childbirth-related causes than white women (Martin and Montagne).

4. Consider, for instance, how easily Ivanka Trump and Sheryl Sandberg assumed the roles of working-mom experts in US popular discourse, leaving little space for stories and representations of working moms of color.

5. But not without some anxiety beforehand. Senator Orrin Hatch expressed concern that a rule reversal could initiate an invasion of babies, asking, "But what if there are 10 babies on the floor of the Senate?" Hatch's question highlights the concern about decorum in the Senate, a serious place for serious business, where noisy and leaky bodies distract from the work of lawmaking. *Vox* writer Sarah Kliff argues that ten babies on the Senate floor would require increased resources for lactation rooms and daycare services, leading to more women in the Senate, more male parents sharing caregiving responsibilities, and a decreasing of the gender wage gap. She concludes, "Come to think of it, a world with 10 babies on the Senate floor doesn't sound so bad at all." Hatch replied to Kliff's article, tweeting, "Seems like a wonderful thing."

WORKS CITED

Buchanan, Lindal. *Rhetorics of Motherhood.* Southern Illinois UP, 2013.

Buzzanell, Patrice M., Rebecca Meisenbach, Robyn Remke, Meina Liu, Venessa Bowers, and Cindy Conn. "The Good Working Mother: Managerial Women's Sensemaking and Feelings About Work-Family Issues." *Communication Studies*, vol. 56, no. 3, 2005, pp. 261–285. *Taylor & Francis Online*, doi:10.1080/10510970500181389.

Calafell, Bernadette M. "Rhetorics of Possibility: Challenging the Textual Bias of Rhetoric through the Theory of the Flesh." *Rhetorica in Motion*, edited by Eileen E. Schell and K. J. Rawson, U of Pittsburgh P, 2010, pp. 104–117.

Cameron, Darla, and Kim Soffen. "For Every Woman in Political Office in the United States, There Are Three Men." *Washington Post*, 1 Feb. 2018, www.washingtonpost.com /classic-apps/for-every-woman-in-political-office-in-the-united-states-there-are-three -men/2018/02/01/46ba0cac-075a-11e8-8777-2a059f168dd2_story.html. Accessed 27 June 2020.

Carey, Allison C. "Beyond the Medical Model: A Reconsideration of 'Feeblemindedness,' Citizenship, and Eugenic Restrictions." *Disability and Society*, vol. 18, no. 4, 2003, pp. 411–430. *Taylor & Francis Online*, doi:10.1080/0968759032000080977.

Chávez, Karma R. "The Body: An Abstract and Actual Rhetorical Concept." *Keywords: A Glossary of the Pasts and Futures of the Rhetoric Society of America*. Spec. issue of *Rhetoric Society Quarterly*, vol. 48, no. 3, 2018, pp. 242–250. *Taylor & Francis Online*, doi:10.108 0/02773945.2018.1454182.

Cho, Sumi, Kimberlé Williams Crenshaw, and Leslie McCall. "Toward a Field of Intersectionality Studies: Theory, Applications, and Praxis." *Intersectionality: Theorizing Power, Empowering Theory*. Spec. issue of *Signs: Journal of Women in Culture and Society*, vol. 38, no. 4, 2013, pp. 785–810. *JSTOR*, doi:10.1086/669608.

Crenshaw, Kimberlé. "Demarginalizing the Intersection of Race and Sex: A Black Feminist Critique of Antidiscrimination Doctrine, Feminist Theory and Antiracist Politics." *University of Chicago Legal Forum*, vol. 1989, no. 1, pp. 139–167.

Cuddy, Amy J. C., and Elizabeth Baily Wolf. "Prescriptions and Punishments for Working Moms: How Race and Work Status Affect Judgments of Mothers." *Gender and Work: Challenging Conventional Wisdom*, edited by Robin Ely and Amy Cuddy, Harvard Business School, 2013, pp. 35–42.

DeBellis Appell, Lauren. "Sen. Tammy Duckworth Bringing Baby to Senate Floor Shines New Light on Working Parents." *Fox News*, 20 Apr. 2018, foxnews.com/opinion/sen-tammy-duckworth-bringing-baby-to-senate-floor-shines-new-light-on-working-parents. Accessed 27 June 2020.

Dolmage, Jay. *Disability Rhetoric*. Syracuse UP, 2014.

Dolmage, Jay. *Disabled Upon Arrival: Eugenics, Immigration, and the Construction of Race and Disability*. The Ohio State U P, 2018.

"Duckworth Announces Support for Legislation Expanding Access to Medicare." *Tammy Duckworth U.S. Senator for Illinois*, 1 May 2018, www.duckworth.senate.gov/news/press-releases/duckworth-announces-support-for-legislation-expanding-access-to-medicare. Press release. Accessed 27 June 2020.

Duckworth, Tammy. "More Women in Congress Could Be a Good Thing for Family Leave Legislation." *LA Times*, 12 May 2019, latimes.com/opinion/op-ed/la-oe-duckworth-family-leave-congress-20190512-story.html. Accessed 27 Apr. 2020.

Endres, Danielle, and Samantha Senda-Cook. "Location Matters: The Rhetoric of Place in Protest." *Quarterly Journal of Speech*, vol. 97, no. 3, 2011, pp. 257–282. *Taylor & Francis Online*, doi:10.1080/00335630.2011.585167.

Farber, Ruth S. "Mothers with Disabilities: In Their Own Voice." *American Journal of Occupational Therapy*, vol. 54, 2000, pp. 260–268. *AOTA*, doi:10.5014/ajot.54.3.260.

Fox, Richard L., and Jennifer L. Lawless. "To Run or Not to Run for Office: Explaining Nascent Political Ambition." *American Journal of Political Science*, vol. 49, no. 3, 2005, pp. 642–659. *JSTOR*, doi:10.2307/3647737.

Foye, Meghann. "Tammy Duckworth Just Brought Her Baby to the Senate Floor." *Working Mothers*, 19 Apr. 2018, workingmother.com/thanks-to-senator-tammy-duckworth-babies-are-now-allowed-on-senate-floor. Accessed 27 June 2020.

Garland-Thomson, Rosemarie. *Extraordinary Bodies: Figuring Physical Disability in American Culture and Literature*. Columbia UP, 2017.

Gatrell, Caroline J. "Maternal Body Work: How Women Managers and Professionals Negotiate Pregnancy and New Motherhood at Work." *Human Relations*, vol. 66, no. 5, 2013, pp. 621–644. *SAGE Journals*, doi:10.1177/0018726712467380.

Gerrity, Jessica C., Tracy Osborn, and Jeanette Morehouse Mendez. "Women and Representation: A Different View of the District?" *Politics & Gender*, vol. 3, no. 2, 2007, pp. 179–200. *Cambridge UP*, doi:10.1017/S1743923X07000025.

Joyce, Amy. "Few Mothers Could Do What Tammy Duckworth Did, but She May Still Pave a Way for Working Parents." *Washington Post*, 19 Apr. 2019, washingtonpost.com/news/parenting/wp/2018/04/19/few-mothers-could-do-what-tammy-duckworth-did-but-she-may-still-pave-a-way-for-working-parents/. Accessed 27 June 2020.

Kahn, Mattie. "Tammy Duckworth Wishes She Wasn't Always the First." *Elle Magazine*, 10 Apr. 2018, medium.com/elle-magazine/tammy-duckworth-wishes-she-wasnt-always-the-first-9ee0c807fd69. 27 June 2020.

Kellman, Laurie. "Senate Allows Babies in Chamber Despite Concerns from Older, Male Senators." *Chicago Tribune*, 18 Apr. 2018, chicagotribune.com/news/nationworld/ct-senate-babies-chamber-duckworth-20180418-story.html. Accessed 27 June 2020.

Kliff, Sarah. "The Tantrum over Babies on the Senate Floor, Explained." *Vox*, 19 Apr. 2018, vox.com/policy-and-politics/2018/4/19/17256390/tammy-duckworth-baby-senate-orrin-hatch. Accessed 27 June 2020.

Koerber, Amy. "Rhetorical Agency, Resistance, and the Disciplinary Rhetorics of Breast-feeding." *Technical Communication Quarterly*, vol. 15, no. 1, 2006, pp. 87–101. *Taylor & Francis Online*, doi:10.1207/s15427625tcq1501_7.

Ladd-Taylor, Molly, and Lauri Umansky. Introduction. *"Bad" Mothers: The Politics of Blame in Twentieth-Century America*, edited by Molly Ladd-Taylor and Lauri Umansky, New York UP, 1998.

Lai, Stephanie. "Destigmatizing Asian American Breastfeeding Is Aim of Photo Exhibits in Temple City and Downtown LA." *Pasadena Star-News*, 5 Aug. 2019, pasadenastarnews .com/2019/08/05/destigmatizing-asian-american-breastfeeding-is-aim-of-photo -exhibits-in-temple-city-and-downtown-la/. Accessed 27 June 2020.

Lerner, Sharon. "The Real War on Families: Why the U.S. Needs Paid Leave Now." *In These Times*, 18 Aug. 2015, inthesetimes.com/article/18151/the-real-war-on-families. Accessed 27 June 2020.

Lett, Phoebe. "Tammy Duckworth and Working Moms like Mine." *New York Times*, 24 Apr. 2018, nytimes.com/2018/04/24/opinion/tammy-duckworth-working-mothers.html. Accessed 27 June 2020.

Lewiecki-Wilson, Cynthia, and Jen Cellio, editors. *Disability and Mothering: Liminal Spaces of Embodied Knowledge*. Syracuse UP, 2011.

Lindgren, Kristin. "Reconceiving Motherhood." *Disability and Mothering: Liminal Spaces of Embodied Knowledge*, edited by Cynthia Lewiecki-Wilson and Jen Cellio, Syracuse UP, 2011, pp. 88–97.

Mandel, Bethany. "Tammy Duckworth's Senate Vote with a Baby in Tow Is a Model of Accommodation for Working Mothers." *NBC News*, 19 Apr. 2018, nbcnews.com/think /opinion/tammy-duckworth-s-senate-vote-baby-tow-model-accommodation-working -ncna867611. Accessed 27 June 2020.

Martin, Nina, and Renee Montagne. "Nothing Protects Black Women from Dying in Pregnancy and Childbirth." *ProPublica*, 7 Dec. 2017, propublica.org/article/nothing -protects-black-women-from-dying-in-pregnancy-and-childbirth. Accessed 27 June 2020.

McCall, Leslie. "The Complexity of Intersectionality." *Intersectionality and Beyond Law, Power and the Politics of Location*, edited by Emily Grabham, Davina Cooper, Jane Krishnadas, and Didi Herman, Routledge, 2008, pp. 65–92.

Nash, Jennifer C. "Home Truths on Intersectionality." *Yale Journal of Law & Feminism*, no. 23, 2011, pp. 445–470.

National Council on Disability. *"Rocking the Cradle: Ensuring the Rights of Parents with Dis-abilities." National Council on Disability*, 27 Sept. 2012, ncd.gov/rawmedia_repository/89 591c1f_384e_4003_a7ee_0a14ed3e11aa.pdf. Accessed 27 June 2020.

Paxton, Pamela M., and Melanie M. Hughes. *Women, Politics, and Power: A Global Perspective*. Pine Forge, 2007.

Powell, Malea, Daisy Levy, Andrea Riley-Muskavetz, Marilee Brooks-Gillies, Maria Novotny, and Jennifer Fisch-Ferguson. "Our Story Begins Here: Constellating Cultural Rheto-rics." *Enculturation*, 25 Oct. 2014, enculturation.net/our-story-begins-here. Accessed 27 June 2020.

Powell, Robyn. "How We Treat Disabled Mothers." *Establishment*, 11 May 2017, medium .com/the-establishment/how-we-treat-disabled-mothers-a765ed94e95a. Accessed 27 June 2020.

Pulia, Shalayne. "Senator Tammy Duckworth on Her History-Making Strides for Working Moms." *InStyle*, 26 June 2018, instyle.com/celebrity/senator-tammy-duckworth-badass -women. Accessed 27 June 2020.

Rivers, Nathaniel, and Ryan Weber. "Ecological, Pedagogical, and Public Rhetoric." *College Composition and Communication*, vol. 63, no. 2, 2011, pp. 187–218. *JSTOR*, www.jstor.org /stable/23131582.

Roberts, Dorothy E. *Killing the Black Body: Race, Reproduction, and the Meaning of Liberty*. Vintage, 1999.

Rossin-Slater, Maya, Christopher J. Ruhm, and Jane Waldfogel. "The Effects of California's Paid Family Leave Program on Mothers' Leave-Taking and Subsequent Labor Market Outcomes." *Journal of Policy Analysis and Management*, vol. 32, no. 2, 2013, pp. 224–245. *Wiley Online Library*, doi:10.1002/pam.21676.

"Senator Becomes First to Breast-feed on Floor of Australia's Parliament." Narr. Laurel Wamsley, *The Two-Way*. *Natl. Public Radio*. 10 May 2017, npr.org/sections/thetwo-way/2017/05/10/527750579/senator-becomes-first-to-breastfeed-on-floor-of-australias-parliament. Accessed 27 June 2020.

"Sen. Tammy Duckworth's Pregnancy Set to Be Another First for the Illinois Democrat." Narr. Scott Neuman, *The Two-Way*. Natl. Public Radio. 24 Jan. 2018, npr.org/sections/thetwo-way/2018/01/24/580182083/sen-tammy-duckworths-pregnancy-set-to-be-another-first-for-the-illinois-democrat. Accessed 27 June 2020.

Siebers, Tobin. *Disability Theory*. U of Michigan P, 2008.

Sins Invalid. Skin, Tooth, and Bone. The Basis of Movement Is Our People: A Disability Justice Primer. 2nd ed. *Sins Invalid*, 2016.

Tseng, To-wen. "Helping Mothers of Color Reach Their Breastfeeding Goals." *Moms Rising*, 15 Aug. 2017, momsrising.org/blog/helping-mothers-of-color-reach-their-breastfeeding-goals. Accessed 27 June 2020.

Turner, Paaige K., and Kristen Norwood. "Unbounded Motherhood: Embodying a Good Working Mother Identity." *Management Communication Quarterly*, vol. 27, no. 3, 2013, pp. 396–424. *SAGE Journals*, doi:10.1177/0893318913491461.

Viebeck, Elise. "'It's about Time': Sen. Duckworth's Newborn Daughter Becomes First Baby Permitted on Senate Floor." *Washington Post*, 19 Apr. 2018, washingtonpost.com/news/powerpost/wp/2018/04/19/its-about-time-sen-duckworths-newborn-daughter-becomes-first-baby-permitted-on-senate-floor/. Accessed 27 June 2020.

Whitaker, Charles. "Looking Behind the Myths of Asian American Parenting." *University of Chicago School of Social Service Administration Magazine*, vol. 22, no. 2, Summer 2015, ssa.uchicago.edu/ssa_magazine/looking-behind-myths-asian-american-parenting. Accessed 27 June 2020.

Wong, Alice. "Tammy Duckworth Is Unapologetically Paving the Way for Disabled Mothers of Color." *Bitch Media*, 11 May 2018, bitchmedia.org/article/disability-visibility-tammy-duckworth. Accessed 27 June 2020.

10

CRIMINALS AND VICTIMS
The Embodied Rhetorics of Unaccompanied Latinx Children as Represented in Spanish- and English-Language Media

Megan Strom (University of Wisconsin–La Crosse)

INTRODUCTION

The more than ninety thousand unaccompanied Latinx children who arrived at the United States southwest border in 2014 (Krogstad and Gonzalez-Barrera) were fleeing extreme poverty, brutal gangs, and limited educational opportunities (Kehaulani Goo). In this light, it is not difficult to see such individuals as victims, particularly when this reality is coupled with what these humans were subjected to during their journey to the United States. However, media coverage of such children paints a rather different picture wherein the children, rather than being victims, are something more sinister: a threat (Strom and Alcock), animals, and criminals (Catalano). This study postulates that print media in English and Spanish—published in the United States—use embodied language to create an embodied rhetoric of unaccompanied Latinx children that has direct and lasting impacts on the lives and bodies of these children.

Attention to the framing bodies of immigrants is central to Jennifer Wingard's work in *Branded Bodies, Rhetoric, and the Neoliberal Nation-State*—". . . neoliberal economics has affected the rhetoric of media and politics and [how] in very direct, material ways it harms the bodies of some of the United States's most vulnerable occupants" (ix). Wingard illustrates how bodies are "branded" and "assembled" by texts (media, policies, etc.) in a way that bodies are turned into " 'others,' into rhetorical products, much like consumable products in advertising" (ix). Of that process, Wingard states that the larger implication is that branding bodies "creates an object upon which the American public can focus their emotions" (ix).

This chapter focuses on public media's representation of a particular kind of body—unaccompanied Latinx children—and how the selective rhetorical options of varying media outlets subsequently shape embodied

https://doi.org/10.7330/9781646422012.c010

realities for unaccompanied Latinx children. Many fields broadly discuss the arrival of unaccompanied Latinx children to the United States: anthropology (see Heidbrink), critical discourse studies (see Strom and Alcock), education (see Catalano), rhetorical studies (see Hesford; Ribero), and social work (see Schmidt). What is troubling is that, overall, this research points to the continued injustices children endure after their arrival. The results of the current analysis underscore these injustices, as the public's imagination of unaccompanied Latinx children is fraught with contradictions that likely will not lead to improvements in their situation. Articles published in two Spanish-language newspapers—*El diario/La prensa* and *La opinión*—and in two English-language newspapers—the *New York Times* and the *Los Angeles Times*—employ the lexical items *ilegal* and *illegal*, respectively, to textually represent children as criminals while simultaneously employing the passive voice to textually represent them as victims. That is to say, overall, the data point to an embodiment of Latinx immigrant children that has already been attested for adult immigrants (see Delbene; Merolla, Ramakrishnan, and Haynes; Santa Ana; Strom "Spanish-Language Print Media").

An important consideration is whether the findings of previous research, which has considered only English-language data, hold for alternative media—that is, media in other languages—where alternative representations of immigrants should be expected given their different readership (see Gutiérrez). In order to do so, the current chapter brings together the fields of rhetoric (specifically embodied rhetoric) and critical discourse studies to analyze the representations of unaccompanied Latinx children in Spanish- and English-language print media in the United States. This approach allows for a rich and nuanced understanding of the power of rhetoric to "write" the bodies of said children (Knoblauch 60). It also constitutes a multidisciplinary perspective that sheds light on how the United States print media have "assembled" these bodies (Puar; Wingard) to become the rhetorical place where the emotions of the United States public regarding immigration play out.

REVIEW OF LITERATURE
Critical Discourse Studies

Critical discourse studies (CDS) identifies a social problem—rather than a particular text or discourse (Chouliaraki and Fairclough)—as the object of study because the approach is not interested in analysis for the sake of analysis; rather, it is interested in analysis for the sake of social change. As Norman Fairclough, Phil Graham, Jay Lemke, and

Ruth Wodak note, "The critical objective [of CDS] is not only to identify and analyze the roots of social problems, but also to discern feasible ways of alleviating or resolving them" (1). As a methodological approach, critical discourse studies does not limit researchers to which elements they include in their analyses (Wodak and Meyer); instead, researchers address the elements that help them identify and analyze the roots of social problems. Importantly, such analyses can include discursive elements (e.g., headlines, lexical items) and nondiscursive elements (e.g., authors, context) or any combination thereof. The current study analyzes two lexical items (*ilegal illegal*) and a grammatical item (the passive voice); thus, it is helpful to consider previous research that has also addressed these discursive items.

Critical discursive analyses of the term *illegal* used to refer to immigrants have been carried out in print media in Australia (Leach and Zamora; O'Doherty and Lecouteur), Ireland (Burroughs), Malaysia (Mohd Don and Lee), Spain (Leach and Zamora; Martín Rojo and van Dijk), and the United States (Delbene; Merolla, Ramakrishnan and Haynes; Santa Ana). What remains unclear in critical discourse studies is whether and how non-English-language media in the United Sates employ this term and what ideological effects this use may call forth. Such information is particularly important for this theoretical and analytical approach given its intent on achieving social justice by identifying discursive avenues to alleviate social problems (Kehualani Goo).

Previous critical discourse analyses of the passive voice have centered on the ideological effect of this grammatical construct. Teun Van Dijk (*Discourse and Power*) has shown how the mainstream media employ the passive voice to hide the negative actions of majority groups, thereby highlighting the (often negative) actions minoritized groups experience. Echoing Fairclough's theory that lack of grammatical agency is indicative of less power, Strom ("Social Hierarchy"; "Spanish-Language Print Media") has shown that Latinx social actors in Spanish-language media published in the United States are less powerful than their non-Latinx counterparts because they are rarely the agents of transitive verbs. Megan Strom and Emily Alcock corroborate the powerlessness of unaccompanied Latinx children in the United States English-language media, a powerlessness represented by a lack of grammatical agency for these social actors. Thus, previous research in critical discourse studies indicates that negative representations of adult immigrants should be expected for print media in English and Spanish; however, no predictions can be made regarding the representation of children in either language.

Embodied Rhetorics

Given that a number of critical discourse analyses have demonstrated how public media can create and project particular embodiments for immigrants—such as that of a *criminal*—it is useful to have a multidisciplinary theoretical approach that specifically considers this phenomenon; in particular, it is key to consider notions of rhetorical embodiment. Knoblauch explains the nuance in the ways rhetorical scholars treat embodiment: embodied language, embodied knowledge, and embodied rhetoric (Knoblauch). For this particular chapter, I reference Knoblauch's definition of *embodied rhetoric*: "a purposeful decision to include embodied knowledge and social positionalities as forms of meaning making within a text itself" (52). While the embodied-language portion of my study is indeed present—I discuss the metaphors with which media reference the bodies of Latinx children immigrants—the most salient point of my analysis is that the patterns indicated show, clearly, "a purposeful decision to include"—and, I argue, construct— "social positionalities as forms of meaning making" within the representative texts (Knoblauch 52).

Overall, scholarship in rhetoric and embodiment has engaged with rhetorics of immigration and the embodiments of immigrants (Dolmage; Ribero; White), but not in multilingual publications, nor has there been work that considers how media's uptake in embodied language creates an embodied rhetoric of Latinx children that has direct and lasting impacts on the lives and bodies of child immigrants in current constructions. Thus, this current study provides an important contribution to understanding how mainstream and alternative media in the United States rhetorically embody unaccompanied Latinx immigrants and what such embodiments mean for those such representations embody in this manner.

METHODS

The current study addresses how United States media rhetoric in two languages embodies unaccompanied Latinx children. The dataset includes news articles published in newspapers that represent the widest possible readership in Spanish and English in order to warrant greater generalizations. In order to allow geographical comparisons, newspapers representing the same cities were chosen. Thus, the dataset includes two of the most widely circulated Spanish-language newspapers in the United States: *El diario/La prensa*, which represents New York City, and *La opinión*, which represents Los Angeles. Similarly, the dataset includes the second and third most widely circulated English-language newspapers in the United States in order to reflect the same cities as the Spanish-language newspapers: *the New York Times* and the *Los Angeles Times*, respectively. The articles were published between January 2014 and December 2014, the year with the greatest number of unaccompanied Latinx children arriving to the United States. The search term *unaccompanied minors* yielded thirty-six articles from *the New York Times* and fifty-one articles from the *Los Angeles Times*, or eighty-seven total articles in English. The search term *niños inmigrantes* was used for the Spanish-language newspapers. Because these newspapers belong to the same parent company, ImpreMedia, and most of the articles appeared in both *El diario/La prensa* and *La opinión*, all of the 118 Spanish-language articles were grouped together. Unfortunately, this foreclosed the possibility of making comparisons across cities.

The overarching question is, How does media discourse in Spanish and English embody unaccompanied Latinx child immigrants, particularly given the power of the ideologies represented by these media to shape the way the public views these children. Data analysis involves determining how two lexical items, *ilegal* and *illegal*, and a grammatical item, the passive voice, embody a vulnerable, at-risk group. To carry out the lexical analysis, the grammatical function of each use of *ilegal* or *illegal* was noted; for example, we noted whether it appeared as an adverb in "unaccompanied young people crossing the border illegally" or as a noun in "este ingreso masivo de ilegales" ("this massive influx of illegals")? To analyze the passive voice, it was important to note which term appeared as the past participle, such as "apprehended" in "unaccompanied youths who have been apprehended" or "deportados" in "estos menores no son deportados de inmediato" ("these youth are not deported immediately") and whether a verb agent could be retrieved from the context. These results were then analyzed overall for the ways the language embodied Latinx immigrant children, leaving two patterns clear, media rhetoric in Spanish and English offer contradictory representations of children by embodying them as both criminals and victims.

EMBODYING LATINX CHILD IMMIGRANTS AS ILEGALES OR ILLEGALS

On April 2, 2013, the Associated Press (AP) announced, "The Stylebook no longer sanctions the term 'illegal immigrant' or the use of 'illegal' to describe a person. Instead, it tells users that 'illegal' should describe only an action, such as living in or immigrating to a country illegally"

(Colford). With this announcement, the AP sanctioned the use of *illegal* as an adverb but not as a noun or as an adjective. The *Los Angeles Times* followed suit on May 1, 2013, with "Stories will no longer refer to individuals as 'illegal immigrants' or 'undocumented immigrants' but instead will describe a person's circumstances" (Edgar). While it is clear the *Los Angeles Times* would not allow the adjectival use of *illegal*, it is not clear (although it is highly unlikely given the AP's statements) whether the newspaper would allow *illegal* in its nominal form nor whether it would allow this term as an adverb. *The New York Times* took a different approach and responded on April 23, 2013, with, "Illegal immigrant may be used to describe someone who enters, lives in or works in the United States without proper legal authorization. But be aware that in the debate over immigration, some people view it as loaded or offensive" (Shapiro). Although *the New York Times* acknowledges the fraught nature of this term, it still sanctions the adjectival use of *illegal*; it remains unclear whether the newspaper would allow its nominal or adverbial use. We can gather from the quick succession and content of these announcements that the news sources in question were well aware of the impact of the term *illegal* in its many grammatical forms in news reporting. For reasons unknown, the United States Spanish-language media did not weigh in on this decision. What follow are the results of an analysis of this term in news reporting on the arrival of unaccompanied Latinx children to the United States in both Spanish- and English-language newspapers less than a year after these announcements were made.

In light of the aforementioned announcements and the findings of previous research that show how *illegal* dehumanizes immigrants, it is surprising this word was used to describe unaccompanied Latinx children or their actions eighty-one times in the English-language data. On the other hand, even in the absence of any definitive editorial decisions by Spanish-language media, the Spanish-language newspapers used *ilegal* to describe unaccompanied Latinx children or their actions only eighteen times. Perhaps one indicator of heightened awareness is the fact that none of the newspapers in the dataset, in either language, used the term in its nominal form. However, the data show *illegal* is still the preferred term in English, with fewer than five uses of *undocumented* and *unauthorized* to refer to unaccompanied Latinx children. Of note is that the Spanish-language newspapers strongly prefer the term *indocumentado* to any other (including *ilegal*) to refer to these children, with no uses of *no autorizado* occurring. This marked difference across languages will be taken up in the discussion section as it underscores the potential for alternative media, in this case media in Spanish, to create a space to resist the hegemonic structure through alternative rhetorical strategies (see Strom "Social Hierarchy"). At any rate, the existence of alternative forms of expression point to the decisions journalists make when writing about child immigration. Just as ideological implications and the power of rhetoric (Dolmage) are clear in this decision (see Fairclough; van Dijk, *Discourse and Power*), power and ideology are also revealed in the choice to use *ilegal* or *illegal,* even as adjectives and adverbs. Thus, this section illustrates the patterns and preferences of the use of *ilegal* and *illegal* in adjectival and adverbial forms and, more important, the resulting rhetorical strategy of embodying unaccompanied Latinx children as criminals.

Of the eighteen uses of *ilegal* in the Spanish-language data, only one appeared in the adjectival form; seven of the eighty-one uses of *illegal* in the English-language data appeared in the adjectival form. Thus, both languages strongly disprefer using *ilegal* or *illegal* as an adjective. The one adjectival use of *ilegal* can only be connected to unaccompanied Latinx children through the metaphor CHILDREN ARE DANGEROUS WATERS (see Strom and Alcock):

1. La "Operación Coyote" durará aproximadamente 90 días para combatir el flujo migratorio *ilegal* que llega por la frontera sur del país. (*El diario / La prensa*; emphasis added)
   "Operation Coyote" will last approximately 90 days in order to combat the *illegal* migratory flow that is arriving at the country's southern border.

Important in example 1 are the terms that collocate, or co-occur (see Fairclough), with "*ilegal*" to establish the embodiment of unaccompanied Latinx children as criminals. The first that occurs is "*Operación Coyote*" ("Operation Coyote"), which, according to the Obama Administration's White House Web page, includes "[a] 60-person investigative team [that] was sent to south Texas to dismantle *criminal* organizations smuggling people into the U.S." (emphasis added). Although this explanation was not readily available to readers of this newspaper, the collocation of "*operación*" ("operation") with "*ilegal*" is sufficient to conjure up images of extensive government-backed military efforts to stop something inherently bad, inherently criminal. The second term that collocates with "*ilegal*" is "*flujo*" ("flow") which, as mentioned above, calls upon the notion that children are a dangerous natural disaster that must be stopped. Overall, the rhetorical strategy writes criminality onto unaccompanied Latinx children and makes it clear a military-like operation is necessary to stop them. However, this embodiment occurs only once in 118 articles in Spanish, meaning it would likely have little lasting effect on the mindset of readers with regards to the way they view unaccompanied Latinx children.

A similar embodiment of children as criminals occurs in the English-language data with a slightly higher frequency of seven uses in a total of eighty-seven articles. Examples 2 and 3 are representative of the majority of the uses of *illegal* in these articles in that they use this term to directly modify "immigrant children" or "minors," respectively:

2. Immigration advocates also credit Mr. Johnson with speaking up about a border crisis that both Democrats and Republicans say the White House was slow to notice, even as the number of *illegal* immigrant children surged in the last year. (Steinhauer; emphasis added)

3. "Aside from being part of an obvious humanitarian crisis, these unaccompanied *illegal* minors have left the federal government scrambling to triage the results of its failed border security and immigration policies" Perry said. (Hennessy-Fiske)

There is no doubt that "illegal" as a direct modifier of immigrant children/minors functions in the way previous research has attested: it criminalizes the children and thus allows, or perhaps even requires, a less-humane reaction to them. Again, we notice the collocation of "surged" with "illegal" in example 2 that works in concert with the CHILDREN ARE DANGEROUS WATERS metaphor to underscore the dangerous nature of unaccompanied Latinx children.

News articles in both languages strongly preferred to associate illegality with unaccompanied Latinx children by means of their actions. Of the eighteen uses of *ilegal* in the Spanish-language data, seventeen appeared in the adverbial form; seventy-four of the eighty-one uses of *illegal* in the English-language data appeared in the adverbial form. The data in Spanish show that the adverb *ilegalmente* ("illegally") is used to modify the verbs *cruzar* ("to cross"), *entrar* ("to enter"), and *llegar* ("to arrive"). The example that follows is a curious juxtaposition of the expression of compassion for the plight of unaccompanied Latinx children and the embodiment of these children as criminals by way of their criminal actions:

4. El presidente Barack Obama destacó que su país tiene "una gran compasión" por los miles de niños que han llegado solos a la frontera intentando entrar *ilegalmente* a Estados Unidos. (Peña, "Obama"; emphasis added)
    President Barack Obama noted that his country has "great compassion" for the thousands of children who have arrived at the border alone trying to *illegally* enter the United States.

In example 4, President Obama offers one potential response to the arrival of unaccompanied minors who have suffered greatly in their journey to the United States: compassion. However, this is immediately followed by "*ilegalmente*" ("illegally") as a modifier of the verb "*entrar*" ("to enter"). Although *ilegal* describes an action rather than a person, the people who carried out this action in example 4 are "*miles de niños*" ("thousands of children"). It is not difficult to map criminality onto the body of one who does illegal, criminal actions. Therefore, this example and the others like it in the dataset embody unaccompanied Latinx children as criminals. The specification of the large number of children only adds to the potential threat by communicating that now there are thousands of criminals arriving at the border. It is impossible to determine whether readers would follow President Obama's explicit message in feeling compassion for these children or the implicit message sent through the adverbial use of *ilegal* that these children are criminals. These conflicting ideas do appear to be a hallmark of this dataset and are likely indicative of United States mainstream society's desire to embody all immigrants as criminals but also their recognition that children should be treated differently than adults.

The English-language dataset patterns in much the same way, with *illegally* modifying the verbs *cross, enter, live*. Example 5 leaves no doubt in the reader's mind that unaccompanied minors have committed a crime because they have "crossed the border illegally":

5. When law enforcement officials detain unaccompanied minors who have crossed the border *illegally*, they have 72 hours to place them in a program within the federal Office of Refugee Resettlement. (Smith; emphasis added)

Inherently, cross, enter, and live are not troubling processes. We all cross streets, enter rooms, and live our lives without problem on a daily basis. However, when these actions are done illegally, they become more sinister, particularly when they happen across a tightly controlled international border. The next logical conclusion is that the unaccompanied Latinx children who carry out these illegal, criminal actions are themselves criminals.

To summarize, *ilegal* appeared only eighteen times in a total of 118 Spanish-language articles, while *illegal* appeared more frequently, eighty-one times, in the 87 English-language articles. Reporting in both languages preferred this adverbial use of this term to describe children's actions rather than the children themselves. Although the clear preference for the adverbial use of *ilegal* or *illegal* indicates journalists are heeding the suggestions of editors, does qualifying the actions as *ilegal* or illegal rather than the people themselves as *ilegal* or illegal constitute a substantive change in the way this rhetoric embodies unaccompanied Latinx children? While at first blush *ilegal* or *illegal* as modifier of a verb does not appear to have the same effect as *ilegal* or *illegal* in the adjectival form, ultimately it does the same rhetorical work by embodying children as criminals. That is to say, it does not require much of the reader to conflate the idea of someone who does illegal activities, or crimes, with a criminal because criminals commit illegal activities. In this way, the adverbial use of *ilegal* or *illegal* is a highly productive rhetorical strategy in this dataset that inevitably achieves the embodiment of unaccompanied Latinx immigrants as criminals.

It must be noted that news articles in both languages used *ilegal* or *illegal* in its adjectival form much more frequently to refer to adult immigrants. Given that the dataset was selected based on the topic of unaccompanied Latinx child immigrants, this is a possible indicator that age does, in fact, play a part in the use of this term. That is to say, although the mainstream and alternative news sources considered in this project rhetorically embody children as criminals, this embodiment is not nearly as pervasive as that of adults. It is possible this points to some agency and awareness on the part of authors in their rhetorical strategies whereby they try to avoid inhumane embodiments of an at-risk group. Indeed, this struggle is evident in the ways authors simultaneously embody children as victims, which is addressed below.

EMBODYING LATINX CHILD IMMIGRANTS AS VICTIMS

Analyses of the passive voice can aid in our understanding of how media rhetoric embodies certain social actors because writers use this grammatical construct to bring to the fore the resulting action of a verb rather than the agent of a verb. It is important to note that journalists make a decision (consciously or not) when they use the passive voice; thus, this decision is ideologically motivated (again, consciously or not) (see Fairclough; van Dijk, *Discourse and Power*). Van Djik writes that the passive voice does rhetorical work by hiding the negative actions of Us (i.e., the majority group) and the positive actions of Them (i.e., minoritized groups), and in this way reinforces the ideology of blameless Us and victimized Them ("Discourse and Power"). Furthermore, Roger Fowler demonstrates how the passive voice underscores the role of the patients or experiencers of verbs, thereby foreclosing their agency. In the current study, the passive voice hides the negative actions of the immigration system against unaccompanied Latinx children, thus allowing the focus to shift to those who are the patients or experiencers of the

Table 10.1. Frequency of past participles representing processes in passive
constructions; Spanish-language data

Processes	Frequency
Detenido (detained)	26
Deportado (deported)	18
Trasladado (moved)	16
Enviado (sent)	10

Table 10.2. Frequency of past participles representing processes in passive
constructions; English-language data

Processes	Frequency
Deported	33
Released	33
Apprehended	27
Allowed	24
Placed	22
Sent	22
Detained	21
Caught	14

verbs. For this reason, it is imperative to consider not only the agents who are obfuscated through the use of the passive voice but also the past participles (the processes [Richardson]) indicative of the new focus of the passive structure.

Table 10.1 gives the terms *El diario / La prensa* and *La opinión* most frequently use as processes of the passive voice; table 2 gives the terms *the New York Times* and the *Los Angeles Times* most frequently use as the processes of the passive voice. All of the processes in tables 10.1 and 10.2 are directly related to the detaining, processing, and moving of unaccompanied Latinx children through the justice system until their court hearings, often with the outcome of deportation. Because all occurrences of the passive voice in the dataset were considered, it is noteworthy that the processes related to the negative aspects of child immigration were most frequent, rather than those associated with more positive aspects of child immigration such as, say, the reunification of children with their parents or a child acquiring Special Immigrant Juvenile (SIJ) status.

One question that arises is, Why does the passive voice appear so frequently with negative processes in this dataset? It is reasonable to argue that the focus on these negative processes through the use of the passive voice may lead to an enhanced understanding of the plight of these children by the United States public and thus an insistence in the improvement of their situation. However, in light of Lilie Chouliaraki's study on the representation of suffering in the media, this seems unlikely. Chouliaraki has demonstrated that the representation of immigrants and refugees as victims leads to inaction by audiences who feel the situation is so dire there is nothing they can do to remedy it. However, Chouliaraki also found that the expression of an opposing idea through another mode (i.e., images) can result in action by the audience. This idea is taken up in this discussion as it relates to the potential for opposing embodiments of unaccompanied Latinx children to incite readers to do something to improve this inhumane and unjust situation.

The next question to be addressed concerns the rhetorical strategy that results from this grammatical construct. It bears repeating that the passive voice allows readers to focus on the patients or experiencers of the processes rather than the social actors who carry them out. In this dataset, this focus means the passive voice hides the identity of those who carry out the negative aspects of the immigration process and instead focuses on the patients or experiencers of these actions: unaccompanied Latinx children. The examples that follow illustrate the rhetorical work carried out by the passive voice that embodies children as victims (and, of no lesser importance, represents federal government entities as blameless bystanders).

All the agents hidden by the most frequently occurring use of passive voice in the dataset were federal-government entities. In the examples that follow, United States immigration court is the hidden agent of the passive voice:

> 6a. Estos menores no *son deportados* de inmediato sino que tienen que pasar procesos individuales en tribunales. (Marrero; emphasis added)
> These children *are not deported* immediately, but rather have to go through individual processes in court.
>
> 6b. Children could *be deported* within a few months, instead of years. (Stewart; emphasis added)

In examples 6a and 6b, the passive voice hides the agents who *deportan/* deport unaccompanied Latinx children. The use of the passive voice here implies that the newspapers, whether they realize it or not, may not consider it prudent to reveal the agents of the deporting process, that is, immigration court. In other words, the preference for the passive voice for these processes acknowledges their negativity and that to be associated with them is not desirable. By disassociating immigration court from the deportation process, the newspapers in this dataset also distance immigration court from the results of deportation, which for many youths could arguably be death at the hands of gangs in their home countries. By suppressing the agency of immigration court, the newspapers focus on the process of deportation. The rhetorical result of this focus is the embodiment of unaccompanied Latinx children as victims of the immediate immigration process in the United States and of any consequences that happen after their deportation.

The newspapers in this dataset also suppress border patrol as the agents of negative processes against unaccompanied Latinx children.

7a. Sólo [*sic*] en el sector del Valle del Río Bravo, en Texas, cerca de 300 menores indocumentados *son detenidos* a diario. (Peña, "Oleda de niños"; emphasis added)

> Just in the Rio Grande Valley sector, in Texas, close to 300 undocumented youth *are detained* daily.

7b. More than 57,000 unaccompanied minors have *been detained* crossing the southwest border illegally since Oct. 1. (Preston; emphasis added)

In examples 7a and 7b, the passive voice hides the agents who *detienen/* detain unaccompanied Latinx children. In this way, the Spanish- and English-language newspapers in the dataset use the passive voice to distance and dissociate the border patrol from the detention of immigrant children. If the border patrol were represented as "tough on immigration" and as immediately sending back all children, as would be the likely interpretation if the active voice were used, some would (justly) criticize them for inhumane treatment. However, because it is not represented that way, the focus shifts to the process, detention, and those who are the experiencers of this process, immigrant children. Being a minor who is detained by a powerful government entity in a foreign country must be a frightening experience and likely amplifies the feeling of victimization for these children. Indeed, the rhetorical strategy of using *detener/*detain as the process highlighted by the passive voice embodies unaccompanied Latinx children as victims. At the same time, it allows readers to dissociate the border patrol with these detentions, thus making it seem as though the process simply happens.

The fact that the active voice appears in the dataset with all but one of the processes appearing in tables 1 and 2 indicates it is a viable, though uncommon, option for journalists. Examples 8a and 8b illustrate the active voice for the verb *detener/*detain:

8a. Desde octubre de 2013 y para el pasado 15 de junio, *las autoridades en la frontera detuvieron* a 52,000 niños indocumentados no acompañados. (Peña, "Niños migrantes"; emphasis added)

> From October 2013 until June 15, *border authorities detained* 52,000 undocumented and unaccompanied children.

8b. *Officers . . . had detained* a group of migrants ahead of Alejandro's group. (Leland; emphasis added)

While in examples 7a and 7b above, the agent of the verb *detener/detain* was suppressed, in examples 8a and 8b, it is clear who carried out these actions against unaccompanied Latinx children: in example 8a, the agent of the verb is "*autoridades en la frontera*" ("border authorities"), while in example 8b the agent of the verb is "officers," both of which refer to border patrol. Here the active voice communicates with more transparency the actions of this powerful government group against unaccompanied Latinx children. The active voice was far less common with these processes than the passive voice, meaning that the overall representation of immigrant children is that of victims. However, of note is how examples like 8a hint at the potential for alternative media, in this case Spanish-language media, to constitute a place for transparent immigration reporting. Similarly, example 8b challenges the hegemonic structure because the mainstream media rarely, if ever, highlight the role of the majority group in carrying out negative actions against members of non-majority groups, particularly if they are children. That is, this example provides readers with an alternative and more transparent understanding of what happens at the United States' southwest border. However, these instances of the transparent allocation of agency with regards to negative immigration processes are very few in the dataset. Thus, the passive voice embodies Latinx children as victims of the border patrol and of the results of their interactions with border patrol. Importantly, this embodiment can function without the explicit expression of the border patrol (or, as in previous examples, federal-government entities); in fact, it is amplified by their suppression. Thus, this grammatical structure allows these social actors to remain blameless in the face of yet another troubling situation for unaccompanied Latinx children in their journey to the United States.

To conclude, the English- and Spanish-language media in this dataset prefer the passive voice over the active voice to avoid blaming powerful officials for actions like detaining and deporting they carry out against unaccompanied Latinx children. This rhetorical choice shifts the focus to the children as those who must face and experience these traumatic processes without their parents in a foreign country. It is not difficult to see how this grammatical structure embodies children as victims and that this rhetorical embodiment calls for compassion. The section that follows considers whether compassion is the likely reaction from readers or if the simultaneous embodiment of unaccompanied Latinx children as criminal forecloses this possibility.

DISCUSSION

This study postulates that print media in English and Spanish published in the United States use embodied language that creates an embodied rhetoric of unaccompanied Latinx children. That creation has direct and lasting impacts on the lives and bodies of these children through the power these representations have to shape the way the public views and reacts to immigrant children. By embodying children as victims through the use of the passive voice, the news articles in both languages pointed readers in the direction of compassion. On the other hand, by writing criminality onto their bodies through the use of *ilegal* and *illegal*, the articles, particularly in English, led readers to a very different reaction, one of brutal exclusion. Drawing on critical discourse studies and social semiotics, it is possible this study does unexpected rhetorical work wherein the cognitive dissonance of opposing embodiments captures the attention of the reader, who may not typically pay much attention to such reporting. Given that previous research has shown dissonant ideologies across modes in the same medium may incite audiences to action (for example, to buy a product) (see Strom, "¿Inglés *Sin* Barreras?") or to react with compassion to suffering (Chouliaraki), the same could be possible for dissonant ideologies presented within the same mode. In the case of the current study, the simultaneous embodiment of children as criminals and victims may demand the attention of readers. Of course, this increased attention would beg the question, What kind of reaction would result? Rejection is the expected reaction to criminals, but acceptance and compassion are expected for victims. Unfortunately, given that the current study only includes one mode (the verbal mode), it is difficult to postulate how successful this dissonance would be in inciting audience action. What can be said is that these dissonant embodiments of unaccompanied Latinx children in *the New York Times*, the *Los Angeles Times, El diario / La prensa*, and *La opinión* likely reflect the mixed opinions of society. Such opinions are based in the understanding that children are innocent but also that immigrants are inherently criminals.

The resulting rhetorical dichotomy of cautious inclusion versus brutal exclusion has material implications that bear out across the lifetime of these children. Here we can draw upon an idea presented in the introduction to this volume, that the body itself is socially constructed, is discursively and linguistically constructed (Knoblauch and Moeller, chapter 1). In this analysis, we see a discursive-linguistic representation of the social construction, deconstruction, and reconstruction of Latinx child immigrants' bodies: they are constructed as innocent children who are victims, only to be later deconstructed and then reconstructed as criminals on the same order of magnitude as a natural disaster. Of course, these rhetorical processes are not haphazard but rather are motivated by, or perhaps are mere reflections of, society's construction, deconstruction, and reconstruction of such bodies. What, then, are the material implications of these processes that are indicative of the simultaneous inclusion and exclusion of child immigrants in United

States society? We cannot say with certainty what the result will be given the recent nature of this immigration, but it is not hard to imagine the physical and psychological toll it would take on anyone, not least of all on children, to constitute the rhetorical place where the emotions of the United States public regarding immigration play out. Indeed, in recent years we have seen exclusionary practices that create hostile environments for these children based on their putative "illegality" (Negrón-Gonzales; Paret) and their linguistic (in)capabilities (cf. Leeman; Zentella), both of which have obvious consequences for their future education, employment, and residence in the United States (Negrón-Gonzales; Unzueta Carrasco and Seif). Thus, these rhetorical processes serve to reestablish who can be cautiously included (children in the role of victims) and who must be brutally excluded (children in the role of criminals), always at the expense of the children.

This collection points to the endless possibilities of embodiments in a number of contexts, taking into account a number of variables, in a number of media, through a number of lenses. In this light, I emphasize the importance of considering the possibilities of embodiments across languages. *Illegal* appeared far more frequently in the English-language data in this study than *ilegal* appeared in the Spanish-language data. Furthermore, passive constructions with children as experiencers of negative processes and powerful government entities as the hidden agents were much more common in the English-language data. These results may add support to the notion that alternative media, in this case media in Spanish, constitute a space to resist the hegemonic structure through alternative rhetorical strategies (see Strom, "Social Hierarchy"). Put another way, there is a very real possibility for resistance through the comparative study of rhetorical embodiments across languages. Thus, this study serves as a call to carry out future research on other rhetorical structures in Spanish-language media that can shed light on the potential for more humane and ethical embodiments of unaccompanied Latinx children.

Until the United States immigration system is reformed, it is likely similar immigration events will occur. At the time of the preparation of this chapter, the country had just experienced the arrival tens of thousands of immigrants—adults and children—from this same region. Further research is needed from a number of theoretical and analytical approaches to allow a more nuanced understanding of the role of mainstream and alternative media in offering representations of immigrants that call for humane and ethical responses to what they experience before and after arriving to the United States.

WORKS CITED

Burroughs, Elaine. "Discursive Representations of 'Illegal Immigration' in the Irish Newsprint Media: The Domination and Multiple Facets of the 'Control' Argumentation." *Discourse & Society*, vol. 26, no. 2, 2014, pp. 165–183. *SAGE Journals*, doi:10.1177/0957926514556029.

Catalano, Theresa. "When Children Are Water: Representation of Central American Migrant Children in Public Discourse and Implications for Educators." *Journal of Latinos and Education*, vol. 16, no. 2, 2017, pp. 124–142. *Taylor & Francis Online*, doi:10.1080/15348431.2016.1205988.

Chouliaraki, Lilie. *The Spectatorship of Suffering*. SAGE, 2006.

Chouliaraki, Lilie, and Norman Fairclough. *Discourse in Late Modernity: Rethinking Critical Discourse Analysis*. Edinburg UP, 1999.

Colford, Paul. "'Illegal Immigrant' No More." *AP. The Definitive Source*, 2 Apr. 2013, blog.ap.org/announcements/illegal-immigrant-no-more. Accessed 20 Jan. 2016.

Delbene, Roxana. "Discourse Practices of De-humanization in the Representation of *Unauthorized Immigrants* in the U.S. Press." *Readings in Language Studies: Language and Power*, edited by John Watzke, Paul Miller, and Miguel Mantero, vol. 2, International Society for Language Studies, 2010, pp. 219–239.

Dolmage, Jay. *Disabled Upon Arrival: Eugenics, Immigration, and the Construction of Race and Disability*. The Ohio State UP, 2018.

El diario/La prensa. "EEUU lanza 'Operación Coyote' para frenar tráfico de inmigrantes." 23 July 2014.

Edgar, Deirdre. "L. A. Times Updates Guidelines for Covering Immigration." *Los Angeles Times*, 1 May 2013, articles.latimes.com/2013/may/01/local/la-me-rr-la-times-guidelines-immigration-20130501. Accessed 20 Jan. 2016.

Erdal, Marta Bivand, and Ceri Oeppen. "Forced to Leave? The Discursive and Analytical Significance of Describing Migration as Forced and Voluntary." *Aspiration, Desire and the Drivers of Migration*. Spec. issue of *Journal of Ethnic and Migration Studies*, vol. 44, no. 6, 2018, pp. 981–998. *Taylor & Francis Online*, doi:10.1080/1369183X.2017.1384149.

Fairclough, Norman. *Language and Power*. 2nd ed. Longman, 2001.

Fairclough, Norman, Phil Graham, Jay Lemke, and Ruth Wodak. "Introduction." *Critical Discourse Studies*, vol. 1, no. 1, 2004, pp. 1–7. *Taylor & Francis Online*, doi:10.1080/17405900410001674489.

Fowler, Roger. *Language in the News. Discourse and Ideology in the Press*. Routledge, 1991.

Gutiérrez, Félix. "Spanish-Language Media in America: Background, Resources, History." *Journalism History*, vol. 4, no. 2, 1977, pp. 34–68. *Taylor & Francis Online*, doi:10.1080/00947679.1977.12066840.

Heidbrink, Laura. *Migrant Youth, Transnational Families, and the State: Care and Contested Interests*. U of Pennsylvania P, 2014.

Hennessy-Fiske, Molly. "More Youths Crossing Border Alone." Los Angeles Times, 22 Feb. 2014.

Hesford, Wendy. *Spectacular Rhetorics: Human Rights Visions, Recognitions, Feminisms*. Duke UP, 2011.

Kehaulani Goo, Sara. "Unauthorized Immigrants: Who They Are and What the Public Thinks," *Pew Research Center*, 15 Jan. 2015, www.pewresearch.org/key-datapoints/immigration/. Accessed 24 Jun. 2015.

Knoblauch, A. Abby. "Bodies of Knowledge: Definitions, Delineations, and Implications of Embodied Writing in the Academy." *Composition Studies*, vol. 40, no. 2, 2012, pp. 50–65. *JSTOR*, www.jstor.org/stable/compstud.40.2.0050.

Krogstad, Jens Manuel, and Ana Gonzalez-Barrera. "Number of Latino Children Caught Trying to Enter U. S. Nearly Doubles in Less Than a Year." *Pew Research Center*, 10 Jun.

2014, www.pewresearch.org/fact-tank/2014/06/10/number-of-latino-children-caught
-trying-to-enter-u-s-nearly-doubles-in-less-than-a-year/. Accessed 25 Jun. 2015.

Leach, Michael, and Anna Zamora. "Illegals/*Ilegales*: Comparing Anti-Immigrant/Anti-
Refugee Discourses in Australia and Spain." *Journal of Iberian and Latin American Studies*,
vol. 12, no. 1, 2006, pp. 51–64. *Taylor & Francis Online*, doi:10.1080/13260219.2006.1
0426842.

Leeman, Jennifer. "Illegal Accents: Qualifications, Discrimination, and Distraction in Arizona's Monitoring of Teachers." *Arizona Firestorm: Global Immigration Realities, National
Media, and Provincial Politics*, edited by Otto Santa Ana and Celeste González de Busta-
mante, Rowman and Littlefield, 2012, pp. 145–166.

Leland, John. "Fleeing Violence in Honduras, a Teenage Boy Seeks Asylum in Brook-
lyn." *New York Times*, Dec. 7, 2014. https://www.nytimes.com/2014/12/07/nyregion
/fleeing-violence-in-honduras-a-teenage-boy-seeks-asylum-in-brooklyn.html.

Marrero, Pilar. "Existe poca ayuda legal para niños migrantes." *El diario/La prensa*, 17
June 2014.

Martín Rojo, Luisa, and Teun van Dijk. " 'There Was a Problem and It Was Solved!': Legiti-
mating the Expulsion of 'Illegal' Immigrants in Spanish Parliamentary Discourse."
Discourse & Society, vol. 8, no. 4, 1997, pp. 523–566. *JSTOR*, www.jstor.com/stable/
42888841.

Merolla, Jennifer, S. Karthick Ramakrishnan, and Chris Haynes. " 'Illegal,' 'Undocumented,' or 'Unauthorized': Equivalency Frames, Issue Frames, and Public Opinion
on Immigration." *Perspectives on Politics*, vol. 11, no. 3, 2013, pp. 789–807. *JSTOR*, www
.jstor.org/stable/43279647.

Mohd Don, Zuraidah, and Charity Lee. "Representing Immigrants as Illegals, Threats and
Victims in Malaysia: Elite Voices in the Media." *Discourse & Society*, vol. 25, no. 6, 2014,
pp. 687–705. *SAGE Journals*, doi:10.1177/0957926514536837.

Negrón-Gonzales, Genevieve. "Undocumented, Unafraid and Unapologetic: Re-articulatory
Practices and Migrant Youth 'Illegality.' " *Latino Studies*, vol. 12, no. 2, 2014, pp. 259–278.
ResearchGate, doi:10.1057/lst.2014.20.

O'Doherty, Kieran, and Amanda Lecouteur. " 'Asylum Seekers,' 'Boat People' and 'Illegal Immigrants': Social Categorization in the Media." *Australian Journal of Psychology*,
vol. 59, no. 1, 2007, pp. 1–12. *Taylor & Francis Online*, doi:10.1080/00049530600941685.

Paret, Marcel. "Legality and Exploitation: Immigration Enforcement and the US Migrant
Labor System." *Latino Studies*, vol. 12, no. 4, 2014, pp. 503–526.

Peña, María. "Niños migrantes: La Casa Blanca quiere contener la crisis." *El diario/La
prensa*, 20 June 2014.

Peña, María. "Obama: 'Los niños serán repatriados.' " *El diario/La prensa*, 25 July 2014.

Peña, María. "Oleada de niños migrantes atiza debate sobre reforma migratoria." *El
diario/La prensa*, 10 June 2014.

Preston, Julia. "Most in Poll Say Children at Border Merit Relief." *New York Times*, July 29,
2014. https://www.nytimes.com/2014/07/30/us/amid-fears-of-open-door-poll-finds
-qualified-support-for-child-migrants.html.

Puar, Jasbir. *The Right to Maim: Debility, Capacity, Disability*. Duke UP, 2017.

Ribero, Ana Milena. " 'Papá, Mamá, I'm Coming Home': Family, Home, and the Neo-
liberal Immigrant Nation in the National Immigrant Youth Alliance's 'Bring Them
Home' Campaign." *Rhetoric Review*, vol. 37, no. 3, 2018, pp. 273–285. *Taylor & Francis
Online*, doi:10.1080/07350198.2018.1463499.

Richardson, John. *Analysing Newspapers: An Approach from Critical Discourse Analysis*. Palgrave
Macmillan, 2007.

Santa Ana, Otto. *Brown Tide Rising: Metaphors of Latinos in Contemporary American Public
Discourse*. U of Texas P, 2002.

Schmidt, Susan. " 'They Need to Give Us a Voice': Lessons from Listening to Unaccompanied Central American and Mexican Children on Helping Children Like Themselves."

Journal on Migration and Human Security, vol. 5. no. 1, 2017, pp. 57–81. *SAGE Journals*, doi:10.1177/233150241700500104.

Shapiro, Rebecca. "NY Times Tweaks Entry on 'Illegal Immigrant.'" *Huffington Post*, 23 Apr. 2013, https://www.huffpost.com/entry/ny-times-illegal-immigrant_n_3141724. Accessed 20 Jan. 2016.

Smith, Morgan. "With Uncertainty, Schools Brace for New Arrivals." *The New York Times*, 3 Aug. 2014.

Steinhauer, Jennifer. "Open to Both Sides, Homeland Security Chief Steps into Immigration Divide." *The New York Times*, 6 Aug. 2014.

Stewart, Nikita. "Program to Give Legal Help to Young Migrants." *The New York Times*, 23 Sept. 2014.

Strom, Megan. "¿Inglés *Sin* Barreras? A Multimodal Analysis of Ideology and Power." *International Journal of the Linguistic Association of the Southwest*, vol. 32, no. 1, 2013, pp. 49–73.

Strom, Megan. "Social Hierarchy in Local Spanish-Language Print Media: The Discursive Representation of Latino Social Actors in the United States." *Discourse & Society*, vol. 26, no. 2, 2015, pp. 230–252. *SAGE Journals*, doi:10.1177/0957926514556019.

Strom, Megan. "Spanish-Language Print Media in the United States: A Critical Discourse Analysis of Ideological Representations." *Selected Proceedings of the 16th Hispanic Linguistics Symposium*, edited by Jennifer Cabrelli Amaro, Gillian Lord, Ana de Prada Pérez, and Jessi Aaron, Cascadilla Proceedings Project, 2013, pp. 253–267.

Strom, Megan, and Emily Alcock. "Floods, Waves, and Surges: The Representation of Latin@ Immigrant Children in the United States Mainstream Media." *Critical Discourse Studies*, vol. 14, no. 4, 2017, pp. 440–457. *Taylor & Francis Online*, doi:10.1080/1740590 4.2017.1284137.

Unzueta Carrasco, Tania A., and Hinda Seif. "Disrupting the Dream: Undocumented Youth Reframe Citizenship and Deportability through Anti-deportation Activism." *Mexican (Im)Migrant Students and Education*. Spec. issue of *Latino Studies*, vol. 12, no. 2, 2014, pp. 279–299. *SpringerLink*, doi:10.1057/lst.2014.21.

Van Dijk, Teun. *Discourse and Power*. Palgrave Macmillan, 2008.

White, Kate. "'We Learn the Customs of our New Country, America': Listening to Immigrant Women in the Twentieth Century." *Rhetoric Review*, vol. 35, no. 1, 2016, pp. 10–21. *Taylor & Francis Online*, doi:10.1080/07350198.2016.1107824.

White House. "The Obama Administration's Government-wide Response to Influx of Central American Migrants at the Southwest Border." *White House*, 1 Aug. 2014, obamawhitehouse.archives.gov/the-press-office/2014/08/01/obama-administration-s -government-wide-response-influx-central-american-. Accessed 28 Dec. 2018.

Wingard, Jennifer. *Branded Bodies, Rhetoric, and the Neoliberal Nation-State*. Lexington, 2013.

Wodak, Ruth, and Michael Meyer. "Critical Discourse Analysis: History, Agenda, Theory and Methodology." *Methods of Critical Discourse Analysis*, edited by Ruth Wodak and Michael Meyer, SAGE, 2009, pp. 1–33.

Zentella, Ana Celia. "TWB (Talking While Bilingual): Linguistic Profiling of Latina/os, and Other Linguistic Torquemadas." *Latino Studies*, vol. 12, no. 4, 2014, pp. 620–625. *SpringerLink*, doi:10.1057/lst.2014.63.

PART III

Textuality, Multimodality, Digitality

11

THE SUCCESSFUL TEXT IS NOT ALWAYS THE ONE THAT MURDERS ME TO PROTECT YOU

Vyshali Manivannan (Pace University-Pleasantville)

Δ I wrote an essay in 2017. It traces relationships between chronic pain, digital imaging, clinical and academic scholarship, metaphor. It argues for a new poetics of pain. It's 12-point Times New Roman, two columns, with 1-inch margins, paragraphs, section breaks. It was peer reviewed, published after a revise-and-resubmit in a SAGE special issue. Its citation alone suggests rigor.

Δ I am told the successful scholarly text, the publishable text that will earn me contract renewal, promotion, tenure-track conversion, is the one that kills me.* I'm told it comes in unisex, one-size-fits-all, 12-point serif fonts, lines spaced the width of a baby's fingerbone. It observes the margins. It's not a Twitter thread, a lyric essay, handwritten marginalia, a series of hidden comments couched in HTML, a bulleted list. It is not, but really always is, one long authorial body told in muddy tripwire.

Δ I have written and published for several years with fibromyalgia, an incurable, nonprogressive chronic pain condition characterized by widespread pain, heightened pain sensitivity, affective dysfunction, and fatigue. My body is unpredictably unruly, but you'd never know it from my scholarship. The ways I express and account for my pain are radically constrained by the formats we expect and materially reward in academia: logocentric, rigidly formatted journal publications with headings, subheadings, linear argumentation, error-free writing disinfected of embodied language, meaning language that evokes bodily actions and functions, and other proofs of an attentive, rational mind unfettered by the urges of the flesh (Knoblauch 52). Mastery of knowledge conflated with mastery over a body so disciplined it disappears. Pages anesthetized to heights this author can't reach.**

---

* The resulting ghosts banished to the extratextual margins. https://tinyurl.com/yx9rd 547.

** You don't have to squint to see the execution taking place. Sick bodies, curable only by death, make sick drafts (Dolphin-Krute, *Ghostbodies*). The signs are there if you can apprehend them. My body hangs from the running header by bound wrists, striated by

---

https://doi.org/10.7330/9781646422012.c011

Δ   *Linearity* is another word for chronology. To extend crip time, the
    constant temporal shifting experienced by a disabled body, fibromyal-
    gic time is measured in multiple temporal structures, as well as their
    loss (Kuppers). Here are four categories in chronic illness literature:
    clock time, biographical time, past-present-future time, and inner
    time (Jowsey 1093–1094). Clock time is endurance. Biographical time
    is the disruption of the rhythm of the social world and of futurity.
    Past-present-future time refers to the formation of bodily experience
    and habit over time. Inner time is the cacophony of all the body's
    metronomes: heartbeat, breath, peristalsis (Jowsey 1095–1098). All
    of this, all at once, is fibromyalgia: a never-ending, cyclical degenera-
    tion, annihilation, and becoming, unpredictably and without end,
    intercalation that corresponds to no one's timekeeping but my own.

Δ   My body of scholarship is an exercise in eugenics, reproducing the
    illusion of homogeneous (able-bodyminded†) academic writers with
    Western/rationalist notions of legitimate expertise. Even in papers
    representing and analyzing my patient expertise, I have to make that
    expertise something to be analyzed in place of knowledges, prac-
    tices, and processes with inherent value. In the institution, *expert* is a
    status attained through reproducible, confirmable, objective analysis;
    revealing through craft what we already know, that pain is an interior
    and intersubjective experience, destabilizes that rank.

Δ   Step lightly or enflesh "the ghosts who appear in the stories we tell
    each other here in the academy" (Powell 12).

Δ   What becomes of the rhetoricity of a body chronically in pain if its self-
    hood is conceived as isolated, incommunicable, shameful? If our schol-
    arship panders to this by favoring dominant discursive practices that are
    purportedly neutral to not only perpetuate the illusion of normative
    scholars but also protect a readership afraid of being either disturbed
    by suffering bodies or stigmatized for not being disturbed enough?

Δ   The Greek uppercase delta signifies change. The asterisk is used to
    correct errors, censor profanity, cut off a piano's prolonged sound.
    The dagger was for cutting dubious content or indicating death. The
    section sign, for law. The double dagger, checkmate. Each of these
    signs appears here. But we're taught symbols only signify in literary
    texts. In scholarship, they're just bullet points.

Δ   A well-organized essay would go like this.*

2.0 spacing, big toes straining to find the footer of a page that fails to accommodate, legs
spread into wishbone. You, trained to be academic inquisitor, cut or stretch me in your
procrustean pages to conform into the only kind of corporeality you're willing to admit.

† "Because mental and physical processes not only affect each other but also give rise
to each other—that is, because they tend to act as one, even though they are conventionally understood as two—it makes more sense to refer to them together, in a
single term" (Price, "Bodymind Problem" 269). But if you prefer a Cartesian split (as
so many of you do), you know what to do with a wishbone.

* Linearity strands me wherever I go, with navigational equipment incompatible to
the task. Chronicity is mythic time, self-renewing, propelling me forward at a halt,

This chapter attempts to account for the ways successful, publishable scholarship deemed worthy of material reward privileges able-bodyminded, neurotypical layouts that implicitly center Western, masculine, linear representations of attention and thought processing (Cole; Dolmage; Hawkins). Such layouts do not include embodied rhetoric, which implies that bodies are rhetorical and that rhetorical arguments align with bodies and indicate an author's intentional efforts to rhetorically represent embodied experience (Knoblauch; Wilson and Lewiecki-Wilson;). It similarly avoids embodied knowledge, the material conditions of production, the corporeal processes and the default epistemological orientation of the fibromyalgic author, whose chronic pain and brain fog mean her body is never invisible or unnoticed to her. Her embodied language describes the flesh of a world that is palpable threat. Anything can fatally hurt. Everything is depletion.

Our expectations of scholarly texts and pained subjects are predetermined by academic discourse, which configures legitimate textual knowledge as antiseptic, cleansed of appeals to sensation. Postanesthetic culture makes pain eradicable and therefore taboo, and so the exposure of pain is seen as a willfully licentious act done to attract curiosity (Garland-Thomson, *Staring* 63; Halttunen 304). Pain is affective contagion. A text that conveys pain, potentially infectious, imperils the "civilized" reader.[†] "Curiosity in the service of mastery tames the extraordinary" (Garland-Thomson, *Staring* 64), but if that curiosity results in bodily arousal, the peril of absorbing carnal sensations contravenes academic expertise; it threatens the knowledge-making endeavor.

Academic knowledge making, from drafting to publication, vanishes the epistemology and ontology of the chronically pained body, cultivating ableist genre conventions like linearity and clinical language,[‡]

---

generating rhythms particular to me, which is to say my body keeps its own time, and linearity is a choreography I clumsily perform for you.

† It's a purposeful choice, this embodied language, as alienated and alienating as I feel, testament to the fact that "the page is not a pool but a skin, a skin is there to hold in and it can feel you touching it. Did you really think it would just lie there and do nothing?" (Atwood 79). If the successful text seeks to murder me, creative destruction and disability masquerade[*,†,‡,§] are the only ways I survive (Siebers).

‡ I'm Léon Foucault's pendulum when pushed, visual proof of rotation, ball and cable swinging unidirectionally while the onlooker and earth turn beneath it. Like it, my direction appears to change relative to your perspective. If you snapped my legs to make a wish, look down, the blood spatter will tell you the axis of my world doesn't match yours. As long as I don't react, I can feign an uncluttered mind. I tell a colleague about my agonizing marathon-drafting sessions, necessary to maximize my moments of full clarity, and she says if I didn't have such a disorganized work ethic, it wouldn't hurt so much to write. Seven years later, I still lie and say a daily writing schedule, chapter divisions, a single mode of (beginning-to-end) reading is how I

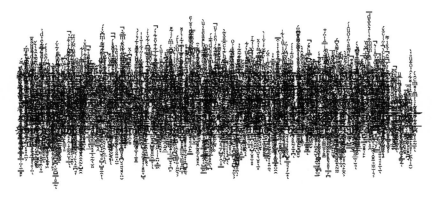

Figure 11.1. Translation: The timekeeping of a body chronically in pain becomes linear in publication, chronological, forward moving. But fibromyalgia is multiple time, incoherent velocity, disjointedness, shock, flight paths predicted and never flown because the endpoint is always calculated to be "better," or even better, "cured." No matter how much I imitate the normative scholarly text, I will never be better or cured. I exist. I endure.

denying chronically pained authors a presence in scholarship. The able body is represented in scholarly craft as the able mind, while the pained subject, to readers and to academic culture, is a liability. Enabling the chronically pained body to visibly impact textual representations of knowledge challenges scholarly gatekeeping as it pertains to embodiment, morality, and intellectual endeavor.[†]

Δ   As the Zalgo text generator[*] indicates, my text, going up, middle, down, is *maxi fucked up*. Maybe it's the closest visual analog to thinking-through fog, thinking-with pain. Simultaneity to the point of chaos, fibromyalgia's temporality. The linearity and typeface of academic discourse can't reveal this. To do so would be to violate the implicit denunciation of the composing body (Dolmage, "Writing Against Normal" 119). Hence being a *fuckup*.

Δ   Maia Dolphin-Krute uses the metaphor of ghosts to describe chronic illness, the body unbound by and abounding with pain that's invisible

---

compose. I'm never called on it. Because of what the product looks like, no one thinks to ask.

†   "I will make less of an attempt to convince my readers than to provoke them into musing along certain lines that are informed not by the traditional rules of argumentation, but by an alternative, nontraditional predisposition . . . a nondisciplinary, nonrational, nonargumentative basis" (Vitanza 44).

*   The Internet meme Zalgo points to something terrible lurking in the margins, the feeling of chaos simulated through scrambled text, coming and coming soon, and in its always-imminent coming exists a reminder that at any moment you might become me (http://www.eeemo.net/).

to everyone else, saying, "[I]f linear continuity is the absence of disruption, the continuity of the ghostbody is the presence of perpetual disruption" (*Ghostbodies* 44). The unappeased ghost is eternal, outside of time, but participant in and witness to its flow. Composing with/in a chronically pained body means composing while disrupted by the absence of normalcy and normal time, the ghostly imperative to haunt your own homes. My epistemological production is most authentic when crafted like a timeline perturbed by its own lack of logical clarity. So the straightforward versions you publish with my name, doctored to look less circuitous, look like I didn't write them at all.

Δ   The successful scholarly text does not convey pain, even if/when the author radiates nothing but.

Δ   Maybe you can't see it here, at this resolution, sized for this page, but the words are there, calcified in Zalgo's white noise. With it, a dangled promise, a desperate need to believe, if I just look long enough, if I wait long enough, the veil will part, everything I need will rise.

Δ   Scholarly texts display as little as possible the embodied circumstances and processes of their production. By conforming to disembodiment, conventional academic discourse problematically valorizes the mode of thinking of Western, heteronormative, masculine, able-bodyminded intellectuals by centering hegemonic voices and recognizable theoretical rigor (Cole; Powell). It's designed to prove authors possess the *cognitive* capital to produce academic work, to engage in *intellectual* endeavor, to *mentally* "fit"* into a university department, a scholarly discipline, and an academic canon whose genre conventions alchemize body into insensate brain.

Δ   Scholarly texts designed to discomfit and arouse expose a (fibromyalgic) author as nonacademic. Her work becomes tabloid sensationalism. Unauthorized expertise. Creative literature. Ghost stories.

Δ   Mel Y. Chen reminds us that the university's insistence on always-sharp, always-on acuity not only excludes the disabled but also pretends the able-bodyminded never experience cognitive fatigue. Writing a conference paper or journal article demands the display of what she calls "a *comprehension*—a word that suggests both finality but also wholeness of grasp" (172). I don't remember the last time I had this.† Brain fog is lethologica, anomia, disordered thinking, dissociation. It makes linearity and sustained focus difficult. I have to trust that revision will let me reorganize in a way that makes sense to everyone but me. I kill myself so the product conforms. Success erases disability (Davis 9).

---

*   "A misfit occurs when the environment does not sustain the shape and function of the body that enters it" (Garland-Thomson, "Story"). I fit the page better with broken legs.

†   For academics, speed is of the essence. It's a bloodletting if you stumble. In the past I cut myself to find the "wholeness of grasp" to meet exceptionally tight deadlines (Chen). The last time I relapsed was that R&R, but respectability politics makes this distasteful to share. You'd prefer not to know. I'm supposed to make it even with broken legs.

Δ   Academic success means having an "unaffected" brain[†] (Price, *Mad* 104).

Δ   Academia positions itself as a moral enterprise, despite being built "in service of and on top of the history of eugenics, lifting some bodies upwards toward privilege upon the footings of segregation and oppression" (Dolmage, *Academic* 50). The nineteenth-century US university bore the markers of a religious and cultural heritage while emulating the research agenda of the German model (Marsden 3–7). Even when intellectualism divested itself of unscientific spirituality, the university retained the humanitarian sensibility, notions of bodily indulgence, "civilized" rhetoric, and "respectable" dispositions of/towards pain.

Δ   The conventions of the scholarly text—namely, its visual layouts, structure, and language—operate to maintain and administer the dominance of Western epistemology. Because writing and epistemology are directly related since language constructs reality, owing its meanings and affective charge at least partially to its chosen conventions, we should pay critical attention to the ethos inscribed into how we write, how our writing looks, whose skins we're asked to wear.

Δ   Words and sentences communicate, and how we visually represent them affects not only the message but also how you perceive the author.

Δ   The craft of letterforms has historically been more about invisible conformity than conspicuousness. Ames Hawkins argues that the standardization of Times New Roman and other serif fonts created a visual frame for the legacy of masculine, colonialist, "civilized" (i.e., not unruly) epistemology, conveying authority, clarity, objective truth, and dispassionate distance (163). Straight-edged and capitalistically designed to fit more words on a page, Times New Roman was created to be efficient, powerful, appealing to rational intelligence. Its uses in newspaper design link it to journalistic principles like truth, objectivity, speed, vertical thinking. Its serifs are trustworthy, older than defaults like Calibri and other sans serif fonts designed for screen reading, and trustworthy *because* they're older members of the elite journalistic knowledge-making enterprise. The font you use is often taken as an evaluative measure of your intelligence, class, taste level, race, gender, capability (Turner 90). DeVoss suggests typeface is transparent; we only notice it when it challenges our expectations ("Matters"). Similarly, Times New Roman, whose use is required in most university courses and journals, makes all authors straight, white, able-bodied, neurotypical men, sustaining the imperialist myth of the default identity, the absence of race, sexuality, able-bodiedness.

---

†   "Brain fog" is actively unwanted in academic spaces, and the potential for spontaneous agonistic encounters in these spaces exacerbates fogginess. In these spaces, cognitive difference or disability represents the unthinkable. When I'm forced to cop to it, I say it like a dismissal of self or an apology to others, with that pervasive polite attitude that accepts and forgives the university's structural discrimination against chronic illness and the temporal rhythms that go with it, and I hate myself just a little bit more.

"Professional" fonts like Times New Roman, Arial, Cambria, Calibri ask me to take up less space. To be rational, not creative.

Δ   Pain is personal and interpersonal, subjective and intersubjective, intensely private and isolating, infinitely communicable and sharable (Morris: Scarry). It's not always hidden from view. Language constructs it. It speaks affectively. In official discourse, pain is monolithic, disruptive, and unendurable; in pop culture, expressing it, or even having it, is constructed as a physical and moral flaw.*

Δ   Like Dolmage asserts, "[A]s we dictate that the word must bear no trace of the non-normative body, we grant the word (and the technologies that produce it) a normative imperative" ("Writing" 111).

Δ   "Although typefaces are a subtle part of everyday life, at best innocuous and at worst invisible, they, in fact, contribute to larger systems of power, control, and oppression by serving as visible marks of identities, tastes, levels of expertise, and social positions," all of which are embodied (Turner 104). Calibri, MS Word's default font since 2007, might abolish serifs in favor of a "hip," modern sensibility, but I've read how its creator defended it against criticism, likening it to a modern replacement for Times New Roman, novel and playful but not frivolous, and most significantly, *neutral*, saying, "If you're eating soup, you shouldn't remember the shape of the spoon" (Arbes). Which is another way of saying the page is the realm of the (neurotypical) mind, not the (dis-eased) body.

Δ   If spoons are widely used as the analogy for how those with chronic pain and fatigue ration a finite amount of energy, then forgetting the shape or supply of spoons is a luxury I don't have.

Δ   Dolphin-Krute says, "Having a deadline implies having a product that must be due by that time. The deadline of death means optimizing your pain and time-management strategies to produce a narrative of how well you survived before you die. Death is a failure of management" ("Daily"). By writing this, I'm failing to manage your perception of me, risking eviction from the neurotypical academy, a variant of this death.

Δ   In the absence of embodied rhetoric, the text becomes the corporeal substitute for the authorial body. The presumption that text is transparent and the body invisible, and "real" pain is neither, forecloses an epistemology informed by chronic pain. "Real" pain is sanitized out of the scholarly text, so any claims of chronic pain in this genre look like malingering.

Δ   "It matters who reads, it matters who engages, and it matters who is conceptualized as a reader" (Yergeau et al.). How you choose to read says a lot about your politics of knowledge.

---

*   My cervical spine, upper traps, ribs, and psoas have needed a coddling I can't give them since June 2018. Recovery time is so often denied by publishing schedules. We can't forget the myth of the marathon, which is that its first runner died of exhaustion on reaching the finish line. He was a courier. There are consequences for not doing your job. I can't get tired of being your pendulum. I can't refuse what you wish.

Δ   Successful scholarship, the kind that "counts" on a CV, models writing in which agonistic logos and straightforward thesis-and-support argumentation are deeply, ideologically entrenched (Lee 94). Melanie Lee describes the formatting requirements for her dissertation as a rhetoric of distance, that is, impersonal disembodiment, necessary to portray herself as credible and authoritative. This comes packaged with gendered assumptions about expertise, neutrality of representation, what kinds of bodies get to be *neutral.*

Δ   Margaret Price's work on intellectual disability and school: the academy (re)produces able minds in its sociality, procedures, formats, exit examinations. Neurodiversity is not welcome (*Mad* 104–106). Or, welcome only within the parameters of what Chen calls the "disciplined cognator": able to name, retrieve, taxonomize in service to the aesthetic of modern rationality (178). We are ideal candidates when our disabilities don't show.

Δ   Academic productivity, sociality, and success rely on mainstream notions of able-bodymindedness (Chen 176–177). What/where we publish impacts other fields of academic activity, so traditional academic writing is configured to impress journal and book editors, colleagues, search committees, tenure committees.* The scholarly genre thus "not only shapes content and sways understanding but it constrains what we are permitted to say" (Morris 34). When we enter a discipline, we must fit in.

Δ   If you were to photocopy this one sided and cut these bullet points into playing cards, use the footnotes like game currency, shuffle once you have a complete deck, designate the top twenty a common pool, then gather a group of scholars, deal out your hands, and play it like a card drafting game, it's a closer simulation of how I must compose through pain+fog.** But you won't. And even if you do, you won't win.

Δ   So much of this essay is disability masquerade, an "alternative method of managing social stigma through disguise [by] relying not on the imitation of a dominant social role but on the assumption of an identity marked as stigmatized, marginal, or inferior" (Siebers 5). After all, "serious" documents, like scholarly publications, reflect the

---

*   At a college where I adjuncted, I was informally told the department's search committee had just rejected a promising TT candidate because he had followed up his dissertation with a novel. *He should have published the novel first, then the dissertation,* the chair said. *It looks like his theoretical rigor and self-discipline are on the decline. Make sure you don't make the same mistake.* Well. Look at what I'm doing now. No wonder I have to hang.

**   I'm composing this essay in Sangha Kali, a font inspired by the Brahmic scripts of Dravidian languages, like Tamil, my parents' native language. I write in English but prefer letterforms that remind me it isn't the only way. For similar reasons I don't like capitalizations or quotation marks, which Dravidian languages don't use. I play with orthography to signal connective tissue. I write with line breaks, white space, handwriting, all visualizations of my bodymind's processing. I practice murder in the dark, light pale fires, and play hopscotch in invisible cities, where the watchmen and the sluts practice their oeuvres. Puzzles. Layered narratives. Nothing spoonfed, like nothing's ever spoonfed to me.

cultural premium placed on invisibility—on "design that masks the reality of any human or personal history behind it" (Nichols 39). There's nothing painful about Times New Roman. It imports what's "intellectual" about me and discards the pain+fog that spurs me to occupy the social/scholarly positions I do.

Δ   Most traditional academic writing effaces the producer of knowledge as embodied, as well as the means of production as an embodied process. According to Rosalind Gill, "[W]riting remains, for the most part, invisible, naturalized, and treated as if it were simply the neutral disinterested recording of research" (18–19). Acceptable scholarship is well ordered, linear, cohesive, concise, conforming to surface features like 12-point Times New Roman, 1-inch margins, citation styles, while Othered scholarship overlaps with literary genres, is creative, concerned with aesthetics, indirect, digressive, recursive, experimental, breaking the laws of format and genre, and making space for usage errors (Dolmage, "Writing," 115–117).

Δ   Pain scholar† David Morris tells us, "In a scholarly journal, discourse about suffering will normally take the form of 25-page essays. There will be footnotes to contemporary thinkers, correct grammar, titles with colons. Obscenities and profanities will be expunged. Readers may notice that the essays place a premium on intelligence, employ difficult or specialized diction, avoid familiar ideas, and strive to appear original" (33–34).

Δ   Professionalism becomes a matter of x-height and slope of letterforms. "The literary mode of typographic representation, borrowing from the convention of the unmarked text, posited the existence of an absent author whose authority was reworked through the seemingly transparent, speaking-itself, character of the words on the page. The subversive disruption of this authority and its impact on the structure of subjectivity, ideology, and power in the text were effected through typographic manipulation" (Drucker 103). As decolonized as Sangha Kali or the Sino-Tibetan Jura, in which this was composed, as cripped as chaotic Zalgo.

Δ   Academic style seems informed by postanesthetic culture, which views pain as distasteful and deviant and also asserts that a cultivated mind is repulsed by publicized displays of pain (Halttunen).‡

Δ   With the body made invisible, identity, process, and experience disappear as well. What's left are the values of dominant discourse. Peter Cole, in poetic form, sketches the dominance of Western experience in scholarly texts, describing how chapters, paragraphs, punctuation, capitalization, and other mechanisms of academic codification are meaningless and antithetical to Aboriginal frames of

---

†   The dagger symbol is the closest I come in traditional academic writing to a visualization of pain; anodyne though it is, at least it represents something capable of wounding.

‡   The hanging, the snapped wishbones, marathons, murders, daggers, written as a sign that a pained body is writing this, always murdered for her text to succeed.

thinking, orality, and temporality (448–449). He notes, "[I]n order to enter those realms of anointed power/those racially predestined orbs those p/reserves of academ(ent)ia . . . it is deemed I am to follow western epistemologies"† (450).

Δ   We imagine the authorial body upright at a computer, at a desk. Composition is, for me, a collaboration between authorial body and the writing technologies (laptop, pen) and rehabilitative technologies (yoga mat or bed, foam roller, heating pad, neck brace, lumbar support, 90–90 cube, tDCS device, etc.) with which I am entangled. "Making knowledge is not simply about making facts but about making worlds, or rather, it is about making specific worldly configurations—not in the sense of making them up *ex nihilo*, or out of language, beliefs, or ideas, but in the sense of materially engaging as part of the world in giving it specific material form" (Barad 91).‡

Δ   I had to cleanse that SAGE essay of its composition processes: sans serif font, 11-point, no indentations, single spaced with white space to signify and simulate cognitive hiccups. I was able to retain my metaphors, but at one point the quantity of poetics was questioned, so to meet the word count, I cut. You were involved in that intersubjective construction of my pain, whether you like it or not (Manivannan, "Author Draws a Blank").

Δ   Editing and revising become a purification of language, intended to correct linguistic and generic errors as well as bodily aberration (Dolmage, "Writing").

Δ   When the body disappears, what upswells are respectability politics, deference to disciplinary authority in the form of jargon, citation, allegedly objective empirical practice, a disregard for the affective power of letterforms and words.

Δ   Entering an academic discipline, "becoming disciplined" as it were, still involves this form of writing. Leonard Cassuto and Paul Jay, in examining the dissertation genre, observe that "the thesis cannot be separated from the conditions under which the student writes it," despite the fact that we are trained to separate them (84). It's in accordance with the biopolitical imperative to govern the body, especially those deemed deviant, unruly, potentially intractable.

---

†   It's harder to break wishbones than it is to break me. A body so easily shattered can't be seriously committed to being a body, or a text.

‡   If you do cut this body or text, you can divine from her entrails how some of these technological permutations open up possibilities while other combinations foreclose them. I allot hours to creating and refining potential workspaces that never fully work. While revising the essay that received an R&R, I asked for an extension after vomiting the second time and was given a day. There's a paragraph in there about burnout, I think. I halved my daily dose of medication to stay up all night, and barely recognized myself in the mirror, or in the reformatting I'd made myself do.

Δ   We become "prisoners of ancient orientations imbedded in the languages we have inherited" (Hayakawa 9).*

Δ   Traditional academic writing fits well within infrastructures founded on able-bodymindedness, crafted to make (marginalized) bodies invisible, privileging a standard of conformity and coherence built for linear, rational logos (Yergeau et al.). This tells future scholars with alternate ways of knowing and processing to expect to perform additional labor to represent knowledge similarly, and to conceal that labor.†

Δ   To create a body of scholarship is to act on the body of the world.‡

Δ   Academic language "seeks to represent the phenomenological world, and the grammar it's developed to do so is disembodied, depersonalized, careful to avoid provoking affective reaction, objective, crafting the only appropriate response as cerebral. We can intellectualize about pain all we want, but to experience it is to be both utterly bored and driven mad with desire to repeatedly stab the sites of pain, as though only violence of greater intensity will persuade the unwanted tenant to leave. Solely cerebral expression, which seeks a solely cerebral response, will never be sufficient to the task" (Manivannan, "What We See," 11).** How many times have I written this? Why do I still feel the need to write it down? Pain+fog means being prone to forgetting; chronicity makes it a repetition that never ends.

Δ   Carl Rhodes, paraphrasing Ginsburg: "The minds of my generation, the best and the worst, insofar as they consider themselves to be writers, have been haunted by the spectre of scientific discourse, shoehorned into dry genres and bullied by audit regimes that try to wring out the passion and romance of thought" (289–290).

Δ   Anna Gibbs: "[T]he direct action of a few startling words on an unsuspecting body can threaten the integrity of the self" ("Writing" 310). The impartial rhetoric of academic style skirts the danger of affective contagion whereby embodied rhetoric provokes sympathetic response, a heightened sensory receptivity to the author's

---

*   "[P]aper has long been the form whereon the academy has held the forest hostage" (Cole 451).

†   *It's not fair,* says that colleague when my scholarship is recognized, *Some people work really hard.* The implication is that I don't because in me work looks fitful, sporadic, not like the deep focus of overwork. But work, for me, is always overwork, while overwork is suicide. If that's what the cult of overwork in academia expects at its altars as celebration, then my habits have been better than yours all along.

‡   In the past, I only ever self-injured for focus when creating scholarship, not art. Both activities require focus. But I wonder if the latter inculcates a disposition towards the body that is more accommodating, if the literary allowances that tolerate embodied knowledge put my bodymind at ease. I wonder how much less pain I'd be in if I could merge the creative and critical without fearing for my career.

** I'm always writing with internal noise; I externalize the sounds with "torture porn" to write entangled with the noise of others and attend less to mine. For this paper, the lineup was *Saw VI, Hostel* (1 and 2), the entire *Wrong Turn* franchise. The plot is always the same: someone violates established mores and must be put to death.

corporeal suffering (Gibbs, "Panic" 141). Paralleling Lee's rhetoric of distance, Karen Halttunen writes that the eighteenth-century rise of spectatorial sympathy was predicated on social distance, catering to middle-class sensitivity to pain. Pain is entertaining, interesting, informative, but not without a fourth wall.

Δ   According to Halttunen, the cult of humanitarian sensibility—which saw pain as unacceptable and revolting—originated in intellectual strains. Sensation to knowledge was constructed as *reason*, different from sensation to pain, or irrational *intuition*. The reasonable individual was a virtuous individual, able to imagine a sufferer's plight—but also a tormentor's cruelty. We secretly compare ourselves to the sufferer and congratulate ourselves on our exemption; like the inflictor, like *logos*, we imagine ourselves in total control (309–312). Scholarship contains itself. It doesn't scream.

Δ   Mastery and bodily revelation don't go together. The body is flawed. It isn't mastery. It's weakness.*

Δ   Over the course of the eighteenth century, Quaker concerns over the deliberate infliction of pain on Black slaves redefined (white) concepts of cruelty. These objections were concerned with white slaveholders' salvation more than Black slaves' pain: slavery was an indulgent luxury, luxury signaled moral laxity, and this hinged on the slaveholders' (violent, disciplinary) obsessions with (their slaves') flesh (Abruzzo 17–24). Cultivating the soul, cultivating the mind, meant abandoning the flesh, which meant the corporeal experience of pain had to be designated morally and intellectually bankrupt. Viewing it became pornographic (Halttunen). Omitting it, academic.

Δ   Writing this is excruciating. I don't want to be in pain, or hurt you, but I wonder what we mean by immersing ourselves in knowledge. In that published essay, I quote Deborah Padfield: "Chronic pain disrupts narrative, and perhaps having that seen, heard, and acknowledged is more important than trying to frame the narrative linearly," allowing us to frame our knowings freely instead of focusing on how we should order our experience (253).

Δ   I have to construct the scholarly text in the grasp of destructive plasticity, form produced in the annihilation of form, the exhaustion of possibility, the refusal of what *is* in favor of *what could be*, a negation that surfaces an alternative subjectivity (Malabou 85–89). It's *Hellraiser*'s waiting room. A bored but anticipatory attitude towards intensities that are unplanned but expected, the expectation of the arrival of a new form of being unrecognizable even to itself.

Δ   I argued with my editors about the aesthetic alterations. They let me keep my creative subheading titles but created columns, added indentations, attached floating lines to body paragraphs, removed all

---

*   Especially because chronicity makes pain mundane, even though it episodically reasserts its presence through flare-ups or altered intensity according to activity, position, or other visceral presences like menstruation and its particular brand of pain (Leder 72).

my white space.* Embodied language aside, their product resembled a cleanly formatted, traditional academic essay. Not even a footnote explaining why I'd wanted to include white space, to perform the material circumstances of fibromyalgia. The embodied knowledge inherent to form—cleansed.

Δ   Knowledge informed by pain looks like knowledge impeded by pain, antithetical to the successful (mind) text. What is this, you might ask, but a list of ideas and quotes with a loose weave that I want you to labor over, unstitch and resew with your own knowledges, viscerally feel how it comes from a particular body. "An embodied rhetoric that draws attention to embodied knowledge—specific material conditions, lived experiences, positionalities, and/or standpoints—can highlight difference instead of erasing it in favor of an assumed privileged discourse" through language and the visuality and materiality of the page (Knoblauch 62). Conceptualizing a kind of reader possessed of more than solely scholarly orientation who can become attuned to pained bodies the way those bodies must attune to themselves. Acknowledging that to even write these words, my body did not passively serve as a conduit of objective observation but acted as a meaning maker, in/through/with the scholarly text.

Δ   "The call to adopt an attitude of epistemic uncertainty is paradoxical to what we come to know academically, where claims to know are cherished, where contributions to cultivating specifics of disciplines are notarized to ensure upward mobility, and, above all, where accumulated knowledges provide the credibility that underpins belonging in the academy" (Herising 141). The idea of an autopoietic text collaged out of literary detritus is antithetical to both professional, routinized scholarship in which genre deviations are immoral aberrations, and the regime of middle-class sensibility and bodily normalcy to which it subscribes (Dolmage, "Writing Against Normal"; Halttunen). Inscribing scholarship with the embodied knowledge of chronicity/suffering that reflects the realities of fibromyalgia is tantamount to jeopardizing success in academic culture.

Δ   Morris says genre shapes suffering and determines how suffering will be perceived. When academic rhetoric negates the embodied experiences of nonnormative bodies, it encourages the suppression of corporeal sympathy between writers and readers, such that academic publishing becomes an instrument of social control. Embodying pain in language and layout would acknowledge that writing is an intrinsically painful act and, through affective contagion, would encourage empathy and challenge the position of academic style as a manufacturer of morals and decency.

---

*   White space imbues a page with (crip) time. Your eyes travel more slowly, or skip ahead more quickly. The visual space it occupies indicates physical (temporal) distance. Lacking white space, the scholarly page is timeless, measured in the minutes it takes your eyes to spatially glide over it without accounting for the process of digestion.

Δ   Embodied language that breaks the taboos around pain—its sensory
    evocation, its pornographic nature—can provoke in the scholarly
    community a tolerance of (feeling) undesirable bodily sensation and
    allow it to play its role in knowledge making.

Δ   Through conveying embodied knowledge in language and form,
    writers can stage an empathetic reader response. Instead of implic-
    itly apprehending chronic pain and fatigue as dysfunctional, ineffi-
    cient, or a failure to be/think normally because it's textually erased,
    we can add Other/Othered bodies, frames, structures, knowings to
    academic canons that privilege objective, authoritative voice and lin-
    ear argumentation. Not agonism, but intersubjective construction of
    pain and sharing of embodied experience.

Δ   The merit badges we award in academia are these: *Burned out.
    Exhausted. Overcaffeinated. No time. Haven't eaten. Last-minute deadlines.*
    But I have to eat. I can't last-minute. I can't opt out of enervation. I
    feel scrutinized and vulnerable writing about how forbidden it feels
    to embody in our genres.*

Δ   Nick Sousanis, arguing against privileging particular composition
    forms over others in his philosophical comic: "While standardization
    has its uses, conforming to another's expectations is detrimental . . .
    to ignore our differences and the configuration of threads from
    which we are uniquely composed robs us of our inherent nimble-
    ness. Rather than funneling our time here down narrow paths, fol-
    lowing a series of prescribed steps, let us open this out . . . and see
    what possibilities emerge when we author paths as uniquely our own
    as our feet themselves" (146–148).

Δ   If you're looking for a conclusion, it's that writing this is a choice
    but also not a choice. I tell myself myths about the vast gulf between
    choice and not-choice, but that space itself is an illusion. Let me
    believe that as I am, I am enough is good enough.

WORKS CITED

Abruzzo, Margaret Nicola. *Polemical Pain: Slavery, Cruelty, and the Rise of Humanitarianism.*
    Johns Hopkins UP, 2011.
Arbes, Ross. "Calibri's Scandalous History." *New Yorker,* 24 Jul. 2017, www.newyorker.com
    /magazine/2017/07/31/calibris-scandalous-history. Accessed 25 June 2020.
Atwood, Margaret. *Murder in the Dark.* Coach House, 1983.
Barad, Karen. *Meeting the Universe Halfway.* Duke UP, 2007.
Cassuto, Leonard, and Paul Jay. "The PhD Dissertation: In Search of a Usable Future."
    Pedagogy, vol. 15, no. 1, 2015, pp. 81–92. *Duke UP,* doi:10.1215/15314200-2799212.

---

*   The cult of sensibility forbids letting me die on your watch, but the cult of mastery
    insists you prove you can read me through the blood I produce, so I must bleed in a
    way that can be processed cognitively. For me, it's a question of how best to enact dis-
    ability masquerade in the margins since no one would believe from my writing that
    I'm always the hanged woman, swinging in pain (Siebers); for you, it's a question of
    how language and formatting might keep my recalcitrant scholarly body tamed.

Chen, Mel Y. "Brain Fog: The Race for Cripistemology." *Journal of Literary & Cultural Disability Studies*, vol. 8, no. 2, 2014, pp. 171–184. *Liverpool UP Online*, doi:10.3828/jlcds .2014.14.

Cole, Peter. "Aboriginalizing Methodology: Considering the Canoe." *Qualitative Studies in Education*, vol. 15, no. 4, 2002, pp. 447–459. *Taylor & Francis Online*. doi:10 .1080/09518390210145516.

Davis, Lennard. *Enforcing Normalcy: Disability, Deafness, and the Body*. Verso, 1995.

DeVoss, Dànielle Nicole. "Matters of Type." *Kairos*, vol. 14, no. 2, 2010, kairos.technorhetoric .net/14.2/reviews/devoss/index.html. Accessed 27 Dec. 2018.

Dolmage, Jay. *Academic Ableism: Disability and Higher Education*. U of Michigan P, 2017.

Dolmage, Jay. "Writing Against Normal: Navigating a Corporeal Turn." *Composing (Media)=Composing (Embodiment): Bodies, Technologies, Writing, the Teaching of Writing*, edited by Kristin Arola and Anne Wysocki, Utah State UP, 2012, pp. 115–131.

Dolphin-Krute, Maia. "Daily Survivor #1." *Full Stop*, 25 Nov. 2015, full-stop.net/2015/11 /25/features/essays/maiadolphinkrute/daily-survivor-1. Accessed 27 Dec. 2018.

Dolphin-Krute, Maia. *Ghostbodies: Towards a New Theory of Invalidism*. Chicago UP, 2017.

Drucker, Johanna. *The Visible Word: Experimental Typography and Modern Art, 1909–1923*. Chicago UP, 1994.

Garland-Thomson, Rosemarie. *Staring: How We Look*. Oxford UP, 2009.

Garland-Thomson, Rosemarie. "The Story of My Work: How I Became Disabled." *Disability Studies Quarterly*, vol. 34, no. 2, 2014. *DSQ*, doi:10.18061/dsq.v34i2.4254. https://dsq -sds.org/article/view/4254.

Gibbs, Anna. "Panic! Affect Contagion, Mimesis, and Suggestion." *Panic*. Spec. issue of *Cultural Studies Review*, vol. 14, no. 2, 2008, pp. 130–145. *DOAJ*, doi:10.5130/csr.v14i2.2076.

Gibbs, Anna. "Writing and the Flesh of Others." *Australian Feminist Studies*, vol. 18, no. 42, 2003, pp. 309–319. *Taylor & Francis Online*, doi:10.1080/0816464032000171403.

Gill, Rosalind. "Dialogues and Differences: Writing, Reflexivity and the Crisis of Representation." *Standpoints and Differences: Essays in the Practice of Feminist Psychology*, edited by Karen Henwood, Christine Griffin, and Ann Phoenix, SAGE, 1998, pp. 18–44.

Halttunen, Karen. "Humanitarianism and the Pornography of Pain in Anglo-American Culture." *American Historical Review*, vol. 100, no. 2, 1995, pp. 303–334. *Europe PMC*, doi: 10.2307/2169001.

Hawkins, Ames. "Why I Hate Times New Roman, and Other Confessions of a Creative-Critical Scholar." *Type Matters: The Rhetoricity of Letterforms*, edited by Christopher Scott Wyatt and Dànielle Nicole DeVoss, Parlor, 2017, pp. 159–186.

Hayakawa, S. I. "The Revision of Vision." *Language of Vision*, by Gyorgy Kepes, Theobald, 1969, pp. 8–10.

Herising, Fairn. "Interrupting Positions: Critical Thresholds and Queer Pro/Positions." *Resistance as Resistance: Critical, Indigenous, and Anti-Oppressive Approaches*, edited by Leslie Brown and Susan Strega, Canadian Scholars' Press/Women's Press, 2005, pp. 127–153.

Jowsey, Tanisha. "Time and Chronic Illness: A Narrative Review." *Quality of Life Research*, vol. 25, no. 5, 2016, pp. 1093–1102. *PubMed*, doi:10.1007/s11136-015-1169-2.

Knoblauch, A. Abby. "Bodies of Knowledge: Definitions, Delineations, and Implications of Embodied Writing in the Academy." *Composition Studies*, vol. 40, no. 2, 2012, pp. 50–65. *JSTOR*, www.jstor.org/stable/compstud.40.2.0050.

Kuppers, Petra. "Crip Time." *Tikkun Magazine*, vol. 29, no. 4, Nov. 2014, pp. 29–31. *Duke UP*, doi:10.1215/08879982-2810062.

Leder, Drew. *The Absent Body*. U of Chicago P, 1990.

Lee, Melanie. "The Melancholy Odyssey of a Dissertation with Pictures." *Pedagogy*, vol. 15, no. 1, 2015, pp. 93–101. *Duke UP*, doi:10.1215/15314200-2799228.

Malabou, Catherine. *The Ontology of the Accident: An Essay on Destructive Plasticity*. Polity, 2012.

Manivannan, Vyshali. "The Author Draws a Blank." Affect Inquiry/Making Space. Capacious Conference. 2018. Creative-Critical Performance, Millersville University, Lancaster, PA, 8–11 Aug. 2018. www.youtube.com/watch?v=f6aKEj5bxFQ&feature=youtu.be.

Manivannan, Vyshali. "What We See When We Digitize Pain: The Risk of Valorizing Image-Based Representations of Fibromyalgia over Body and Bodily Experience." *Senses and Digital Health*. Spec. issue of *Digital Health*, vol. 3, 2017, pp. 1–15. *SAGE Journals*, doi:10.1177/2055207617708860.

Marsden, George M. *The Soul of the American University: From Protestant Establishment to Established Nonbelief*. Oxford UP, 1993.

Morris, David. "About Suffering: Voice, Genre, and Moral Community." *Social Suffering*, edited by Arther Kleinman, Veena Das, and Margaret Lock, U of California P, 1998, pp. 29–46.

Nichols, Garrett W. "Type Reveals Culture: A Defense of 'Bad' Type." *Type Matters: The Rhetoricity of Letterforms*, edited by Christopher Scott Wyatt and Dànielle Nicole DeVoss, Parlor P, 2017, pp. 32–61.

Padfield, Deborah. "'Representing' the Pain of Others." *Another Way of Knowing: Art, Disease and Illness Experience*. Spec. issue of *Health*, vol. 15, no. 3, 2011, pp. 241–257. *SAGE Journals*, doi:10.1177/1363459310397974.

Price, Margaret. "The Bodymind Problem and the Possibilities of Pain." *New Conversations in Feminist Disability Studies*. Spec. issue of *Hypatia*, vol. 30, no. 1, 2015, pp. 268–284. *Wiley Online Library*, doi:10.1111/hypa.12127.

Price, Margaret. *Mad at School: Rhetorics of Mental Disability and Academic Life*. U of Michigan P, 2011.

Powell, Malea. "Listening to Ghosts: An Alternative (Non)Argument." *ALT DIS: Alternative Discourses and the Academy*, edited by Christopher L. Schroeder, Helen Fox, and Patricia Bizzell, Heinemann, 2002, pp. 11–22.

Rhodes, Carl. "Writing Organization/Romancing Fictocriticism." *Culture and Organization*, vol. 21, no. 4, 2015, pp. 289–303. *Taylor & Francis Online*, doi:10.1080/14759551.2014.882923.

Scarry, Elaine. *The Body in Pain: The Making and Unmaking of the World*. Oxford UP, 1985.

Siebers, Tobin. "Disability as Masquerade." *Literature and Medicine*, vol. 23, no. 1, 2004, pp. 1–22. *PubMed*, doi:10.1353/lm.2004.0010.

Sousanis, Nick. *Unflattening*. Harvard UP, 2015.

tchouky. *Zalgo Text Generator*. 2009, www.eeemo.net. Accessed 25 June 2020.

Turner, Heather Noel. "The Development of Typeface Personas and the Consequences of Perceived Identities." *Type Matters: The Rhetoricity of Letterforms*, edited by Christopher Scott Wyatt and Dànielle Nicole DeVoss, Parlor, 2017, pp. 89–108.

Vitanza, Victor. "Critical Sub/Versions of the History of Philosophical Rhetoric." *Rhetoric Review*, vol. 6, no. 1, 1987, pp. 41–66. *JSTOR*, www.jstor.org/stable/465949.

Wilson, James C., and Cynthia Lewiecki-Wilson. "Disability, Rhetoric, and the Body." *Embodied Rhetorics: Disability in Language and Culture*, edited by James C. Wilson and Cynthia Lewiecki-Wilson, Southern Illinois UP, 2001, pp. 1–26.

Yergeau, Remi M., Elizabeth Brewer, Stephanie Kerschbaum, Sushil K. Oswal, Margaret Price, Cynthia L. Selfe, Michael Salvo, and Franny Howes. "Multimodality in Motion: Disability and Kairotic Spaces." *Kairos*, vol. 18, no. 1, 2013, kairos.technorhetoric.net/18.1/coverweb/yergeau-et-al. Accessed 29 Dec. 2018.

12

HOOKING UP EMBODIED TECHNOLOGIES, QUEER RHETORICS, AND GRINDR'S GRID

Caleb Pendygraft (Massachusetts Maritime Academy)

The boundary between machine and body has been theorized for some time now, and it seems Donna Haraway's cyborg figure no longer is a matter of speculation (Balsamo; Haraway). If we are not already cyborgs, then, at minimum, our somatic worlds are so tethered to technologies they've largely become diffuse and ubiquitous, reaching a level of integration at which we begin to question our identities—even our embodiment—in their absence. This body-technology line can intersect, and at moments, overlap and blur (Arola and Wysocki). "Technologies, especially in the case of small tech, are never distinct objects," rhetoricians have pointed out, "they are only experienced in relation to other entities arranged in complex constellations to form particular environments" (Hawk and Rieder xvii). Ben McCorkle has suggested "the thin chrome line, the literal contact zone between the human body and the personal computer" is a site where scholars must "focus our critical attentions because soon that line will become blurred and indistinguishable, or will even disappear altogether" (174). In this chapter I theorize this contact zone as an emergent effect of *embodied technologies*, or the technologies that are used by, come in contact with, are worn on, and/or interact with our bodies *and* contain potential to alter how we experience and what we do in our bodies.

I argue not only that embodied technologies have the possible agency to change our embodiment but also that, in doing so, they require reconsideration of their role in embodied rhetorics. New materialist rhetorics have argued that objects, machine or otherwise, have their own rhetorical agency (Barnett and Boyle; Gries), and we shouldn't ignore that agency when it concerns embodied rhetorics. In attempts to call for a new materialist approach to visual rhetorics, Laurie E. Gries defines agency as "an act of intervention" that is "not some capacity that

https://doi.org/10.7330/9781646422012.c012

any single person has" (57). This reshifting of agency in new materialist thought can be largely credited to Karen Barad's definition that agency is "an enactment, not something that someone or something has" (178). Instead, agency is reconceived as relational, forming between entities, what Barad calls an "intra-action": "Agency is not an attribute but the ongoing reconfigurings of the world. The universe is agential intra-activity in its becoming" (141). Here interaction, understood as action between two distinct whole entities, is reimagined as intra-action, in which entities are no longer distinctly separate but entangled. This intra-action is an entanglement that makes up agency, which underscores how I frame embodied technologies in this chapter.

When I say embodied technologies have agency, and potentially queer agency at that, I do so in accordance with other queer rhetoricians who draw from new materialism, such as Gavin Johnson. Johnson writes that "when we intra-act, agency emerges from the entanglement of matter and meaning; however that agency is in constant flux as it orients different bodies, cultures, places, histories, objects, and futures" (125). Embodied technologies, as I expand on in the next section, are caught up in this fluctuation. Overall, my chapter adds to the copious discussions centered around the intersections of technologies, rhetoric, and embodiment (e.g., Chávez; Garland-Thomson; Grosz; Hawisher and Selfe). Similar to Kristin L. Arola and Anne Frances Wysocki's claim that books "extend us toward each other but then work back on us," ultimately shaping "how we are embodied in the world" (5), I believe embodied technologies contain the same rhetorical potentiality to affect our embodiment.

This chapter offers a continuation of A. Abby Knoblauch's position that "[w]e are all situated beings, bodies situated in culture and language" (58) and argues that technologies play a role in rhetorically situating our bodies. Moreover, because of the ubiquity of embodied technologies manufacturing a state of embodiment "in which we are likely to forget" our bodies, I turn to queer theory in order to expose embodied technologies' capacity to shape bodies (McCorkle 176). Much as queer theory makes use of queerness to expose the normalization of heterosexuality, I believe examining queer embodied technologies can reveal the agential capabilities of embodied technologies to reshape our embodied lives. In turn, I ask what it would mean to contemplate how embodiment, technologies, and queerness intersect. What could tenets of queer rhetorics lend in understanding the impact of technologies on embodied rhetorics?

This chapter is organized into two parts. The first half unpacks embodied technologies and how they can become queer. I argue they do so not only when they are used to procure queer-sex hookups but also when their use rhetorically affects our own embodiment insofar as how we come to understand our own sex and sexuality. In other words, by examining how embodied technologies shape how we have sex and experience our sexualities in our bodies, we can better understand how these technologies fit into embodied rhetorics. In the second half, I illustrate how LGBTQ hookup smartphone applications offer insight into how our bodies are rhetorically impacted by technologies. More specifically, I look closely at phone apps, using Grindr as my primary site of analysis.[1] I conclude with a gesture towards what impact embodied technologies may have elsewhere and in the future.

DEFINING EMBODIED TECHNOLOGIES

To flesh out my definition of embodied technologies, I start with an explanation of terms, borrowing from various ruminations on the body. Embodiment "calls us to attend to what we just simply do, day to day, moving about, communicating with others, using objects that we simply use in order to make things happen" (Wysocki 3). This point runs parallel with feminist thinkers who argue that embodiment is a doing and a practice (Grosz; McWhorter). Embodied rhetorics bolster these views on embodiment, inquiring how embodiment becomes purposeful, asking "the rhetor to reconnect thinking with our particular bodies, understanding that knowledge comes from the body" (Knoblauch 60). To engage with embodied rhetorics is to acknowledge "the purposeful effort by an author to represent aspects of embodiment within the text he or she is shaping" (Knoblauch 58). Drawing from these definitions within a new materialist conceptualization of agency, I understand embodiment as the lived, mundane practices that exist on a continuum of intra-actions between flesh, meaning making, and materiality-outside-the-body. Embodiment, as I use the term here, isn't limited to simply *my body* but also includes how my body brushes up against and is shaped by other material agents in the world, always emerging anew. My inclusion of materiality here raises the following questions: What would it mean to think of embodied rhetorics not only in terms of how the body is represented in text but also how bodies themselves come to be affected? What if embodied rhetorics included both the bodies using objects as well as objects using bodies? What would happen to theories of embodied rhetorics if instead of asking how a rhetor's body affects a text we asked how texts affect our bodies?

Margaret Syverson has engaged similar inquiries in her text *The Wealth of Reality: An Ecology of Composition*. Syverson understands the relationships between technologies and bodies as "situated in an ecology, a larger system that includes environmental structures, such as pens, paper, computers, books, telephones, fax machines, photocopiers, printing presses, and other natural and human-constructed features" (5). Embodiment is key to her ecological model of writing and rhetoric because rhetors, she writes, "have physical bodies and consequently not only the content but the processes of their interaction is dependent on, and reflective of, physical experience" (12). Syverson lays a foundation for the framing of embodied technologies. However, where she sees these ecological components as separate entities within systems, I argue that embodied technologies suggest the boundaries between technologies and bodies are more malleable. Embodied technologies, in other words, make room for all actors in such an ecological framing to have more agency. The recent theorization of wearable technologies, or *wearables*, may lend more clarity in understanding embodied technologies.

Catherine Gouge and John Jones, in a special issue of *Rhetoric Society Quarterly* on wearable technologies, define wearables "as those technologies, electronic or otherwise, whose primary functionality requires that they be connected to bodies" (201). In particular, they consider "what it means 'to wear' and reframe how we ought to pay attention to acts of wearing within broader understandings of embodiment and rhetoric" (201). In the issue there are investigations of breast pumps, Fitbits, smartphones, ostomy bags, and more, all discussed as rhetorical wearables. It's clear that wearables are embodied technologies, but as I frame embodied technologies, not all embodied technologies must be wearables. Embodied technologies allow for more literal space—a continuum, if you will—between bodies and technologies; most important, they allow for the *impact* of technologies to shape our understanding of embodiment. Wearables are worn by bodies, but can wearables wear bodies?

My point: technology isn't always acknowledged for having agency to affect the bodies that wear them. However, embodied technologies impact our sense of embodiment and thus shape how we come to rhetorically understand our embodiment. When a body uses embodied technologies to reach desired outcomes, the body's involvement is a prerequisite to the function of the technology. My iPhone X, for instance, can bypass its security measures with a glance; it recognizes my face better than I do. Facial recognition is certainly a technological advancement, but it also requires us to pay attention to how we embody our face—it is changing the way we position our bodies and gaze, rhetorically torquing us to be aware of and potentially change our embodiment. If my phone doesn't recognize my face, maybe I remove my hat, move into brighter light, or change my expression. Consider, too, that we've reached a juncture at which phantom-phone syndrome is a real concern amongst behavioral scientists (Deb; Krueger and Djerf). Phantom-phone syndrome is only one example of not only how technology is being used by people for their own ends but also how technologies are shaping our embodiment in their use. Embodied technologies are formed in this relationship between technology and bodies by shaping embodied rhetorics in both directions.

Finally, I'd also like to add that, in many ways, when I speak of embodied technologies as relational and emergent, I am invoking notions of performativity. Largely indebted to Judith Butler's notion that subjectivity—with a particular regard for one's gender—is an ongoing production of performances, performativity helps us understand that embodied technologies shape our behavior and how we exist in the world, in our bodies (*Gender Trouble* 133). Butler writes, "One is not simply a body, but, in some very key sense, one does one's body" ("Performative" 272). When we *do* our bodies, we mustn't overlook the web of relationships between our bodies and technologies. Machines and tech have the potential to allow us to do our bodies in new ways. As an analog to Gerald Jackson's notion of digital performativity, which he theorizes as an intricate mix of coding, gendered performances, and computation (52), I believe we can bring the materiality of technologies into the theoretical fold of embodied rhetorics by understanding how machines and bodies perform together. How we perform with our technologies can affect how we do our bodies. In sum, embodied technologies are relational, in that they require both machine and flesh to various spatial and rhetorical degrees; cause various types of embodiments to emerge from these relations; challenge us to reimagine how we live daily life in our bodies; ask us to consider how our bodies are lived in a world so enmeshed with technologies; and rest on the notion that agency doesn't lie within single entities.

QUEER RHETORICS AND EMBODIED TECHNOLOGIES

Turning attention to the overlap of bodies and sexualities can demonstrate the potential rhetorical effects when attending to embodied technologies. More specifically, queer rhetorics can put into perspective how embodied technologies can influence what choices we make with our bodies.[2] Queer theories are underscored by the "debunking of stable sexes, genders and sexualities," framing "identity as a constellation of multiple and unstable positions" (Jagose 1). What makes rhetorics queer are the practices aimed not at "affirming an identity, but rather disrupting norms for thinking, particularly norms that reinforce heterosexist ways of being" (Rhodes and Alexander). As Jonathan Alexander and Jacqueline Rhodes astutely describe, queerness "is indeed a radical, disruptive, even abnormalized invocation of body, gender, desire, fear and sensation. It is a spectacular act, in which we might make use of our converging alienations, our mesh of desire and want, in order to position ourselves to be—if only for a particular, rhetorical moment" (207).

Embodied technologies are caught up in a "mesh of desire and want" because they are capable of enabling alternative, perhaps even abnormalized, understandings and enactments of bodies. Furthermore, embodied technologies that become queer inundate bodies with the possibility of abnormalized sensation—they can make sensation in our bodies in new ways for particular rhetorical situations that resist normalized perceptions of embodiment. I am thinking, for example, of sex toys that can cause new ways to hook up with the desires and pleasures in our embodied lives.

Queerness can also disrupt interactions between bodies, desires, and identities with objects. That is to say, queer theory can offer a lens to reorient ourselves towards objects, in turn exposing how embodied technologies turn queer. Queer embodiment requires "rethinking how the bodily direction 'toward' objects shapes the surfaces of bodily and social space" (Ahmed 68). It's been argued that it is "impossible (and irresponsible) to separate the producer of the text from the text itself" (Banks, "Written through the Body" 33). A theory of embodied technologies creates the possibility of destabilizing the relationship between rhetor and text, as such a theory acknowledges that the machinery used by a producer of a text is actively participating in the process of meaning making. This intra-action among rhetor, machine, and meaning, in turn, has the potential to become queer when those technologies affect the way we experience our sexualities, desires, and even pleasure.[3] The rhetor's decision to interact with these technologies is met with their ability to alter our embodiment. In short, how we position our bodies with, around, and for embodied technologies is a rhetorical matter.

Queer rhetorics can also lend insight into the limitations and possibilities of embodied technologies: since queer rhetorics expand notions of what can exist in the realm of sex, sexuality, and desire, queer rhetorics might lead us to ask what technologies are not embodied? A simple answer: a technology that no longer serves a purpose to the body using it. I argue that as long as a technology's utility is tethered to the body in a meaningful way *and* the technology has the potential to impact the body, it can be defined as an embodied technology. Invoking my earlier definition, home-integrated technologies such as smart speakers and even smart refrigerators can be thought of as embodied technologies. They are designed to influence the bodies that use them, and through their use, a body makes rhetorical decisions. The ever-listening Google Home or Amazon's Alexa can radically shape how you move about your space. They can offer hands-free directions while you cook, which frees up the body, or set timers, which sets bodies into motion. In fact, they have been called to bear witness regarding homicide cases, illustrating how technologies impact decisions that have very real consequences on material bodies (McLaughlin). While these speakers may not be directly located *on* the body, they still affect the body rhetorically.

Smart refrigerators provide another example of how technologies can work remotely to impact embodiment. These appliances actively keep track of what food is typically purchased in a household and how frequently certain types of foods are consumed and send push notifications to users alerting them when it's time to replenish groceries. As an embodied technology, smart refrigerators demonstrate how bodily interaction with the technology influences ways bodies can exist in the world, guiding rhetors in their decision making. In this case, the refrigerator causes a body to move to and through a grocery store, bringing awareness to consumption, and so on. Perhaps even more pointedly, smartphone apps that track fertility moderate and influence cishet couples' sex schedules in order facilitate conception. Arguably, these types of technologies are being so integrated into our worlds we forget how they are rhetorically influencing our embodiment.

LOCATING GRINDR

While scholarship may not directly point to embodied rhetorics when it concerns queer technologies, there is an abundance of rhetorical scholarship on LGBTQ communities in digital spaces (Alexander; Alexander and Banks; Banks, "Beyond Multimodality"; Gray; Pullen and Cooper; Rhodes and Alexander). This scholarship has centered primarily around digital LGBTQ writing in places like the writing classroom and in online platforms such as YouTube. It's been argued that online LGBTQ communities require us to "understand issues such as the subjectivity of 'queer' identity, the potential of social construction, and the contemporary setting of reflexivity" (Pullen 10). New communicative technologies enable new identities and change how we view LGBTQ online spaces (10). Rhetoricians have explored such intersections, from recognizing how video blogging can create online communities (Alexander and Losh) to learning from LGBTQ students in pedagogy (Peters and Swanson), and scholars have emphasized the importance of paying attention to LGBTQ online communities.

Outside the analyses of LGBTQ writing in digital communities, scholars have also examined the rhetoric of online dating sites but have largely done so through a heteronormative lens. For example, Elizabeth C. Tomlinson argues that dating-profile design on sites like Match.com or eHarmony.com are rhetorically viable loci of understanding digital identity construction and audience awareness amongst users. Similarly, Jen Almjeld has assessed how gendered narratives and template design function in online dating sites. Only recently have scholars began to recognize the import of applications like Grindr in changing LGBTQ digital spaces and their intersection with dating (McGlotten).

If embodied technologies have the potential to affect a user's body, then Grindr's rhetorical purpose is clear: the app is designed to move queer bodies in physical space. Grindr may queer otherwise nonqueer spaces by way of the bodily interaction with the app: you can cruise for sex during your lunch break, while you shop, or at a family reunion. Grindr uses the phone's locative technology to place gay, bisexual, queer and/or trans users, who mainly identify as men, in proximity to other queer (primarily) male-identified people in their area. The user is placed into a virtual grid in order to hook up in person, for sex or otherwise.

Situating Grindr both within rhetorical scholarship and as an embodied technology draws attention to a pivotal—but often overlooked—factor in theorizing these LGBTQ and queer digital spaces: the body. What happens to our bodies when these technologies are in our pockets, carried with us daily? What are the embodied consequences of apps like Grindr, which are rhetorically torqued to provide sexual hookups?

PLATFORMS AND GRINDR.COM

As a prerequisite to analyzing Grindr as an embodied technology, I turn to platforms themselves to signal a distinction between the *participation within* these technologies and the somatic, embodied *interactions with* the machinery that contains them. Platforms are extensions of their devices—the software imbricated in the tangible objects of embodied technologies—offering a way to explore how these devices cause rhetors to move and act. When I say *platform*, I'm drawing from Tarleton

Gillespie's critique of the term's circulation in digital discourse. He examines platforms up close on a number of levels, bringing into relief how platforms (e.g., Google or YouTube) may appear to offer democratic spaces, imbuing constituents with agency, but in reality "are not mere intermediaries for content distribution and circulation" (Edwards 62). Simply put, platforms actively shape the meaning making that takes place. Gillespie's arguments subsequently inspired a *Present Tense* issue on platform rhetorics. "Platforms promise to be catalysts for public participation," the editors write, "but they also mask their role in facilitating or occluding that participation" (Edwards and Gelms 2). Platforms sit "at the intersections of software, hardware, culture, and production," a place I find rich for queer critique (Edwards and Gelms 3).

Further, the embodied technologies that use platforms warrant analysis because the platforms are guiding the bodies that are connected. Platforms can be implicated in rhetorics of embodiment by paying attention to how they rhetorically regulate participation with/in embodied technologies. To merely scrutinize platforms' content, affordances, and limitations isn't enough to conceive of how they come to be embodied, though. Through using platform terminology, I aim to show platforms are equally important in fleshing out embodied technologies and their rhetorical capabilities. A look at Grindr's platform can shed light on how platforms are actively working within embodied technologies to affect the embodiment of users.

As part of its embodied technology, Grindr's platform and interface rhetorically place emphasis on organizing certain bodies, specific queer identities, and racial hierarchies that exclude other types of queer being. This premise requires parsing out the nuances of Grindr's platform as rhetorically constructing bodies and the embodied practice of engaging with the application in order to hook up for sex. Downloading Grindr onto one's phone and logging on requires the creation of an account, with an alternative option to sync either with an existing Facebook profile or with a Google profile. Before a user can to customize a profile or engage with other users, the locative technologies of the device must be enabled. Once permission is granted to access the device's location, the user is inundated with other users' profile images arranged side by side to form a grid. It's obvious the interface is designed according to the proximity of bodies: your profile remains in the upper-left-most position, while the squares around it shift according to the locale of users: the closer the profile to yours, the closer the user. Displaying actual distance between users is an option that can be featured in the profile, measuring distance between users precisely in feet (or meters).

Profile descriptions alone may not create an embodied technology; however, it's important to acknowledge how the many categories available turn the onus of rhetorical invention on the user's body. In other words, the embodied technology's platform has the agency to cause users to (re)assess their own embodiment. This becomes clear by the arrangement of profiles, where images are privileged over alphabetic text. Any text shown on the grid is either a Display Name accompanying a picture or ads across the bottom of the screen. When customizing a profile, the picture is the first editable content, with text fields beneath.[4] The limited fifteen characters for a Display Name don't leave much room for text on the main interface.[5] As Grindr's developer, Joel Simkhai, explained, "Grindr is a very, very visual experience. I'm not really a big believer in words" (qtd. in Trebay).

Michael Faris looks specifically at the interface design and platform rhetorics of Grindr, especially the discursive and computational infrastructure of Grindr's platform (2). Faris argues the ads on Grindr and its users' bigoted rhetoric "reinforce a normative gay sensibility that idealizes toned, white, youthful, and masculine bodies" (3). I agree: the "public of Grindr" is oftentimes seen as "a space less welcoming—even hostile—to bodies that don't meet white, masculine ideals" (6). "Grindr's platform rhetoric," Faris writes, "elides a tension between its explicitly progressive political rhetoric and the practices on the app that can make it unwelcoming to nonnormative users and that privilege normative beauty standards" (3). Pushing Faris's arguments further, it's important not to overlook how bodies are impacted by Grindr's platform rhetoric. What embodied consequences can result from such rhetoric?

A potential answer is that Grindr makes room for queer rhetorical silence, as Johnathan Smilges posits. Smilges argues that "the dichotomy between speech and silence breaks down when it comes into contact with the queer body, given the particular significations and stigmatizations that often accompany queerness" (80). Because Grindr's platform allows a user to forego uploading a picture or remove their face from their profile, users are able to "negotiate their profiles to engage the queer community without fully exposing their identities. This balancing act between disclosure and withholding encourages us to more closely attend to the rhetoric of queer persons who may not be 'out' or live as openly as queer people" (Smilges 80).

Smilges isn't looking at the body-machine contact zone as I am, but his theorization of queer rhetorical silence exposes how the platform of Grindr moves users in virtual space in ways that may otherwise be damaging for the bodies using their devices. Some users may not be able to live visibly queer lives; Grindr enables a different sort of embodiment for those who can't or choose not to openly embody queerness outside the app.

Important, Smilges is making room for a sort of absent queer participation in understanding a blank Grindr profile as "a portal out of the digital interface and into the physical world where the referent queer body exists. Blank profiles, then, do not conceal queerness but exacerbate its material presence" (88). What isn't exposed on Grindr's platform is as important as the bodies that are. I would add, however, that Grindr is moving bodies around in physical space even if the profiles attached are queerly silent. By proxy of the machinery, the app platform is its users' embodiments regardless. I'd like, then, to broaden the analysis of Grindr's platform beyond user interface to Grindr's brand overall in order to underscore how the platform is using bodies and embodiments to other ends.

Take *Kindr Grindr*, launched by Grindr in 2018. Its aim? To reassure users Grindr "is into diversity, inclusion, and users who treat each other with respect" and "not into racism, bullying, or other forms of toxic behavior" ("Kindr"). Its main page displays videos and images of real individuals, including recognizable LGBTQ celebrities, with their perspectives of kindness both on Grindr and in queer communities. Among these images are nonnormative queer bodies—bodies not necessarily legible as white, masculine, and young and not always thin or "athletic." For example, an individual named Mars displays a bare chest and mastectomy scars; most persons are people of color; some individuals embody both/neither masculine and feminine gender expressions; there are bodies of all sizes; and a user named Andrew sits shirtless in his wheelchair with a tattoo on their chest that reads "Queer Cripple." These bodily depictions attempt to construct an image of embracing the nonhomonormative (see Duggan; Halberstam), a reflection of Grindr's purported inclusivity in hopes of allowing users with nonhomonormative bodies a safe space to interact with the app.

Underlying Grindr.com's impetus for inclusion is the online uproar against the racism, ageism, ableism, and femme-, fat-, and transphobia that has become synonymous with stereotypical Grindr users. You don't have to look far to find such rampant toxic masculinity. It has been commonplace in the Grindr universe to read profiles that include phrases like "Masc4Masc," meaning no femme guys; "No Asians;" or even "looking for BBC," standing in for "big Black cock." *Douchebags of Tumblr* is an online blog of screenshots from people who expose the profiles and conversations that use these hateful sentiments. The amount of content is testament to the blatant bodily exclusion practiced by users on Grindr. The *Kindr* project's inception marks an attempt to dissuade such behavior.

Kindr Grindr was created with Landen Zumwalt, head of communications at Grindr, explaining how the "'Kindr' initiative is a rallying call for Grindr and our community to take a stand against sexual racism and all forms of othering;" Grindr, they say, "will work to maintain a welcoming and inclusive environment and end the need for people to include exclusionary statements on profiles" ("Grindr Takes"). The result? Users now can report hate speech, and profiles are surveilled for bigoted language. These measures are not in themselves wrong; awareness and efforts to thwart instances of bigotry point to a more inclusive horizon for queer platforms and their embodied technologies. The issue lies in the lack of accountability on the part of those working to make Grindr kinder, for Grindr's ethos is culpable in such exclusions.

Putting bodies on display calls into question how the embodied use of the app may still propagate such exclusionary tactics. Of course, Grindr is part of the problem: it has enabled these bodily exclusions since its initial launch in 2009. How does a platform remedy the symptoms of ideological and cultural oppression when the platform created a venue for bigots? If Grindr is in fact now "kinder," how does its use as an embodied technology foster such inclusion? In order to answer that question, it's important to explain how the platform's interface organizes users based on their embodiment.

It's naïve for *Kindr* to abruptly act as though it's on the right side of identity politics without acknowledging the complicity of the app's interface (one based on arranging users by their embodiment) in the exclusionary practices it's now claiming to try to address. Think of the bodies on display at *Kindr*'s Web site. While now showcasing trans/nonnormative bodies, Grindr uses these bodies as visual markers of its new inclusive modus operandi, muffling any talk about how the platform itself played a role in the exclusionary rhetorics it now opposes. A less generous, but perhaps accurate, read is that the platform is using such bodies as spectacle, and, in doing so, further entrenching the issue at hand by way of tokenization. Because it's an embodied technology, Grindr's refusal to take responsibility affects which bodies download and interact with the app or which bodies feel safe enough to hook up. The exclusionary climate of Grindr's platform reveals how embodied technologies can force bodies apart, not just bring them together.

EMBODIED TECHNOLOGIES AND THEIR QUEER FUTURES

To queer technology, as scholar Matthew A. Vetter writes, "is to realize the ways in which digital tools, and the cultures-of-use that build up around them, are directing our lives." Vetter is using "queer" in its verb form, indicating that rhetors have the agency to disrupt the platforms and technologies we participate with/in. As I've hoped to make clear, agency emerges between the embodied technology and user, between machine and body. Although Vetter's statement intends to limit agency to the rhetor, it still implies that technologies are directing our lives. The machines are also doing the directing, which underscores my argument that technologies cause rhetors to perform in their bodies in new ways. As I conclude this chapter, I reflect on Grindr not only as a space where users are queer, can search for queer sex, and can explore their queer embodiment but also as an example of how queer technologies bear witness to how technologies and their platforms are directing, reorienting, and moving our bodies in the world in queerer ways.

All of Grindr's profile features enable users to reveal as much or as little as they want about themselves and their sexual preferences. A user's profile, then, might be said to reflect a kind of embodied knowledge, which Knoblauch defines as "specific material conditions, lived experiences, positionalities, and/or standpoints" (62). In particular, Grindr exposes a queer embodied knowledge; Alexander and Rhodes explain that "queer representation" relies on "the experience—and the potentially critical re-experience—of being 'oriented'" (202). What is laid bare in the profile can dictate the use of the app and how users choose to perform both digitally and in person, impacting how both literal and virtual bodies will potentially move through space. Embodied technologies, then, orient bodies in various directions, having within them the capacity to direct bodies into space via the rhetor's decision making. While Grindr's profile categories are intended to help users have a better experience on the grid, these choices carry problematic ideological weight and implications for embodied technologies, as well as for users' physical bodies.

Sara Ahmed's ideas on physical interaction, a necessary component of embodied technologies, are helpful on this point. Touch, says Ahmed, involves "a differentiation between those who can and cannot be reached"; she notes that "touch then opens bodies to some bodies and not others" (107). Embodied technologies enable a different type of touching. Investigating the interplay of bodies and technologies and the potential violence of touch, Scot Barnett (chapter 2) argues that, despite its violent potential, "touch is one of the primary ways we have for initiating, establishing, and sustaining meaningful relations with others in the world." Embodied technologies, then, can reinforce and challenge the means by which we come to touch others by way of touching our technology. With Grindr, for instance, you touch your phone with the prospect of possibly touching someone else when that touching may not have otherwise been able to occur. Grindr queerly orients bodies because it puts "within reach bodies that have been made unreachable" through normalized means (Ahmed 107). Grindr, in this way, exemplifies how embodied technologies can queer the relationship between meaning making with/in digital spaces, technologies, and bodies because of the types of touching they can enable.

As is the case with Grindr, it's when queer bodies, sex, and sexuality are being altered that embodied technologies can most clearly queer our understanding of embodiment. Shaka McGlotten writes on this point, stating that, with Grindr, "[w]hat you chose to disclose, and how, matters . . . you have to change a profile to stay interesting and relevant, to matter. Then there are categories that can make or break your chances" (128). In other words, rhetorical digital decision making impacts chances of hooking up and also pressures users into living "interesting" lives. As a result, the user is faced with having to decide how they represent their embodiment and whether they want to change their embodiment in order to stay relevant. This option wasn't a mistake; the valuation of displayed bodies on a grid was intentional. Simkhai, Grindr's creator and former CEO, says that the pressure of seeing a litany of bodies is intended to have an effect on Grindr's users: "'Grindr made me get fit and go to the gym more, get better abs,' said Mr. Simkhai, who occasionally posts a shirtless photograph on his own profile. 'People criticize it for being superficial, but I didn't invent that in human nature. What Grindr does is makes you raise your game'" (qtd. in Trebay). Simkhai declares that his body is caught up with the rhetorical influence of Grindr as an embodied technology. Implicit in his statement is the message that what you see on Grindr is meant to reach beyond the user-interface experience. To this end, while the intended use of the app is to hook up with others for sex, it is also geared toward making a user aware of their body, how they live in their body, and how they possibly act on their body (e.g., working on fitness in order to increase the chances of having sex).

When accounting for embodied technologies and their agency to affect bodies in such ways, it's critical to be aware of the relationship between the user's body and the user's identities, especially when those bodies are queer. If "interface designs are a series of semiotic messages that support hierarchical regimes along the axes of identity" (McCorkle 179), we must be mindful of how identities are rhetorically sutured to the bodies attached to embodied technologies. For example, Grindr allows users to sift through their grid based on desired body types via "tribes," a problematic term in itself. Tribes entered Grindr's interface in late 2013: a tribe allows you to further categorize yourself beyond the general user information. Options include Bear, Clean-Cut, Daddy, Discreet, Geek, Jock, Leather, Otter, Poz, Rugged, Trans, and Twink.[6] The tribes to which you belong purport to delineate the type of embodiment you possess. Your tribe is an indication of the body behind the screen, for each tribe is based on bodily assumptions. The tribal references mark how you identify, as well as how you act and what type of body you have.

Grindr's tribe-lore novelty lies in the user's capability to generate searches for members based on tribe. By enabling users to filter their grids by "tribal affiliation," Grindr encourages users to categorize themselves and others into specific, embodied roles. The rhetorical process of choosing to belong to a tribe carries certain embodied limitations concerning the user's identity and body. Queer rhetorics recognize the danger in doing so because "categories that render individuals socially interchangeable" are "bound up with the process of *normalization*" (Butler, *Undoing* 55). While "tribes" contribute to user experience customization, they can also work to reify exclusion of bodies. What's more disconcerting, you can search for the nearest one hundred guys on the basis of tribal affiliation alone or in combination. The filter feature enables searching for proximate users based also on Age and what you are Looking For: chat, dates, friends, networking, relationships, right now, or not specified. Admittedly, searching by age allows users to refine potential hookups due to generational differences. However, ageism isn't obsolete in LGBTQ communities; prejudice around age is real, as is the stereotyping of weight and race.[7]

Ultimately my point in discussing these interface search features is this: embodied technologies not only have the capacity to move bodies through space but can also enable rhetors to discriminate against bodies in virtual and physical space. Such interface features come to represent "the values of our culture," acting like maps "constituting a complex set of material relations among culture, technology, and technology users" (Selfe and Selfe 485). In other words, "the maps of computer interfaces order the virtual world according to a certain set of historical and social values that make up our culture" (485). Being able to sort through bodies on a virtual platform makes apparent that Grindr's grid is an obvious map, mapping potential hookups: how you hook up in the world, how you hook up with your phone, how your desires are oriented toward other users, the types of bodies you desire, and what your embodiment entails by its platform-based categories.

While this mapping is not conventionally geographic but, instead, proximal, we can't ignore the implications of accessing virtual bodies in a digital landscape based on embodied stereotypes. In the future, we must recognize how embodied technologies are enmeshed within systems of power, as we see with Grindr. That is to say, "the interface serves to organize raced and gendered bodies," often according to the "logical of digital capitalism: to click on a box or link is to acquire it, to choose it" (Nakamura 17). Embodied technologies, even when geared towards queer and/or inclusive communities, are still sites of power that require analysis. McGlotten notes this issue, too, explaining that "Grindr is at once celebrated for allowing men to find other men nearby, and critiqued for producing anxiety as men feel subjected to a surveillance" because "proximate men are laid out on a grid, available for one's perusal like an endless rows of nearly indistinguishable cereal boxes at the supermarket" (130).

Unpacking these technologies as sites of embodied rhetorics that have the queer potential to hook up bodies with other bodies for sex reveals much about the way we also hook up to devices and machinery around us. To attend to embodied rhetorics and technologies such as Grindr is also to regard the systemic pressures of capitalism, along with cultural and identificatory exclusion that can occur with both technological and bodily interaction.[8] As embodied technologies, apps like Grindr show that as much as it is essential to question the rhetorical choices we make in digital spaces, it is equally important to pay attention to how our technologies rhetorically participate in our embodied lives. Our bodies, our identities, and even queer rhetorics do not stop at the surface of our skin. Consequently, there is a need to continue examining embodied technologies outside Grindr. It is important to ask, for instance, How do we deal with embodied technologies that are biologically integrated to alter our bodies permanently? What ways are embodied technologies changing the landscape of gender and sexuality? As technologies advance to influence our embodiment, we must be ever mindful of how they rhetorically privilege some bodies and exclude others. Conceptually, embodied technologies offer a lens through which we can continue to question the boundaries around embodied rhetorics and the technologies that shape our bodies.

NOTES

1.   Grindr was released in 2009 and soon "exploded into the largest and most popular all-male location-based social network out there" ("Learn More"). No longer restricted by the personal computer, online dating discourse radically shifted because of Grindr. The basic version is free but has a number of limitations.

2.   My engagement with *queer* draws from rhetorical theories (e.g., Alexander; Banks; Dadas; Rhodes) and wider queer studies (e.g., Ahmed; Halberstam; Jagose).

3.   Granted, not all embodied technologies are queer or require the potential to queer our embodiment. For instance, Snapchat allows users to send customizable pictures and videos that disappear after they are received. I argue that Snapchat is an embodied technology because it interacts with the body and allows users to make rhetorical choices. Such decisions don't queer the user's embodiment, *per se.* However, under certain circumstances, one's embodied life may be affected when those photos are licentious, screen captured, then leaked online (Binder), queering the intended embodied effects.

4.   While it's true that both adding an image and a Display Name are optional, having a blank profile may impede interaction.

5.   There's more space to write a personal description (up to 250 characters) in the About Me section. There are other optional categories to explore in Grindr's profile design: age, "tribe," height, weight, body type, ethnicity, looking for, and relationship status.

6.   The deeply problematic appropriation of the Indigenous term *tribe* notwithstanding, there are many repercussions in choosing an identity along such lines. Each "tribe" name has been circulated in queer discourse for some time. Take the etymology for Bear and Otter, which can be traced back to George Mazzei's 1979 article "Who's Who at the Zoo?," in which Mazzei attempts to "blithely categorize other gay men and lesbians as types of animals" (n.p.).

7.   You only are permitted one "tribe" if you don't pay for Grindr Xtra. A subscription to Xtra enables three "tribal affiliations." For a 99¢ download and a monthly subscription, Grindr Xtra comes with extended "benefits" and a whole array of perks: saved phrases for chatting, access to five hundred more users, ad-free browsing, the ability to filter through other profile aspects, and more. I'm not suggesting that by clicking through profiles you can purchase the user behind the screen (although personal escorts do advertise), but Xtra allows you to organize what types of embodiments appear on your grid map to peruse. You are paying for more "ground" to cover, more men to "search," and ultimately more possibility to hook up. Accompanying Xtra is the (purchased) freedom to be selective about the bodies you choose to cruise. Your map can literally be segregated by race, for example, or by waist size or height.

8.   There is something to be said about the fact that money enables more opportunity in a space that aims for equitable inclusion.

WORKS CITED

"Learn More." *Grindr*, 21 May 2015. *Internet Archive*, web.archive.org/web/20150315014350/http://grindr.com/learn-more.

Ahmed, Sara. *Queer Phenomenology: Orientations, Objects, Others.* Duke UP, 2006.

Alexander, Jonathan. *Literacy, Sexuality, Pedagogy: Theory and Practice for Composition Studies.* Utah State UP, 2008.

Alexander, Jonathan, and William P. Banks. "Sexualities, Technologies, and the Teaching of Writing: A Critical Overview." *Computers and Composition*, vol. 21, no. 3, 2004, pp. 273–293. *ScienceDirect*, doi:10.1016/j.compcom.2004.05.005.

Alexander, Jonathan, and Elizabeth Losh. "'A YouTube of One's Own?': 'Coming Out' Videos as Rhetorical Action." *LGBT Identity and Online New Media*, edited by Christopher Pullen and Margaret Cooper, Routledge, 2010, pp. 37–50.

Alexander, Jonathan, and Jacqueline Rhodes. "Queerness, Multimodality, and the Possibilities of Re/Orientation." *Composing (Media)=Composing (Embodiment): Bodies, Technologies, Writing, the Teaching of Writing*, edited by Kristin L. Arola and Anne Frances Wysocki, Utah State UP, 2012, pp. 188–212.

Almjeld, Jen. "A Rhetorician's Guide to Love: Online Dating Profiles as Remediated Commonplace Books." *Computers and Composition*, vol. 35, 2014, pp. 71–83. *ScienceDirect*, doi:10.1016/j.compcom.2014.04.004.

Arola, Kristin L., and Anne Frances Wysocki, editors. *Composing (Media)=Composing (Embodiment): Bodies, Technologies, Writing, the Teaching of Writing*. Utah State UP, 2012.

Balsamo, Anne Marie. *Technologies of the Gendered Body: Reading Cyborg Women*. Duke UP, 1996.

Banks, William P. "Beyond Modality: Rethinking Transmedia Composition through a Queer/Trans Digital Rhetoric." *Routledge Handbook of Digital Writing and Rhetoric*, edited by Jonathan Alexander and Jacqueline Rhodes, Routledge, 2018, pp. 341–51.

Banks, William P. "Written through the Body: Disruptions and 'Personal' Writing." *The Personal in Academic Writing*. Spec. issue of *College English*, vol. 66, no. 1, 2003, pp. 21–40. *JSTOR*, doi:10.2307/3594232.

Barad, Karen M. *Meeting the Universe Halfway: Quantum Physics and the Entanglement of Matter and Meaning*. Duke UP, 2007.

Barnett, Scot, and Casey Andrew Boyle, editors. *Rhetoric, through Everyday Things*. U of Alabama P, 2016.

Binder, Shawn. "Why Snapchat Might Not Be Awesome for Your Relationships." *Mic*, 15 Dec. 2015, mic.com/articles/130487/here-s-how-snapchat-might-be-ruining-our-relationships#.R4KY6iOKW. Accessed 27 June 2020.

Butler, Judith. *Gender Trouble*. Routledge, 1990.

Butler, Judith. "Performative Acts and Gender Constitution: An Essay in Phenomenology and Feminist Theory." *Theatre Journal*, vol. 40, no. 4, 1988, pp. 519–533.

Butler, Judith. *Undoing Gender*. Routledge, 2004.

Chávez, Karma R. "The Body: An Abstract and Actual Rhetorical Concept." *Keywords: A Glossary of the Pasts and Futures of the Rhetoric Society of America*. Spec. issue of *Rhetoric Society Quarterly*, vol. 48, no. 3, 2018, pp. 242–250. *Taylor & Francis Online*, doi:10.1080/02773945.2018.1454182.

Dadas, Caroline. "Messy Methods: Queer Methodological Approaches to Researching Social Media." *Computers and Composition*, vol. 40, 2016, pp. 60–72. *ScienceDirect*, doi:10.1016/j.compcom.2016.03.007.

Deb, Amrita. "Phantom Vibration and Phantom Ringing among Mobile Phone Users: A Systematic Review of Literature." *Asia-Pacific Psychiatry*, vol. 7, no. 3, 2015, pp. 231–239. *Wiley Online Library*, doi:10.1111/appy.12164.

Douchebags of Grindr. 3 July 2011, www.douchebagsofgrindr.com. Accessed 26 June 2020.

Duggan, Lisa. "The New Homonormativity: The Sexual Politics of Neoliberalism." *Materializing Democracy: Toward a Revitalized Cultural Politics*, edited by Russ Castronovo and Dana Nelson, Duke UP, 2002.

Edwards, Dustin. "Circulation Gatekeepers: Unbundling the Platform Politics of YouTube's Content ID." *Computers and Composition*, vol. 47, 2018, pp. 61–74. *ScienceDirect*, doi:10.1016/j.compcom.2017.12.001.

Edwards, Dustin, and Bridget Gelms. "The Rhetorics of Platforms: Definitions, Approaches, Futures." *Rhetoric of Platforms*. Spec. issue of *Present Tense: A Journal of Rhetoric in Society*, vol. 6, no. 3, 2018, pp. 2–10, www.presenttensejournal.org/editorial/vol-6-3-special-issue-on-the-rhetoric-of-platforms/. Accessed 27 June 2020.

Faris, Michael J. "How to be Gay with Locative Media: The Rhetorical Work of Grindr as a Platform." *Rhetoric of Platforms.* Spec. issue of *Present Tense: A Journal of Rhetoric in Society*, vol. 6, no. 3, 2018, pp. 2–12. www.presenttensejournal.org/volume-6/how-to-be-gay-with-locative-media-the-rhetorical-work-of-grindr-as-a-platform/. Accessed 27 June 2020.

Garland-Thomson, Rosemarie. *Extraordinary Bodies: Figuring Physical Disability in American Culture and Literature.* Columbia UP, 1997.

Gillespie, Tarleton. "The Politics of 'Platforms.'" *New Media & Society*, vol. 12, no. 3, 2010, pp. 347–364. *SAGE Journals*, doi:10.1177/1461444809342738.

Gouge, Catherine, and John Jones. "Wearables, Wearing, and the Rhetorics That Attend to Them." *Wearable Rhetorics: Bodies, Cities, Collectives.* Spec. issue of *Rhetoric Society Quarterly*, vol. 46, no. 3, 2016, pp. 199–206. *Taylor & Francis Online*, doi:10.1080/02773945.2016.1171689.

Gray, Mary L. "'Queer Nation Is Dead/Long Live Queer Nation': The Politics and Poetics of Social Movement and Media Representation." *Critical Studies in Media Communication*, vol. 26, no. 3, 2009, pp. 212–236. *Taylor & Francis Online*, doi:10.1080/15295030903015062.

Gries, Laurie E. *Still Life with Rhetoric: A New Materialist Approach for Visual Rhetorics.* Utah State UP, 2015.

"Grindr Takes a Stand against Sexual Racism and Discrimination with 'Kindr' Initiative." *Grindr*, 18 Sept. 2018, grindr.tumblr.com/post/178209018151/grindr-takes-a-stand-against-sexual-racism-and. Accessed 26 June 2020.

Grosz, Elizabeth A. *Volatile Bodies: Toward a Corporeal Feminism.* Indiana UP, 1994.

Halberstam, Judith. *In a Queer Time and Place: Transgender Bodies, Subcultural Lives.* New York UP, 2005.

Haraway, Donna. *Simians, Cyborgs and Women: The Reinvention of Nature.* Routledge, 1991.

Hawisher, Gail E., and Cynthia L. Selfe. "The Rhetoric of Technology and the Electronic Writing." *College Composition and Communication*, vol. 42, no. 1, 1991, pp. 55–56. *JSTOR*, doi:10.2307/357539.

Hawk, Byron, and David M. Rieder. "On Small Tech and Complex Ecologies." *Small Tech: The Culture of Digital Tools*, edited by Byron Hawk, David M. Rieder, and Ollie O. Oviedo, U of Minnesota P, 2008, pp. ix–xxiii.

Jackson, Gerald. *Queer Practices, Queer Rhetoric, Queer Technologies: Studies of Digital Performativity.* Diss. University of Southern Carolina, 2017. *ScholarCommons*, scholarcommons.sc.edu/etd/4248. Accessed 28 June 2020.

Jagose, Annamarie. *Queer Theory: An Introduction.* New York UP, 1996.

Johnson, Gavin. "From Rhetorical Eavesdropping to Rhetorical Foreplay: Orientations, Spacetimes, and the Emergence of a Queer Embodied Tactic." *Pre/Text*, vol. 24, no. 1–4, 2018, pp. 119–138.

"Kindr Grindr." *Kindr*, Grindr.com, 2018, https://www.kindr.grindr.com/.

Knoblauch, A. Abby. "Bodies of Knowledge: Definitions, Delineations, and Implications of Embodied Writing in the Academy." *Composition Studies*, vol. 40, no. 2, 2012, pp. 50–65. *JSTOR*, www.jstor.org/stable/compstud.40.2.0050.

Kruger, Daniel J., and Jaikob M. Djerf. "Bad Vibrations? Cell Phone Dependency Predicts Phantom Communication Experiences." *Computers in Human Behavior*, vol. 70, 2017, pp. 360–364. *ACM Digital Library*, doi:10.1016/j.chb.2017.01.017.

Mazzei, George. "Who's Who at the Zoo?" *Advocate*, 26 July 1979.

McCorkle, Ben. "Whose Body?: Looking Critically at New Interface Designs." *Composing (Media)=Composing (Embodiment): Bodies, Technologies, Writing, the Teaching of Writing*, edited by Kristin L. Arola and Anne Frances Wysocki, Utah State UP, 2012, pp. 174–187.

McGlotten, Shaka. *Virtual Intimacies: Media, Affect, and Queer Sociality.* State U of New York P, 2013.

McLaughlin, Eliott C. "Suspect OKs Amazon to Hand Over Echo Recordings in Murder Case." *CNN*, 26 Apr. 2017, www.cnn.com/2017/03/07/tech/amazon-echo-alexa-bentonville-arkansas-murder-case/index.html. Accessed 26 June 2020.

McWhorter, Ladelle. *Bodies and Pleasures: Foucault and the Politics of Sexual Normalization*. Indiana UP, 1999.

Nakamura, Lisa. *Digitizing Race: Visual Cultures of the Internet*. U of Minnesota P, 2008.

Peters, Brad, and Diana Swanson. "Queering the Conflicts: What LGBT Students Can Teach Us in the Classroom and Online." *Sexualities, Technologies and the Teaching of Writing*. Spec. issue of *Computers and Composition*, vol. 21, no. 3, 2004, pp. 295–313. *ScienceDirect*, doi:10.1016/j.compcom.2004.05.004.

Pullen, Christopher. Introduction. *LGBT Identity and Online New Media*, edited by Christopher Pullen and Margaret Cooper, Routledge, 2010, pp. 1–13.

Pullen, Christopher, and Margaret Cooper. *LGBT Identity and Online New Media*. Routledge, 2010.

Rhodes, Jacqueline. "Homo Origo: The Queertext Manifesto." *Sexualities, Technologies and the Teaching of Writing*. Spec. issue of *Computers and Composition*, vol. 21, no. 3, 2004, pp. 385–388. *ScienceDirect*, doi:10.1016/j.compcom.2004.05.001.

Rhodes, Jacqueline, and Jonathan Alexander. *Techne: Queer Meditations on Writing the Self*. Computers and Composition Digital Press, 2015.

Selfe, Cynthia L., and Richard J. Selfe. "The Politics of the Interface: Power and Its Exercise in Electronic Contact Zones." *College Composition and Communication*, vol. 45, no. 4, 1994, pp. 480–504. *JSTOR*, doi:10.2307/358761.

Smilges, Johnathan. "White Squares to Black Boxes: Grindr, Queerness, Rhetorical Silence." *Rhetoric Review*, vol. 38, no. 1, pp. 79–92. *Taylor & Francis Online*, doi:10.1080/07350198.2018.1551661.

Syverson, Margaret A. *The Wealth of Reality: An Ecology of Composition*. Southern Illinois UP, 1999.

Tomlinson, Elizabeth C. "The Role of Invention in Digital Dating Site Profile Composition." *Computers and Composition*, vol. 30, no. 2, 2013, pp. 115–128. *ScienceDirect*, doi:10.1016/j.compcom.2013.04.003.

Trebay, Guy. "The Sex Education of Grindr's Joel Simkhai." *New York Times*, 13 Dec. 2014, www.nytimes.com/2014/12/14/fashion/the-sex-education-of-grindrs-joel-simkhai.html. Accessed 26 June 2020.

Vetter, Matthew. "Queer-the-Tech: Genderfucking and Anti-Consumer Activism in Social Media." *Harlot*, vol. 11, no. 11, 2014, harlotofthearts.org/index.php/harlot/article/view/195/148. Accessed 26 June 2020.

Wysocki, Anne Frances. "Into Between—On Composition in Mediation." *Composing (Media)=Composing (Embodiment): Bodies, Technologies, Writing, the Teaching of Writing*, edited by Kristin L. Arola and Anne Frances Wysocki, Utah State UP, 2012, pp. 1–24.

13

AVOWED EMBODIMENT
Self-Identification, Performative Strategic Attire, and TRAP Karaoke

Temptaous Mckoy (Bowie State University)

"Bihhhh we going to TRAP Karaoke!" It was the text I sent one of my girls, Jennifer, letting her know I had finally got my hands on some tickets to TRAP Karaoke in DC, at the Howard Theatre. All summer I had been watching this event known as TRAP Karaoke all up and down my Facebook and Instagram scroll. All my friends were tagging me in their posts: "Temp, we need to go!" "Aye, you would love this!" "We need to find out how to get on stage!" From what I gathered, TRAP Karaoke was a movement that curated a space for trap music loving, all up in your face swag surfin', standing together sangin' Black people. In all of TRAP Karaoke's social media posts, you could see Black people singing/ rapping their favorite songs, having the time of their lives! Won't no artist, it was just the people on stage rocking out! But I also saw these dope t-shirts. Everyone had these #Tees4TheTrap on. The shirts my people were wearing had various messages, some funny, some political, but ALL pro-Black. I especially appreciated that if you weren't a part of the Black community, you was 'bout to be left out on the message. Eventually, I concluded these shirts symbolized community in this space that was meant to celebrate Black culture, Black joy, and most important, the outward declaration that you can be as unapologetically Black as you want to be . . . and I wanted in. Not only to be a part of TRAP Karaoke as an event but also of the experience it created for Black people. But look, won't no way I was gonna go to no TRAP Karaoke and wear a basic shirt. I needed to make sure my attire was strategic. I knew I wanted to show I was a member of the community TRAP Karaoke represents, yet be political as well. I knew that in doing both, I would represent the woman I am and the scholar I would soon become. I saw a shirt with the words "Reclaiming My Time—Auntie Maxine" on it. Immediately I knew: that's the shirt I'm wearing to TRAP Karaoke.

One of the ways social-movement organizations such as the Black Panther Party, Brown Berets, and even the Ku Klux Klan develop their collective identity is, I argue, through a shared embodiment among

https://doi.org/10.7330/9781646422012.c013

their members (Caliendo and McIlwain 49; Diani 8; Freeman and Johnson 152; Pulido 15). This shared embodiment forms an identity for the organization, as well as a sense of community amongst organization members. When experienced collectively, this usage of our embodiment can forge new understandings for what it means to hold and enact a self-identified identity, how we see ourselves in relation to individuals around us, and autonomous embodied rhetorical practices.

In this chapter, I employ *embodiment* as a way to refer to how individuals evoke their identity through the physical body to proclaim who they are and what they represent; included in this definition, then, may be the use of the body to call for the need for social change and individual growth. For my working definition, embodiment is the combination of the physical body and one's individual (group) identity. Embodiment is the material physicality alongside the cultural and social experiences that shape the way one moves about or performs in society.

This acknowledgment and awareness of one's positionality can lead to the development and understanding of a personified identity (Merriam et al. 412). A. Abby Knoblauch argues that embodied rhetoric can be seen as a clear "purposeful effort by an author to represent an aspect of embodiment within the text he or she is shaping" (58). I build on the notion of the body itself as text, arguing that social-movement organization members have a duty to utilize their bodies as texts (in various ways) in order to effectively communicate who they are and what they represent. As my chapter focuses on TRAP Karaoke as a site for study, a predominantly Black organization, I centralize Black embodiment. I claim that Black individuals enact embodied rhetoric by default, as every notion of their being, existence, and communicative practices must be intentional and purposeful, thus resulting in the Black body always serving as text.[1] This is not to say only Black bodies serve as text; instead, I argue that the social and cultural privilege Black individuals are not provided *as a result* of their physical bodies leaves them unable to separate their bodies as text from Black embodiment. Embodied practices enacted by Black individuals occur both consciously and subconsciously, in part because for Black individuals, disregarding the physical can lead to unclear understandings of how embodiment shows up in the creation of an individual's identity (Díaz-Andreu et al. 2), ways of knowing, and claimed agency (Harris 2976).

My proposed theoretical framework, avowed embodiment (AE), addresses this inherent embodied rhetoric and illustrates one of the ways Black bodies can serve as text, both in themselves and by the use of performative strategic attire in social movements such as TRAP

Karaoke. TRAP Karaoke is a user-generated concert experience-turned-movement that brings together Black performance, celebration, epistemologies, and a space to be unapologetically Black as f**k. Being unapologetically Black can mean several things, but one of the most important is removing oneself from the white gaze. Or as Damon Young, author of "How to Be Unapologetically Black," states, "Give negative infinity f**ks about what white people think." By confessing their embodiment openly, rhetorically (what I call *avowing embodiment*), an individual within an organization can enact various embodied practices that showcase who/what the individual/organization is, which can lead to understanding and acceptance as a means of *activism, resistance,* and/or *celebration*. One way this happens for TRAP Karaoke participants is by wearing #Tees4Theavowing shirts traditionally worn by attendees and participants. Individuals who wear #Tees4TheTrap hold Black or historically marginalized identities and allow their shirts to showcase their embodiment.

This idea of avowing one's embodiment is not new: it builds on the work of past scholars and their theorization of self-identification and transformation (Banks 30; Craemer and Orey 166; Cross, "The Negro-to Black" 13; Harris and Sim 615; Moses, Villodas, and Villodas 112). Specifically, I build on William Cross's self-identification theory, Nigrescence theory, to develop my theory of avowed embodiment. While much work has been done on identification, rhetorical embodiments, and theories of identity development (Carlson 126; Gowland and Thompson 15; Trautwein 996), an avowed-embodiment framework speaks specifically to and for members of Black communities and the action of showcasing their embodiment however they see fit.

NIGRESCENCE THEORY TO AVOWED EMBODIMENT

Nigrescence theory (NT) is a Black identity model pioneered by William E. Cross Jr.—a Black man, avid African American theorist, and CUNY professor emeritus—to explain the psychological perils of Black-identity recognition during the civil rights era, a time when Black racial identity was oftentimes based on the white gaze (Ilmi 219; Ogbu 18). Cross details one method of identity creation and way of knowing as they track a process of racial identity and self-discovery for Black people. Cross refers to this as the "Negro-to-Black conversion" (*Stereotypic* 107).[2] According to Cross, the Negro-to-Black conversion is a psychological transformation performed by Black individuals by which they initially reject their racial identity and then ascribe to white cultural norms and

222   TEMPTAOUS MCKOY

proposed identity. Yet while embarking on this psychological journey, the individual experiences a transformation, ultimately resulting in racial identity acceptance and empowerment.[3]

The theory served as a response to literature from the 1930s to the 1970s on Black identity grounded in self-hatred (Cross, *Stereotypic* 119). Nigrescence theory, which is also referred to as the "Black identity change," is depicted in five stages: preencounter, encounter, immersion, internalization, and commitment (Cross, *Stereotypic* 8). First, preencounter establishes an individual in their neutral being (8) or the "colonized mind" (109). In the encounter stage, the individual has an experience, mental or physical, that signals a change in identity. This encounter can also be described as a "personal experience that temporarily dislodges the person from his old-world view, thus making him receptive (vulnerable) to a new perspective and/or identity" (Cross, "The Negro-to-Black" 15). Presently, we refer to this moment as becoming "woke." Next, the stage of immersion is the phase of identity transformation that moves to a participant's internalization, which depicts behavior. In the stages of immersion and internalization, an individual is able to sort the positives and negatives associated with their Black identity (15). The process ends in the stage of commitment to the newfound Black identity, assuming the participant accepts and takes on the new identity (Cross, *Stereotypic* 8).

I build on Cross's work to develop my theoretical framework because it is a person's psychological transformation that influences their rhetorical usages of their embodiment, especially in the encounter and immersion stages. For someone to decide to *avow* their embodiment (immersion), they must first be able to identify how their embodiment is situated within the world around them (encounter). I like to think of the immersion stage as one in which someone is weighing the potential risks and advantages associated with avowing their embodiment, as it is imperative to acknowledge that openly identifying oneself will not always result in a positive outcome. For example, only recently have California and New York passed bills to stop discrimination based on natural hair. Dubbed the Crown Act, which stands for Create a Respectful and Open Workplace for Natural Hair, the bill prohibits discrimination against potential and current employees based on the texture/style of their hair—especially if their hair is "ethnic." Before this, Black individuals had to decide whether it was best to wear their natural hair to work or a hairstyle that was more reflective of white standards for professional hair (straightened/weave/short fade). Regardless of their choice, a commitment is made, leading to a conscious decision to outwardly showcase their embodiment.[4] Another example is a famed scene from the classic miniseries *Roots*, in which we see Kunta Kinte, played by LeVar Burton, reject the orders of his slave master by refusing to take on the name Toby, even though it leads to his continued whipping (commitment stage). He is aware of the continued lashings he will receive, but he is also aware of the significance of his name as attached to his embodiment, thus leading to his decision to enact an embodied practice of resistance.[5] These are examples of what I'm calling *avowed embodiment*: the rhetorical act of showcasing one's identity through the physical body, in this case shown as physical resistance. Kinte is well aware of his identity as a slave, yet he does not buckle when commanded. Instead, he intentionally utilizes his body to showcase his resistance by willingly submitting to a lashing.

The choice to utilize avowed embodiment (AE)—however the participant may see fit—requires the participant to take on the stages as described in Nigrescence theory most appropriate to their embodied lived experiences, or as Adrienne Rich might say, their politics of location (32). For example, the encounter stage for someone who is Black may be very different from the experience of someone who has an unseen disability and who is grappling with the choice to be open about their need for assistance while not garnering pity. Not wanting someone to feel bad for us is attached to our sense of pride in who we are and how we identify. This encounter also differs for gay men and lesbians. Society addresses these sexual orientations in different ways, even going so far as to fetishize one (lesbianism) while chastising the other (gayness). Avowed embodiment, then, opens itself up to multiple marginalized (and multiply marginalized) communities and combines Cross's psychological process of acceptance and self-reflection with embodied performance.

While avowed embodiment often serves as a form of resistance, I want to make clear the difference between AE and Julie Ericksen's notion of embodied resistance. Embodied resistance aims to uncover or address issues of social norms attached to certain bodies or oppositional behaviors and can be viewed as political action (Ericksen 794). Avowed embodiment also utilizes different facets of embodiment to address social norms associated with certain bodies but suggests a level of acceptance of social status and critique, utilizing this acknowledgment as the participant sees fit. An example of this would be my choice as a Black woman to not raise my voice during certain interactions to be sure I am not perceived as combative; this a part of my performance of avowed embodiment. There is a psychological process I take on subconsciously (as Cross argues), contextualizing my audience and how I want them to receive what I say. The moment I speak (perform) following this psychological process is a moment I have moved into the avowed-embodiment model. My performance is shaped based upon the previous analytical facets of my Black-woman identity.

It's also useful to think through the implications of Cross's encounters stage. Encounters can be positive, negative, or both. For example, someone who has been raised to have Black pride may have an encounter that makes them question their upbringing; they may later return to their roots and showcase their embodiment as an act of resistance or pride. However, someone who is LGBTQIA+ and has grown up in a conservative home might have a positive encounter with someone they identify with and, as a result, might decide to turn away from their upbringing and more clearly perform their embodied identity. In each case, there is a different catalyzing factor for deciding to enact AE. For some, this can be one way to move *away* from who they have been socialized to be, while for others, AE is how they *appreciate* who they have been socialized to be. While Cross provides us with a psychological framework for this process, AE allows us to see what this change looks like, literally, when manifested and shown through embodied actions.

To clarify, avowed embodiment will not always result in positive performances or outlooks. In fact, there are times when avowed embodiment may restrict one's performative practices, as in my example of not raising my voice (even when raising my voice is a reasonable response, but not for my embodied identity as a Black woman). Furthermore, avowing our embodiment allows for the acknowledgment of and reflection on cultural and social implications, understandings of that embodiment, and our choice to react. In some instances, our performative response may result in backlash, while in other instances our performance may result in a newfound sense of self, community, and uplift.

AVOWED EMBODIMENT: A THEORY OF ITS OWN

Avowed embodiment (AE), which I define as the act of outwardly declaring/showcasing one's identity through the physical body or strategic attire (such as #Tees4TheTrap shirts), has three essential purposes: identify, communicate, and celebrate/resist. First, AE is intended to allow an individual to declare who they are—to themselves and to those who may share features of the same embodied identity. Publicly identifying who you are can be a pivotal moment for self-acceptance. However, I argue that a person cannot truly enact AE without first accepting who they are (what we might see as Cross's commitment stage).[6] I further argue that identifying a sense of self begins with the body (AhnAllen, Suyemoto, and Carter 674), especially, but not solely, for Black individuals (Thompson 44). For example, an "invisible" disability impacts the body, despite its invisibility. I suffer from bipolar disorder II; there is no way to look at me and know that, but it impacts my physical body in a number of ways, including how I move in and out of spaces. In fact, I noticed my physical actions before I was able to identify my mood disorder. I then had to learn what I was facing, how to handle it, and ways I could make myself better before I was able to outwardly share this aspect of my life. So, in identifying it for myself, I am able to also engage and create a sense of community with other people who may have the same disorder. We might see this as the identification stage.

Next, AE serves to communicate one's embodiment. Of course, there are a multitude of intersectional identities someone can have, and while the physical body is an obvious influence, it does not necessarily define identity. For example, a Black person who decides to engage in anime culture may not enact the same embodied practices as an individual who engages in Chopped and Screwed, a hip-hop subculture based on a Djing technique of slowing and reversing hip-hop music. It's also possible that Black and white members of anime culture would choose to avow their embodiment through strategic attire in different ways. But the body still manages to show up, no pun intended, in multiple facets when it comes to creating one's identity.

Finally, AE serves to celebrate someone's newfound self and/or makes it possible to utilize this newfound sense of self as a form of resistance. In order for someone to engage in AE, they must essentially celebrate who they have come to know themselves to be. Even when a person outwardly declares they are a sexual-assault survivor, for example (which might align with the encounter stage), they are celebrating their ability to overcome. Outwardly declaring their ability to overcome is celebration of their commitment (the final stage of NT) to tell their story, engage with the trauma of the assault that occurred upon their body, and understand there are others who, too, hold that identity. Celebration is where communication and identification meet and lead to a potential end goal.

While some may avow their embodiment for a sense of relief, others may do so as a way to resist cultural and social norms. If we use the body as text, we have a better chance of engaging in any form of resistance we choose, even if that resistance does not result in a positive outcome. A white woman protesting for the ability for me, a Black woman, to wear my natural hair at work certainly does not have the same impact as if I were to do it. In fact, the white woman's actions may have a greater

impact because in order for her to do such a thing, she much first identify herself as a white woman, communicating her position by utilizing
her physical body to protest, whereas there may be instances when my
protesting in this way is perceived as combative and nonconforming to
social expectations.

As we can see, it is not possible to remove the physical body in moving
towards AE; our bodies are a very important part of how we form our
own identities. However, I argue that Cross's foundational psychological
principles of transformation can also lead to embodied practices that
can be exemplified and reflected in performative strategic attire. For
many, clothing is an extension of embodiment (Crane 181; Feinberg,
Mataro, and Burroughs 18; Frith and Gleeson 40). Even in its simplest
form, clothing selection is strategic, or, as Carol Mattingly and others
have shown, rhetorical. For example, I like clothing in neutral colors,
not just because neutral goes with anything but also because it gives me
balance and is rarely out of place. This is an example of who I am and
what I embody—I do not like dysfunction, but I can also blend into
multiple settings, and I tend to maneuver through spaces where I see
myself as a solid "fit."

In the remainder of this chapter, I showcase what AE looks like in
the form of performative strategic attire, teasing apart the differences
between performative strategic attire and more general forms of expression. As I later mention, context matters. I then draw connections
between performative strategic attire as a way to embody performative
theory and embodied rhetorics, alongside Cross's Nigrescence theory to
illustrate how the intersections of these concepts serve as an utterance
of avowed embodiment.

AVOWED EMBODIMENT IN PRACTICE: PERFORMATIVE STRATEGIC ATTIRE

In building on Cross's theory to provide an understanding of the psychological transformations that could lead to embodied performance,
we now move to *performative strategic attire* as a way to illustrate avowed
embodiment. As indicated by Dicky Yangzom, "[C]lothing manifests as
a space for distinction where embedded meaning of shared collective
consciousness is made visible" (2). Yet, *performative strategic attire* serves as
a form of rhetoric, exemplified on the body, selected specifically by the
individual based on their identity. We rely on the context of an individual's use of performative strategic attire to better understand how this
serves as a form of avowed embodiment rather than only an utterance

or outward physical expression. Attire can clearly serve as an utterance; however it is not what is uttered (worn) that makes it meaningful but the rationale for why it was uttered (worn) that makes it have performative meaning (Sanders 117). As previously mentioned, performative strategic attire can define the attire of a social-movement organization, thus serving specific visual rhetorical purposes. In donning performative strategic attire, organization participants are able to showcase an extension of their identity and embodiment. Essentially, the attire becomes a part of the text that is contextualized by the physical body.

In *Persuasion and Social Movements,* Charles J. Stewart, Robert E. Denton Jr., and Craig Allen Smith argue that strategic attire can serve to communicate group identity and generate a sense of shared identification (140, 164). In addition, the authors suggest strategic attire becomes an extension of physical interaction that, in turn, influences behaviors rather than operating as a result of behaviors (140). I argue, however, that performative strategic attire occurs as a means to influence behaviors *and* as a result of behaviors. The wearing of the pink pussy hats, for example, did not happen only to influence others interested in women's rights: this performative strategic attire happened as a result of actions that oppressed *women* specifically.[7] Similarly, members of the "new" alt-right, a white nationalist group, situate themselves as "minority victims facing reverse discrimination" (Futrell and Simi 76) and wear polo shirts as performative strategic attire to ensure they are not "cringe worthy" like their predecessors (*NY Times*). Members of this group did not simply decide to shift their attire because they thought it looked better; it was a response to previous perceptions and reactions by those who oppose the (majority *white and male*) alt-right. In order for the new attire to *become* the new attire, the participants in both groups had to engage in a psychological process similar to the one described by Cross and then avow their community identity through the use of performative strategic attire.

The use of performative strategic attire becomes both a means of identifying (for onlookers) and identification (for participants): it's a celebration of shared narratives and experiences and the usage of embodied activism—activism influenced by an advocate's physical body and identity—thus providing ways of avowing participants' embodiment, which can shape the movement overall.[8] For various Black social-movement organizations, such as TRAP Karaoke, the use of performative strategic attire forges a sense of community and togetherness, and, most important, serves to celebrate the avowed embodiment of the organizations.

AVOWED EMBODIMENT AND PERFORMATIVE
STRATEGIC ATTIRE IN TRAP KARAOKE

TRAP Karaoke, founded in summer 2016, is not recognized as an "official" Black Power social movement. Started by DC native Jason Mowatt as a trap-music karaoke event aiming to develop a "user gener-ated concert experience," TRAP Karaoke has grown into a movement all its own, one that engages the lived experience of its attendees (Trap Karaoke). Most important in regard to avowed embodiment, TRAP Karaoke provides its participants the space to be, as their Web site explains, "Unapologetically Black as F**K"—an uncut approach to racial identity (Chappell). This is not your traditional karaoke but rather karaoke centered around traditionally Black, or trap, music. TRAP music finds its roots in the US South. The genre emerged in the early 2000s as a musical outlet detailing the experience of those in troubled neighborhoods (Admin). This became a branch of hip-hop artistry away from what, at the time, dominated "the sound of the hood"—crunk music.

TRAP Karaoke events serve as safe spaces for Black individuals to showcase their AE through various rhetorical practices, such as per-forming on stage, engaging in universal dance, and most important, wearing a #Tee4TheTrap. #Tees4TheTrap are t-shirts worn by TRAP Karaoke event attendees that exemplify and speak to Black lived experi-ences, ways of knowing, and tacit community knowledge. In my forth-coming analysis I present AE in action and illustrate its applicability in understanding Black social movements and Black embodied practices. I show how #Tees4TheTrap as performative strategic attire shape the ways identification, communication, and celebration occur in the TRAP Karaoke movement.

Identification—Maintaining Visibility

Identification and maintained visibility through performative strategic attire are two of the most crucial facets of articulating and amplifying an organization's manifesto and/or identity. TRAP Karaoke is shaped primarily by its participants without one overarching "official" mani-festo but rather a call to celebrate and uplift the Black community and its embodiment. Yet, we can look to performative strategic attire as a way to assist in the structuring of the organization (Stewart, Denton, and Smith 178). The need for maintained visibility is supported by its role as a symbolic identification for participants and onlookers alike (83). #Tees4theTrap act as a key way to identify members of the TRAP

Karaoke organization: what started as a hashtag to virtually link the experiences and attire of TRAP Karaoke attendees is now a pivotal part of the organization's identity. While one is not necessarily "required" to wear a #Tees4theTrap to support the movement, the t-shirts serve to identify members of the overall call to Black celebration.[9] The shirts function as a symbol of solidarity amongst participants.[10]

Although it can be argued that solidarity is important to creating any sense of community, I believe it is especially crucial to the identity of this organization, which is built on shared embodied and lived experiences. #Tees4theTrap shirts include phrases, lyrics, and Black icons that, again, represent the shared experiences of participants. One shirt, for example, includes the phrase "Coretta & Cardi B." If a participant wears this shirt, they are identified as a TRAP Music fan but also as someone knowledgeable of the work of Coretta Scott King, wife of Dr. Martin Luther King Jr.[11] Furthermore, the t-shirts utilize the discursive rules of cohesion and coherence, both of which rely on the default assumption of the audience to ensure the discourse is effective (Bublitz 38). While some onlookers might misidentify (or fail to identify) the references, typically misidentification would not occur amongst TRAP Karaoke participants, as the organization's overall purpose is to celebrate Black lived experiences. However, the possibility for misidentification does welcome additional discourse surrounding Black identity and how that identity is communicated, defined, supported, and avowed amongst other Black people and TRAP Karaoke participants through #Tees4theTrap.

Communication—Symbolic Speech, Community, and Celebration

As we know, communication is not limited to verbal and written context; as I (and many others) have argued, the body serves as communicative text. If we look at someone's body as a lexical template, removed from its clothing or any other objects, we may read the body in a number of ways (Kantz and Marenzi 56). For example, do we read the body as healthy, or do we consider it might be malnourished? The body itself has the ability to communicate and/or to be read. Additionally, when we see the physical body in "daily interactions," these (inter)actions can produce pathological or physiological meanings (55). And of course these interactions in which we use our bodies can be influenced by how we self-identify. Once we add a layer of attire, the physical body may be seen through a different filter or lens and yet can still reflect embodied rhetorical practices. Clothing as symbolic speech can be used as a means to communicate a participant's embodiment to observers. For TRAP Karaoke, the use of performative strategic attire as symbolic speech helps amplify participants' AE but also showcases the organization's commitment to its participants as a community.

TRAP Karaoke utilizes the participatory nature of TRAP music and karaoke to forge community amongst participants. Events are typically held at small venues that curate spaces for intimacy. Furthermore, the participants themselves are the performers on the stage, weakening the boundary between performer and audience. In an interview with *Forbes*, Mowatt attributes the organization's success to its strong sense of community, stating, "[I]t's about personal empowerment, cultural participation, cherished moments, community, and creating a safe space for human connection" (qtd. in Mitchell). Attempting to shape the physical place to be both welcoming and intimate creates a space of intellectual and embodied safety. The social construction of place and space for TRAP Karaoke participants also transfers to their performative strategic attire. These physical spaces are transformed into churches of Black celebration, thus requiring the appropriate apparel. Furthermore, performative strategic attire for TRAP Karaoke is reliant upon assumed shared experiences, which leads to an understanding of the language utilized on #Tees4theTrap. The shirts worn by participants become the clothing version of the embodied cultural "head nod" that lets other participants know "I see you and I feel you."

This sense of community is not only crucial to individual participant's avowed embodiment but also serves as a means to communicate that shared experience and a sense of community to other participants. Utilizing the hashtag #Tees4theTrap connects attendees online and forges a virtual community. Here, participants can discuss t-shirt ideas and can find merchants responsible for selling the shirts—oftentimes Black business owners. Finally, this development of community amongst participants can lead to strategic exclusion, reaffirming who the community is for and what it represents. A shirt with the phrase "#BlackGirlMagic" is not only celebratory but also strategically excludes all other girls who are not Black, and this is okay. Moments of strategic exclusion ensure the identity of the organization remains intact but also protect the avowed embodiment of the participants. Participants' ability to see other members engaged in embodied practices not only showcases the number of organization participants, an argument from quantity, but also signals a sense of togetherness and celebration.

Celebration-Activism

TRAP Karaoke finds its foundation in its ability to engage in the labor of AE and then utilize said avowal to celebrate who they are as an organization for Black people. The embodied lived experiences of its members shape the way moments of celebration and activism occur within the movement. For TRAP Karaoke participants, #Tees4theTrap are celebratory: they include slogans such as "Very Black, Very Lit" and "Black Thighs Matter," which are references to the participants' embodiment and what they celebrate about said embodiment.[12]

Yet, it is also imperative to recognize that this embodied celebration is also utilized to recognize the often-painful experiences of participants. Through validating these experiences, we acknowledge the negative encounters (in Cross's terms) that have inspired participants to engage their embodiment in a specific way—in this case, through performative strategic attire. Often, this approach to engagement can lead to activism. Outrage leads to action. TRAP Karaoke participants see this strength when communicating suggested political change. T-shirts stating "I Can't Breathe," referencing the unjust death of Eric Garner, signal participants' acknowledgment that they, too, could have been Garner (due to their shared embodied Blackness) and shed light on this form of injustice. A shirt that replaces President Trump's "Make America Great Again" with "Deport White Supremacy. Make America Equal for Once" calls out social injustice. When worn, #Tees4TheTrap bring attention to injustice and communicate to participants that they, too, are impacted by these issues. When worn on specific bodies, the shirts can also communicate to outsiders that they are accountable for the injustices and that change must occur.

Sometimes, this line of celebration/resistance-activism can be blurred: a shirt is a shirt even if it is in the middle of the floor, but its rhetorical power changes depending on whose floor it is.[13] I suggest that performative strategic attire does not operate in a vacuum of purpose but rather serves as a form of activism and celebration. Activism *is* a form of celebration: it is the celebration of a group's ability to overcome oppressive instances, learn from them, and then call for change through their shared embodiment.

CONCLUSION

As this chapter details, performative strategic attire is one of many ways we can see Avowed Embodiment take shape as a rhetorical practice. Without Avowed Embodiment, organizations such as TRAP Karaoke risk losing their ability to communicate their identity, solidify their community, and celebrate who they are. I argue that a Black social movement and its participants cannot forge a sense of community identity and understanding without first accepting their Blackness and then outwardly avowing it.

Moving forward, I hope researchers are able to use my theoretical framework to better assess not only social-movement organizations and their participants but also their embodied identities while still respecting the narratives and agency of those identities. I also hope this frame can help individuals, scholars and nonscholars alike, in understanding and navigating their lived experience. I see this type of continued research as one way I enact a responsible approach to my scholarship. Because I am a scholar of socially just work, it is important that the scholarship I produce can take shape outside the academy and be utilized to amplify the voices of those who sometimes go unheard. In order for a theory to be effective and tangible, it should make sense theoretically, practically, and outside "formal" education spaces. Finally, as scholars seek to better understand AE, it is imperative that they think about how they situate their personal embodied experiences in the theoretical framework they wish to take up. Even though I've created AE to speak specifically to Black lived experiences, I do not see it as a way to ignore the lived embodied experiences of other historically marginalized groups; instead, it is a theoretical framework that can be adapted to apply to various embodiments in different spaces and times. Avowed Embodiment is one way embodied rhetorics can take shape and be recognized in various fields of study.

NOTES

1. "We often need to be reminded that the human body produces meaning physiologically not just through language and discourse, but in an integrated way that *inter alia* associates voice quality, gesture, gaze, body posture and movements" (Kantz and Marenzi 54).
2. I suggest the *Negro* in Negro-to-Black conversion is actually a reference to the work of Charles W. Thomas (whom Cross references in "Encountering Nigrescence") who coined the psychological condition "Negromachy" to describe the confusion experienced by Black people in understanding their racial identity, or when "a person is confused about his self-worth and depends on white society for self-definition" (Cross, "Encountering Nigrescence" 31). Cross and Thomas suggest the way to overcome Negromachy is with a psychological shift and an understanding of racial identity, thus birthing the Negro-to-Black conversion, or Nigrescence theory.
3. In aiming to support the labor and research of Black scholars, and the importance of recognizing and amplifying lived experience in informing our research, I recognize Cross's theory but note that the application of his work may not traverse boundaries of self-identification for people who are not Black. In fact, *nigrescence*

is Latin for "the process of becoming Black or developing a racial identity," which suggests that those who are not Black cannot undergo this process; nonetheless, I welcome scholars to responsibly and consciously refer to Cross's work in theorizing Avowed Embodiment (AE) to fit in the context of other historically marginalized communities ("Nigrescence"). Essentially, AE can serve as a theoretical framework that provides space for the foundational principles, identity perception, and acceptance, of Cross's work to be utilized across various embodiments and fields of study.

4. I think it is important to note that discussing hair, especially weaves, can be a bit tricky. It is not that in order to avow your embodiment as a Black individual you must wear your natural hair; instead, making the choice to wear your hair in a way that may be closely aligned with your identity can be a part of your transformation. Yet, I acknowledge there is a lot of history behind Black women and their choice to rock a weave. And as I believe in preserving some histories and knowledge associated with my community, I will not point toward specific sources but rather call on my readers to do their own research to better understand this issue.

5. Or activism.

6. Of course, one might have a false sense of self as well (e.g., those who suffer from body dysmorphia), but this project focuses on a "true" sense of self, despite the slipperiness of that term.

7. The movement has also been criticized by women in Black communities, however, for its disembodied nature, what Knoblauch might call an attempt to "erase or ignore markers of difference" in their activism (58).

8. There are times I capitalize *avowed embodiment* and times I do not. To clarify, *Avowed Embodiment* refers to the transformative process that takes place for participants, while *avowed embodiment* refers to this process in action, or its verb form. It's important that readers can identify the difference between the transformation process and the actual performance that happens as a result of said transformation.

9. And, of course, fashion is a major part of Black social movements (James).

10. See socratemp.com for images.

11. When a #Tee4TheTrap is placed on the body of an academic like myself, we might ask what aspects of my identity I'm also *not* avowing. What does it mean for a Black, trap-music-loving woman scholar to wear a #Tee4TheTrap shirt at an academic conference?

12. See socratemp.com for images.

13. We can also look at the shirt as an actual object. In other words, if a "Deport White Supremacy" shirt is lying on my floor it, has a very different type of rhetorical effect than if it is on the floor of my best white friend.

WORKS CITED

Admin. "Trap Music: Under Lock and Key." *DJ*, 28 Feb. 2013, djmag.com/content/trap-music-under-lock-key. Accessed 25 June 2020.

AhnAllen, Julie M., Karen L. Suyemoto, and Alice S. Carter. "Relationship between Physical Appearance, Sense of Belonging and Exclusion, and Racial/Ethnic Self-Identification among Multiracial Japanese European Americans." *Cultural Diversity and Ethnic Minority Psychology*, vol. 12, no. 4, 2006, pp. 673–686. *APA PsycNet*, doi:10.1037/1099–9809.12.4.673.

Banks, William P. "Written through the Body: Disruptions and 'Personal' Writing." *The Personal in Academic Writing*. Spec. issue of *College English*, vol. 66, no. 1, 2003, pp. 21–40. *JSTOR*, www.jstor.org/stable/3594232.

Bublitz, Wolfram. "Cohesion and Coherence." *Discursive Pragmatics*, edited by Jan Zien-kowski, Jan-Ola Östman, and Jef Verschueren, John Benjamins P, 2011, pp. 37–49.

Burton, LaVar, performer. *Roots*, directed by Alex Haley. Wolper Productions, 1977.

Caliendo, Stephen M., and Charlton D. McIlwain. *The Routledge Companion to Race and Ethnicity*. Routledge, 2011.

Carlson, A. Cheree. " 'You Know It When You See It:' The Rhetorical Hierarchy of Race and Gender in *Rhinelander v. Rhinelander.*" *Quarterly Journal of Speech*, vol. 85, no. 2, 1999, pp. 111–126. *Taylor & Francis Online*, doi:10.1080/00335639909384249.

Chappell, Terrence. "Unapologetically Black Is the New Black." *EBONY*, 5 Apr. 2016, www.ebony.com/life/social-activism-movement/. Accessed 25 June 2020.

Craemer, Thomas, and D'Andra Orey. "Implicit Black Identification and Stereotype Threat among African American Students." *Social Science Research*, vol. 65, 2017, pp. 163–180. *PubMed*, doi:10.1016/j.ssresearch.2017.02.003.

Crane, Diana. *Fashion and Its Social Agendas: Class, Gender, and Identity in Clothing*. U of Chicago P, 2012.

Cross, William. "Encountering Nigrescence." *Handbook of Multicultural Counseling*, edited by Joseph G. Ponterotto, J. Manuel Casas, Lisa A. Suzuki, and Charlene M. Alexander, SAGE, 2001, pp. 30–44.

Cross, William E. "The Negro-to-Black Conversion Experience." *Black World*, vol. 20, no. 9, 1971, pp. 13–27.

Cross, William. *Stereotypic and Non-Stereotypic Images Associated with the Negro to Black Conversion Experience: An Empirical Analysis*. 1976. Diss. Princeton University, 1976. *ProQuest Dissertations and Theses*. https://www.proquest.com/openview/6bc5f9afcc2e64473c23c2eaf36a86cb/1?pq-origsite=gscholar&cbl=18750&diss=y.

Diani, Mario. "The Concept of Social Movement." *Sociological Review*, vol. 40, no. 1, 1992, pp. 1–25. *SAGE Journals*, doi:10.1111/j.1467-954X.1992.tb02943.x.

Díaz-Andreu, Margarita, Sam Lucy, Staša Babić, and David N. Edwards. *The Archaeology of Identity: Approaches to Gender, Age, Status, Ethnicity and Religion*. Routledge, 2005.

Ericksen, Julia A. "Embodied Resistance: Challenging the Norms, Breaking the Rules." *Embodied Resistance: Challenging the Norms, Breaking the Rules*, edited by Chris Bobel and Samantha Kwan. Vanderbilt UP, 2011.

Feinberg, Richard A., Lisa Mataro, and W. Jeffrey Burroughs. "Clothing and Social Identity." *Clothing and Textiles Research Journal*, vol. 11, no. 1, 1992, pp. 18–23. *SAGE Journals*, doi:10.1177/0887302X9201100103.

Freeman, Jo, and Victoria Johnson. *Waves of Protest: Social Movements since the Sixties*. Rowman & Littlefield, 1999.

Frith, Hannah, and Gleeson, Kate. "Clothing and Embodiment: Men Managing Body Image and Appearance." *Psychology of Men & Masculinity*, vol. 5, no. 1, 2004, pp. 40–48. *APA PsycNet*, doi:10.1037/1524-9220.5.1.40.

Futrell, Robert, and Pete Simi. "The [Un]Surprising Alt-Right." *Contexts*, vol. 16, no. 2, 2017, p. 76. *SAGE Journals*, doi:10.1177/1536504217714269.

Gowland, Rebecca, and Tim Thompson. *Human Identity and Identification*. Cambridge UP, 2013.

Harris, Angela P. "Critical Race Theory." *International Encyclopedia of the Social & Behavioral Sciences*, edited by Neil J. Smelser and Paul B. Baltes, Elsevier, 2012, pp. 2976–2980.

Harris, David R., and Jeremiah Joseph Sim. "Who Is Multiracial? Assessing the Complexity of Lived Race." *American Sociological Review*, vol. 67, no. 4, 2002, pp. 614–627. *JSTOR*, doi:10.2307/3088948.

Haynes, Gavin. "The white polo shirt: how the alt-right co-opted a modern classic." *The Guardian*, Aug. 30, 2017. https://www.theguardian.com/fashion/2017/aug/30/the-white-polo-shirt-how-the-alt-right-co-opted-a-modern-classic.

Ilmi, Ahmed. "The White Gaze vs. the Black Soul." *Race, Gender & Class 2011 Conference.* Spec. issue of *Race, Gender & Class,* vol. 18, no. 3/4, 2011, pp. 217–229. *JSTOR,* www .jstor.org/stable/43496844.

James, Danielle. "An Illustrative Identity of Fashion and Style Throughout African-American History and Movements." *Huffington Post,* 10 Feb. 2015, www.huffingtonpost .com/danielle-james/the-illustrative-identity_b_6519244.html. Accessed 25 June 2020.

Kantz, Deirdre, and Ivana Marenzi. "Language Functions and Medical Communication: The Human Body as Text." *Teaching Medical Discourse in Higher Education.* Spec. issue of *Language Learning in Higher Education,* vol. 6, no. 1, 2016, pp. 53–76. *De Gruyter,* doi:10.1515/cercles-2016–0003.

Knoblauch, A. Abby. "Bodies of Knowledge: Definitions, Delineations, and Implications of Embodied Writing in the Academy." *Composition Studies,* vol. 40, no. 2, 2012, pp. 50–65. *JSTOR,* www.jstor.org/stable/compstud.40.2.0050.

Mattingly, Carol. *Appropriate[ing] Dress: Women's Rhetorical Style in Nineteenth-Century America.* Southern Illinois UP, 2002.

Merriam, Sharan B., Juanita Johnson-Bailey, Ming-Yeh Lee, Youngwha Kee, Gabo Ntseane, and Mazanah Muhamad. "Power and Positionality: Negotiating Insider/Outsider Status within and across Cultures." *International Journal of Lifelong Education,* vol. 20, no. 5, 2001, pp. 405–416. *Taylor & Francis Online,* doi:10.1080/02601370110059537.

Mitchell, Julian. "TRAP Karaoke: The User-Generated Concert Creating a New Live Event Category." *Forbes,* 31 July 2017, www.forbes.com/sites/julianmitchell/2017/07/31/trap -karaoke-the-user-generated-concert-creating-a-new-live-event-category/#5040561 361ad. Accessed 25 June 2020.

Moses, Jacqueline O., Miguel T. Villodas, and Feion Villodas. "Black and Proud: The Role of Ethnic-Racial Identity in the Development of Future Expectations among At-Risk Adolescents." *Cultural Diversity & Ethnic Minority Psychology,* vol. 26, no. 1, 2019, pp. 112–123. *APA PsycNet,* doi:10.1037/cdp0000273.

"Nigrescence." *Merriam-Webster,* www.merriam-webster.com/dictionary/nigrescence. Accessed 25 June 2020.

Ogbu, John U. "Collective Identity and the Burden of 'Acting White' in Black History, Community, and Education." *Urban Review,* vol. 36, no. 1, 2004, pp. 1–35. *SpringerLink,* doi:10.1023/B:URRE.0000042734.83194.f6.

Pulido, Laura. *Black, Brown, Yellow, and Left: Radical Activism in Los Angeles.* U of California P, 2006.

Rich, Adrienne. "Notes Towards a Politics of Location." *Feminist Postcolonial Theory: A Reader,* edited by Reina Lewis and Sara Mills, Routledge, 2003, pp. 29–41.

Sanders, Robert E. "Utterances, Actions, and Rhetorical Inquiry." *Philosophy & Rhetoric,* vol. 11, no. 2, 1978, pp. 114–133. *JSTOR,* www.jstor.org/stable/40237061.

Stewart, Charles J., Robert E. Denton Jr., and Craig Allen Smith. *Persuasion and Social Movements.* Waveland, 2012.

Thomas, Charles W. "Boys No More: Some Social Psychological Aspects of the New Black Ethic." *American Behavioral Scientist,* vol. 12, no. 4, 1969, pp. 38–42.

Thompson, Vetta L. Sanders. "African American Body Image: Identity and Physical Self-Acceptance." *Black Psychology: African-Centered Epistemology.* Spec. issue of *Humboldt Journal of Social Relations,* vol. 30, no. 2, 2006, pp. 44–67. *JSTOR,* www.jstor.org/stable /23263216.

Trautwein, Caroline. "Academics' Identity Development as Teachers." *Teaching in Higher Education,* vol. 23, no. 8, 2018, pp. 995–1010. *Taylor & Francis Online,* doi:10.1080/135 62517.2018.1449739.

Yangzom, Dicky. *Clothing and Social Movements: The Politics of Dressing in Colonized Tibet.* 2014. Master's thesis. City University of New York, 2014. *ProQuest Dissertations and Theses.*

Young, Damon. "How to Be Unapologetically Black." *The Root,* 26 Feb. 2016, verysmartbrothas .theroot.com/how-to-be-unapologetically-black-1822522165. Accessed 25 June 2020.

14

MATTERS THAT (EM)BODY

Kellie Sharp-Hoskins (New Mexico State University)
and Anthony Stagliano (Florida Atlantic University)

The report from the Intergovernmental Panel on Climate Change issued in October of 2018 paints a dire picture. Responding to the transnational Paris Agreement (made just two years earlier) to keep global temperature increase to below 2º C, the report recommends 1.5º C as the absolute cap, explaining that even "[l]imiting global warming to [only] 1.5º C would require rapid, far reaching and unprecedented changes in all aspects of society." As panel member Hans-Otto Pörtner explains, "[W]arming of 1.5º C or higher increases the risk associated with long-lasting or irreversible changes, such as the loss of some ecosystems" ("IPCC Press Release" 1). In short, if radical change to the world economy is not undertaken within a few years, global catastrophe is imminent, with the effects of change happening as soon as 2040. The international community of climate scientists and experts is making urgent, unequivocal statements about the necessity of making "unprecedented changes in all aspects of society" with the goal of giving "people and ecosystems more room to adapt and remain below relevant risk thresholds" (1). In other words, even unprecedented changes won't reverse or halt global warming or its disastrous effects, but they will allow us to (hopefully) adapt.

At its core, this adaptation—of social, cultural, and economic processes and practices—would fundamentally revise relations between bodies and matter: not only how we imagine and use matter (as commodity, as resource, as disposable, as renewable) but also possibilities for embodiment itself. Embodiment, as N. Katherine Hayles defines it, emerges within material relations: "In contrast to the body, embodiment is contextual, enmeshed within the specifics of place, time, physiology, and culture" (196). It not only names this enmeshment but also our experience of it—the names we have for feeling at *home*, at *ease*, *comfortable* in our bodies. Or not. It both acknowledges and resists the idea

https://doi.org/10.7330/9781646422012.c014

that we are (or can be) separate from our bodies. Embodiment reminds us that bodies are not merely containers for our *selves* and that how *we* seem to inhabit *them* is a necessary rhetorical reduction of a much more complex relation. As indicated by the IPCC, in the early twenty-first century this relation—or the specifics of place, time, physiology, and culture that characterize the emergence of embodiment—must be understood as anthropocenic, characterized by the geological impact of human activity.

Writing on the anthropocene, like the IPCC report, is largely grim, as testified by the title of Roy Scranton's 2015 book *Learning to Die in the Anthropocene: Reflections on the End of a Civilization.* Written as a sort of manifesto for learning to *live* differently with our new reality, as grim as that reality may seem, Scranton's book accords with the appeal for total change issued by the IPCC. To Scranton, if we are to survive as a species, if the planet is to continue to be able to survive, we must admit that the current civilization, capitalist modernity, is dead. Admitting that learning to let a civilization die and learning to live radically differently, is, according to Scranton, our only hope.

Like a lot of people concerned about the possibility of a future, Scranton is worried that we won't manage to do what is necessary and that we will remain haunted totally by the already-dead modernity that has poisoned the planet. In other words, our future embodiments will be haunted by our current consumption; our possibilities for living will be haunted by our current habits. We share this worry. But we also see haunting as a provocation, an invitation to unflinching analysis of the ghosts of the earth haunting embodiment *now*. Because as frightening as anthropocenic futures may be, the anthropocenic now is already haunted, sponsoring differential embodiment on a global scale. From massive deposits of e-waste in places like Guiyu, China, to the complex software-hardware systems that shape how writers and activists do their work and live their lives, all bodies and embodiments are haunted by the weight of materiality in digital writing.

Compelled by this provocation, in this chapter we engage Jacques Derrida's concept of *hauntology* to investigate how disciplinary embodiments emerge from and entangle with anthropocenic technologies, the ghosts of the earth. To understand this entanglement, and as an exemplary case, we investigate the human and nonhuman relations that contribute to theories and practices of digital writing. Insofar as embodiment provides a rhetorical account of relations between matter and context, we acknowledge it cannot be limited to describing human bodies. Digital hauntology suggests how embodiment can also be enlisted to describe *how* objects and things and energy emerge and take shape, how they are inhabited and oriented, or, following Jane Bennett, "the curious ability of inanimate things to animate, to act, to produce effects dramatic and subtle" (6). While a haunting embodiment affecting all manners of matters threads through this chapter's argument, we explore mostly how human embodiments are haunted and affect life now in the anthropocene.

We begin with the premise that traces of the materiality of digital devices are not well accounted for in emerging engagements with ecologies of writing and rhetoric. That is, even with an eye to ecologies, a myopic focus on human embodiments that *use* technology disavows the ways other embodiments—human and nonhuman—participate in the conditions of possibility for digital writing (and digital writing scholarship). In response, we propose *digital hauntology* as a rhetorical methodology that accounts for the fraught relations among digital bodies and the differential embodiments they sponsor by looking for the ghosts of digital writing. To understand and work with these ghosts is to undertake the inventive task of imagining living *otherwise*.

HAUNTING ECOLOGIES OF DIGITAL WRITING

Within the broader field of rhetoric and writing studies, ecologically oriented theory and research seems to be best equipped to consider the embodying work of materiality, writ large. Indeed, even with its history and some current use focused on ecology as a metaphor,[1] ecological thinking in the field is premised on a (human) body in the (material) world. As Marilyn Cooper suggested of an ecological model of writing in 1986, for example, its "fundamental tenet is that writing is an activity through which a person is continually engaged with a variety of socially constituted systems" ("Ecology" 366–367). With an explicit focus on the social ecologies of writing, Cooper does not so much as mention bodies, technologies, embodiment, or materiality. And yet she invokes what is established as a commonplace in 1986: "That is, writing and what writers do during writing cannot be artificially separated from the social-rhetorical situations in which writing gets done, from the conditions that enable writers to do what they do" (qtd. in Cooper, "Ecology" 367). As scholarship on ecologies evolves in the field following Cooper's early work, this premise continues to ground ecological reasoning; further, the "conditions that enable writers" multiply as scholars move from conceptualizing ecology metaphorically to insisting on its materiality. Cooper's "ecological model . . . of an infinitely extended group of people who interact through writing, who are connected by the various systems that constitute the activity of writing" ("Ecology" 372), then, is extended beyond people and texts to all manner of material bodies and relations through which they emerge.

In 1999, for example, Margaret A. Syverson posed an "ecology of composition" as a unit of analysis that moves beyond complex system of "writers, readers, and texts" and their "dynamic interactions" to account for "ecology [as] a larger system that includes environmental structures, such as pens, paper, computers, books, telephones, fax machines, photocopies, printing presses, and other natural and human-constructed features, as well as other complex systems operating at various levels of scale, such as families, global economies, publishing systems, theoretical frames, academic disciplines, and language itself" (5). This shift away from conceptualizing ecologies as only social systems is echoed in the disciplinary scholarship that followed. Christian R. Weisser and Sidney I. Dobrin's 2001 edited collection *Ecocomposition*, for example, "places ecological thinking and composition in dialogue with one another in order to both consider the ecological properties of written discourse and the ways in which ecologies, environments, locations, places, and natures are discursively affected" (2). Again without considering bodies or embodiment explicitly, their work nevertheless centers questions of the relationships between humans—their writing practices and consumption practices—and ecologies. Weisser's chapter, for instance, calls for a "greening of identity" that acknowledges how "[w]e are as influenced by the places we inhabit and our connections with the other organisms that share those sites as we are influenced by human relationships" (86). Colleen Connelly uses an ecofeminist perspective to reject Western concepts of nature that have "been used to justify the degradation of nature and oppression of women" (187) as well as reinforce racism and classism (186). And Christopher J. Keller investigates how ecocomposition enables compositionists to study how "place affects individual writers in different ways in relation to history, race, class, gender, and a host of other forces" by considering the stark racial divide amongst students hailed (and not) by the invitation to "retreat" to nature for a writing assignment (203).

These contributors and others pave the way to understanding relationships among embodiment and ecology by foregrounding identity. Identity categories and identity claims, they show, are bound to ecological systems; in Weisser's terms, "our identities are always already ecological; we are who we are as a result of the people, places, things, animals, and plants that have touched our lives" (93). As Cooper notes in her forward to the collection, however, the problems of the field in understanding and representing the complexity of the relationships between humans and ecology persisted in 2001: "[I]t is still a struggle to see relationships as primary rather than focusing on—especially on—the human actors relating to human and nonhuman others, and even harder to see writing as part of a whole, interrelated, ceaselessly changing environment rather than as a social system through which humans act on and make conscious choices about the nonsocial other system, the natural environment" (xiv). Cooper's articulation of this struggle is prescient: in the two decades since, scholars in rhetoric and writing studies have continued to pursue ecological thinking to grapple with and account for the relationships between humans and nonhuman others. Although bodies and embodiment evade direct representation in this work, they haunt the discourse under the signs of labor, work, practice, roles, habits, and agency, as well as students, teachers, writers, and researchers, inviting scholars to more nuanced ecological accounts of *how* we inhabit bodies. Moreover, such accounts are also increasingly shaped by scholarship and intellectual work that pursues non-Western epistemologies to consider relations among humans and nonhumans and critique ecology as adequate to the task of (re)imagining relations among humans and nonhumans. Gabriela Racquel Ríos, for example, uses the concept of "'land' to shift the ontological presuppositions inherent in the term 'ecology'" toward "an ontological position that sees humans as 'the Earth being conscious of itself'" (64).

Whereas, as Ríos argues, Indigenous and decolonial scholars contextualize land/body relations and embodiment as a long-held intellectual and cultural concern (see also Driskill; Haas; Powell), it is only in the last few years that attention to embodiment has begun to emerge more explicitly within rhetoric and composition studies as scholars bring ecological thinking to bear on digital writing. Thus in 2010, for example, Cooper writes declaratively that writing is "an embodied interaction with other beings and environments" ("Being" 18). And, specifically redressing the "neglect of the body" in a critique of technorhetorics, M. Jimmie Killingsworth turns to ecorhetoric to "conceptualiz[e] technology's relation to the body and earth" (79). For Killingsworth, the mechanic metaphors of technorhetoric encourage us to "think of the body—and by extension, other people—as something we use," in which case "we are prone to *overuse* or even *abuse* the body" (83). Giving the example of his own experience immersed in writing a research project, he explains, "My body had become this uncooperative *thing*, this *other* that resisted my technological ambitions. . . . I had overextended my body, favoring certain postures (sitting), certain behaviors (reading screens), and certain senses (especially sight), while neglecting others (walking, standing, listening)" (81). He goes on to explain how this use, overuse, and abuse is not limited to human bodies—"What is happening to the body is happening to the earth on a larger scale" (82)—and is not merely parallel but interdependent: "A nice clean connection to a virtual world depends upon a much dirtier connection to a coal-fired plant somewhere near somebody's homeplace" (88).

This connection among embodiment, habits, and ecologies also underwrites Nathaniel A. Rivers's argument that we reconsider how the concept of environmental "footprints" need not only represent a quantitative relation between humans and environments but could also "motivat[e] qualitatively different *ways of being* in the world" (183; emphasis added). This shift from a quantitative to qualitative assessment informs his acknowledgment that there is "no way of moving that does not leave marks" (186). Responding to this premise, Rivers asks, "What is it to place one's feet and to inscribe with one's own body? In making environmentalism a question of a footprint's *size*, do we lose the nuance of *kind?* Everything leaves its mark upon the world. Not all marks are the same, of course, but the simple presence of marks cannot ultimately ground critique" (175). Importantly, this attention to different kinds of marks begins to acknowledge—if only tacitly—ecological relations to *differential* embodiment. That is, different kinds of footprints imply different kinds of feet, different shoes, different gaits, different access to walking paths or sidewalks or beaches. Writing about how toxins pollute bodies differentially (in racialized and classed patterns), Phaedra C. Pezzullo explains that differences do not exist outside bodies— "Bodies . . . are not pre-given, 'natural' entities with boundaries that are beyond questioning and whose 'truth' is somehow transparently understood"—and neither do they preexist embodiment (10). As Jay Dolmage argues, "We have ongoing and ineluctable rhetorical relationships with other bodies, objects, and networks—and these rhetorical relationships shape and reshape us" ("Open" 264).

Dolmage is specifically interested in how digital texts circulate (and not) and become accessible (and not) to different bodies with different literacies and possibilities for access. Investigating the rhetorical shortcomings of open-access scholarship vis-à-vis accessibility, he reminds us that "even when a composition is primarily text based, its reception is bound to be multimodal—it will be accessed through screen readers, enlarged, read across platforms, etc." ("Open" 264). These technological requirements that indicate different needs for different bodies are further entangled with additional issues of access: "[A] huge chunk of scholarly publishing is both expensive and inaccessible, ensuring that the discourse circulates easily through certain bodies. When disabled people need to access these texts, this can be provided only through the bodies of the more able and privileged" (266). Insisting on the knotty relationships among embodiment and materiality, Dolmage implicitly responds to Killingsworth's misgiving that "techno-rhetoric may seem to be covering this crucial connection of body with identity politics, but without a clear account of the material foundation of such problems . . . political insensitivity and quietism can slip in the back door" (Killingsworth 89). Indeed, Dolmage's attention to the materiality of circulation and access insists embodied difference does not preexist relations of power. The circulation of texts across bodies—human and nonhuman—marks their difference, granting or denying access, shaping experiences, producing affect.

Synthesizing this scholarship, we see how ecological questions in digital writing studies can simultaneously sponsor rhetorical attention to human embodiment and push us to ask questions about its forms and futures. Pairing Killingsworth with Rivers, for example, we can ask about the "the electrical uptake required to make thousands of computers run all day and all night in most every house and office around the country" to sponsor our teaching and writing, and we can insist that our "measurements will not settle the question" (Killingsworth 88; Rivers 186). Drawing together Rivers, Dolmage, and Ríos we can question both how our embodied practices impact our environments and how such environments "shape and reshape us," revealing our kinship (Dolmage, "Open" 264). Our ecological footprint, from this perspective, not only bespeaks differential privilege and access—where certain bodies are encouraged to make their mark—but disciplines normate embodiments: marks are expected to fit within extant frames of recognizability and economic profitability. Given these resources for thinking ecologically, however, the field has yet to grapple with the impact of our digital writing practices on a large scale; in the words of Killingsworth, "[We] have never read an environmental impact statement as part of a plan to install a computer classroom or to increase the use of computers in a writing program" (88).

DIGITAL HAUNTOLOGY

Coined by Derrida in his *Specters of Marx*, hauntology as a concept and analytical tool has come to function in a wide variety of fields as a way of analyzing the remnants or remains of ideas long thought dead. Pierre Macherey, in his contribution to *Ghostly Demarcations*, calls Derrida's hauntology "a science of ghosts, a science of what returns" (18). Put otherwise, in Lisa Blackman's 2019 *Haunted Data*, "hauntologies raise the important ethical and methodological questions of how one can follow ghosts, or be followed by ghosts, interpret ghosts, interrogate ghosts, and listen to ghosts" (18). For his part, Derrida sees haunt*ology* not only as a science, as an -ology of haunting, but as the very hauntings of being itself that come to presence and, by haunting it, divide it. Mark Fisher, the British critical theorist and cultural critic who popularized the term several years after Derrida's book, defines it this way: "The concept of hauntology was in part a restatement of the key deconstructive claim that 'being' is not equivalent to *presence*. Since there is no point of pure origin, only the time of the 'always-already,' then haunting is the state proper to being as such" (44). In Fisher's hands, hauntology is a tool for seeing the ways seemingly dead cultural tropes continue to haunt the present, in, for instance, retro cultural consumption. Fisher sees this, in keeping with the specter of Marx haunting the term, as a function of pernicious cultural capitalism. But a revisit to Derrida's *Specters* reminds us that for him, the ghost, the "revenant" that haunts, complicates tidy distinctions between the ephemeral (spectral) and the physical (embodied). That is, in his usual fashion, he traces through *Specters of Marx* all the ghosts that haunt Marx's materialism while simultaneously showing that these specters do not simply *return* (they indeed do that) but that their presence, as that which should be gone, divides up presence itself, revealing the separation of immaterial and material unsustainable.

Following that logic out, we can argue that what haunts the digital is the fact that its material character cannot be reduced to mere substrate. In other words, the poles of haunting are reversed: the ephemeral immaterial (digitality and information culture itself) is not what haunts but what is haunted by the physical, the material, the oppressive *weight* of history and our inescapable planetary fate. That is, our devices, software (that can never exist in the absence of devices), and networks all are *embodied ghosts* haunting our writing practices, reminding us of the dark inseparability between our own (often quite ecoconscious and ethical) practices, our embodied habits and orientations, and the end of the earth. Put differently, the spectral physicality of the digital comes, at once, from the past and the future. It haunts because it surfaces what we attempt to repress: that the technologies of the digital age do not stand outside the processes destroying the earth (and thus enable us to comment from that position) but participate in those very processes. A digital hauntology, then, builds on extant scholarship in digital writing studies that seeks accounts adequate to the complexity of differential embodiment. It frames questions of embodiment like those asked by Kristin Arola and Anne Wysocki—"How do differing media encourage—or discourage—particular senses of bodies in the world and bodies in relation to others? How have changes in media, over time, entwined with differing possibilities for bodies and relations with others?"—in anthropocenic terms (24). And, we argue, it offers possibilities for living otherwise.

THE HAUNTING OF DIFFERENT BODIES, THE DIFFERENTIAL HAUNTING OF BODIES

In the documentary *Examined Life*, Judith Butler and disability activist Sunaura Taylor go for a walk through San Francisco, discussing disability, embodiment, and ability. When Butler asks Taylor, "[W]hat environments make it possible for you to take a walk," Taylor replies that she moved to San Francisco because it was the "the most accessible place in the world," with curb cuts on nearly every corner, a fully accessible public transportation system, and a large number of accessible buildings. That physical, infrastructural accessibility, Taylor argues, leads to social acceptance. This physical accessibility invites a wider range of embodiments to public spaces and social environments, fundamentally shifting possibilities for who (or which bodies) participates in public and social life and *how* they can do so. "Physical access," Taylor argues, "leads to a social access and acceptance." Moments after that exchange, Taylor and Butler pass a shoe lying in the gutter, and Taylor comments, "That's somebody's shoe. I wonder if they can walk without it," reminding us that *all* bodies depend in our daily activities and movements on enabling technologies. Butler adds that we have a false idea that the "able-bodied" person is radically self-sufficient. That is, much like normed embodiments are taken for granted in dominant cultural (and infrastructural) imaginaries, technologies that underwrite those embodiments—shoes, touchscreens, seatbelts—are normed and unmarked; they are there, haunting all lived reality nevertheless. But they haunt different bodies differently, sponsoring differential embodiment. As noted above, Ríos and Dolmage remind us that we are always entwined with other bodies (human and nonhuman), that our embodiment is not simply reducible to the biological singular body since the relationships that compose embodiment involve us with other bodies, entities, and networks.

In a similar key, Jennifer Cole writes on *Gimpgirl* of the technologies that help her do her work, like the enabling technologies Taylor finds essential in San Francisco:

> I will use myself as a working example to further comment on. I am writing this article on my laptop, using speech to text technology (Dragon Dictate) to type my thoughts for me while I talk to my computer. I'm sitting upright in my adjustable hospital-style bed, supported by an almost entirely metal spine that was implanted to keep my spine from collapsing. My laptop is on a rolling metal table to keep it from putting pressure on my legs. I am literally surrounded by technology to lift me out of bed, help me do necessary personal activities, and to help me take part in my household as a wife and individual. When I leave this house, you see me in my power wheelchair, or perhaps using my adapted minivan or the ramp on the light rail. I am alive because medical technology was developed to treat blood clots. I exist because I have an almost symbiotic relationship with technology.

These examples show us that when we say digital writing practices are always haunted, we must acknowledge not all bodies encounter the same ghosts, nor do they encounter them in the same ways. When Taylor and Butler have their peripatetic conversation through San Francisco, they remind us to ask, as Butler does, citing Gilles Deleuze, "[W]hat can a body do?" (*Examined*). For Deleuze, Butler says, that is a question that is "supposed to challenge the traditional ways in which we think about bodies" and that takes us away from self-present essences to relations between capacities and possibilities. The haunting of embodiment, in other words, shifts attention from bodies as singular or discrete to embodiment as emergent, lived always in relation. And it is the erasure of the gap between present (and *em*bodied) and absent (and spectral) that the ghost of digitality performs, enabling us to imagine and invent different possibilities for bodies.

Sara Ahmed helps us imagine embodiment as mediating histories and futures through her concept of orientations. "Over time," she explains, "we acquire our tendencies, as the acquisition of what is given. Bodies could be described as 'becoming given.' Orientations thus take time. If the orientations are an effect of what we tend toward, then they point to the future, to what is not yet present. And yet, orientations are shaped by what is behind us, creating a loop between what is toward and behind. In other words, we are directed by our background" (247–248). For Ahmed, being directed by our background invokes both discursive accumulations and material objects—like Derrida, for example, she considers the physical writing table—and thus orientations neither elide nor can be reduced to disembodied perspectives or paradigms. Moreover, Ahmed considers how seemingly benign objects participate in differential work: they invite specific bodies at the expense of others. Such bodies are not only differentiated in terms of ability; differential embodiment is not merely metonymy for physical ability. As Ahmed argues, for example, "Gender is an effect of how bodies take up objects, which involves how they occupy space by being occupied in one way or another" (251); she also reminds us that orientation always "involves racial and class-based divisions of labor" (253). To be clear, these different possible embodiments are not divorced from ability, nor can they be separated from technology. As Dolmage argues in *Disabled Upon Arrival*, for example, it was (and continues to be) technologies of immigration—including photography, archives, and the medical gaze and glance—that paired disability and racialization, creating acceptable categories of inclusion and abjection such that physical disability rhetorically "darkens" some bodies while race "disables" others. In addition to shaping immigration practices proper, and the possibilities for embodiment marked acceptable (or not) for immigrant bodies, these technologies and their attendant eugenic rhetorics shaped social relations writ large—training us to assess each other in terms of acceptable embodiment, haunting us through norms of whiteness and ability.

Moreover, these norms circumscribe and narrate access to and use of technologies. Angela M. Haas (Cherokee) explains, for example, that "there is a long Western rhetorical tradition of constructing American Indians—via print, visual, oral, and digital compositions—in stereotypical, essentialized, and fetishized ways that contribute to a larger, monolithic fiction of who/what is 'the American Indian'" (189), and these "colonial scripts . . . prescribe how we interface with digital and visual rhetorics" (190). Western orientations to technology, in other words, identify specific objects, bodies, and practices as technology rich and assume others to be technology poor or illiterate: Western educated and affluent bodies are understood to be producers and users of technology; American Indians, citizens of the Global South, women, and racialized others are imagined as not needing, wanting, or using technology at all. The effect of these orientations is to exacerbate divisions of access. As Adam J. Banks argues in the context of Black bodies, for example,

> Not only are Black people forced to catch up on technological tools and systems and educational systems to which they have been denied access, but they are required to do so in a nation (or system) in which the struggle they endure to gain any access to any new technology, any acquisition of any new literacies, is rewarded by a change in the dominant technological

systems and the literacies used to facilitate access to them, and thus the same struggle over and over again. (xxi)

As Banks's description of Black technology users illustrates, orientations draw together embodied pasts and futures. Racialized, gendered, classist, and colonial haunting, among others, then, must contextualize how we imagine relationships between technologies and embodiment, which cannot be disarticulated from their ecological entanglements.

While differential technology access haunts embodiment, so too does technology production and use. Our digital technologies *are* contributing to climate change, as the accumulation of e-waste in the dystopian city-scapes forming in Guiyu, China, and elsewhere reminds us. Once an all-too-literal metaphor for the mountains of waste produced by obsolescent technologies, Guiyu responded to media scrutiny of working conditions—especially for children—by shifting its "recycling" activities indoors. As Davor Mujezinovic relates of his visit to Guiyu in 2019, "In the city center, there is no sign of toxic waste nor appalling working conditions. Guiyu is relatively clean and well developed, and the spaces previously occupied by recycling workshops have been rented out to other businesses. There is little sign of e-waste except for the occasional litter and the bags outside the few remaining workshops. Were it not for the constant sight of trucks and rickshaws hauling e-waste around the city, one might even momentarily forget Guiyu's past" ("Electronic Waste"). A closer look, however, reveals a continued practice of exploitation of resources, land, and people:

> Inside, people are working on mechanically disassembling the waste with simple tools: hammers, screwdrivers, wire cutters, and pliers. The protective gear is likewise basic: gloves and a mouth-mask are worn by most, and some wear protective goggles. Further in, obscured by heaps of waste, workers submerge motherboards and other devices into vats filled with a corrosive substance; above them fans, lead the air away into filtering instruments meant to reduce the environmental impact of the emissions. Despite the fans, the ventilation is rather poor and the air reeks of a strong chemical smell, which hurts my lungs when breathing. (Mujezinovic, "Electronic Waste")

As this image suggests, the sheer accumulation of the material waste generated by digital culture haunts us even while we see in the digital *new* possibilities. A productive digital hauntology would remind us that, for instance, a broken smartphone screen is not just a discrete body suddenly haunting our practices but *also* that the kinds of easy accessibility a smartphone user enjoys are *always* haunted by different forms of embodiment, different relationships to what is too unthinkingly taken to be ordinary. As

Wysocki explains of embodiment *in general*, "[T]echnologies and media enable us to extend what we can do with our given sensory apparatus. . . . extend[ing] our reach but . . . also modif[ying] our sense of engagement: it shifts how we feel what is around us or how we sense those with whom we communicate; our senses reflex and shift in response to these mediated engagements, and in further response we then modify our media toward our shifting ends" (4). Accordingly, not only do our "senses reflex and shift" when we use the latest smartphone technologies (as our facial expressions respond to recognition technology, as our voices adapt to please Siri, and as our fingers learn how to zoom in and out or take screenshots), but the senses of the people of Guiyu (including children) also reflex and shift as they pull apart our "recycled" smartphones: joints and postures respond to repetitive movements, eyes and hands learn how to differentiate useful parts, cells transform from exposure to toxic waste.

Like the ghosts Derrida analyzes, then, the conditions of digital writing are embodied in multiple ways that emerge from and reinforce differential access, power inequity, and asymmetrical value. Embodiments in Guiyu are demanded by embodiments of smartphone users. Digital writing is haunted, as noted above, by the embodied materiality of the putatively ephemeral realm of the digital: we update apps and software whose function is "no longer supported," we replace hardware that does not support updated apps and software. This haunting looks like capitalism itself, capitalizing on consumer desire, "cheap" labor, and the different(ial) embodiments of each. In other ways, meanwhile, as Cole reminds us, the haunting embodiment of digital writing is a tool that opens up access for bodies excluded by writing machines that depend on specific bodily abilities not shared by all.

HAUNTING ECO-CONSCIOUSNESS

It is not enough, then, to see in digital hauntology the call to be eco-conscious, in a simple sense. No such consciousness is possible, undivided, without contradiction. Rather, it is only possible riven by fissures, dividing against itself, haunted by all the possibilities and dangers inherent in the ever-spectral materiality of digital life (and writing).

For instance, eco-conscious environmental activism and disability activism collided in California in 2018 over a bill (ultimately signed into law by Governor Brown in September of that year) that would ban single-use plastic straws from restaurants in the state unless specifically requested by the consumer (Assembly). Environmentalist arguments that such plastics were wasteful and accumulated in landfills came up against disability-activist arguments that such tools are enabling technologies and outright bans conceal ableist biases. The point of drawing attention to this conflict is to underline that being conscious of the ghosts that haunt contemporary technology use entails a different practice than simply *opposing* certain kinds of technologies, out of hand. In "Better Footprints," Rivers points in this direction when he says, complicating "leave no trace" policies in national parks, that "trails are made of our footprints, which, rather than leaving marks upon some static substrate, make up the threads weaving that very surface" (185). That is, the challenging thing is not to leave *no* trace but to understand how one's movement through the world, one's engagements with and interactions with the world and the technological devices made of it, *affect* the ecology in which they and we are all implicated. Reduction of use, then, is not the only way to engage in eco-consciousness. As Dolmage notes, "[W]hen, for instance, a digital text circulates, the ways that it moves, moves through, and (sometimes selectively) moves past bodies must be interrogated" ("Open" 264).

Or, in other words, we must engage *differently* with the material haunts of digital culture and digital writing. It is flawed to see the ghost of e-waste in the devices used by Cole and give into a desire to ban such equipment; this, in effect, elides different embodiments, bans specific bodies. But we simultaneously are haunted by the ways these machines affect embodiment in Guiyu and other such e-waste sites. Better footprints and better engagements with the ghosts that haunt the relationship between digital technologies and living bodies are what is needed. In that way, our digital hauntology might ask, echoing Deleuze's question noted above, *What can a ghost do?* What can these contradictory ghosts of digital technology do? What can they be made to do?

WHAT CAN A GHOST DO?

One aspect of Derrida's own notion of *hauntology* rhetorical scholars may be particularly attuned to is that for Derrida, the ghost *does work*. Haunting is an activity of transformation; it *effects* changes in the world. It is, in short, wholly rhetorical. Our concern then is not just with *what* haunts (or who or what is haunted) but how the haunting effects embodiment and what work it can be made to do.

A productive digital hauntology, we are suggesting, is one in which we enter into dialogue with the ghost instead of trying to exorcise it, chase it away, or flee from it. What Derrida teaches us with hauntology is that what seems used up, depleted, exhausted, haunts us, comes back. Carbon that is burned up doesn't go away but returns, this time as a threat to planetary existence, to all that is present. And as Derrida notes in his treatment of Hamlet, it is necessary to acknowledge the ghost, enter into dialogue with it, even as its (non)presence undermines and threatens our own discrete identity. With respect to digital writing practices, such acknowledgment needn't only be the sudden, overwhelming physicality of our media that often comes with broken screens, hard-drive crashes, lost signals, and so forth. Rather, it can (and should) be productively sought as part of the writing practice. For instance, acknowledgment could take such forms as tracking the origins and destinies of the devices used or mapping the physical networks subtending the digital. This is our understanding of digital hauntology as a method, as a way of answering the how-to-*be*-otherwise question.

This form of inventive being otherwise, though, is not simple, especially when we recognize the affordances and constraints an academic discipline's material and social ecologies enact. It cannot simply be, for instance, *more* digital production labs. Not, at least, without more conscious understanding of the impact of those labs, as Killingsworth reminds us. Nor can it be a retreat away from those sites and tools, in an eco-conscious key, because *access* for all bodies in the ecologies of digital writing requires that we understand eco-consciousness differently too. Thus, we are faced with a number of questions, including that posed by Arola and Wysocki invoked earlier: "How can we work with available media and media technologies to open new possibilities for embodiment?" (24). Tackling such a question within the disciplinary formations of digital writing as a practice and pedagogy means engaging in a hauntology that reveals to us how to work not just with particular new media technologies that enable different forms of embodiment but also with the haunting embodiment of their material, environmental impact, and how to work with *that* to make different futures. In that way, the environmental impact study—that Killingsworth notes we have never read—would take the form of inventive engagement with all manners of *impact*, including the enabling and limiting ways such technologies (and their labs) intersect with different kinds of bodies, both human and nonhuman, and the capacities and possibilities of each that rely on each other.

NOTE

1.   Drawing on Matthew Ortolova, Gabriela Racquel Ríos critiques the field of composition for its tendency to "dematerialize discussions of ecology" and proposes "exploring the relationship between ecocomposition and ecological literacy [to] illuminate more fully the consequences that our literacy practices have on our ecological communities" (70).

WORKS CITED

Ahmed, Sara. "Orientations Matter." *New Materialisms: Agency, Ontology, and Politics*, edited by Diana Coole and Samantha Frost, Duke UP, 2010, pp. 234–257.

Arola, Kristin L., and Anne Frances Wysocki. *Composing (Media)=Composing (Technology): Bodies, Technologies, Writing, and the Teaching of Writing.* Utah State UP, 2012.

Assembly Bill 1884. Ch. 576. 20 Sept. 2018. *California State Legislature*, 20 Sept. 2018, leginfo .legislature.ca.gov/faces/billNavClient.xhtml?bill_id=201720180AB1884. Accessed 26 June 2020.

Banks, Adam J. *Race, Rhetoric, and Technology: Searching for Higher Ground.* NCTE, 2006.

Bennett, Jane. *Vibrant Matter: A Political Ecology of Things.* Duke UP, 2010.

Blackman, Lisa. *Haunted Date: Affect. Transmedia, Weird Science.* Bloomsbury, 2019.

Butler, Judith, and Sunaura Taylor, perf. *Examined Life.* Dir. Astra Taylor. Zeitgeist Films, 2008.

Cole, Jennifer. "Original Cyborgs: Disability and Technology on Yahoo Accessibility." *GimpGirl*, 23 May 2011, www.gimpgirl.com/2011/05/23/original-cyborgs-disability-and -technology-on-yahoo-accessibility/. Accessed 13 Oct. 2018.

Connelly, Colleen. "Ecology and Composition Studies: A Feminist Perspective on Living Relationships." *Ecocomposition: Theoretical and Pedagogical Approaches*, edited by Christian R. Weisser and Sidney I. Dobrin, State U of New York P, 2001, pp. 179–192.

Cooper, Marilyn M. "Being Linked to the Matrix: Biology, Technology, and Writing." *Rhetorics and Technologies: New Directions and Writing and Communications*, edited by Stuart A. Selber, U of South Carolina P, 2010, pp. 15–32.

Cooper, Marilyn M. Foreword. *Ecocomposition: Theoretical and Pedagogical Approaches*, edited by Christian R. Weisser and Sidney I. Dobrin, State U of New York P, 2001, pp. xi–xviii.

Cooper, Marilyn M. "The Ecology of Writing." *College English*, vol. 48, no. 4, 1986, pp. 364–375. *JSTOR*, doi:10.2307/377264.

Derrida, Jacques. *Specters of Marx.* Routledge, 1994.

Dolmage, Jay Timothy. *Disabled Upon Arrival: Eugenics, Immigration, and the Construction of Race and Disability.* The Ohio State UP, 2018.

Dolmage, Jay Timothy. "Open Access(ibility)." *Circulation, Writing, and Rhetoric*, edited by Laurie E. Gries and Collin Gifford Brooke, Utah State UP, 2018, pp. 262–277.

Driskill, Qwo-Li. "Decolonial Skillshares: Indigenous Rhetorics as Radical Practice." *Survivance, Sovereignty, and Story: Teaching American Indian Rhetorics*, edited by Lisa King, Rose Gubele, and Joyce Rain Anderson, Utah State UP, 2015, pp. 57–78.

Fisher, Mark. "The Metaphysics of Crackle: Afrofuturism and Hauntology." *Dancecult: Journal of Electronic Dance Music Culture*, vol. 5, no. 2, 2013, pp. 42–55. *DOAJ*, doi:10.1280 1/1947-5403.2013.05.02.03.

Haas, Angela M. "Toward a Decolonial Digital and Visual American Indian Rhetorics Pedagogy." *Survivance, Sovereignty, and Story: Teaching American Indian Rhetorics*, edited by Lisa King, Rose Gubele, and Joyce Rain Anderson, Utah State UP, 2015, pp. 188–208.

Hayles, N. Katherine. *How We Became Posthuman: Virtual Bodies in Cybernetics, Literature, and Informatics.* U of Chicago P, 1999.

"IPCC Press Release." *IPCC*, 1 Oct. 2018. Press release. Accessed 13 Oct. 2018. https://www .ipcc.ch/site/assets/uploads/2018/11/pr_181008_P48_spm_en.pdf.

Keller, Christopher J. "The Ecology of Writerly Voice: Authorship, Ethos, and Persona." *Ecocomposition: Theoretical and Pedagogical Approaches*, edited by Christian R. Weisser and Sidney I. Dobrin, State U of New York P, 2001, pp. 193–208.

Killingsworth, M. Jimmie. "Appeals to the Body in Eco-Rhetoric and Techno-Rhetoric." *Rhetorics and Technologies: New Directions and Writing and Communications*, edited by Stuart A. Selber, U of South Carolina P, 2010, pp. 77–93.

Macherey, Pierre. "Marx Dematerialized, or the Spirit of Derrida." *Ghostly Demarcations: A Symposium on Jacques Derrida's Specters of Marx*, edited by Michael Sprinker, Verso, 2008, pp. 17–25.

Mujezinovic, Davor. "Electronic Waste in Guiyu: A City under Change?" *Environment & Society Portal*, Summer, no. 29, 2019. Accessed 15 Oct 2021. https://www.environment andsociety.org/arcadia/electronic-waste-guiyu-city-under-change.

Pezzullo, Phaedra C. *Toxic Tourism: Rhetorics of Pollution, Travel, and Environmental Justice*. U of Alabama P, 2007.

Powell, Malea D. "2012 CCCC Chair's Address: Stories Take Place: A Performance in One Act." *College Composition and Communication*, vol. 64, no. 2, 2012, pp. 383–406. *JSTOR*, www.jstor.org/stable/43490757.

Ríos, Gabriela Racquel. "Cultivating Land-Based Literacies and Rhetorics." *Literacy in Composition Studies*, vol. 3, no. 1, 2015, pp. 60–70.

Rivers, Nathaniel A. "Better Footprints." *Tracing Rhetoric and Material Life: Ecological Approaches*, edited by Bridie McGreavy, Justine Wells, George F. McHenry Jr., and Samantha Senda-Cook, Palgrave, 2018, pp. 169–196.

Scranton, Roy. *Learning to Die in the Anthropocene: Reflections on the End of a Civilization*. City Lights, 2015.

Syverson, Margaret A. *The Wealth of Reality: An Ecology of Composition*. Southern Illinois UP, 1999.

Weisser, Christian R. "Ecocomposition and the Greening of Identity." *Ecocomposition: Theoretical and Pedagogical Approaches*, edited by Christian R. Weisser and Sidney I. Dobrin, State U of New York P, 2001, pp. 81–96.

Weisser, Christian R., and Sidney I. Dobrin, editors. *Ecocomposition: Theoretical and Pedagogical Approaches*. State U New York P, 2001.

Wysocki, Anne Frances. "Introduction: In Between—On Composition in Mediation." *Composing (Media)=Composing (Technology): Bodies, Technologies, Writing, and the Teaching of Writing*, edited by Kristin L. Arola and Anne Frances Wysocki, Utah State UP, 2012, pp. 1–24.

INDEX

ability, 12, 244. *See also* disability
academia, 196; aesthetic alterations in, 194–95; and disabled, 187–88; writing in, 191, 193–94
access, accessibility, 15, 17*n2*, 244
accountability, ethic of, 140
active voice, media use of, 173–74
activism, 11, 30, 90, 93, 94, 107, 129, 140, 221, 227, 231, 223*n5*, 223*n7*, 248; discomfort training, 108–9; political, 107–8.
adaptation, to climate change, 236–37
AE. *See* avowed embodiment
affect, affectivity, 25, 75, 86*n1*, 94; emotion and, 77–78; museums, 79–80; negative, 83–84; negotiation of, 84–85
affect theory, 76–77, 86
African Americans, viii, 16, 78, 81, 134; avowed embodiment, 224–26; bodies, 246–47; bodies as text, 220–21; character of, 135–36; citizen-women, 123, 128; education and employment, 138–39; Greensboro sit-in, 74, 77; negative affective attachments to, 83–84; nigrescence theory and, 221–24; piety of, 136–37; and sexual savage myth, 129–32; women's suffrage movement, 114–15
agency, 101, 211, 212; and active voice, 173–74; as intervention, 199–200; and passive voice, 170–72
agism, 213
Agmon-Levin, Nancy, 63
Ahmed, Sara, xi, 4, 5, 49, 76, 77, 78, 79, 90, 98, 109, 110, 111, 114, 115, 117; embodied technologies, 211–12; on orientations, 245–46
Alabama, 15
Albright, Ann Cooper, 112
Alcock, Emily, 163
Alerby, Eva, 46
Alerby, Jo´runn Eli´ do´ttir, 46
Alexander, Jonathan, 204
Almjeld, Jen, 206
American Indians, constructing, 246
Americans with Disabilities Act, 154
animation, and materiality, 125

anthropocene, 237–38
anti-Dakota Pipeline protest, 6
antiprison activism, 11. *See also* Tamms Year Ten Campaign
antiracist work, 50, 53
Anzaldúa, Gloria, x, 9, 134, 141
Arbery, Ahmaud, murder of, viii
Aristotle, 26, 27, 57
Arola, Kristin L., 200, 244, 250
Aryan Nations Web site, 77
Asian Americans, stereotypes of, 151, 152–53
Associated Press (AP), on immigrant terms, 165–66
attire, performative strategic, 226–27
Austin, 16
Australia, 152, 163
authorial body, 189, 192
autoimmunity, and smell, 63
autopoetic texts, 195, 233*n8*
avowed embodiment (AE), 12, 221, 223, 231–32; purposes, 224–25; resistance and, 225–26

bacteria, 4, 66
bacterial rhetorics, 63
Banks, William P., 9, 40, 53, 82; on Black bodies, 246–47
Barad, Karen, 90, 94, 200
Barber, Lucy G., 114
Belcourt, Billy-Ray, 4
Bernard-Donals, Michael, 30–31
Berne, Patricia, 146
"Better Footprints" (Rivers), 249
Biddle, Jennifer, 90
biological bodies, 12
biological essentialism, 62
BIPOC, 16
Black Lives Matter, 6, 16, 44, 54
Blackman, Lisa, 243
Black people. *See* African Americans
Blair, Carole, 74, 75
Blair, Ezell, Jr. (Jibreel Khazan), 74
Board of Lady Managers (Columbian Exposition), 125, 127
bodies, body, viii–ix, 8, 25, 28, 36, 48, 63, 83, 89, 101, 115, 141*n3*, 143, 194, 199,

203; authorial, 189, 192; Black, 130–31, 246–47; chronic pain in, 184, 185–86; as communicative texts, 229–30; as cultural object/sign, 109, 110–11; defining, 3–7; difference in, 80–81; and identities, 212–13; languaging, x–xi; and mind, 75–76; ownership of, 4–5; as rhetorical, 23–24; as text, 10, 155–56, 220–21, 229–230; violence against, 32–33
bodying, 120, 124
bodymind, 5, 184, 184n, 185, 187, 190, 193
Bodyminds Reimagined: (Dis)Ability, Race, and Gender in Black Women's Speculative Fiction (Schalk), 5
Boler, Megan, 115, 121n1
border patrol, media portrayal of, 172–73
Bosnian war, violence, 28–29
Bostock v. Clayton County Georgia, vii
boundaries, 4, 61, 77; body-technology, 199, 202; smell and, 65–66
Bowlsbey, Maile Pearl, 143, 144, 148–49, 150, 154
Bradford, Kevin D., on smell, 60–61
Branded Bodies, Rhetoric, and the Neoliberal Nation-State (Wingard), 161
breastfeeding, rhetorics of, 150–51
Brennan, Teresa, 4, 59, 90, 96
Brookes, Jennifer C., 63
Brooms, Derrick, 81
Brown, Gerry, 248
Bryant, Levi Paul, 25
Buchanan, Lindal, 150
Burke, Kenneth, 28, 34, 100
Burton, LeVar, 221
Butler, Judith, 109, 203, 244

Calafell, Bernadette Marie, 9, 155
California: anti-discrimination bills, 222; environmental activism, 248–49
capital, cognitive, 187
Carby, Hazel, 130
Carolis, Catarina De, 63
Cassuto, Leonard, 192
CCCC, x, 44–45, 54, 156
CDS. *See* critical discourse studies
celebration activism, 231
Cellio, Jen, 147
Ceraso, Steph, 65
chastity, 136
Chávez, Karma R., 8, 124, 145
children, 12, 43, 44, 94, 97, 109, 118, 130, 152–54. *See also* Latinx child immigrants
Choi, Yoonsun, 152
Chouliaraki, Lilie, 171

Christianity, Black women and, 136–37
chronic illness, 184, 186–87
chronic pain, 185–86, 194; and knowledge, 194–95
citizen-woman, 125; Black, 123, 128; developing, 134–37; education and employment, 138–39; liberty, 139–40; materiality, 137–38; reanimating, 134–39; role of, 140–41
civil rights museums, 74–75, 79–86
Civil Rights Act (1964), vii
Clare, Eli, 4
climate change, 247; adaptation to, 236–37
clothing: performative, 226–27; as symbolic speech, 229–30, 231. *See also* attire
Clough, Patricia, 76
Cobos, Casie, 82
COGFA. *See* Commission on Government Forecasting and Accountability
Cole, Peter, 191–92, 249
colonialism, xi, 6, 246–47; embodied rhetorics, 9–10
commemoration, ethical, 80
Commission on Government Forecasting and Accountability (COGFA), 97
communication, 34, 85; body as text in, 229–30; touch and, 27–28
communities: digital, 206–7; TRAP Karaoke as, 230
composition, x, 30, 37, 192, 196, 240, 241, 246; ecology of, 239
Congress of Representative Women, 130
Connelly, Colleen, 239
contemporary theory, 80
Cooper, Marilyn, on ecological model of writing, 238–40
Corbett, Edward, 58
corporeality, 9, 90, 109, 110, 120, 124, 125, 128, 133, 137, 184n, 185, 194, 195. *See also* intercorporeal
COVID-19 pandemic, vii–viii, 15–16
Crenshaw, Kimberlé, 145
criminals: Latinx child immigrants represented as, 164, 166–70, 175; rehabilitation of, 102
crip time, 184, 196n
critical discourse studies (CDS), 162–63, 175
Cross, William E., Jr., nigrescence theory, 221–22, 232–33n3
Crown Act (Create a Respectful and Open Workplace for Natural Hair), 222
cruelty, as pain, 194
cultural violence, 31, 38
culture: body, 81; postanesthetic, 185, 191
Cvetovich, Ann, 67

Dahomey Village (Columbian Exposition), 130–31, 132
dance, dancers, ix, 107, 109, 110, 112–14, 119–20, 127, 132, 228; of Florence Fleming Noyes, 112–14
Dance of Freedom, 113, 119
dating profile design, 206
Davis, Diane, 100–101
deadlines, 189
death, vii, 100, 172, 183*n*, 184, 189, 193*n*, 231
Deleuze, Gilles, 245, 249; on affect, 76–77
Denton, Robert E., Jr., 227
Derrida, Jacques: on hauntology, 237–38, 242–43, 249
Desrochers, Debra M., on smell, 60–61
diario, El/La prensa (newspaper), 171; on child immigrants, 162, 164
Dickinson, Greg, 75
digital texts, circulation of, 241–42, 249
direct violence, 31
disability, 6, 30, 147, 148, 152, 190–91, 244, 246; and motherhood, 145, 153–55
disability activism, and eco-consciousness, 248–49
Disability and Mothering (Lewiecki-Wilson and Cellio), 147
disability justice (DJ) movement, 146
Disability Rhetoric (Dolmage), 147
disability studies, 5, 80–81
disabled bodies, 6, 14–15, 184; academia and, 187–88
Disabled Upon Arrival (Dolmage), 246
discomfort, 120; endurance of, 109–10; women's embodiment in, 111–19
discomfort training, 110–11, 118, 119; for activists, 108–9
discrimination, 139, 222
disorientation: embodied, 48–49, 51–52; of white bodies, 49–50
DJ. *See* disability justice movement
Dobrin, Sidney I., 239
Dolmage, Jay, 59, 80, 81, 147, 244, 246; digital texts, 241–42, 249
Dolphin-Krute, Maia, on chronic illness, 186–87
Douchebags of Tumblr, 209–10
Duckworth, Tammy, 12, 156*n1*, 156–57*n2*; body as text, 155–56; career of, 143–44; motherhood, 151–52, 153–55; work and motherhood, 148–51
Durham, Jeremy, 118

Ecocomposition (Weisser and Dobrin), 239
eco-consciousness, 248–49

ecofeminism, 239
ecology, of digital writing, 238–42
ecorhetoric, 240
Edbauer Rice, Jenny, 76, 78, 79
Eddy, Martha, 110
editorials, 149
education, 97, 108, 123, 138, 161, 162, 176, 232, 246
election, 2016, 107
embodied knowledge(s), 8–9, 78–9, 83, 108–9, 112, 119, 120, 144, 148, 164, 185, 193*n*, 195, 196, 211
embodied technologies, 199, 211–12, 214; facial recognition and, 202–3; queer theory, 200–201
embodiment, viii–ix, 3, 7–8, 25, 26, 62, 63, 201, 204, 220, 221, 236, 247, 249; disability, 244–45
emergencies, bodily reactions to, 89
emotions, 79, 162; and affect, 77–78
employment, African American women, 138–39
endurance, discomfort, 109–10
Engels, Jeremy, 48
enmeshment, 236
enslavement, 78
environmental activism, 241; and disability activism, 248–49
Ericksen, Julie, 223
ethics, of touch, 26, 27–28, 39–40
eugenics, 154, 184, 188
European Parliament, 152
e-waste, 237, 247, 248, 249
Examined Life, 244
experience, 33, 76

facial recognition, 202–3
Fairclough, Norman, 162–63
families, 92, 94, 143, 153, 239
Faris, Michael, 208
fat, identity, 13, 14
fat studies, 5
feminist(s), 6, 108, 109, 117, 145, 201, 239; discomfort training, 108–9
feminist theory, 62
fibromyalgia, 183, 185, 186, 195
Fisher, Mark, 243
flesh, fleshy forms, 3, 4, 7, 9, 10, 26–7, 49, 54, 90, 111, 124, 135, 146–7, 155, 183, 184, 185, 194, 201, 203
Floyd, George, murder of, viii, 16
fonts, serif, 188–89
Foster, Susan, 110
Fowler, Roger, on passive voice, 170
Frost, Samantha, 62

Gage, Scott, 31
Galtung, Johan, 31, 32
gas, odorants in, 60
Gatens, Moira, 124
Gatrell, Caroline, 149
Georgia, white nationalism in, viii
ghost analogy, of chronic illness, 186–87
Ghostly Demarcations, 243
Gibbs, Anna, on academic writing, 193–94
Gill, Rosalind, 191
Gillespie, Tarleton, on digital platforms, 206–7
Glenn, Cheryl, 43
Gouge, Catherine, 202
governance, and motherhood, 145, 151–53
Graham, Phil, 162
Greensboro Four, 74–75, 77; ICRCM depictions of, 85–86
Gries, Laurie: on agency, 199–200; and racial slur, 44–46, 50–53; Watson keynote address, 44–45, 49, 52
Grindr, 201, 205, 215*n1*, 215*n5*; inclusion, 209–10; platforms, 206, 207–9, 211–14; and tribes, 213, 215, 216*n6*, 216*n7*
Grosz, Elizabeth, 7, 81, 124, 135; ontothetics, 126–27
guilt, and scent, 61–62
Guiyu, e-waste in, 237, 247, 248, 249
Gut Feminism (Wilson), 4–5

Haas, Angela M., 82, 246
Haber, Honi Fern, 7
hair, natural, 222, 233*n4*
Halberstam, J., 6
Halley, Jean, 76
Halttunen, Karen, 194
haptic rhetorics, 57, 66
Haraway, Donna, 4, 6, 47, 199
hate speech, 210
Haunted Data (Blackman), 243
hauntology, 237–38, 242; digital, 243–44, 247–48, 249–50
Hawhee, Debra, 3–4, 23, 57, 67, 80
Hawk, Byron, 64
Hayles, N. Katherine, 8, 236
Haynes, Cynthia, 30
health care, socialized, 6
Held, Virginia, 47
Hephaestus, 80
heteronormative, 187, 206
heterosexist, xi, 204
heterosexuality, normalization of, 200
Hindman, Jane E., 9
hooks, bell, 48
"How to Be Unapologetically Black" (Young), 221

human conduct, scent and, 60–61
humanitarian sensibility, 194
humanities, 25
hygiene, 60

ICRCM. *See* International Civil Rights Center and Museum
ideality, 126–27, 129, 133–140
identification(s), 12, 13–14, 66, 100, 101; touch and, 28, 33–34; and TRAP Karaoke, 228–29
identities, 6, 149, 172, 233*n4*; and bodies, 212–13; disabled and mothering, 153–55; LGBTQ, 205–6; mothering, 156, 157*n3*; nigrescence theory and, 221–24; and queer theories, 203–4; social-movement organizations, 219–20
identity construction, on dating-profile sites, 206
Illinois, Supermax in, 90, 91
illness, chronic, 184, 186–87
immigrants, 163, 164; inclusion and exclusion of, 175–76; negative processes against, 170–72; terms used for, 165–66; unaccompanied Latinx children, 161–62, 166–70
immigration, immigration system, 162, 176, 246; media portrayals of, 170–73
incarceration, impermeability of, 93
inclusion, Grindr's efforts, 209–10
indirection, 50–51, 52
Inessential Solidarity (Davis), 100–101
injustices, 74, 85, 140, 162, 231
Inoue, Asao, 46, 54
intelligence, body and, 110
intercorporeal, 27, 33–34
interface design, Grindr, 208
Intergovernmental Panel on Climate Change (IPCC), 236, 237
International Civil Rights Center and Museum (ICRCM), 74–75; affect negotiation in, 84–85; structure of, 82–84
International Women's March, 107
interruption, touch as, 33
intersectionality, intersectional analysis, 5, 145–46
intervention, agency as, 199–200; social, 77
intrabody resonance, 11, 90–91, 96–97, 101; prisoner testimony, 98–99; prison reform, 102–3; in Tamms prisoner testimonies, 99–100
invention, 8, 80, 144, 146–48, 155, 156, 208
IPCC. *See* Intergovernmental Panel on Climate Change

isolation, 95, 100; at supermax prisons, 92–94
Italy, COVID-19 pandemic, 15

Jackson, Gerald, 203
Jay, Paul, 192
JHA. *See* John Howard Association
Jim Crow, 74, 75; museum depictions of, 83, 85
John Howard Association (JHA), on prisoner condition, 91–92
Johnson, Gavin P., 45, 200
Johnson, Jenell, 58
Johnson, Mark, 5
Johnson, Maureen, 10
Jones, John, 202
journalism, passive voice in, 170–71
Joyce, Amy, 149

Kant, Immanuel, on smell, 64–65
Keller, Christopher J., 239
Kessler, Molly, 4
Killingsworth, M. Jimmie, 240–41, 242, 250
Kindr Grindr, 209–10
Kirsch, Gesa E., 3
Kittay, Eva Feder, 154
Koerber, Amy, 150
Kozel, Susan, 25; *Telematic Dreaming* performance, 35–38, 39–40

Ladd-Taylor, Molly, 148
language, 12, 17n4, 57, 65, 193, 210; active voice, 173–74; bodies and, x–xi; in describing immigrants, 163, 165–67, 169–70, 176; of pain, 189, 195–96; passive voice, 170–73
language norm, 13
Latinx child immigrants, 12, 161–62, 163; inclusion and exclusion of, 175–76; public response to, 174–75; represented as illegal/criminals, 164, 166–70; as victims, 170–74
Lawrence et al. v. Texas, vii
Learning to Die in the Anthropocene: Reflections on the End of a Civilization (Scranton), 237
Lee, Melanie, 190
Lemke, Jay, 162
letterforms, 188–89, 190n, 191
Levinas, Emmanuel, 30
Levy, Daisy, 10
Lewiecki-Wilson, Cynthia, 7, 147
LGBTQ+/LGBTQIA+, vii, 16, 213, 223, 224; communication, 205–6; and community, vii, 205, 206, 208, 209, 213, 214
liberty, 139–40

Lindgren, Kristin, 153
linearity, 184
listening, multimodal/multisensory, 65
Livingston, Ira, 6
lobbying, 109, 111, 120; discomfort, 118–19; training for, 117–18
Loe, Kelin, 66
Los Angeles, 164
Los Angeles Times, 171; on child immigrants, 162, 165, 166
Louisville (Ky.), viii, 16

Macherey, Pierre, 243
machine, and body, 199. *See also* technologies
MacKaye, Hazel, 112
Madsen, Annelise K., 115
Manning, Erin, 33, 38–39, 40, 41n3
Manthey, Katie, 10
marginalization, vii, 12, 75–81, 83–84, 112, 114–45, 155, 193, 221
Martin, Trayvon, 16
masculinity, 151; toxic, 209
Massie, Pascal, 26
Massumi, Brian, 9
mastery, and bodily revelation, 194
materiality, materialism, 12, 13, 30, 59, 125, 126–27, 133; citizen-woman, 137–38
maternal bodies, 12, 143, 144, 149; disability and, 147, 154–55; leakiness of, 150–51
Mattingly, Carol, 226
McCain, Franklin, 74
McCorkle, Ben, 199
McGlotten, Shaka, 212
McNeil, Joseph, 74
media, 161–62; on terms for immigrants, 165–70; use of active voice, 173–74; use of passive voice, 163, 170–73
mediation, 27, 36, 37–38
Mejia, Robert, 60
memory project, 120
Merleau-Ponty, Maurice, 27; on touch, 28, 39, 40
Michel, Neil, 74
migraines, and scent, 59–60
Milholland, Inez, 119
mind, and body, 4–5, 75–76
Minh-ha, Trinh T., indirection, 50–51
Minneapolis, Floyd murder in, viii, 16
modernity, 237
Moraga, Cherríe, x, 9
Morris, David, 191
motherhood, 157n3; and disability, 153–55; and governance, 151–53; and work, 145, 148–51, 157n4

Mowatt, Jason, on TRAP Karaoke, 228, 230
Mujezinovic, Davor, 247
murders, of people of color, viii, 16
Murphy, G. Patrick, 92
museums, 87*n3*, 87*n4*; affects of, 79–80;
    visitors, 81–82
music, TRAP, 229, 230. *See also* TRAP
    Karaoke

Nancy, Jean-Luc, on violence, 28–29, 40
Nashville: Women's Day on the Hill, 108,
    117; women's marches in, 107, 121,
    111–12
National American Woman Suffrage Asso-
    ciation (NAWSA), 112, 114, 119
National Council of Disability (NCD), 154
NAWSA. *See* National American Woman
    Suffrage Association
NCD. *See* National Council of Disability
NCTE, 44
Negro-to-Black conversion, 221–22, 232*n2*
Nelson, Brian, 102; as Tamms prisoner,
    94, 95, 97
neoliberal economics, 161
neurodiversity, 190
newspapers: terms for immigrants in,
    165–66; Spanish- and English-language,
    162, 164–65; use of active voice, 173–
    74; use of passive voice, 163, 170–73
New York (state), anti-discrimination bills,
    222
New York City, 15, 89, 164; women's suf-
    frage performances, 112, 119
New York Times, 171; on child immigrants,
    162, 165, 166
nigrescence theory (NT), 225, 232–33*n3*;
    as Black identity model, 221–24
normal, as pathology, 15
normate body, 47–50, 53, 242
Norwood, Kristen, 151
Novotny, Maria, 10
Noyes, Florence Fleming, 12, 107, 111,
    115; women's suffrage movement,
    108–9, 112–14, 119–20
Noyes Rhythm, 109
NT. *See* nigrescence theory

Obama, Barack, 167; on child immigrants,
    168–69
Obergefell et al. v. Hodges, vii
Obermark, Lauren, 79, 82
odor, bacteria and, 66
odorants, gas and, 60
odor cues, 63
Oklahoma City National Memorial
    Museum, 79

olfaction: ontologies of, 62–63, 67–68;
    vibration theory of, 63–64
olfactory rhetorics, 58–59, 64–65, 67;
    human conduct and, 60–61; interrela-
    tion in, 68–69
ontoethics, of materiality, 126–27
Operación Coyote/Operation Coyote, 167
Opinion, La (newspaper), 171; on child
    immigrants, 162, 164
orientations, 49, 193, 243, 245–47
Ott, Brian, 75
"Our Story Begins Here: Constellating
    Cultural Rhetorics" (Levy), 146–47

pageants, woman's suffrage, 112, 113*f*,
    114–15, 119
pain, 12, 24, 26, 28, 36, 39–40, 40*n2*, 99,
    111, 150, 183, 189; chronic, 185–86,
    194; embodied language, 195–96
pandemic, COVID-19, vii–viii, 15–16
parades/marches, 121; women's' suffrage,
    112, 113*f*, 114–15
parental leave, 158–59
passive voice, media use of, 163, 170–72,
    175
pathos, in prisoner testimonies, 99–100
patriarchy, xi, 129; US Senate, 152, 157*n5*
patriotism, African American, 137
Paul, Alice, 114
"Pedagogy of Rhetorical Looking: Atrocity
    Images at the Intersection of Vision
    and Violence, A" (Fleckenstein, Gage,
    and Bridgman), 31
people of color, xi, 5, 11, 60, 83, 85, 87*n5*,
    114, 137, 141*n4*, 143–6, 146–9, 152–55;
    representation of, 79, 156*n1*, 157*n4*
performative strategic attire, 226–27
performativity, 3, 203
permeability, incarceration, 93
Perricone, Carlo, 63
Perricone, Roberto, 63
persuasion, 11, 57, 63, 67, 76, 90, 102,
    146, 147
Persuasion and Social Movements (Stewart,
    Denton, and Smith), 227
Pezzullo, Phaedra C., 241
phantom-phone syndrome, 203
Phillips, Lisa, 58, 61
philosophy, ethical, 30; of touch, 24,
    26–27
piety, of African American women, 136–37
plasticity, destructive, 194
platforms: digital, 206–7; Grindr, 207–14
Plato, 57; and Platonic philosophies, 25
poetics, of pain, 183
politics, of scent, 59–60

politics of location, 223
Politics of Touch: Sense, Movement, Sovereignty (Manning), 33
Pörtner, Hans-Otto, 236
positionality, 9 13, 78, 79, 83, 108, 109, 128, 164, 195, 211
postanesthetic culture, 185, 191
post-partum bodies, 147–48
Powell, Malea, x, 9–10
Presumed Incompetent: The Intersections of Race and Class for Women in Academia (Gutiérrez y Muhs et al.), 5–6
Presumed Incompetent II (Flores Niemann et al.), 6
Price, Margaret, 5, 190
Pride Month, vii
prisoners: intrabody resonance and, 98–99; mental illness, 91–92; in Tamms, 94, 95–96, 97–98
prison reforms, 90; activism, 94, 98, 102
professionalism, 150, 191
professionalization, 138–39
profiles, Grindr, 209, 211, 215*n5*
prostitution, decriminalization of, 120
psychoses, 91, 95
Puar, Jasbir K., 6
puberty, and scent, 60
public(s), and Latinx child immigrants, 174–75; visceral, 67
public media. *See* media
public memory, 75, 76, 79, 80
publishing, academic, 194–95
punishment, and touch, 92–94
Puwar, Nirmal, 47

Quakers, on slavery, 194
queerness, 15, 200, 204, 211; rhetorical silence, 208–9
queer rhetorics, 203, 204–5, 213
queer theory, 12, 203–4; embodied technologies, 200–201

racial slurs, 46, 50; use of, 43, 44, 45, 52; and violence, 46, 53
racism, 45, 47, 53, 75, 78, 83, 84; Dahomey Village exhibit, 130–31
Ratcliffe, Krista, 43
reanimation, 135–36, 137, 138
reflection, silences of, 46–47
Reflection in the Writing Classroom (Yancey), 46
refrigerators, smart, 205
rehabilitation, of criminals, 102
relationality, 147
resistance, xi, 47, 61, 66, 94, 102, 176, 221; avowed embodiment and, 223–31

resonance, 89, 101; intrabody, 90–91
Reynolds, Laurie Jo, 94
Rhetorical Bodies (Selzer), 29–30
rhetorical education, 23, 85
Rhetorical Touch: Disability, Identification, Haptics (Walters), 23
Rhetoric in Tooth and Claw (Hawhee), 57
Rhodes, Carl, 193
Rhodes, Jacqueline, 204
Rich, Adrienne, 223
Richmond, David, 74
Richmond, Tyler, 46
Right in Maim: Debility, Capacity, Disability (Puar), 6
Ríos, Gabriela Raquel, 82, 240, 244
risks, in touch, 25, 35
Rivers, Nathaniel A., 152, 241, 249
Roberts, Dorothy, 147
Rogers, Brandon, 60
Ronzulli, Licia, 152
Rosch, Eleanor, 7
Royster, Jacqueline Jones, 3, 9, 81

Sackey, Donnie Johnson, 82
safe spaces, TRAP Karaoke, 228
Saltmarsh, Jennifer, 63, 66
Sangha Kali, 190*n*, 191
Sano-Franchini, Jennifer, 82
scent, 57, 65; guilt and, 61–62; and human conduct, 60–61; intimacy of, 62–63; politics of, 59–60; rhetoric of, 58–59, 69*n1*
Schalk, Sami, 5
Schoenfeld, Netta, 63
Scranton, Roy, 237
security housing unit (SHU) syndrome, 91
Sedgwick, Eve Kosofsky, 76, 110; on affect, 77–78
segregation, 77, 78, 114; rationale for, 83–84; at supermax prisons, 92–93
self-hatred, Black, 222
self-identification theory, 221
self-recovery, 120
Selzer, Jack, 29–30
semiotics, social, 175
sensation, ix, 3, 11, 24, 26, 28–29, 34, 36, 39, 58, 62–63, 67, 69*n3*
sensory engagement, 79
sensory rhetorics, 11, 64
Sermon, Paul, 35
settler colonialism, 6
sexism, Tennessee legislature, 118, 121*n3*
sexuality, sexualities, 131, 188, 201, 203–4; Black, 131–34
sexual savage myth: Black females and, 129–32; and white patriarchal culture,

133–34; at World Columbian Exposition, 132–33
Shaw, Anna Howard, 113
Shaw, Marian, 132
Sheridan, Mary, Thomas R. Watson conference, 44, 45
Shoenfeld, Yehuda, 63
SHU. *See* security housing unit syndrome
SIJ. *See* Special Immigrant Juvenile status
silence: and power, 43–44; queer rhetorical, 208–9; as reflection, 45, 46–47
Simkhai, Joel, 208, 212
Sins Invalid, 146
skin, as outer boundary, 4
Skin, Tooth, and Bone. The Basis of Movement Is Our People: A Disability Justice Primer (Sins Invalid), 146
slavery, slaves, pain and, 194
smell, ix, 57, 58, 61, 63; and boundaries, 65–66; Kant on, 64–65
Smilges, Johnathan, on queer rhetorical silence, 208–9
Smith, Craig Allen, 227
Smitherman, Geneva, x
smuggling, immigrant, 167
social justice, lobbying, 118–19
social movements, bodies as text in, 220–21; organizations, 219–20
solitary confinement, 90, 91–94, 97
somatic(s), 49, 51, 110, 112, 119, 120, 199, 206
sonic rhetorics, 57–58, 64–65
Sousanis, Nick, 196
South, On the (Aristotle), 26
space, virtual, 208–9
Special Immigrant Juvenile (SIJ) status, 171
Specters of Marx (Derrida), 242, 243
speeches: clothing as symbolic, 229–30; at Columbian Exposition, 125–26
Spinoza, Baruch, on affect, 76
Stacey, Jackie, 4, 90
stereotypes, 77, 157$n3$; of Asian Americans, 152–53
sterilizations, forced, 153–54
Stewart, Charles J., 227
Still Life with Rhetoric (Gries), 44
structural violence, 31, 32, 34, 35, 41$n3$
suffering, 92, 94, 95, 100, 102, 175, 184; and academic writing, 191, 193–95; media on, 171–72
Suffrage Allegory pageant (MacKaye), 112, 113f, 119
suffragists: embodied experiences, 111–19; Florence Fleming Noyes performances, 108–9

supermax prisons, 11, 90; description of, 91–92; isolation in, 92–94; prisoner treatment in, 97–98
Swastika Counter Initiative, The (Gries), 44
Syverson, Margaret, 201–2, 239

Talking and Testifyin: The Language of Black America (Smitherman), x
Tamms C-MAX prison: description of, 91–92; isolation at, 92–94; prisoner experiences in, 95–96, 97–98
Tamms Year Ten campaign, 94, 95; prisoner testimonies at, 99–100
Taylor, Breonna, viii, 16
technology, technologies, 249; communicative, 205–6; digital, 247; queer rhetorics, 204–5, 211. *See also* embodied technologies
technorhetorics, 240, 242
#Tees4theTrap, 229, 231
Telematic Dreaming installation, 25, 41$n4$; performance in, 35–38; violence in, 39–40
Tennessee, 12, 121$n2$, 121$n3$: lobbying, 109, 117–18; women's marches in, 111–12
Terborg-Penn, Rosalyn, 114
Thinking Through the Skin (Biddle), 90
This Bridge Called My Back (Moraga and Anzaldúa), x
Times New Roman, 188–89
Tomlinson, Elizabeth C., 206
torture, 84, 93, 193n; Bosnian war, 28–29
touch, ix, 15, 95; ethics of, 26, 27–28, 39–40; identification and, 33–34; as punishment, 92–94; as relational, 31–32; rhetorics of, 23–24, 30; and violence, 24–25, 28–29, 34–35, 38–39
transgender people, vii, x, xi, 11, 146, 148, 206, 210, 213
Transmission of Affect, The (Brennan), 4, 90
TRAP Karaoke movement, 13, 219, 220–21; avowed embodiment and, 231–32; clothing and communication in, 229–30; identification and visibility, 228–29
trauma, 6, 16, 82, 87$n3$, 174, 225
Trump, Donald, vii, 107
Turner, Paaige K., 151
typefaces, 188–89, 190n

Umansky, Lauri, 148
US Senate, 157$n5$; Tammy Duckworth in, 143–44, 150–52

Van Dijk, Teun, 163, 170
ventilators, COVID-19 pandemic, 15–16
Vetter, Matthew A., 211

victims, 227; Latinx child immigrants as, 170–74, 175
violence, viii, 6, 11, 16, 41*n3*, 84; against bodies, 32–33; of racial slurs, 46, 53; rhetorical, 30–31; and touch, 24–25, 28–29, 34–35, 38–39, 93
virtue, 128, 135–37
visibility, TRAP Karaoke, 228–29
Visible and the Invisible, The (Merleau-Ponty), 27
visitors, museum, 81–82
visual rhetorics, 57, 155
vulnerability, body, 25, 27–28, 36, 59, 61, 66

Walters, Shannon, 10, 23, 93; on touch, 26, 27–28
Washington, DC, women's suffrage parades and pageants in, 112, 114–15
Waters, Larissa, 152
Watson Conference, Thomas R., 11, 43; Laura Gries' speech, 44–45
Wealth of Reality: An Ecology of Composition, The (Syverson), 201–2
wearable technologies, 202
Weber, Ryan, 152
Weiss, Gail, 5, 7
Weisser, Christian R., 239
Wells-Barnett, Ida B., 114
Westefer v. Snyder, 92
white bodies, 47, 53, 54; embodied disorientations of, 48–50, 51–52; indirection, 50–51
White City, 125, 141*n4*
white nationalists/supremacy, viii, xi, 54, 227
whiteness, 11, 46; acknowledgment of wrongdoing, 52–53; embodied disorientation, 48–50; identity, 13–14
whites: antiracist work, 50; and citizen-woman, 134–39; and sexual savage myth, 129–30, 133–34
willfulness, 109
Willful Subjects (Ahmed), xi
Williams, Fannie Barrier: on citizen-woman, 123, 128, 134–39; at Columbian Exposition, 125–26, 127; on

cultural stereotypes, 131–32; on liberty, 139–40; on sexual savage myth, 129–32, 133–34
Wilson, Elizabeth, 4–5, 62
Wilson, James, 7
Wilson, Woodrow, inauguration, 114, 115, 116*f*
Winderman, Emily, 60
Wingard, Jennifer, 161
Wodak, Ruth, 163
women: African American, 129–30, 135–36, 138–39; Christian devotion, 136–37; embodied experiences, 111–19; white and black progress, 123–24. *See also* citizen-woman
Women's Day on the Hill protest (Nashville), 12, 108, 117
Women's March (2017), 115
women's marches, 119; Nashville, 111–12, 121; suffrage, 114–15, 116*f*
women's suffrage movement: embodied experiences, 111–19; Florence Fleming Noyes performances, 108–9
Wong, Alice, 154
Woolworth lunch counter sit-in, 74, 77
work, and motherhood, 145, 148–51, 157*n4*
working class, whiteness, 14
Working Mother (publication), 149
World's Columbian Exposition, 12, 123, 141*n2*, 141*n4*; Dahomey Village at, 130–31; and sexual savage myth, 132–33; Fannie Barrier Williams speech at, 125–26, 127, 128–30
World's Congress of Representative Women, 12, 123, 141*n1*
writing: academic, ix, 191; aesthetic alterations, 194–95; digital, 238–42, 248
Wysocki, Anne Frances, 30, 200, 244, 248, 250

Yancey, Kathleen Blake, 46
Yangzom, Dicky, 226
Young, Damon, 221
Young, Iris Marion, 47

Zumwalt, Landen, 210